Timothy J. M. Ling is Ministry Development
Officer for the Canterbury Diocese of the
Church of England.

The Judaean Poor and the Fourth Gospel

Judaean society in the first century did not conform to the stereotypical 'Mediterranean honour culture', in that it lacked a significant gentile population and was dominated by a powerful religious elite. Timothy Ling argues that this demands a new social-scientific approach to the Gospel and Letters of John that moves away from the accepted 'sectarian' interpretation. He attributes their distinctiveness instead to their roots in Jesus' Judaean ministry, as contrasted with the Galilean ministry, which has attracted much recent study. In particular, Ling contends that the numerous references to 'the poor' in the New Testament can be better understood in the context of the 'alternative' ideologies found among pietistic religious groups practising asceticism, renunciation, and other forms of 'virtuoso religion' in first-century Judaea. In doing so, he mounts a convincing challenge to the current dominant reading of the Gospel of John as a product of early Christian sectarianism.

TIMOTHY J. M. LING is Ministry Development Officer for the Canterbury Diocese of the Church of England.

SOCIETY FOR NEW TESTAMENT STUDIES

MONOGRAPH SERIES

General Editor: John Court

136

THE JUDAEAN POOR AND THE FOURTH GOSPEL

SOCIETY FOR NEW TESTAMENT STUDIES

MONOGRAPH SERIES

Recent titles in the series

The Judaean Poor and the Fourth Gospel

TIMOTHY J. M. LING

CAMBRIDGE
UNIVERSITY PRESS

CAMBRIDGE UNIVERSITY PRESS
Cambridge, New York, Melbourne, Madrid, Cape Town, Singapore, São Paulo

Cambridge University Press
The Edinburgh Building, Cambridge CB2 2RU, UK

Published in the United States of America by Cambridge University Press,
New York

www.cambridge.org
Information on this title: http://www.cambridge.org/9780521857222

First published 2006

Printed in the United Kingdom at the University Press, Cambridge

A catalogue record for this publication is available from the British Library

ISBN-13 978-0-521-85722-2 hardback
ISBN-10 0-521-85722-8 hardback

CONTENTS

PREFACE

This study is a revised version of my Ph.D. thesis, submitted to the University of Kent in 2003. The thesis was the result of three years' research funded by the Arts and Humanities Research Board of the British Academy; I am grateful to the Research Board for the opportunity and the financial support.

Its origins may be located in the inspirational and passionate teaching of the Revd Dr Eric Franklin and Dr Brian Capper, who opened up the New Testament world for me and set me on my course. I am particularly grateful for the occasion on which Brian passed me a battered copy of Michael Hill's *The Religious Order: A Study of Virtuoso Religion*, and started me thinking about 'a sect within the church'.

The process of developing the ideas contained in this study has been greatly assisted by a number of opportunities to present and discuss seminar papers: at the British New Testament Conference, in the Johannine Literature Seminar (2000), the Hermeneutics Seminar (2001), and the Synoptics Seminar (2002); also, at a Symposium hosted by St Andrews University on Anthropology and Biblical Studies (2004). I am grateful to all those who contributed to these discussions.

The revision of the thesis for publication has also been assisted by the comments and criticisms of my examiners, Professor Chris Rowland and the Revd Dr Jeremy Law, and by Dr John Court, the chair of my panel. The shortfalls in the work naturally remain my own.

Finally, I must acknowledge the support and encouragement I have received from friends and family. Thank you, Andy and Lucy, Andrew and Elisabeth, Denisa, Nathan and Esther, John, Denis and Chris, John and Olive, and especially my wife Ruth and children Joseph and Beth, for making this journey with me.

ABBREVIATIONS

AA	*American Anthropologist*
AAA	American Anthropological Association
ABD	D. N. Freedman, ed., *The Anchor Bible Dictionary* (6 vols.; London: Doubleday, 1992)
ABQ	*American Baptist Quarterly*
AmEth	*American Ethnologist*
ANT	L. E. Vaage and V. L. Wimbush, eds., *Asceticism and the New Testament* (London: Routledge, 1999)
AntRev	*Antioch Review*
ApL	*Applied Linguistics*
AQ	*Anthropological Quarterly*
ARA	*Annual Review of Anthropology*
ASR	*American Sociological Review*
BA	*Biblical Archaeologist*
BBB	Bonner biblische Beiträge
Bib	*Biblica*
BI	*Biblical Interpretation*
BJRL	*Bulletin of the John Rylands Library*
BK	*Bibel und Kirche*
BTB	*Biblical Theology Bulletin*
BZAW	Beihefte zur Zeitschrift für die alttestamentliche Wissenschaft
CA	*Current Anthropology*
CBQ	*Catholic Biblical Quarterly*
CHJ	W. Horbury, W. D. Davies, and J. Sturdy, eds., *The Cambridge History of Judaism*, (Cambridge: Cambridge University Press, 1999)
CritA	*Critique of Anthropology*
CSSH	*Comparative Studies in Society and History*
DJD	Discoveries in the Judaean Desert
DJG	J. Green, S. McKnight, and I. Howard, eds., *Dictionary of Jesus and the Gospels* (Downer's Grove, IL: InterVarsity Press, 1992)
DNTB	C. A. Evans and S. E. Porter, eds., *Dictionary of New Testament Background* (Leicester: InterVarsity Press, 2000)
DPL	G. F. Hawthorne and R. P. Martin, eds., *Dictionary of Paul and his Letters* (Downer's Grove, IL: InterVarsity Press, 1993)

EDSS	L. Schiffman and J. VanderKam, eds., *Encyclopedia of the Dead Sea Scrolls* (New York: Oxford University Press, 2000)
ESCA	A. Barnard and J. Spencer, eds., *Encyclopedia of Social and Cultural Anthropology* (London and New York: Routledge, 1996)
ETL	*Ephemerides Theologicae Lovanienses*
EthEu	*Ethnologia Europaea*
FI	*Feminist Issues*
HBT	*Horizons in Biblical Theology*
HJPAJC	G. Vermes, F. Millar, and M. Black, *The History of the Jewish People in the Age of Jesus Christ* (rev. edn; Edinburgh: T. & T. Clark, 1973–87)
HO	*Human Organisation*
HTKNT	Herders theologischer Kommentar zum Neuen Testament
HTR	*Harvard Theological Review*
HTS	*Hervormde Teologiese Studies*
HWW	P. S. Pantel, ed., *History of Women in the West* (Cambridge, MA: Harvard University Press, 1992)
IDB	G.A. Buttrick, ed., *The Interpreter's Dictionary of the Bible* (4 vols.; Nashville: Abingdon, 1962)
IEJ	*Israel Exploration Journal*
IJSCC	*International Journal for the Study of the Christian Church*
Int	*Interpretation*
ISBE	G. W. Bromiley, ed., *International Standard Bible Encyclopedia* (Grand Rapids, MI: Eerdmans, 1988)
JAAR	*Journal of the American Academy of Religion*
JBL	*Journal of Biblical Literature*
JFSR	*Journal of Feminist Studies in Religion*
JJS	*Journal of Jewish Studies*
JQR	*Jewish Quarterly Review*
JRA	*Journal of Roman Archaeology*
JRel	*Journal of Religion*
JRS	*Journal of Roman Studies*
JSNT	*Journal for the Study of the New Testament*
JSNTS	*Journal for the Study of the New Testament*, Supplement Series
JSSR	*Journal for the Scientific Study of Religion*
JTS	*Journal of Theological Studies*
MAS	*Modern Asian Studies*
Neo	*Neotestamentica*
NICNT	New International Commentary on the New Testament
NTS	*New Testament Studies*
NovTest	*Novum Testamentum*
OCD	S. Hornblower and A. Spawforth, eds., *The Oxford Classical Dictionary* (Oxford: Oxford University Press, 1996)
Rel	*Religion*
RelTh	*Religion and Theology*
RevQ	*Revue de Qumran*
RIDA	*Revue internationale des droits de l'antiquité*
RSR	*Religious Studies Review*

SA	*Sociological Analysis*
SB	*Scripture Bulletin*
SBAZ	Studien zur Biblischen Archäologie und Zeitgeschichte
SBLDS	Society of Biblical Literature Dissertation Series
SJSJ	Supplements to the *Journal for the Study of Judaism*
SLJT	*Saint Luke's Journal of Theology*
SRel	*Studies in Religion*
TDNT	G. Kittel and G. Friedrich, eds., *Theological Dictionary of the New Testament* (10 vols.; Grand Rapids: Eerdmans, 1964–)
ThT	*Theology Today*
TS	*Theological Studies*
VC	*Vigiliae Christianae*
WUNT	Wissenschaftliche Untersuchungen zum Neuen Testament
ZAW	*Zeitschrift für die alttestamentliche Wissenschaft*
ZDMG	*Zeitschrift der deutschen morgenländischen Gesellschaft*
ZNW	*Zeitschrift für die neutestamentliche Wissenschaft*
ZTK	*Zeitschrift für Theologie und Kirche*

1

INTRODUCTION

This book grapples with the question of how we can understand a text produced in an ancient social world which was, in all probability, quite different from our own. In order to answer this question it draws on resources from the social sciences and therefore may appropriately be called a work of social-scientific interpretation. In New Testament studies, the field of social-scientific interpretation is no longer in its infancy.[1] Part of the broader purpose of this book, a generation on, is to take stock. It advocates a more integrated approach to conceiving the social worlds which we construct in order to assist us in the interpretative process. In doing so it draws attention to the liminal interface between values and practices, which I believe has been obscured in much of our application of social-scientific resources, which has tended to privilege either values or practices, social structures or social agency. The book's main thesis is that forms of piety which are frequently evident at this liminal interface and which were indigenous to first-century Judaea are particularly pertinent for our understanding of both the New Testament's 'poor' and the Johannine tradition, and that further they help account for the literature's distinctiveness, vis-à-vis the Synoptic tradition, in a more credible manner than the sectarian readings which currently dominate social approaches to the literature.

---

[1] The label 'social-scientific' finds its contemporary origins in the methodological debates of the Society of Biblical Literature's 1973 working group The Social World of Early Christianity: see J. Z. Smith, 'The Social Description of Early Christianity', *RSR* 1 (1975), 19–25. Also, P. Van Staden and A. Van Aarde, 'Social Description or Social-scientific Interpretation? A Survey of Modern Scholarship', *HTS* 47 (1991), 55–87.

1   The problem of incommensurability

New Testament texts, like all texts, presuppose and encode information regarding the social world in which they were produced. For example, this text, amongst other things, presupposes a degree of biblical literacy and encodes the conventions of Western academic discourse. Therefore when we attempt an interpretation of a text, especially an ancient text like the New Testament, it is prudent to provide some means of revealing and discriminating differences between our context, i.e. the Western academy, and that of the authors or objects to be interpreted, i.e. the ancient world. To interpret a New Testament text one has to contend with both the contemporary point of view, the 'etic' perspective, and the first-century point of view, the 'emic' perspective.[2] In acknowledging such constraints on our understanding of texts the issue arises: to what extent is the translation of alien cultural forms into the categories of the interpreter possible, if at all? I strongly believe that it is possible, and the contents of this book demonstrate some of the pitfalls, and some of the possibilities, involved in social-scientific readings of New Testament texts.

The question of the relationship between 'emic' and 'etic' categories is called the problem of incommensurability.[3] Categories derived from one social context may be incommensurable with those derived from another. They may obscure or distort meaning. This is evident

[2] The terminology 'emic' and 'etic' is derived from anthropologists' appropriation and adoption of the label from linguists. It owes its origins to the phonetic–phonemic distinction: see R. Feleppa, 'Emics, Etics, and Social Objectivity', *CA* 27/3 (June 1986), 243. This terminology, however, is the subject of debate within anthropology. One concern is the danger of excessive rigour in the elaboration of question sets so that inquirers are blinded and attribute platonistic, alien, rigid formal structures to social realities that are less structured and more fluid, 244. C. Geertz, 'From the Native's Point of View: On the Nature of Anthropological Understanding', in *Meaning in Anthropology* (ed. K. Basso and H. Sleby; Albuquerque: University of New Mexico Press, 1976), pp. 221–37, notably has misgivings about the terminology and prefers the contrast 'experience–near' and 'experience–distant'. Also, P. Craffert, 'Is the Emic-etic Distinction a Useful Tool for Cross-cultural Interpretation of the New Testament?', *RelTh* 2/1 (1995), 14–37.

[3] See S. R. Garrett, 'Sociology of Early Christianity', *ABD* VI, p. 93. Also, A. Pennycook, 'Incommensurable Discourses?', *ApL* 15/2 (1994), 115–38, who, from the perspective of applied linguistics, uses the problem of incommensurability as a metaphor for the problematic theoretical underpinnings of discourse analysis. There are strong parallels with his understanding of theoretical movements in his discipline and those identified in this book. His advocacy of a (later) Foucauldian understanding of discourse analysis may hold potential for biblical interpretation and merits attention in another context.

in contemporary contexts and can be seen where the language of the business school is imported unmediated into the voluntary sector, with distorting and sometimes negative results. The distance between a first-century agrarian society, i.e. a postulated context for New Testament texts, and the contemporary interpreter is far greater than that which lies between contemporary private and voluntary sectors. The greater this distance, combined with the limited array of first-century cultural artefacts, the greater the challenge for the contemporary interpreter. Two explicit approaches to this challenge are currently in vogue in New Testament studies: 'Modelling' and 'Interpretivist' strategies. These broadly reflect debates within the social sciences that focus on the relationship between the individual social agent and the contexts they may inhabit, social structures.

The 'Modelling' strategy has been vigorously promoted by members of the Context Group of scholars, e.g. Bruce Malina.[4] Its methods have recently been defended by Philip Esler in a series of articles in the *Journal for the Study of the New Testament*.[5] The strategy derives its theoretical underpinning from Berger and Luckmann, who have argued that reality is a social construct, such that both the knowledge of the interpreter and that of those examined are constrained by their historical social experiences.[6] The social worlds which we inhabit are therefore deemed to be discernible, i.e. stable, so that it is possible to reconstruct 'normative social values' and 'social locations' and produce the sort of 'models' necessary for cross-cultural analysis and thereby facilitate understanding.[7] Whilst the problem of incommensurability is understood to be profound, it is

---

[4] See B. Malina, *The New Testament World: Insights from Cultural Anthropology* (revised edition; Louisville, KY: Westminster, John Knox Press, 1993). For a succinct discussion of the work and outlook of the Context Group, see D. G. Horrell, *Social-Scientific Approaches to New Testament Interpretation* (Edinburgh: T. & T. Clark, 1999), pp. 13f., and their webpages: http://www.serv.nt/~oakmande/index.html.

[5] 'Models in New Testament Interpretation: A Reply to David Horrell', *JSNT* 78 (2000), 107–13.

[6] P. Berger and T. Ludemann, *The Social Construction of Reality* (Middlesex: Penguin, 1966); see also G. Ritzer, *Sociological Theory* (4th edn; New York: McGraw-Hill, 1996), pp. 215f. for a brief discussion of this book's influence and antecedents.

[7] 'Social location' refers to all the factors that influence a person or group, their socialisation, experiences, rationality, and views of reality. For a full theoretical treatment, see R. L. Rohrbaugh, ' "Social Location of Thought" as a Heuristic Construct in New Testament Study', *JSNT* 30 (1987), 103–19, and for its application, 'The Social Location of the Markan Audience,' *Int* 47 (1993), 380–95. Rohrbaugh's application is, however, ultimately a disappointment: having provided clarity in the use of the term 'social location' he renders the term redundant with a focus on the Lenskis' 'social level' and an undifferentiated use of the social term 'class'.

argued that it may also be overcome by modelling the social location of contemporary agrarian societies, which have a greater cultural affinity with the first century. In particular, members of the Context Group stress that biblical texts should be read as products of a 'pre-industrial advanced agrarian society of the circum-Mediterranean region',[8] that is a 'viciously agonistic, group-orientated and honour-obsessed culture of finite goods'.[9] This modelling of normative social values, combined with an 'abductive' strategy of working from evidence to hypothesis in a back-and-forth movement of suggestion checking, is presented as a means to circumvent the problem of incommensurability.[10] However, modelling is about discerning typical patterns, which are liable to become, if they have not already, caricatures or stereotypes which may interfere with understanding rather than illuminate it.[11] This is a theme that is extensively developed in the following chapter and throughout this book.

The 'Interpretivist' strategy has most recently been restated by David Horrell in dialogue with Philip Esler.[12] Horrell, following

[8] J. H. Elliott, 'Social-scientific Criticism of the New Testament: More on Methods and Models', *Semeia* 35 (1986), 49, citing G. Lenski, J. Lenski, and P. Nolan, *Human Societies: An Introduction to Macrosociology* (6th edn; New York: McGraw-Hill Book Co., 1991), and G. Sjoberg, *The Preindustrial City, Past and Present* (New York: Free Press, 1965).

[9] P. F. Esler, 'Review: The Social Ethos of the Corinthian Correspondence (Horrell)', *JTS* 49/1 (April 1998), 259f.

[10] See J. H. Elliott, *Social Scientific Criticism of the New Testament: An Introduction* (London: SPCK, 1995), p. 48, citing L. Woodson, *A Handbook of Modern Rhetorical Terms* (Urbana, IL: National Council of Teachers of English, 1979), p. 1. This methodological approach is strikingly similar to that of C. Geertz, *Local Knowledge: Further Essays in Interpretive Anthropology* (New York: Basic, 1983), p. 69, who suggests that the interpreter achieves a conjunction of emic and etic categories by 'Hopping back and forth between the whole conceived through the parts that actualize it'.

[11] D. G. Horrell, *The Social Ethos of the Corinthian Correspondence* (Edinburgh: T. & T. Clark, 1996), pp. 287–9.

[12] D. G. Horrell, 'Models and Methods in Social-scientific Interpretation: A Response to Philip Esler', *JSNT* 78 (2000), 83–105. Whilst not personally adopting the term he places himself firmly, by implication, within the Interpretivist camp. This identification was accepted as appropriate in my own conversation with Horrell at the British New Testament Conference, Manchester, 2001. There is, however, a problem with locating Horrell. He published with many members of the Context Group in Esler's social-scientific volume *Modelling Early Christianity: Social Scientific Studies of the New Testament in its Context* (London: Routledge, 1995). In his own *The Social Ethos*, pp. 26–32, he describes his approach as 'socio-historical'. He suggests that if the dimension of time is added to the sociological approach, the distinction between sociology and history is effectively removed. More recently, though, Horrell appears ambivalent about surrendering the label 'scientific' to the model users and wishes to identify his more Interpretivist approach as equally if not more scientific: see 'Models and Methods'.

Anthony Giddens' critique of Berger and Luckmann, stresses the primacy of human agency.[13] Giddens views the structural properties of social systems, i.e. normative values, as both the medium and the outcome of practices that constitute those systems. Social structures are therefore deemed to have only a virtual existence, existing only in so far as they are reproduced and transformed by acting human subjects. Horrell, as a result of these insights, wishes to rehabilitate the individual's capacity for social transformation. Therefore, he does not seek to model a 'social location', which would emphasise a common structural position within a social system, and thereby limit the range of experience open to an individual; rather, his focus is on the 'social ethos' or 'life-style' expressed.[14] These are more general, practice-orientated, and aesthetic categories, which leave space for the transformational dimension of embodied meaning. The 'Interpretivist' approach to the problem of incommensurability may be characterised as seeking to overcome the interpreter's distance from any text's context of origin, by 'tacking between the most local of detail and the most global of structure in a continuous dialectical process', which brings both into simultaneous view, whilst keeping the transformative dimension of socially embodied meaning always in mind.[15] However, Giddens' critique of Berger and Luckmann, which emphasises the recursive character of social life and gives primacy to human agency, so that social structures have only a virtual existence, obscures the relations of individuals to social structures which repeated empirical studies suggest order people's lives.[16] In addition, when reading the New Testament we are dealing with ancient texts, where the quest for any real knowledge about the various particularities of social

---

[13] A. Giddens, *Central Problems in Social Theory: Action, Structure and Contradiction in Social Analysis* (Cambridge: Polity Press, 1979), pp. 69f. See also Horrell's extensive discussion in his *The Social Ethos*, pp. 45–53.

[14] Following C. Geertz, 'Ethos, World View and the Analysis of Sacred Texts', *AntRev* 17 (1957), 421, and L. E. Keck, 'On the Ethos of Early Christians', *JAAR* 42/3 (September 1974), 440, who links 'ethos' with 'life-style'.

[15] Garrett, 'Sociology', pp. 91ff., following Geertz, *Local*, p. 69.

[16] D. Layder, *Understanding Social Theory* (London: Sage Publications, 1994), pp. 140f. and 218f., argues cogently that the layers of society are more durable than Giddens acknowledges. There is a 'depth' ontology to society which his structuration theory tends to flatten out: see also Ritzer, *Theory*, pp. 533f., and M. Archer, *Culture and Agency: The Place of Culture in Social Theory* (Cambridge: Cambridge University Press, 1988).

practice is an extreme challenge, given the paucity of evidence.[17]
Preoccupation with the particular may result in a failure to produce
the interpretative framework necessary for the sort of cross-cultural
analysis which New Testament interpretation requires.[18]

How, then, do we address the problem of incommensurability?
The first stage is to acknowledge that whilst differences exist in the
approaches of Modellers and Interpretivists, striking and helpful
similarities are also evident which are frequently obscured by the
adversarial rhetoric that has framed much of the methodological
debate to date.[19] For example, the Modellers' 'abductive' strategy
clearly resonates with the Interpretivists' 'continuous dialectical
process'. In addition, they both emphasise the limitations of their
approaches and ultimately surrender their results to the critical
scrutiny of their peers. The second stage is to recognise that the
debate within the social sciences has moved on. It is now widely
regarded as a multi-paradigm science which focuses on both social
structures and social actors with correspondingly divergent theoretical positions;[20] and even the relative analytical comfort of these
positions is being challenged by appeals for a more integrated social
paradigm.[21] It is this latter position that I wish to advocate as the
most fruitful for conceiving social worlds as we seek to address the

[17] Meggitt suggests that it is an impossible one: see *Paul, Poverty and Survival*
(Edinburgh: T. & T. Clark, 1998), pp. 39f.
[18] Esler, *Modelling*, p. 6, following P. Descola, 'Societies of Nature and the
Nature of Society', in *Conceptualising Society* (ed. A. Kuper; London: Routledge,
1992), p. 108.
[19] E.g. B. Malina, 'The Received View and What it Cannot Do: III John and
Hospitality', *Semeia* 35 (1986), 171–94, which is a polemical attack on 'social history'.
[20] R. Friedrichs, *A Sociology of Sociology* (New York: Free Press, 1970), has
identified prophetic and priestly paradigms; the prophetic viewing themselves as
agents of social change and the priestly viewing themselves as 'value-free' scientists.
More recently Ritzer, *Theory*, pp. 637–42, has suggested a threefold conception of
sociology: the social-facts paradigm, focusing on structures; the social-definition
paradigm, focusing on actors; and the social-behaviour paradigm, focusing on
unconscious behaviour.
[21] Notably by Ritzer, *Theory*, pp. 642ff., who identifies the major levels of
sociological analysis as the macro-objective, the macro-subjective, the micro-
objective, and the micro-subjective. These clearly resonate with the work of
D. Layder, *Modern Social Theory: Key Debates and New Directions* (London: UCL
Press, 1997), pp. 19ff., who advocates a theory of 'social domains' with which to
conceive the social world: 'contextual resource', 'social setting', 'situated activity', and
'psycho-biography'. Also, 'habitus' and 'field' in the work of P. Bourdieu, *Outline of
a Theory of Practice* (trans. R. Nice; Cambridge: Cambridge University Press, 1977),
and its application in S. B. Ortner, *High Religion: A Cultural and Political History of
Sherpa Buddhism* (Princeton: Princeton University Press, 1989), pp. 11f., who in this
ethnographic history talks of 'structure', 'actor', 'history', and 'practice'.

problem of incommensurability. It is clear that social 'structures' are a significant element of any social world; a social world is made up of cultural norms and values.[22] In addition, a social world is made up of 'actors', who, whilst constrained by cultural norms and external material limits, may still act upon rational interests.[23] Furthermore, the social world is 'practised': human agency is not neutral, but occurs in a context of power interests. 'Practice' emerges from, reproduces, and transforms structure. It is a measure of conformity or non-conformity to social norms. Finally, social worlds have 'histories' made up of both external forces, impinging upon the political economy of society, and internal dynamics, which may mediate, reinterpret, and transform such forces. Any reconstructed social world cannot be adequately understood by giving primacy to either agency or structure. It is more adequately conceived of as being made up of structures, actors, practice, and histories. It is necessary to give due consideration to each of these elements and their interrelatedness, as we seek to imagine the social worlds of texts, in order to avoid the dangers of either stereotyping or losing oneself in an alien world.

2   Social structures and religious aspirations

What working with a more integrated view of the social world means in practice is developed in the following chapters, the first of which presents a critical revision of the model of a normative Mediterranean honour culture which has been proposed and applied in interpretation by members of the Context Group. This revision differs from recent criticisms, which have predominantly focused on Greco-Roman social material, e.g. the work of Gerald Downing.[24] The critique not only addresses such source material but also engages in substantive and methodological criticisms of the

---

[22] This understanding of 'structure' is consciously closer to Giddens' 'structural dualism' than Malina's understanding of structure, which privileges the constraining and ordering side of 'structure'. It is an understanding that desires to acknowledge the dynamic realities of structure, structure as conflicting discourses, not simply ordering principles.

[23] To think of actors as entirely cultural products, as Modellers appear at times to do, generates the danger that they become merely the inverse of the overly Westernised actor: see A. Cohen, *Self Consciousness: An Alternative Anthropology of Identity* (London: Routledge, 1994), pp. 1–22.

[24] *Making Sense in (and of) the First Christian Century* (JSNTS 197; Sheffield: Sheffield Academic Press, 2000).

anthropological literature used. It highlights how this structural view has unnecessarily homogenised the social world and obscured cultural and historical diversity, especially the anomalous character of Judaea. In addition, it demonstrates how methodological assumptions underlying the approach preclude the identification of the religious and moral dimensions of the social world. In contrast, the critical revision demonstrates the utility of a hermeneutical strategy that seeks a more integrated view of the social world, by revealing the prominence of the religious social actor at the liminal interface of values and practices. It also reveals that in such contexts the presence of such actors has a significant impact on perceptions of poverty and gender.

These insights are built upon in chapter 3, which introduces resources from the social sciences not previously drawn into the interpretation of New Testament texts that help us to understand the role of the religious actor in their social world. In the process it exposes a theoretical legacy within the sociology of religion that has either totally assimilated such actors within, or marginalised them from, their social worlds. This pattern is shown to be repeated in discussions of the ascetic in the New Testament. In response, recent comparative studies of 'virtuoso religion', i.e. forms of piety that may lead to the establishment of religious orders, are introduced. 'Virtuoso religion' is a category, first formulated by Weber, to differentiate particular forms of religiosity from 'mass religion'.[25] The concept has recently been the subject of significant revision by Silber, following Hill, which has taken due consideration of the sociology of religion's tendency either to assimilate or to marginalise such actors.[26] Their descriptions of forms of virtuoso practice provide a means of discussing and discriminating between the possible roles and potential significance of such actors within their social worlds which neither assimilates nor marginalises them. This material reveals the potential for such actors, in particular social conditions, to have a disproportionate impact on their social worlds. These conditions appear to resonate significantly with

---

[25] M. Weber, *The Sociology of Religion* (trans. T. Parsons; London: Methuen & Co., 1963), pp. 162–5.

[26] I. Silber, *Virtuosity, Charisma, and Social Order: A Comparative Sociological Study of Monasticism in Theravada Buddhism and Medieval Catholicism* (Cambridge: Cambridge University Press, 1995), and M. Hill, *The Religious Order: A Study of Virtuoso Religion and its Legitimation in the Nineteenth-century Church of England* (London: Heinemann, 1973).

first-century Judaea. The validity of 'virtuoso religion' as a heuristic construct is then tested by scrutinising this apparent resonance. These discussions not only confirm structural parallels but also highlight the presence of virtuoso religion in the practices of the Essenes and other pietists, which notably offered cultural resources that radically addressed the situation of the poor within their social world, a piety of poverty. This scrutiny helps reveal a distinct Judaean, as opposed to Mediterranean, social world that is highly suggestive for our understanding of both the New Testament 'poor' and the Johannine traditions. These become the focus of chapters 4 and 5.

3   The 'poor'

Before applying the insights which the discussion of virtuoso religion provides, chapter 4 starts by reviewing recent social approaches to the identity of the New Testament's 'poor'.[27] These are shown to place such a stress on the social and economic dimensions of the social world that its religious dimension is obscured. In contrast, the heuristic potential of virtuoso religion is demonstrated, by reference to a survey of the *ptōchoi*, the 'poor', in the New Testament. In this context an *excursus* on the first beatitude, i.e. makarism (Matt. 5:3/Luke 6:20), demonstrates how a more broadly conceived view of the New Testament world, which accommodates cultural diversity, proves a valuable heuristic aid and suggests the inversion of the commonly held view of Lucan 'originality'. This analysis of the *ptōchoi* moves beyond the socio-economic categories of previous social approaches and draws attention to their pious practices and the predominantly Judaean location for these traditions. It is argued that these features are most credibly understood against the backdrop of the particular Judaean social world presented, as opposed to any normative Mediterranean honour culture.

---

[27] This review examines: L. Schottroff and W. Stegemann, *Jesus and the Hope of the Poor* (trans. J. O'Connell; Maryknoll, NY: Orbis, 1986); B. Malina, 'Interpreting the Bible with Anthropology: The Case of the Poor and the Rich', *Listening* 21 (1986), 148–59, and P. Hollenbach, *Defining Rich and Poor Using the Social Sciences* (SBL Seminar Papers; ed. Kent Richards; Atlanta, GA: Scholars Press, 1987), pp. 50–63.

4   Transcending Johannine sectarianism

The preceding discussion of virtuoso religion and the Judaean poor has prepared the ground for a re-examination of the popular social thesis that the Johannine literature's distinctiveness may be accounted for by reference to its sectarian origins.[28] Chapter 5 of this book starts by revealing a number of critical problems with this sectarian identification, not least of which is the Gospel's marked tension between insularity from and involvement in the world, e.g. 17:15–18. It argues that if a social thesis is to be advanced as an explanation for the Gospel's literary distinctiveness, it must take seriously its social witness. This witness has been paradoxically neglected in 'social' readings, which have suppressed the Gospel's distinctive Judaean focus with their reconstructions of community history. However, when this social world is illustrated by reference to the Gospel's idiosyncratic presentation of the *ptōchoi* and women, the relevance of the Judaean context is clear. The Gospel's presentation is more convincingly understood in terms of Judaea's indigenous forms of virtuosity, a social form that may indicate distinctive perceptions of poverty and gender, than it is by some late-first-century social schism. Indeed, the virtuoso's unique potential to form an alternative structure within society at large, which distinguishes it from other social forms such as a sect, is shown to help illuminate the very features that unsettle the sectarian reading, i.e. the Gospel's evident tension between insularity and involvement with the world is a defining feature of virtuoso religion. This social scenario, which takes seriously the Gospel's social witness, renders the sectarian thesis redundant by accounting for the Johannine distinctiveness in terms of its origins within the context of Judaea's indigenous virtuosity.

---

[28] E.g. J. L. Martyn, *History and Theology in the Fourth Gospel* (New York: Harper and Row, 1968), and W. Meeks, 'The Man from Heaven in Johannine Sectarianism', *JBL* 91 (1972), 44–72.

2

THE NEW TESTAMENT WORLD

1   Introduction

This chapter is entitled 'The New Testament World' as an appropriate testimony to the classic status in the field of social-scientific interpretation which Bruce Malina's book of the same title has gained.[1] Malina's book, and the model of a normative Mediterranean honour culture which it and other works by members of the Context Group promote, has been widely adopted.[2] According to members of the Context Group, the most appropriate models for the sort of cross-cultural analysis necessary for New Testament interpretation are those constructed on the basis of research and data pertaining to the geographical, social, and cultural region inhabited by the biblical communities.[3] New Testament texts are therefore to be read as the products of an 'advanced agrarian circum-Mediterranean region'. In order to

---

[1] *The New Testament World.*

[2] For example, Neyrey 'presumes' the characterisation of 'honour' in antiquity, and proceeds to depend on secondary material, 'Loss of Wealth, Loss of Family and Loss of Honour: The Cultural Context of the Original Makarisms in Q', in *Modelling Early Christianity* (ed. P. F. Esler; London: Routledge, 1995), p. 140. He cites in his secondary material the ubiquitous Malina, *The New Testament World*; J. H. Neyrey and B. J. Malina, 'Honour and Shame in Luke–Acts', in *The Social World of Luke–Acts* (ed. J. H. Neyrey; Peabody, MA: Hendrickson Publishers, 1991), pp. 25–66, and P. F. Esler, *The First Christians in their Social Worlds: Social Scientific Approaches to New Testament Interpretation* (London: Routledge, 1994). Likewise, R. L. Rohrbaugh, 'Legitimating Sonship – A Test of Honour: A Social-scientific Study of Luke 4:1–30', in Esler, ed., *Modelling Early Christianity*, pp. 183–97. Even deSilva, who 'supplements' the anthropology with critical reflections from classical sources, fails actually to engage with the anthropology: see, e.g., his *Despising Shame* (Atlanta: Scholars Press, 1995), where he appears simply to follow the route set by Malina. However, Downing, *Making Sense*, has recently gone some way to stem this trend. Yet his focus is very much on the ancient sources (from a particular Cynic perspective), and he does not directly engage in challenging the Context Group on their own ground.

[3] E.g. B. Malina, 'The Social Sciences and Biblical Interpretation', *Int* 36 (actual issue misprinted and published as 37/3) (1982), 241.

facilitate the reading of these texts, social-scientific resources, predominantly from cultural anthropology, have been adopted to help provide a model of this 'region'. The resulting model of a defining 'normative Mediterranean honour culture' has four essential characteristics: it is public in nature, paramount in practice, rooted in gender distinctions, and agonistic in character. The intended purpose of this model is to bring values into the open for critical scrutiny, to sensitise the reader to another culture, to provide a reading scenario, and so to 'fill in the context', i.e. to facilitate interpretation.[4] The prominence of this particular model makes it a natural starting point for any discussion of the social world of the New Testament. However, as hinted in the previous chapter, the utility of this model is questionable. In an attempt to practise a more integrated approach to social-scientific interpretation, this chapter critically reviews the relationship between the anthropology evident in this defining model and the first-century text world. It examines each of the model's elements in turn, starting with the anthropology upon which the element was based, and then explores its relation to the first-century text world. This discussion highlights how the adoption, and subsequent unchecked promulgation, of limited and at times flawed anthropology in the foundational statements of this model has obscured the complexity of first-century social relations. Indeed, it reveals the inadequacy of this crude normative view, especially in relation to perceptions of poverty and wealth, gender relations, and religious and moral values, i.e. prominent New Testament themes.

2   Honour, public in nature

The primary source for the model of a normative Mediterranean honour culture, which has been disseminated by Malina,[5] is the anthropologist Julian Pitt Rivers and his essay in his and Peristiany's edited volume *Honour and Shame: The Values of Mediterranean Society*. Indeed, members of the Context Group

---

[4] See J. H. Neyrey, ed., *The Social World of Luke–Acts* (Peabody, MA: Hendrickson Publishers, 1991), pp. xviii, 22.

[5] Also typical of the adoption and promotion of the model in this form are K. Hanson and D. E. Oakman, *Palestine in the Time of Jesus: Social Structures and Social Conflicts* (Minneapolis, MN: Fortress Press, 1998), p. 6, and Esler, *The First Christians*, pp. 25–59.

appear, at times, almost totally dependent upon this source, and Malina's reading of it, for their anthropology.[6] The first element of their 'model' is to stress the public nature of honour. Mediterranean honour is both displayed and competed for in public. Moxnes is typical in stating that: 'Honor is fundamentally the *public* recognition of one's social standing.'[7] The following review of this element of the model reveals how anthropologists' concentration on the 'other' has generated a false and programmatic dichotomy between guilt and shame cultures, and that this antithesis lies behind the limited appropriation of Pitt Rivers' otherwise subtle definition of honour as '... the value of a person in his own eyes, but also in the eyes of his society. It is his estimation of his own worth, his *claim* to pride, but it is also the acknowledgement of that claim, his excellence recognised by society, *his right* to pride.'[8] The particular adoption of this definition by members of the Context Group has in turn become self-perpetuating. Revising this definition to include both internal and external dimensions, virtue and repute, is an important and necessary corrective to prevent obscuring the complex social realities of the first-century social world.

2.1   The anthropology

Pitt Rivers' definition of honour is predominantly the source adopted by members of the Context Group in their presentation of a

---

[6] More recently, D. D. Gilmore's edited volume *Honor and Shame and the Unity of the Mediterranean* (Special Publication no. 22; Washington, DC: AAA, 1987) has been widely cited as literature supportive of this reading. However, despite reservations expressed by some of Gilmore's own contributors, the defining characteristics of the model, as outlined above, remain constant and are affirmed, predominantly uncritically, in biblical studies. Less frequently cited are: J. K. Campbell, 'Honour, Family and Patronage: A Study of Institutions and Moral Values in a Greek Mountain Community', in *Friends, Followers and Factions* (ed. S. W. Schmidt, J. C. Scott, C. H. Lande, and L. Guasti; Berkeley, CA: University of California Press, 1977), pp. 250–63, and the more problematic, for any normative model, J. Peristiany and J. Pitt Rivers, eds., *Honour and Grace in Anthropology* (Cambridge: Cambridge University Press, 1991).

[7] H. Moxnes, 'Honor and Shame', in *The Social Sciences and New Testament Interpretation* (ed. R. Rohrbaugh; Peabody, MA: Hendrickson, 1996), p. 20, his italics.

[8] J. Pitt Rivers and J. Peristiany, eds., *Honour and Shame: The Values of Mediterranean Society* (London: Weidenfeld & Nicolson, 1965), p. 21, his italics Whilst the Context Group are consistent in their adoption of this definition, Pitt Rivers is not. For a full discussion of Pitt Rivers' analysis and various attempts at defining honour see F. Stewart, *Honor* (Chicago: University of Chicago Press, 1994), pp. 12f.

normative Mediterranean culture.[9] The adoption of Pitt Rivers'
definition has been accompanied by a stress upon an alleged
antithesis between 'our Western guilt-orientated society'[10] and
the first-century Mediterranean honour/shame society:

> shame cultures differ from industrialized 'guilt cultures'
> in that their members are group-orientated and governed
> in their attitudes and actions primarily by the opinion
> and appraisals of significant others. In contrast to 'guilt
> cultures' with their developed sense of individualism, an
> internalized conscience, and an interest in introspection,
> in 'shame cultures' what 'other people say' serves as the
> chief sanction of conduct. This means that honor and
> shame, as all other virtues, are primarily assessed by the
> court of public opinion.[11]

However, this antithesis does not bear close scrutiny. Indeed, the
utility of the antithesis has been attacked by Cairns, following
Lloyd-Jones,[12] who describes 'shame *versus* guilt' as an 'empty
set'.[13] All societies rely on both internal and external sanctions.
The distinctions made by anthropologists have frequently

---

[9] Typical of such adoption is Esler, *The First Christians*, p. 25.

[10] B. Malina and R. Rohrbaugh, eds., *Social-Science Commentary on the Synoptic Gospels* (Minneapolis: Fortress Press, 1992), p. 309.

[11] J. H. Elliott, 'Disgraced Yet Graced: The Gospel according to 1 Peter in the Key of Honor and Shame', *BTB* 25 (1995), 168. Cf. the classic anthropological statement of the same in R. Benedict, *The Chrysanthemum and the Sword: Patterns of Japanese Culture* (London, 1947), p. 223, which was used by Dodds when he first applied the antithesis to ancient Greece: E. Dodds, *The Greeks and the Irrational* (Berkeley and Los Angeles: University of California Press, 1951).

[12] H. Lloyd-Jones, 'Honour and Shame in Ancient Greek Culture', in *Greek Comedy, Hellenistic Literature, Greek Religion, and Miscellanea: The Academic Papers of Sir Hugh Lloyd-Jones* (Oxford: Clarendon Press, 1990), p. 253: 'among the cultures of which I have any knowledge, there is none in which both shame and guilt do not both play some part'. See also the more recent discussion in P. Horden and N. Purcell, *The Corrupting Sea: A Study of Mediterranean History* (Oxford: Blackwell, 2000), pp. 508f.: 'Older distinctions between shame cultures and guilt cultures no longer seem fruitful.'

[13] D. Cairns, *Aidōs* (Oxford: Clarendon Press, 1993), p. 42. Indeed, Cairns, pp. 27ff., convincingly demonstrates that the antithesis stands in a direct line of descent from Weber's Protestant ethic – truly internal sanctions can only exist in a society in which children are socialised by parents who stress the kind of imperatives, the absolute Good and Evil, which are hypostatised in the figure of a patriarchal deity; hence the apparent lack of drive for progress in shame cultures.

been arbitrary.[14] The antithesis is ethnocentrically conceived. It labels as guilt any form of shame which makes reference to internalised standards. There is no simple antithesis to be found. For a society to rely simply on external sanctions alone would imply that it possessed no norms of culturally approved behaviour at all; that the initiators and recipients of external sanctions would see no intrinsic value in any standard behaviour. Indeed, as Downing has helpfully pointed out, even Pitt Rivers and Peristiany have more recently expressed their doubts about the utility of the antithesis: 'for the sentiment shame seems to be universal and guilt is simply internalised shame'.[15] Nonetheless, as noted above, members of the Context Group[16] rigidly characterise the Mediterranean as a shame

[14] This is clear in Benedict's seminal discussion of the antithesis in relation to Japanese codes of honour, where the presence of internalised standards appears to preclude the discussion of Japan as a shame culture. Instead, and in spite of, the many indications that Japanese society was construed in terms of shame (displaying a clear emphasis on notions of honour, status, and reciprocal obligations), it is labelled as a 'shame culture with an admixture of guilt': see the discussion in Cairns, *Aidōs*, p. 28. Cairns' examples continue; he cites M. Mead, ed., *Cooperation and Competition among Primitive Peoples* (New York, 1937), and D. Leighton and K. Kluckhohn, *Children of the People: The Navaho Individual and his Development* (Cambridge, MA, 1948), as representative of works which strip shame cultures of their internal dimension in their focus on the 'other'. Returning to Benedict he notes, p. 41, n. 98: 'The presence of the stock, the pillory, and the ducking stool in the public market place offers eloquent refutation to the statement [quoting Benedict, *Chrysanthemum*, p. 223] that "the early Puritans who settled in the United States tried to base their whole morality on guilt"'.

[15] Downing, *Making Sense*, p. 22, citing Pitt Rivers and Peristiany, eds., *Grace*, p. 6. See also Campbell, 'Honour, Family and Patronage', p. 327, again less cited by the Context Group, who notes that 'any act may, of course, produce both a sense of guilt and a sense of shame. Which term will be used depends on whether the act is more generally regarded under the aspect of transgression or a failure to live up to an ideal pattern of behaviour.'

[16] Elliott, 'Disgraced Yet Graced', does take seriously the religious dimension of the 'honour' complex, arguing that 1 Peter is transposing the issue of honour and shame into a theological key. Indeed, this is one of the few occasions when Pitt Rivers and Peristiany, eds., *Grace*, is cited. However, he remains wedded to the idea of the Mediterranean as a 'shame culture': see p.168, where individuals are described as 'governed by their attitudes and actions primarily by the opinion and appraisal of significant others'. Therefore his thesis of theological transposition is read against the 'conventional [response]' of returning insult for insult'. He appears locked into the Mediterranean anthropological mindset so that he is unable to engage fully with the stress on divine justice evident in Greco-Roman honour culture: see §2.2. below. See also H. Moxnes, 'BTB Readers' Guide: Honor and Shame', *BTB* 23 (1993), 174, who relates honour to patronage in the Roman world, as ultimately a relation with the supreme patron 'god', the Emperor. However, Elliott and Moxnes are the exceptions in taking up these more nuanced positions concerning honour.

culture, and consequently 'honour' is predominantly conceived of in terms of external repute: 'At stake is how others see us, and so how we see ourselves. Unlike Western culture, cultures in which honour is a dominant value depend *totally* for their sense of worth upon this acknowledgement by others as "honourable".'[17] This stands in contrast to the work of Campbell, whose important (in terms of the anthropological literature) study on 'honour' in the Greek mountain village discusses three concepts: 'honour', *timē*, 'honourable', *timios*, and 'loving honour', *philotimos*. Although *timios* and *philotimos* indicate, in different degrees, some concern about other men, 'all three are essentially self-regarding terms. In each case it is a question of a man attempting to realize a particular ideal pattern of conduct. What interests him is the success of his quest, not the effect of his actions on others.'[18] The tendency by members of the Context Group to stress external repute, i.e. to give primacy to social structures over internal virtue, has the effect of excluding a significant dimension of the social world, i.e. the social agency of the particular, and frequently religious, social actor.[19] It has the added effect of narrowing the semantic field so that it is predominantly the language of repute that is examined. This obscures the lexical reality, also documented by Stewart, that words for 'honour' regularly display both internal and external dimensions.[20] Unfortunately, the repeated focus on its external dimension has become somewhat of a self-perpetuating orthodoxy in biblical studies, which has in turn secularised

---

[17] Neyrey and Malina, 'Honour and Shame', p. 26, my italics.

[18] J. K. Campbell, *Honour, Family, and Patronage: A Study of Institutions and Moral Values in a Greek Mountain Village* (Oxford: Clarendon Press, 1964), p. 295.

[19] Pitt Rivers and Peristiany, eds., *Grace*, is a valuable corrective to this emphasis, which associates honour and shame with the sacred. However, it is rarely discussed in the biblical literature. It does appear in Moxnes, 'BTB Readers' Guide: Honor and Shame', p. 169, and 'Honor', p. 33, where it is acknowledged that Peristiany and Pitt Rivers dissociate themselves from the 'Mediterranean' as a fixed cultural area. However, because few of the contributors to the *Grace* volume relate 'honour and shame' to gender distinctions, and instead discuss honour in terms of virtue, this work is not viewed as a valuable corrective: rather, Moxnes suggests that it does not 'disprove the thesis of Gilmore'. This view is highly problematic because the Gilmore volume is not uniform in its commendation of the model of honour as outlined; see further §3 below.

[20] Stewart, *Honor*, pp. 34–43, presents a lexical history of 'honour' in Europe, concluding that the most helpful means of understanding it is as a right, at times internalised.

conceptions of honour. Indeed, this dogmatic approach obscures a significant anomaly in the anthropological literature. Whilst the external values of wealth and social status appear to be important features within elements of some manifestations of Mediterranean culture, in the Arabic Mediterranean they play little or no part.[21] However, rather than viewing honour within either a 'shame-' or 'guilt-' cultural frame it is more appropriate, as will be further argued below, to approach our texts without imposing *a priori* such distinctions.

2.2   The first century

Members of the Context Group have placed a consistent emphasis on the public dimension of honour: 'What sort of personality sees life nearly exclusively in terms of honor? For a start, such a person would always see himself or herself through the eyes of others. After all, honor requires a grant of reputation from others. So what others tend to see is all important.'[22] This emphasis is, however, unsustainable. The stress upon external repute obscures both a more complex Hellenic and a more complex first-century reality. The Homeric *timē*, 'honour', whilst derived from one's ancestors, had to be defended by one's *aretē*, 'heroic excellence', which consisted in being *agathos*, 'good'.[23] In the assertion of his *aretē* the

---

[21] See J. Davis, *People of the Mediterranean: An Essay in Comparative Social Anthropology* (London: Routledge and Kegan Paul, 1977), pp. 91, 98: 'The essential characteristics of honour are first that it is a system of stratification: it describes the distribution of wealth in a social idiom.' Also, J. Pitt Rivers, 'Honour', *International Encyclopedia of the Social Sciences* (compiled and ed. D. Shills; New York: Macmillan and Free Press, 1968), p. 507: 'Honor is always bound to wealth and possessions.' Cf. Stewart, *Honor*, pp. 131f., who, discussing the Arabic Mediterranean, notes: 'honor, as we have indicated, was in essence equally distributed among all adult men, and to the extent that one can talk about differences in honor, they were not based on wealth'.

[22] Malina, *The New Testament World*, p. 63. See also Neyrey, 'Loss', p. 141: 'Honour is not honour unless publicly claimed, displayed and acknowledged'; B. Malina, 'The Received View and what it Cannot Do: III John and Hospitality', *Semeia* 35 (1986), 187: 'Honor cannot be achieved or lost without an audience, a public that ascribes or withholds it.' Also, D. deSilva, 'Honor and Shame', *DNTB*, pp. 518-22: 'First-century Mediterranean people were orientated from early childhood to seek honor and avoid disgrace, meaning that they would be sensitive to public recognition or reproach.'

[23] For an excellent summary of the scheme of values that centred on honour in Homeric thinking see Lloyd-Jones, 'Honour and Shame', pp. 254ff. For a more general discussion of how Homeric society was characterised by the warrior's quest for honour, see M. Finley, *The World of Odysseus* (London: Penguin Books, 1962).

individual had to observe limits, which the gods had set, to avoid their *phthonos*, 'envy'.[24] These limits were observed out of a concern for *dikē*, 'justice', that is the proper order of the universe which Zeus in particular maintained. It was necessary for the man to combine his *aretē* with the virtue of *sōphrosynē*, 'safe thinking', to avoid *hybris*, exceeding the limits set by the gods.[25] Lloyd-Jones is surely correct to observe that 'The culture Homer presents is one in which honour and shame are prominent; but their interplay with guilt and justice is constantly to be observed.'[26] Homeric society was, however, profoundly different from that of the first century. It is not appropriate to extrapolate from this primarily polytheistic and maritime society to the emerging monistic and complex hybrid societies of the first century.[27] The development of, at the very least,

On how this emphasis was replaced by 'softer values', see Moxnes, 'Honor', p. 34, citing A. Adkins, *Merit and Responsibility* (London: Clarendon, 1960). See also de Silva, *Despising*, p. 19, who highlights Dodds, *Greeks*, and B. Williams, *Shame and Necessity* (Berkeley: University of California Press, 1993), corrective to Adkins, *Merit and Responsibility*. They both highlight a shift in Greek culture away from the agonistic stress on external 'honour' above all else towards the development of a guilt culture alongside the older shame culture. This started with the notion that the gods envied human success and developed into a doctrine of punishment for the *hybris* exhibited by mortals, *Greeks*, p. 33. Likewise, the violation of the honour of another placed one in a situation which might incur the indignation of the gods, *nemesis*. Indeed, *aidōs* and *nemesis* served to bond people together rather than just divide, *Shame*, p. 81. This corrective has since, in turn, been critically revised by N. Fisher, *HYBRIS* (Warminster, England: Aris & Phillips, 1992), p. 5, who argues that *hybris* and *nemesis* do not simply refer to an offence against the gods but highlight the significance of personal honour: 'central to all these concepts, and especially to *timē*, *aidōs* and *hybris*, is the individual's own sense of personal honour and shame'.

[24] See P. Walcot, *Envy and the Greeks* (Warminster: Aris & Phillips, 1978), pp. 22–3.

[25] Indeed, Dodds suggests that whilst Greek culture began as a shame culture, by the fifth century BC it had become a guilt culture, *Greeks*, pp. 28f. H. Lloyd-Jones, *The Justice of Zeus* (Berkeley and Los Angeles, University of California Press, 1971), p. 26, argues for a more nuanced position: from the first, Greek culture contained important elements of a guilt culture, and even after the fifth century BC it continued to preserve elements of a shame culture.

[26] Lloyd-Jones, 'Honour and Shame', p. 259.

[27] On the differences between 'agrarian', 'hybrid', and 'maritime' societies, see G. Lenski, J. Lenski, and P. Nolan, *Human Societies: An Introduction to Macrosociology* (6th edn; New York: McGraw-Hill Book Co., 1991), pp. 208f. Maritime societies are to be differentiated from agrarian ones for a number of reasons. Commerce, rather than agriculture, is the main source of economic surplus in a maritime society, and consequently merchants are much more favourably located in the political and distributive realms than they are in purely agrarian societies. Indeed, maritime societies were historically more likely to be republican and plutocratic, in contrast to the monarchical model of agrarian societies. Whilst the antithesis between an agrarian and a maritime society is appropriate at a generalised level of abstraction, the first-century Mediterranean was more complex than this

a monistic outlook is evident in the Greek philosophical literature. Heraclitus spoke scornfully of traditional observances and perceived a world governed by a divine law that gave expression to the divine *logos*. Xenophanes openly derided anthropomorphism and argued in favour of a form of monotheism which paved the way for a natural theology.[28] Plato was essentially monotheistic in his religion, and this in turn affected his ethics. He strongly disapproved of the notion that one should help one's friends and harm one's enemies as the early Greek code of honour required. Aristotle, 'closer to the beliefs and attitudes of the ordinary Greek',[29] continued in not too dissimilar fashion.[30] Indeed, *megalopsychia*, 'great-spiritedness', is presented, in book 4 of his *Nicomachean Ethics*, as a mean in respect of honour and dishonour; excess is *chaunotēs*, 'vanity'; a deficiency is *mikropsychia*, 'small-spiritedness'. The great-spirited man is as polite to those of moderate fortune as to the great.[31] He cares more for truth than for what people think.[32] His sense of honour must relate to what is truly honourable, that is, *aretē*.[33] However, *aretē* has moved on from its Homeric heroic connotations to a clear stress upon being and doing good, which in turn is closely linked

---

antithesis suggests. It is important to consider whether it would best be represented as a 'hybrid society', part maritime and part agrarian. Does the relationship between Tyre and Sidon and Galilee suggest that a more hybrid view is appropriate? See P. Schmitz, 'Sidon', *ABD* VI, pp. 17–18, and particularly D. Edwards, 'Tyre', *ABD* VI, pp. 686–92, who discusses the social and economic relationship in detail. When classical Greek texts are used as sources, another problem arises: are they most appropriately viewed as the products of maritime, agrarian, or hybrid societies? Millar's discussion of the significance of the Roman occupation of the cultivatable arc of territory in the Near East and this land's relation to the surrounding mountains and steppe perhaps underlines the importance of being sensitive to this relational quality of first-century societies: *The Roman Near East, 31 BC–AD 337* (Cambridge, MA: Harvard University Press, 1993), pp. 16ff., 506ff.

[28] C. Kahn, 'Xenophanes', *OCD*, p. 1628, who suggests that rather than being viewed as a monotheist he should be described as preaching a 'harmonious theism without conflict among the gods'. In place of the Homeric pantheon he offered a vision of a supreme god, 'greatest among gods and men, like unto mortals neither in body nor in mind' (fr. 23), who without effort sways the universe with his thought.

[29] 'Honour and Shame', p. 274.

[30] *NE* 1.5.4f.; cf. 4.4.10f.

[31] *NE* 4.6.

[32] *NE* 4.7.

[33] *NE* 4.3. 'It would be nearer the truth to say that greatness of spirit is the beautiful completion of virtues, for it adds to them its own greatness and is inseparable from them. And this makes it hard for a man to be truly great in spirit. Without a fine moral sense it is impossible.'

to justice.[34] In parallel with this philosophical shift runs a political one. Homeric society had its roots in maritime society, whilst the first-century Mediterranean was marked by the emergence of an agrarian empire. The differences between such societies are significant. The former generates its surplus through trade and consequently may support a broad elite and republican political organisation.[35] The latter depends for its surplus upon the exploitation of the masses engaged in agricultural production and tends to be monarchical in its political organisation with a narrow elite.[36] It is not surprising that in the transition between these two forms of social organisation social structures and values were transformed. The rise of empire distilled the honour competition so that heroic competition was transferred to the narrowest clique of elite families.[37] Indeed, Lloyd-Jones suggests that the honour complex of values had been rendered almost meaningless by the development of history:

> As the city states lost their independence and much of their importance, the philosophers turned away from the active world to create ethical systems designed no longer to serve the citizen of a complex and highly organised community competing for wealth and honours with its peers, but to offer comfort to the individual human being in his life as a denizen of a vast incalculable universe.[38]

A cultural shift of such profound significance had taken place that the Epicureans advocated that one should care for reputation only to prevent oneself from becoming an object of contempt. The Stoics suggested that one should value virtue and not honour, and the Cynics explicitly criticised the system of public honours. Yet the official religion and official ideology continued to preserve elements of the system when neither the ethical systems of philosophers nor

[34] *NE* 4.3. 'But in truth it is only the good man who is to be honoured.' This may manifest itself in the practice of public benefaction, but is as much a disposition as a practice.
[35] See Lenski, Lenski, and Nolan, *Human Societies*, p. 209: 'The explanation of the republican tendency in maritime societies seems to be that commerce, rather than warfare and the exploitation of peasant masses, was the chief interest of the governing classes.'
[36] *Ibid.*, pp. 195f.
[37] Lloyd-Jones, 'Honour and Shame', pp. 277f. This distillation process was further reinforced by the emergence of the ruler cult.
[38] 'Honour and Shame', p. 278; cf. H. Baldry, *The Unity of Mankind in Greek Thought* (Cambridge: Cambridge University Press, 1965).

most of the religions practised by ordinary men retained these values.[39]

There is little appreciation of such complexity in the bold assertions about the public nature of honour presented by members of the Context Group. Moxnes, who perhaps applies the 'model' with the lightest touch, still maintains a narrow focus on the external public dimensions of honour. He draws a parallel between the small-scale nature of the communities which Mediterranean anthropologists have examined and Homeric society in Greece. On the basis of this parallel he suggests that the 'model' of 'Mediterranean honour culture' is applicable to 'tribal and local communities in Palestine in the first and second Temple periods'.[40] Whilst this narrowing of application to 'tribal and local communities' is a helpful corrective to its blanket application to the 'New Testament world', problems still remain. Which texts reflect these 'tribal and local communities'? Where in the social world of Palestine is this external dimension of 'honour' to be located? The preceding discussion of the Greco-Roman honour complex is highly suggestive of an elite and urban context, as opposed to 'small-scale and local'. How are such anomalies to be reconciled? Indeed, Moxnes' emphasis neglects the presence, within Greco-Roman honour's conceptual field, of *hybris* and *nemesis*. 'Honour' is located not simply before a public but before the gods and within a context of a limited moral autonomy.[41] This emphasis upon external repute leads to the secularisation of the honour complex of values. This is most evident in Neyrey's adoption of the model in his discussion of Luke's makarisms, discussed in detail in chapter 4, §3.2 below. In this discussion he suggests that the Queen of Sheba honours Solomon because of his external qualities, his 'sumptuous palace' (1 Kgs. 10:1–10).[42] However, this identification is not simply made

[39] 'Honour and Shame', p. 279. He notes how Cicero was sceptical in his attitude towards the official religion yet participated, 'carrying out his duties as an augur with a secret smile'.

[40] See Moxnes, 'Honor', p. 34.

[41] Cairns, *Aidōs*, p. 350. He notably identifies an increase, in post-Solonic literature, of 'explicit statements of the autonomy of one's own judgement of one's actions'. He also asserts that 'Behind the idea of one's own *timē*, moreover, lies a subjective claim to honour and an internalized self-image that is not wholly dependent on the opinions of others; to be concerned for one's self image in Greek is to be concerned for one's *timē*, but at no stage does this necessarily imply concern for one's outward reputation to the exclusion of one's image in one's own eyes', p. 432.

[42] 'Loss', p. 157.

on the basis of his prosperity but rather on his more 'internal' qualities of wisdom, justice, and righteousness before God. Such readings, far from avoiding ethnocentrism and anachronism, impose a completely alien construct on the text.

2.3   Summary

The nature of 'honour culture' is more complex than suggested by the Mediterranean caricature of 'public repute' which has been promoted by members of the Context Group. The concept of 'honour' is neither static nor simple. It may be based on types of behaviour, always winning in battle, or always keeping one's promise. It may be based on certain external qualities, wealth, health, or high status; or it may be based on various internal moral qualities linked to notions of virtue and justice. These elements of honour are all interconnected, yet at times may be identified as competing discourses with which social actors, in particular historical contexts, must grapple. The ever-present tension between values and practices cannot be arbitrarily disposed of by the dogmatic imposition of the 'model'; rather, it is within this tension that we must attempt to locate our texts. It is clear from both the anthropology and the Greco-Roman conceptions of honour which we have just briefly surveyed that a simplistic stress on public repute is an inadequate means of conceiving this complex concept. Indeed, this stress excludes significant dimensions of the first-century text world, most notably the rise of monotheistic world views and a developing moral autonomy. It is difficult for the interpreter to attempt to locate and navigate these competing discourses. The programmatic application of this element of the 'model' precludes such subtlety.

3   Honour, Mediterranean and pivotal

The second element of the model of a normative Mediterranean honour culture promoted by members of the Context Group is that this 'honour' is paramount in practice: 'Honour is the core value of Mediterranean societies.'[43] This feature of the normative model is

---

[43] B. Malina and R. Rohrbaugh, eds., *Commentary*, p. 76. See also Esler, *The First Christians*, p. 25; Malina, *The New Testament World*, pp. 28ff., 63, and similarly, Esler, ed., *Modelling*, p. 8, who talks of the 'world of . . . first century Palestine and the Mediterranean generally'.

once again heavily dependent upon Malina's reading of Pitt Rivers and Peristiany.[44] However, when this element of the model is critically examined, it is apparent that it functions at such a high level of abstraction that it places severe strains on its heuristic value. The review of this element highlights once again the significance of the religious dimension of the social world. In addition, it reveals the particular place of Judaism and Judaea within a wider Greco-Roman honour culture.

3.1   The anthropology

Members of the Context Group have variously asserted that 'Honour is the pivotal social value in Mediterranean society.'[45] However, the pivotal nature of honour is a questionable generalisation. Pitt Rivers is the first to note that 'honour' is not homogeneous: 'What honour is has varied within Europe from one period to another, from one region to another and above all from one class to another.'[46] The idea that a value complex is somehow 'paramount' or 'pivotal' when its conception is dependent upon varied publics is a precarious exaggeration.[47] This is not to deny that 'honour' is a social phenomenon, or phenomena, worthy of discussion. The problem is one of clarity; if honour is elevated to a paramount value, its particular significance to a distinct public may be lost.[48]

---

[44] Pitt Rivers and Peristiany, eds., *Honour and Shame*.

[45] E.g. Esler, *The First Christians*, p. 25.

[46] J. Pitt Rivers, *The Fate of Shechem or the Politics of Sex: Essays in the Anthropology of the Mediterranean* (Cambridge: Cambridge University Press, 1977), p. 1.

[47] Malina, *The New Testament World*, pp. 53f., makes the 'significant clarification' in this revised edition that other values may be present. However, following F. Hsu, 'Passage to Understanding', in *The Making of Psychological Anthropology* (ed. G. Spindler; Berkeley: University of California Press, 1978), pp. 142–73, he remains adamant that honour and shame remain the 'basic pattern of effect'. See also Neyrey and Malina, 'Honour and Shame', p. 26, who state that: 'What is honourable is what people consider valuable and worthy'; specific instances may be quite local, 'Yet all groups are concerned about their honour'. Acknowledging the 'particular' character of honour in this manner leaves the 'basic pattern of effect' for the Mediterranean at such a high level of abstraction as to be a curious state in which people simply understand their values to be valuable. However, having made this 'significant clarification' the assertions boldly continue to the effect that honour remains pivotal, gender-based, agonistic, public and a finite good.

[48] See F. G. Downing, '"Honor" among Exegetes', *CBQ* 61 (1999), 59, who notes that Malina in his *The New Testament World*, pp. 32 and 48, asserts that disagreement among disciples dishonours their teacher but later tells us that in an elective group the leader's honour is guaranteed.

Herzfeld, a prominent anthropologist, has led this criticism, arguing that 'honour' is an inefficient gloss on a wide variety of indigenous terminological systems.[49] Not only do anthropologists debate the idea of 'honour' as a 'paramount value', but they also contest the idea of the Mediterranean, as a clearly definable cultural region.[50] Herzfeld, notably in Gilmore's volume, challenges the idea of the 'circum-Mediterranean stereotype' as being the product of 'an anthropology embedded in its own cultural and historical origins, rather than a set of objectified "Mediterranean societies"'.[51] Herzfeld does not stand alone in this criticism. It is de Pina-Cabral's contention that 'the "honour-and-shame syndrome" and the "Mediterranean culture-area complex" are not as useful as tools for social anthropological comparison as they are as tools for legitimation of academic authority'.[52] In a less ideological fashion,

[49] M. Herzfeld, 'Honor and Shame: Problems in the Comparative Analysis of Moral Systems', *Man* 15 (1980), 349. See also S. Silverman, 'Review: *The Fate of Shechem or the Politics of Sex: Essays in the Anthropology of the Mediterranean*', *Man* 12/3/4 (December 1977), 559, who notes that Pitt Rivers sidesteps any delineation of 'the Mediterranean' by disclaiming an interest in cultural areas: 'Yet if the unit is not specified and justified, on what grounds does one juxtapose data from Andalusia of the 1950's from Western European literature of diverse time and place, and from the Middle East of Genesis? . . . The shift back and forth between concepts taken as heuristic devices and proclaimed socio-structural truths makes for slippery going.'

[50] For recent discussions, see Horden and Purcell, *Corrupting Sea*, pp. 522f., who argue for the logic of a Mediterranean region whilst drawing attention to its diversity. Cf. M. Herzfeld, *Anthropology: Theoretical Practice in Culture and Society* (Oxford: Blackwell, 2001), p. 42, on the trap of viewing regions simply as natural geographical regions that frame research and professional discussion. He notes that there remains a 'logical circularity': more conferences and learned works on 'the Mediterranean' 'lead some scholars to cite critiques of these regional foci as "evidence" for their importance'!

[51] See ' "As in your own House": Hospitality, Ethnography, and the Stereotype of Mediterranean Society', in *Honor and Shame* (ed. D. D. Gilmore; Washington, DC: AAA Special Publication no. 22, 1987), pp. 75f., and 'The Horns of the Mediterraneanist Dilemma', *AmEth* 11 (1984), 439–54.

[52] J. de Pina-Cabral, 'The Mediterranean as a Category of Regional Comparison', *CA* 30/3 (1989), 399–406. This aggressive article, whilst pulling no punches, is perhaps too readily dismissed by D. Gilmore, 'On Mediterraneanist Studies', *CA* 31 (1990), 395–6, as polemic. Indeed, Brandes, one of the contributors to Gilmore's own volume, notes: 'it is hardly coincidental that discussions of honour and shame derive from observations in villages and small towns. These are the settings which anthropologists have selected to differentiate Mediterranean people from themselves. Urbanites presumably provide less striking differences', 'Reflections on Honor and Shame in the Mediterranean', in *Honor and Shame* (ed. D. D. Gilmore; Washington, DC: AAA Special Publication no. 22, 1987), p. 126. See also J. Llobera, 'Fieldwork in Southwestern Europe: Anthropological Panacea or Epistemological Straitjacket?', *CritA* 6/2 (1986), 30, who makes similar observations, and J. P. Mitchell,

Stewart attacks the idea of a distinctive Mediterranean 'honour' complex by simply observing that it is inappropriate to treat the region as a discrete unit.[53] Not all people are affected to the same degree by their proximity to the sea; different groups react differently to similar circumstances, and the physical location is not the only influence. In his particular area of ethnographic study, the Bedouin, he notes that the meanings of Arab words for 'honour' differ greatly from location to location.[54] The two most prominent words, *'ird* and *wajh*, which he respectively glosses as 'personal honour' and 'afronts to dignity', vary their relative force according to both time and place. Importantly, for later discussion on the reflexive nature of honour, §5 below, *'ird* requires immediate defence whilst *wajh* does not. Indeed, most notably, for a cultural region that has witnessed successive waves of Islamic settlement, pre- and post-Islamic notions of *'ird* are at variance. The pre-Islamic sense is much broader.[55] The impact of the new religio-political contexts appears to have narrowed the scope of the reflexive dimension of honour.[56] Such subtleties raise questions of both the coherence of the idea of honour, as a pivotal value, and the sustainability, in the light of such regional diversity, of the idea of the 'Mediterranean'. Islamic settlement and conquest is a recurrent feature of the history of the Mediterranean basin.[57] These chapters of Islamic history stand between the contemporary observer of the Mediterranean and the world of the New Testament texts. Therefore it is essential that we vigorously test the 'model' against the available evidence for Jewish culture and that of the Greco-Roman world.

'Honour and Shame', *ESCA*, p. 280, on 'Mediterraneanism' as a hegemonic discipline comparable to 'Orientalism'.

[53] Stewart, *Honor*, pp. 76f. He also notes that Pitt Rivers, 'Honour', p. 509, is incorrect to assert that the Southern European conception of 'honour' is distinct because it is only in this region that honour is recognised in law. Stewart lists a whole series of exceptions from Northern European countries further undermining the idea of a uniform and distinct cultural region.

[54] Stewart, *Honor*, p. 102, and G. M. Kressel, 'An Anthropologist's Response to the Use of Social Science Models in Biblical Studies', *Semeia* 68 (1994), 153–60.

[55] Stewart arrives at this conclusion by comparing his fieldwork on the modern Bedouin with that of B. Farès, *L'honneur chez les Arabs avant l'Islam* (Paris, 1932), which studied the Bedouin in pre-Islamic contexts.

[56] Stewart, *Honor*, p. 103.

[57] Notably taking in, at times, the focus of Pitt Rivers' and Gilmore's work, 'Andalusia'. The name speaks of the region's Islamic past, coming from the Arabic *Al-Andalus*, a name originally applied to the whole Iberian peninsula by the Moors.

3.2   The first century

If the cultural region of the 'Mediterranean' is a problematic con-struct for the twenty-first-century anthropologist, how helpful is it as a heuristic tool for the first century?[58] The first-century Mediterranean is marked by both regional commonality and diversity. Millar's cautionary tone, in his social and economic history of the 'Roman Near East', is notable: 'nothing is clearer than the fact that in this area above all we cannot speak of constant or enduring patterns of social and economic life'.[59] What he does suggest as possible is the comparison of 'sub-regions', attempting to see how visible and surviving manifestations of each culture 'change over time'.[60] Whilst noting that the various local cultures could find expression in strikingly different ways he suggests that a profound commonality may be identified with the progressive extension of Roman rule.[61] However, this commonality finds a paradox at its heart: Herod, the most vigorous promoter of Greco-Roman culture in the Near East, King of Judaea, a Jew by religion, the son of an Idumaean father and Nabataean mother, and a Roman citizen. For all his cultural imperialism, his own kingdom, Judaea, remains at best ambivalent in its attitudes towards Hellenistic inculturation.[62]

---

[58] B. Malina and R. Rohrbaugh, *Social-Science Commentary on the Synoptic Gospels* (Minneapolis: Fortress Press, 1992), p. 5: 'at a higher level of abstraction there remains a common set of social patterns that pervaded all the cities of the *Mediterranean cultural area*, Jerusalem and Damascus included'. However, is this level of abstraction so general and at such a height as to negate any particular heuristic value?

[59] *The Roman Near East*, p. 225.

[60] *Ibid.*, p. 230. Note also his highlighting of the significance of the Roman occupation of the cultivatable arc of territory in the Near East, and this land's relation to the surrounding mountains and steppe, pp. 2f.; cf. the discussion of Sherpa Nepal in §5 below.

[61] *The Roman Near East*, p. 235.

[62] M. Hengel, *Judaism and Hellenism: Studies in their Encounter in Palestine during the Early Hellenistic Period* (1st English edn; trans. J. Bowden; London: SCM Press, 1981), p. 3, notes that 'Hellenism' is a 'complex phenomenon which cannot be limited to purely political, socio-economic, cultural or religious aspects, but embraces them all'. As A. Momigliano, *Alien Wisdom: The Limits of Hellenization* (Cambridge: Cambridge University Press, 1975), pp. 10f., suggests, an accentuating feature of Hellenism is the interplay between the Jews and the Romans. The Jews were 'convinced of the superiority of their beliefs and ways of life and fought for them. Yet they continuously compared their own ideas with Greek ideas, made propaganda for their own beliefs, absorbing many Greek notions and customs in the process.' See also Millar, *The Roman Near East*, who stresses in a similar fashion the interconnectivity of 'Greek' and 'Orient'. As Josephus notes, Hellenistic culture was a melting pot, first a language and secondly a soul, *Contra Apion* 1 (180).

The ambivalence of the Jews about participating fully in Greco-Roman culture undermines the presentation of a uniform Mediterranean honour culture as a general backdrop to the New Testament.[63] Indeed, in sections of Greco-Roman literature the Jews are noted for their 'hatred of mankind' (Diodorus Siculus, *Bibliotheca Historica* 1.2).[64] This slogan, whilst not normative, is of particular interest because of its frequency in ancient sources.[65] What do the Greco-Roman authors mean when they refer to a *gēnos* as 'haters of humanity'? In a world yet to formulate a universal conception of humanity as understood today in our declarations of human rights, what is this 'humanity' that the Jews allegedly hate? Baldry has argued that a concept of universal humanity does emerge in Greco-Roman literature.[66] He follows the idea's progress through Homer to Cicero, noting that whilst it was never a reality, it emerges as an ideal. However, at the end point of his quest he is forced to acknowledge that Cicero's standard for *humanitas* was far from our comprehension of 'mankind'. Rather, it was more akin to that of the Roman 'gentleman': it was an elite

---

[63] This is not to deny Jewish participation in Greco-Roman life and even in civic cults. Rather, the position of the Jews was one marked by their ambivalence and their frequent habitation in religiously segregated communities within cities, evident in their organisation as *politeumata*. On the nature of the *politeuma* and Jewish participation in city life in the Diaspora, see E. M. Smallwood, 'The Diaspora in the Roman Period before CE 70', *CHJ* III, p. 177.

[64] M. Stern, *Greek and Latin Authors on Jews and Judaism: Edited with Introductions, Translations and Commentary* (Israel Academy of Sciences and Humanities, 1974–84), Vol. I, pp. 181f., no. 63. Of course this is not the only perception of the Jews, as the presence of God-fearers bears full testimony. Nonetheless, as R. Sullivan, 'The Dynasty of Judaea in the First Century', *ANRW* II/8 (1989), 345ff., notes, a strong argument can be made against any full assimilation of Jews as a group into society on the basis of their difficulties in obtaining local citizenship in non-Jewish areas and cities.

[65] Stern, *Greek and Latin Authors*, Vol. I, no. 11, Hecataeus of Abdera, apud Diodorus Siculus, *Bibliotheca Historica* 40.3, pp. 26ff. Stern notes that Hecataeus represents a good example of the aetiological way of thinking characteristic of ancient ethnography, how Greek writers dwelt on their relations with foreigners. *Xenēlasia* was considered to be a custom of all barbarians: see Stern, p. 30, for references. However, Hecataeus' characterisation is distinctive in that it provides context and reason for such an outlook: 'as a result of their expulsion from Egypt [Moses] introduced an unsocial and intolerant mode of life'; I, nos. 48 and 49, Apollonius, apud Josephus, *Contra Apion*, 2.79–80, 89, 91–6, pp.148ff.; I, nos.171f., Apion, apud Josephus, *Contra Apion* 2.121, pp. 411ff.; II, nos. 281f., Tacitus, *Historiae* 5.5, pp. 19 (26), 22 (30), 36, 39, 40, 41, 57, 88f.; II, no. 301, Juvenal, *Saturae* 14.96–106, pp.102f.; also, Seneca, *De Tranquillitate Animi* 15.1 and Pliny, *Naturalis Historia* 7.80.

[66] Baldry, *The Unity of Mankind*.

construct. The mark of humanity was the possession of Hellenistic culture:

> The standard set by Greeks for the true man varied to some
> extent according to the point of view of the thinker, but
> always, with one notable exception, it involved the idea
> that a man really worthy of his name is one fitted to be a
> member of human society and play his part in the life of the
> community. Homer's Cyclops, Protagoras' 'misanthrope',
> and Aristotle's 'cityless' man all stand outside the true
> human pattern because they are incapable of social and
> political association with normal men.[67]

This is particularly pertinent for our understanding of the Greco-Roman perception of the Jews. The honourable man, 'worthy of his name', is fitted, first, to be a member of human society, and secondly, to play his part in that society. Note the antithesis, an inability to hold social and political association with normal men. Therefore key to the standing of a *gēnos* is the degree to which they can and do engage in appropriate society.

In such a context the religious exclusivity of the Jews was a social problem that prejudiced their effective integration within appropriate society.[68] Moses was considered to have introduced an 'unsocial and intolerant mode of life' (Diodorus Siculus, *Bibliotheca Historica* 40.3).[69] This social problem was also a political problem that others sought to exploit. In Josephus, *Ant.* 12 (125f.), we are told that the Ionians aimed to take advantage of the Jews' vulnerability in social relations by insisting that political equality must presuppose the worship of city gods.[70] The honourable man was expected to participate in such worship.[71] Cicero's comments

---

[67] *Ibid.*, p. 202 The exception that proves the rule is the paradoxical view of the Cynics, who regarded the mass of 'civilised' mankind as sub-human and claimed true humanity for those whom others nicknamed 'dogs'.

[68] De Lange paraphrases the problem: 'The Jews are a peculiar people; they have never been able to keep religion out of politics.' 'Jewish Attitudes to the Roman Empire', in *Imperialism in the Ancient World* (ed. P. Garnsey and C. Whittaker; Cambridge: Cambridge University Press, 1978), p. 255.

[69] Stern, *Greek and Latin Authors*, Vol. I, p. 26, no. 11.

[70] Notably the Jews prevail in this particular instance. However, the fact that the Ionians attempted this political manoeuvre suggests a deep-seated vulnerability in the Jews' social relations.

[71] Stern, *Greek and Latin Authors*, Vol. II, p. 340, no. 403, Philostratus, *Vita Apollonii* 5.33–4: 'they cannot share with the rest of mankind in the pleasures of the table nor join in their libations or prayers or sacrifices', that is, they are social outcasts.

on this matter further highlight the problem. The persistent exclusivity of the Jews was an affront to good taste:

> Even while Jerusalem was standing and the Jews were at peace with us, the practice of their sacred rites was at variance with the glory of our empire, the dignity of our name, the customs of our ancestors. (*Pro Flacco* 28.69)[72]

The Jews not only declined to worship the gods of others,[73] but also restricted access to their own.[74] Their sensitivity surrounding the Temple, evident in popular unrest, simply served to accentuate, at the very least, the perception of an unwillingness to engage as a people in a civilised mode of life: Josephus, *Ant.* 17 (146–67).[75] Their adherence to laws on idolatry (Exod. 20:3–5 and Deut. 5:8–9) reinforced the perception that they were different.[76] This difference is noted by Tacitus: 'the ways of their people differed so from those of their neighbours' (*Historiae* 5.12.2).[77] Notably, in this context of engagement in Greco-Roman culture, he also notes: 'they set up no statues in their cities, still less in their temples; this flattery is not paid to their kings, nor is this honour given to the Caesars' (*Historiae* 5.5.4). These observations underline Goodman's thesis that it was less socially desirable among Jewish aristocrats to indulge in the forms of showy expenditure expected of a

---

[72] Note the language used: 'glory', 'dignity', 'name', and 'custom' are all firmly within the 'honour' semantic field. The Jews, at least for Cicero, were excluding themselves from respectable society.

[73] Whilst Herod built many pagan temples, these were constructed in pagan and not Jewish regions: see Josephus, *Ant.* 15.329–30 and *BJ* 1.407; also brief discussion in D. Flusser, 'Paganism in Palestine', in *The Jewish People in the First Century: Historical Geography, Political History, Social, Cultural and Religious Life and Institutions* (ed. S. Safrai and M. Stern; Assen and Amsterdam: Van Gorcum, 1976), p. 1086.

[74] Stern, *Greek and Latin Authors*, Vol. II, no. 301, Juvenal, *Saturae* 14, pp. 96–106. Whilst unclear as to the nature of the Temple rites, Juvenal is aware that access is restricted ('any not worshipping the same rites, and conducting none but the circumcised to the desired fountain').

[75] Also, 18 (261–74), 20 (189-96), *BJ* 1 (648-55), and 2 (170). R. A. Horsley, *Sociology and the Jesus Movement* (New York: Continuum, 1994), pp. 83ff., highlights the popular expression of this exclusive attitude towards the Temple.

[76] See G. Foerster, 'Art and Architecture in Palestine', in *The Jewish People in the First Century: Historical Geography, Political History, Social, Cultural and Religious Life and Institutions* (ed. S. Safrai and M. Stern; Assen and Amsterdam: Van Gorcum, 1976) pp. 971, 976, and 1002, on how the aniconic trend was most prominent during the Second Temple period.

[77] Stern, *Greek and Latin Autors*, Vol. I, p. 133, no. 40, on Jewish sexual *amixia*, highlighting its potential to compromise appropriate social interaction.

Greco-Roman 'gentleman'.[78] Roman rule, far from homogenising the cultural landscape, perhaps heightened regional sensibilities; a parallel may be drawn here between the spread of Islamic and Roman rule. What was the likely impact on indigenous conceptions of honour, such as '*ird*, discussed in §3.1 above? It is worth noting that the most Hellenised cities in Roman Palestine are not to be found in insular and inhospitable 'Judaea', but rather on the fertile coastal plain and trade routes.[79] Herod's building policy, founding cities and erecting temples, notably takes place outside 'Judaea':[80]

> But then, this magnificent temper of his, and that sub-missive behaviour and liberality which he exercised towards Caesar, and the most powerful men of Rome, obliged him to transgress the customs of his nation, and to set aside many of their laws, by building cities after an extravagant manner, and erecting temples, *not in Judaea indeed*, for that would not have been borne, it being forbidden for us to pay any honour to images, or representations of animals, after the manner of the Greeks; but still he did this in the country [properly] out of our bounds, and in the cities thereof. (Josephus, *Ant.* 15 (328-9))

[78] M. Goodman, *The Ruling Class of Judaea: The Origins of the Jewish Revolt against Rome AD 66–70* (Cambridge: Cambridge University Press, 1987), and 'The First Jewish Revolt: Social Conflict and the Problem of Debt', *JJS* 33 (1982), 420. The problem remains that other culturally specific 'showy expenditure' replaces the Hellenic forms (e.g. tombs and funerary practices). However, this is not a problem for this discussion, in that it is sufficient to illustrate that the Jews were to a degree abstaining from cultural forms that would integrate them with respectable society. The further assertion made by Goodman that the adherence to laws on idolatry prevented the general indulgence in the sort of art collections fashionable in Rome is, however, almost impossible to prove. It is also possible to argue both sides of the case from the very limited evidence available, as, indeed, does Goodman! Compare *Ruling Class*, p. 129, 'much ostentatious expenditure of the rich was directed towards the interiors of their earthly and eternal dwellings', with 'The First Jewish Revolt', p. 420, 'private showy expenditure seems to have been considered less socially desirable among Jewish aristocrats'; see his n. 27 for reservations.

[79] G. A. Smith, *The Historical Geography of the Holy Land, Especially in Relation to the History of Israel and the Early Church* (London: Hodder and Stoughton, 1896), p. 597. It is no coincidence that the Hellenistic cities of the Decapolis follow the 'great line of commerce between Damascus and Arabia'. Trading opportunities and Hellenistic culture go hand in hand. See also J. Pastor, *Land and Economy in Ancient Palestine* (London: Routledge, 1997).

[80] On the limits of Judaea, see chapter 3, §3.2 below. For the significance of Herod's building programme and benefactions in relation to Greco-Roman culture, see L. Levine, 'Herod the Great', *ABD*, Vol. III, pp. 161–9, and most recently D. Roller, *The Building Program of Herod the Great* (Berkeley: University of California Press, 1998).

This reluctance to build in 'Judaea' underlines the importance of clarity when considering social context. Neither the 'Mediterranean' nor even 'Palestine' is sufficient for our purposes. Freyne has recently, and helpfully, highlighted that 'There are plenty of surface indicators – everything from geography to wine-making techniques – to suggest a rich cultural diversity within the borders of this relatively small territory [Judaea, Samaria, and Galilee]; and our literary sources for the period are aware of such diversity also.'[81] The degree of inculturation in these particular sub-regions,[82] rather than being taken as a given, should more properly be the subject of investigation.[83] Furthermore, the textual sources that provide our access to Greco-Roman honour culture also require careful investigation. They may be classified as predominantly elite texts which present particularly thorny problems of interpretation.[84] Indeed, Greco-Roman society appears most uniform as an elite construct.[85] Nonetheless, careful reading of such texts highlights both a degree of regional commonality and an attitudinal diversity.[86]

The combination of commonality and diversity problematic renders not only the idea of a 'Mediterranean' cultural region,

---

[81] S. Freyne, 'Behind the Names: Galileans, Samaritans, *Ioudaioi*', in *Galilee through the Centuries* (ed. E. Meyers; Winona Lake, IN: Eisenbrauns, 1999), p. 39.

[82] In dealing particularly with the background to the Gospels, clarity is required in distinguishing between Roman administrative and culturally defined regions. Special sensitivity is required in any discussion of 'Judaea', which often becomes an all-encompassing tag for Palestine.

[83] See chapter 3, §3 for further discussion of the significance of Judaea as a cultural region.

[84] This is less of a problem for F. G. Downing, 'A bas les aristos: The Relevance of Higher Literature for the Understanding of the Earliest Christian Writings', *NovTest* 30 (1988), 229, who suggests that 'ordinary townspeople at least would have had ample opportunity to "consume" in oral form the cultural products emanating from above . . . to provide feed-back, signs of boredom, or positive hostility'. In contrast, J. Meggitt, *Paul, Poverty and Survival* (Edinburgh: T&T Clark, 1998), pp. 15ff., stresses the alien nature of elite culture to the masses. However, his stress on the exceptional and idiosyncratic character of popular culture, whilst a valuable corrective, obscures the familiar. Downing in his *Making Sense*, p. 223, again wishes to stress the attitudinal commonality that makes comprehension possible. What is key in these discussions is that such texts may not simply be appropriated as 'proofs'.

[85] See J. Collins, 'Cult and Culture, the Limits of Hellenization in Judea', in *Hellenism in the Land of Israel* (Christianity and Judaism in Antiquity Series, Vol. 13; ed. J. Collins and G. Sterling; Notre Dame, IN: University of Notre Dame Press, 2001), p. 54. Also, §3.1 above, on the 'unity of mankind'.

[86] This commonality and diversity are most helpfully demonstrated in F. G. Downing's somewhat idiosyncratic *Strangely Familiar: An Introductory Reader to the First Century – to the Life and Loves, the Hopes and Fears, the Doubts and Certainties of Pagans, Jews and Christians* (Manchester: F. Gerald Downing, 1985).

but also the assertion that honour is somehow 'pivotal': 'As in the traditional societies of the region today, so also in biblical times *honour meant everything*, including survival.'[87] This idea of the 'pivotal' nature of honour has recently been critically examined by Downing and so will only be briefly noted here.[88] Downing cogently illustrates that honour is only 'occasionally pivotal and is often negligible, if present at all'.[89] He argues that 'life', 'wealth', and 'poverty' may all come before 'honour'.[90] First, he notes that most people allowed themselves to be sold into the ignominy of slavery rather than die of starvation, a notable example of this being Luke 15:15.[91] Secondly, he cites Martin's conclusions on wealth, slavery, and status: 'wealth emerges as a more important indicator of well-being than (dishonoured) slavery or (honoured) freedom'.[92] Finally, from a Cynic perspective, he argues that poverty, along with hunger, thirst, and physical harm, can be offered as a life that is 'happy', *makārios*,[93] without particular reference to the incidence of others' disrespect. It is clear that people's motivations, even in the first century, are more complex than the Context Group's normative honour culture. Philo, questioning the benefits of public philosophical lectures, paints a picture that resonates to this day:[94]

> For instead of attending, the audience dismiss their minds elsewhere. Some are occupied with thoughts of voyaging and trading, some with their farming and its returns, others

[87] Malina and Rohrbaugh, *Commentary*, p. 76, my italics. See also Neyrey, 'Loss', p. 154: 'loss of honour is more serious to ancient peasants than the mere loss of wealth'.

[88] 'Honour' and *Making Sense*, pp. 19–42. It is also discussed by Lloyd-Jones, 'Honour and Shame', pp. 274f., who argues that both 'affection' and 'good' come before honour and that 'truth' was more important than public perception.

[89] 'Honour', p. 68.

[90] See also de Silva, *Despising*, p. 16: 'people considered safety or advantage to be greater goods than honor'.

[91] See Meggitt, *Paul, Poverty and Survival*, p. 58: 'If a person was "lucky", unemployment would eventually lead, via debt, to slavery.'

[92] *Making Sense*, p. 39, citing D. Martin, *Slavery as Salvation: The Metaphor of Slavery in Pauline Christianity* (London and New Haven: Yale University Press, 1990), pp. 20–2.

[93] *Making Sense*, p. 40, suggests that *contra* K. C. Harrison (surely an error for K. C. Hanson) *makārios* cannot mean 'honourable': see further chapter 4 §3.

[94] Contrary to Malina, *The New Testament World*, p. 66, who suggests that first-century texts have little resonance with the contemporary reader because of an alleged lack of concern for individual motivation. Indeed, he asserts, 'By our standards, first century Mediterranean writings are generally boring.'

with honours and civic life, others with profits they get from their particular trade or business, others with the vengeance they hope to wreak on their enemies, others with the enjoyment of their amorous passions – the kind of thought differing with the kind of person. (Philo, *De Congressu* 64–7)

As this reference neatly illustrates, outward expression, presence in the lecture halls and theatres, may say little for inward disposition.

Notwithstanding these critical reflections, the model promoted by members of the Context Group stresses the pivotal character of their normative honour: 'Honour is the fundamental value.'[95] This is typified in the obscuring of any dimension of social value not overtly constructed in the 'honour' frame, i.e. the religious, and by construing the social context of the New Testament texts as part of a uniform cultural region. Rohrbaugh's discussion of Jesus' rejection at Nazareth is a clear example of this. He argues that application of the 'model' to Luke 4:1–30 provides an explanation for why 'no prophet is accepted in the prophet's hometown' (verse 24).[96] Honour, like all else in antiquity, was allegedly a 'limited good': see further §5 below; to be recognised as a 'prophet' in one's own town meant that honour due to other persons was diminished. Claims to more than one's appointed (at birth) share of honour thus threatened others and would eventually trigger attempts to cut the claimant down to size. However, whilst the reading of the exchanges in Nazareth, in terms of challenges to Jesus' honour, may have some force, it overwrites the notable exceptions from the anthropological literature, which show that religious experience may be viewed as an unlimited good.[97] This exception suggests that all in Nazareth may have benefited, in terms of accrued honour, by having religious prestige conferred on one of their own without anyone losing out.[98] In addition, the dogmatic imposition of the model neglects such

---

[95] Rohrbaugh, 'Legitimating', p. 183.

[96] See Malina and Rohrbaugh, eds., *Commentary*, pp. 308f., and more recently Rohrbaugh, 'Legitimating'.

[97] See J. du Boulay and R. Williams, 'Amoral Familism and the Image of Limited Good: A Critique from a European Perspective', *AQ* 60/1 (January 1987), 14. See further §5 below.

[98] It is notable that Pitt Rivers has commented upon this passage, and it is to this very religious dynamic of the exchange that he refers. See *The Fate of Shechem*, p. 101: 'The character of the sacred as the inversion of the secular is implicit in all mythologies, those which define the status of the Gods and those which recount the

fundamental questions as the redactional interest that Luke may
have had in avoiding *atimos*, present in Matt. 13:57 and Mark 6:4,[99]
and replacing it with *dektos*, 'acceptable'.[100] Does Luke's redaction
reflect a particular Greco-Roman, as opposed to Jewish, preoccupation with honour? Is Luke sensitive to the Greco-Roman sense
of *atimia*, as legal disenfranchisement, compared with the more
nebulous Jewish understanding of divine judgement?[101] We will
return to these questions, as we examine further the question of
Luke's redactional interests, in chapter 4.

3.3   Summary

It has become clear in surveying the anthropological literature that
the idea of a defining 'Mediterranean honour culture' is unsustainable and of questionable heuristic value. The 'model', rather
than being 'richly nuanced',[102] operates at such a high level of
abstraction that its validity for application in cross-cultural
analysis, certainly in its present form, cannot be maintained.
Indeed, it is clear that religious and regional differences have a
significant bearing on the extent to which the public dimension of
the honour culture is complemented, or even supplanted, by other
more internal values. Furthermore, it is clear that the New
Testament texts belong within a cultural context where the position
of Judaea and its relation to the wider Greco-Roman world require
sensitive handling. Unfortunately, the normative model presented
by members of the Context Group inhibits such subtlety and
precludes the identification of values which may otherwise have

origins of the world. Both types of myth set the bounds of the mortal world and, in
doing so, establish the graduations of proximity to the Divine in space and time. The
mortal world is confined by an inversion of that which preceded it and that which
lies beyond it. For this reason, we find Gods of foreign origin in so many parts of
the world and for this reason also no prophet is accepted in his own country ... The
stranger belongs to the "extra-ordinary" world, and the mystery surrounding him
allies him to the sacred and makes him a suitable vehicle for the apparition of the
God, the revelation of a mystery.'

[99] The tradition is also present in John 4:44; John also retains the *timē* root.

[100] It may of course be that all Luke is doing is attempting to generate an ironical
link with verse 19: see, J. Nolland, *Luke*, Vol. I (Dallas: Word Books, 1989), p. 200.
However, if the enterprise is cultural sensitivity, then such questions are necessary.

[101] See A. Lintott, 'Punishment, Greek and Roman Practice', *OCD*, pp. 1278–80;
A. Gomme and P. Rhodes, '*atimia*', *OCD*, p. 208, and R. Bultmann, 'αἰσχύνω',
TDNT I, pp. 189–91.

[102] Elser's recent judgement on the standing of the model: see 'Review: The Social
Ethos of the Corinthian Correspondence (Horrell)', *JTS* 49/1 (April 1998), 259f.

played prominent roles in an emic construction of honour, i.e. the religious dimension of the social world.

4   Honour, rooted in gender distinctions

The third element of the model of a normative Mediterranean honour culture promoted by members of the Context Group is its basis in gender distinctions: 'Honour is always male, and shame always female.'[103] Honour and shame, it is argued, form a value system rooted in gender distinctions. Preservation of male honour requires a vigorous defence of the shame of women, of the family or lineage.[104] Honour, most closely associated with males, refers to one's claimed social status and also public recognition of it. Shame, most closely linked with females, refers to sensitivity towards one's reputation, or in the negative sense, to the loss of honour.[105] However, as with the preceding elements of the model, the picture that is presented of the 'machismo' male and 'oriental seclusion' of women is problematic. The following review reveals that this binary conception of 'honour' and 'shame' is an artificial construction, which is poorly matched at the level of social practice. Revision of this element of the model, whilst acknowledging gender differentiation, highlights regional, socio-economic, and religious dimensions within the social world that undermine any rigid gender stereotype.

4.1   The anthropology

The model of a normative Mediterranean honour culture rooted in gender distinctions once again stumbles at the first fence, the anthropology. Immediately, issue must be taken with the male bias that underlies the definition of the general concept 'honour' in terms of gender differentiation, which principally ascribes honour to men,

---

[103] Malina, *The New Testament World*, p. 51. See also Moxnes, 'BTB Readers' Guide: Honor and Shame', p. 169; Neyrey and Malina, 'Honour and Shame', p. 62, and Esler, *The First Christians*, p. 31.

[104] Moxnes, 'BTB Readers' Guide: Honor and Shame', p. 168: 'To maintain his honor, a man must be able to defend the chastity of women under his dominance. The loss of this chastity implies shame for the family as a whole. Women are therefore looked upon as potential sources of shame.' See also S. Love, 'Women's Roles in Certain Second Testament Passages: A Macrosociological View', *BTB* 17/2 (1987), 50.

[105] Elliott, 'Disgraced Yet Graced', p. 168: 'In such cultures where the division of labour and related spheres of life is determined along gender lines, males are seen to embody the honor of the family and females, the family's shame.'

leaving women with, if anything, only shame.[106] The premise that 'honour' and 'shame' are binary or polar concepts has been vigorously challenged in the anthropological literature. Previous analysis, which focused on the grounds or standards according to which honour is judged, neglected to ask about how and by whom it is judged in actual social relations.[107] The polarisation between competitive men and passive women is contradicted in more extended ethnographic descriptions that observe the range of contexts and processes within which persons are granted honour.[108] This is not simply an issue for feminist revision but also raises questions of how variant masculinities are conceived and portrayed. This is particularly evident upon closer examination of Brandes' seminal work on masculinity in the Mediterranean. For example, P. Loizos pointedly questions the influence on Brandes' research that spending the first months of his observations going almost every day to an all-male bar may have had on his conclusions.[109] To what extent did this gender-exclusive context generate a peculiarly intense and specialised masculine discourse about women?[110] Indeed, the range of experiences that women

---

[106] U. Wikan, 'Shame and Honour: A Contestable Pair', *Man* 19 (1984), 638f. 'In the context of men's "theory" discourse, the allure of "honour" has been so strong that it has blinded anthropologists to the implications of their adopted positions.' See also J. Dubisch, 'Gender, Kinship and Religion: "Reconstructing" the Anthropology of Greece', in *Contested Identities: Gender and Sexuality in Modern Greece* (ed. P. Liozos and A. Papataxiarchis; Princeton: Princeton University Press, 1991), p. 33, and '"Foreign Chickens" and Other Outsiders: Gender and Community in Greece', *AmEth* 20 (1993), 272–87.

[107] Dubisch, 'Gender, Kinship and Religion', p. 638.

[108] N. Lindisfarne, 'Variant Masculinities, Variant Virginities: Rethinking "Honour and Shame"', in *Dislocating Masculinity* (ed. A. Cornwall and N. Lindisfarne; London: Routledge, 1994), p. 84. See also Pitt Rivers, *The Fate of Shechem*, pp. 80f., 'women hold in their hands not merely the power to put pressure on their menfolk but actually to "ruin" them', and most notably, considering the role of widows in the New Testament, 'Once past the age of sexual activity women are no longer a threat to the honour of their menfolk and at the same time they enjoy the deference which is due to age as well as the attachment and esteem of their children whose honour is owed to them. They become therefore in a sense surrogate males... a widow with no grown-up son living in the house possesses a masculine legal status.'

[109] 'A Broken Mirror: Masculine sexuality in Greek Ethnography', in *Dislocating Masculinity*, pp. 78f.

[110] In his later writing Brandes has been notably more reflective than many of those who have appropriated his early work. He displays an awareness of the gender exclusivity which characterised his concentration on male folklore and reflects: 'my scholarly investigation was perhaps more a natural outgrowth than I originally realised of my interest in my own identity'. *Metaphors of Masculinity: Sex and Status in Andalusian Folklore* (Pennsylvania: University of Pennsylvania Press, 1985), pp. 13, 16.

present is subject to substantive variation depending upon local conditions.[111] Women's active participation is most clearly observed in situations of socio-cultural change.[112] In such situations they are sometimes the instigators of change,[113] and sometimes the maintainers of tradition.[114] With even greater significance for the adoption of any normative model of gender distinction, du Boulay has identified and drawn contrasts between cosmological differences in 'village Greece'.[115] She contrasts an Old Testament discourse, of Adam and Eve, and a pre-Christian Hellenic discourse, of sun and moon, with a New Testament discourse, of the Mother of God, with which Christian women can attain a 'kind of superiority of honour'.[116] The normative model of honour overwrites such subtlety. The binary nature of honour and shame is an artificial construction that is poorly matched at a conceptual level; people's understandings of themselves are not constructed in this frame. Rather the concept of 'shame' is a better guide to the emic, experience-near perspective, for both genders.[117] 'Honour', with all its evocative multivalency, is more often the analysts' construct and not the fruit of analytical precision.[118] The semantic field of such

---

[111] See F. Jowkar, 'Honor and Shame: A Feminist View from Within', *FI* 6 (1986), 45, and Wikan, 'Shame', on the differences evident from her field studies in Oman and Cairo. See also Pitt Rivers, *The Fate of Shechem*, p. 45: '... the women of the aristocracy. Not only are they free of the sanctions which enforce the plebeian code of honour, their status marks them off from the duty to respond to its precepts, not like the shameless whose failure to respond established their dishonourable status, but because by the principle of *honi soit* their honour is impregnable and does not therefore depend on male protection.'

[112] J. R. Gregory, 'The Myth of the Male Ethnographer and the Woman's World', *AA* 86 (1984), 319.

[113] S. Rogers, 'Female Forms of Power and the Myth of Male Dominance: A Model of Female/Male Interaction in Peasant Society', *AmEth* 2 (1975), 727–56.

[114] D. Rothenberg, 'The Mothers of the Nation: Seneca Resistance to Quaker Intervention', in *Women and Colonization: Anthropological Perspectives* (ed. M. Etienne and E. Leacock; New York: Praeger, 1980), pp. 63–87. These observations are particularly significant for the investigation of women and their function in the New Testament. For example, how does social change impact on the presentation of women in Luke in comparison to John? Are they conservative agents or agents of change?

[115] J. du Boulay, 'Cosmos and Gender in Village Greece', in *Contested Identities: Gender and Sexuality in Modern Greece* (ed. P. Liozos and A. Papataxiarchis; Princeton: Princeton University Press, 1991), pp. 47–78.

[116] *Ibid.*, p. 75.

[117] G. Kressel, 'Shame and Gender', *AQ* 65 (1992), 34, argues for 'greater attention to the particular in the study of Mediterranean cultures'. He points to 'instances in which comparative measurements have unjustly distracted concern from qualitative differences'.

[118] Wikan, 'Shame', p. 649.

'honour cultures' is dominated by language of 'shame'; 'public honour' is notably less frequently used. The emic language for 'shame' is diverse, relating to both virtue and reputation, and is perceived to work not only at the level of social interaction, but also at a cosmological level. These observations with regard to gender are particularly significant because where an awareness of the critical literature is displayed by biblical scholars, and a defence of the idea of the 'Mediterranean' as a cultural region promoted, it is on the basis of the gender distinctions made in the Mediterranean manifestation of honour culture.[119]

4.2   The first century

The separation of public male honour from private female shame in the model initially appears to be replicated in the first-century text world. Neyrey is typical in citing Philo as representative of this normative perception:[120]

> Market places, and council chambers, and courts of justice, and large companies and assemblies of numerous crowds, and a life in the open air full of arguments and actions relating to war and peace, are suited to men; but taking care of the house and remaining at home are the proper duties of women; the virgins having their apartments in the centre of the house within the innermost doors, and the full-grown women not going beyond the vestibule and outer courts; for there are two kinds of states, the greater and the smaller. And the larger ones are called really cities; but the smaller ones are called houses. And the super-intendence and management of these is allotted to the two sexes separately; the men having the government of the greater, which government is called a polity; and the women that of the smaller, which is called oeconomy. (*De Spec. Leg.* 3.169f.)

Yet, whilst gender distinction is a significant dimension of Mediterranean societies it is also a feature of most agrarian societies, where its importance varies depending upon particular

---

[119] See §2.1 above.
[120] J. H. Neyrey, 'What's Wrong with This Picture? John 4, Cultural Stereotypes of Women, and Public and Private Space', *BTB* 24 (1994), 79.

social location.[121] Regional, socio-economic, and religious dimensions all appear to undermine the rigid gender stereotype. Neyrey's adoption of Philo as indicative of the 'cultural stereotype' is no exception to this.[122] To assert that gender distinctions are fundamental to 'Mediterranean honour culture' when it is subject to such variation is somewhat problematic. Perhaps a more helpful generalisation, in terms of gender, is the contrast between perceptions of women in the Orient and those of the Greco-Roman world. Note the contrast established by Cornelius Nepos:[123]

> They consider that many of the customs we think are appropriate are in bad taste. No Roman would hesitate to take his wife to a dinner party, or to allow the mother of his family to occupy the first rooms in his house and to walk about in public. The custom in Greece is completely different: a woman cannot appear at a party unless it is among her relatives; she can only sit in the interior of the house, which is called the women's quarters; this no male can enter unless he is a close relation. (*De Viris Illustribus, praef.* 6.L)[124]

[121] A. Batten, 'More Queries for Q: Women and Christian Origins', *BTB* 24 (1994), 46: 'Although generally the distinction between public and private is a very real and important one, it varies depending on the social location of one's origins.'

[122] 'John 4', pp. 79f. His perspective, rather than focusing on popular perceptions, is clearly based on Greek elite culture. Indeed, this perspective shapes his reading of his sources; see especially p. 81, where his elite male sources complain about women's behaviour. This apparently indicates a commonplace perception that a woman's place was in the domestic sphere. It does not appear evident to Neyrey that such complaints and instructions may be indicative of common *practice* contrary to the stereotype.

[123] See A. Spawforth and G. Townend, 'Cornelius Nepos', *OCD*, p. 396. Neyrey also cites Nepos, but along with K. Corley, *Private Women, Public Meals: Social Conflict in the Synoptic Tradition* (Peabody, MA: Hendrickson Publishers, 1993), pp. 24–66, regards him as talking about elite women in the Latin West and reinforces his view of the eastern Mediterranean stereotype. However, Neyrey does not consider the impact of Roman colonisation in the East and appears to view the Mediterranean as a tidy east/west split. Perhaps as important in considering Nepos is the extent of the impact of the Augustinian reforms on the seating of women at gladiatorial shows: 'Whilst formerly women had been used to attend gladiatorial shows together with men, [the Emperor Augustus] ordered that they could attend only if they were accompanied and if they sat in the highest rows' (e.g. Suetonius, *Life of Augustus* 64.4–5). However, even after these reforms, women were present, even if they were restricted, at the very public games; a full clampdown on women in public life in Rome did not occur until the second century.

[124] Translation from M. Lefkowitz and M. Fant, *Women's Life in Greece and Rome: A Source Book in Translation* (2nd edn; London: Duckworth, 1992), pp. 164f. Notably, the Herodian dynasty were 'educated' in Rome, and Palestine in the first

The further west, it appears, the greater the degree of female integration in public life. However, this east/west differentiation is still too general; Oepke notes that in detail there existed the 'widest possible variations'.[125] This variety is borne out in honorific inscriptions which testify to women in public roles, as benefactress and patroness, examples of which have been found in Italy, the Balkans, Egypt, and Asia Minor.[126] The rigid gender stereotypes which members of the Context Group present are an inadequate basis from which to attempt the cross-cultural analysis of the New Testament world. Even on the more general basis of the east/west division of the Mediterranean, Judaea occupies the border land between the Orient and the Greco-Roman world. Such a liminal cultural region does not lend itself to a gross typology.

Honorific inscriptions, however, are not indicative of a role for the majority of women in the public sphere. Rather they represent the elite minority of society, i.e. the rich. In the elite honour discourse of the Greco-Roman world, socio-economic status was a necessary element for demonstrating the honourable condition of an individual. To be honourable one had first to be a member of appropriate society, and secondly to be able to participate in that society (see §3.2 above). Participation in society required means of economic support: *timē* has from the first instance had a strong material orientation.[127] Even in philosophical literature, when the concept takes on a more abstract form, the *koine timē* can mean both 'honour' and 'price'.[128] The presence of women in honorific

century was under 'Roman' colonial administration: see Josephus, *Ant.* 18 (143), cf. 18 (165).

[125] Oepke, 'γυνή', *TDNT* I, pp. 776–89, and S. M. Treggiari, *Roman Marriage* (Oxford: Oxford University Press, 1991), pp. 311–19. See also Meggitt, *Paul, Poverty and Survival*, p. 68, n. 161: 'The Empire was not homogeneous and contained a number of distinct legal and social cultures. Egyptian women, for instance, along with those of Asia Minor, seem to have had rather more freedom than Roman and Greek.'

[126] Lefkowitz and Fant, *Women's Life*, pp. 129–62, and U. Eisen, *Amtsträgerinnen im frühen Christentum: Epigraphische und literarische Studien* (Göttingen: Vandenhoeck & Ruprecht, 1996), pp. 34–40. See also H. King, 'Women', *OCD*, p. 1623, and T. A. J. McGinn, 'Widows, Orphans and Social History', *JRA* 12 (1999), 629.

[127] J. Schneider, 'τιμή', *TDNT* VIII, pp. 169–80.

[128] This is particularly evident in the New Testament; of particular interest is the contrast that may be discerned between Synoptic and Pauline usage. Generally, the former focuses on 'price' and the latter on more abstract conceptions of 'honour'. A question for later consideration may be the extent to which the exposure of the Pauline corpus to the urban Greco-Roman world, as opposed to the Galilean and Judean world, facilitates this shift.

inscriptions is indicative of the presence in some dimensions of the public realm of wealthy women. In the person of Phile of Priene, we have a woman *stephanephorus*, a special magistrate with the right to wear a crown, and in Flavia of Phocaea, a benefactress declared 'president for life'.[129] The significance of socio-economic status was, however, uneven in its impact. Whilst there is ample evidence for elite women engaging in public roles, there are more numerous records of high-status women being excluded from the public sphere.[130] Indeed, a degree of wealth was a prerequisite for seclusion.[131] On the other hand, poverty was a great equaliser, even across gender boundaries, forcing women into the public market place.[132] If both the highest-status women and the mass of the poor are variously present in the public sphere, market places and council chambers, then the secluded woman of many Greco-Roman authors, like their *humanitas*, is perhaps exposed as an idealised vision for the elite few.[133]

The clear-cut distinction between male/public and female/private is further undermined by reference to philosophical and religious

---

[129] See Lefkowitz and Fant, *Women's Life*, pp. 159f.

[130] Three elite women stand out in the eastern Mediterranean: Cleopatra VII, Salome Alexandra, and, most strikingly for Judaea, Berenice, who petitioned Florus to spare the Jews: Josephus, *BJ* 2.15.1f. See Sullivan 'Judaea', pp. 310–13, and E. Smallwood and M. Griffin, 'Berenice (4)', *OCD*, p. 239. Cf. the numerous examples of women's exclusion from the public sphere in Neyrey, 'John 4'.

[131] B. J. Capper, 'Public Body, Private Women: The Ideology of Gender and Space and the Exclusion of Women from Public Leadership in the Late First-Century Church', in *Theology and the Body: Gender, Text and Ideology* (ed. R. Hannaford and J. Jobling; Leominster, Herefordshire: Gracewing, 1999), p. 127: 'elite wealth empha-sized the retreat of the virtuous woman'. It also paid for the female slaves and the separation of physical domestic space. It is not so easy to partition a 'peasant' hovel.

[132] *Ibid.*; also Batten, 'More Queries for Q', p. 45; H. King, 'Women', *OCD*, pp. 1623–4, and Lefkowitz and Fant, *Women's Life*, pp. 208–24, on 'Occupations'. It is clear that women worked in the public domain, as grocers, procurers, gilders, fullers, and farmers. Curse tablets are an excellent source for this and are a strong indicator of popular practice in such public professions.

[133] See §3.2 above, which discusses Baldry on Cicero and *humanitas*. There is a very real problem for discerning a normative view in that our texts are predominantly from male elite perspectives: cf. Plutarch, *Bravery of Women* 242EF. Illustrative of this problem is Capper, 'Public Body', p. 129, who cites Livy 1.57–69 to suggest that the 'gender space ideology . . . was also a part of Roman perceptions'. This passage ends praising Lucretia for her virtue for staying at home whilst all her contemporaries were found to be absent dining luxuriously. The problem in a nutshell is that *practice* appears to contradict elite *perceptions* for appropriate behaviour. On this problem, see further King, 'Women': 'In both the Greek and Roman worlds, discrepancies seem to have existed between norms and practice, with "real" women – if it is possible to separate these out from the multiple images of the sources – apparently acting in ways which were contrary to the stated ideals.'

expression. Women participated in philosophical education; Pythagoreanism most notably seems to have been particularly hospitable to them.[134] Women may also be seen as regular participants in the cults.[135] Indeed, within Judaism, both in Judaea and the wider Diaspora, it is becoming clearer that women could hold public roles of authority in religious institutions. Batten has highlighted the inscriptional evidence that Jewish women in the Diaspora served as leaders in the synagogue, a role that entailed 'not only religious but financial and political responsibility'.[136] However, upon closer examination of such surveys, a pattern is apparent: female public authority appears allied to either wealth, discussed above, or to specialised religious or philosophical practice. The religious and philosophical context of women's public roles is especially notable in Batten's discussion, which draws examples from the Therapeutae and the Cynics. This parallel is also present in Crawford's discussion of women in Second Temple Judaism, which focuses on the Essenes,[137] and the discussion of women in philosophy by Harper, who notes the prominence of Pythagoreanism. It appears that the specialised religious or philosophical actor, as with the wealthy elite, transcends the normal prescriptions of *humanitas* and may participate in elements of that society.[138] Meanwhile, the non-elite, whether male or female, simply exist outside this frame and necessarily participate, albeit invisibly, in the public world. Gender issues appear to be sidelined in the contexts of extreme wealth, poverty, and the specialised religious roles. These conditions are not without

[134] See V. Harper, 'Women in Philosophy', *OCD*, p. 1625, and Lefkowitz and Fant, *Women's Life*, pp. 167–70.

[135] See E. Kearns, 'Women in Cult', *OCD*, p. 1624, who notes, 'Women's participation in cults open to both sexes is also amply attested by votive offerings and literary references.' Also, Lefkowitz and Fant, *Women's Life*, pp. 273–334; their section on 'Religion' is notably one of the longest in the book.

[136] 'More Queries for Q', p. 46; she leans heavily in this discussion on both Corley, *Private Women*, and B. Brooten, *Women Leaders in the Ancient Synagogue: Inscriptional Evidence and Background Issues* (Brown Judaic Studies, 36; Chico, CA: Scholars Press, 1982).

[137] S. W. Crawford, 'Mothers, Sisters, Elders: Titles for Women in Second Temple Jewish and Early Christian Communities', in *The Dead Sea Scrolls as Background to Postbiblical Judaism and Early Christianity* (ed. J. R. Davila; Leiden: Brill, 2003), pp. 177–91.

[138] On the relation between celibacy and female autonomy, see R. S. Kraemer, 'Jewish Women and Women's Judaism(s) at the Beginning of Christianity', in *Women in Christian Origins* (ed. R. S. Kraemer and M. A. D'Angelo; Oxford: Oxford University Press, 1999), p. 70, n. 84.

significance when considering the background of the New Testament.

Notwithstanding these observations, this element of the model stresses that a binary opposition dominates gender roles: e.g. 'A woman's place is within the private place of the household. The public realm belongs to men.'[139] This programmatic dichotomy tends to obscure considerations of wealth, poverty, or religious social practice as significant dimensions for the understanding of the role of women in public roles in the New Testament.[140] This is clearly the case with Mary and Martha in Luke 10:38–42. This passage is considered by Malina and Rohrbaugh to be a curiosity, and the phrase 'her house' in verse 38 is passed over as 'strange'.[141] The domestic and private view of women is derived from their 'model' of Mediterranean honour culture and drives the reading 'Mary and Martha are known only in terms of the interior of their house.'[142] Neither the etymology of 'Martha', related to the Aramaic 'Master',[143] nor that of the probable location of the scene, 'Bethany', meaning 'house of the poor',[144] is considered. Whilst the roles of Mary and Martha are not clear, and many questions remain to be asked of this passage, these are simply obscured by the application of the Context Group's normative model.

4.3   Summary

Whilst gender distinctions are evident within both the Mediterranean of contemporary anthropology and the first-century

---

[139] Love, 'Women's Roles', p. 50.

[140] Torjesen has noticed the significance of asceticism and its relation to the honourable position of women: see her 'In Praise of Noble Women: Gender and Honour in Ascetic Texts', *Semeia* 57/1 (1992), 41–64. However, on the basis of predominantly elite Greek texts, she remains wedded to the public/private dichotomy. This results in an underlying contradiction in her paper, which outlines inscriptional evidence of women's participation in public life, whilst locating them essentially within the private sphere.

[141] *Commentary*, p. 348.

[142] Neyrey and Malina, 'Honour and Shame', p. 62. No consideration is given to the account in John 11:20, where Martha 'goes out' to greet Jesus. Such differences may indicate a redactional interest in Luke in 'domesticating' the text for urban Greco-Roman auditors. In attempting to generate culturally sensitive scenarios, such questions should, at the very least, be addressed.

[143] See J. Nolland, *Luke*, Vol. II (Dallas: Word Books, 1993), p. 603.

[144] For the suggestion that the etymology of Bethany is 'house of the poor', see B. J. Capper, 'Two Types of Discipleship in Early Christianity', *JTS* 52 (2001), 105–23. Also note the extended discussion of Martha and Mary in chapter 5, §3.3 below.

text world, their significance, as defining features, has been questioned. The review of the anthropology has highlighted the selective view of gender roles which has in the past dominated Mediterraneanist studies. It has only been in recent years that a greater sensitivity and sophistication has revealed the significance of particular social locations for the perceptions of gender. It is evident from the above review of elements of the first-century Mediterranean social world that women honourably participated in religious cults, and were present in council chambers, and they were necessarily present in the market place. First-century texts and inscriptions bear testimony to women's public honour. Emancipation was far off, as their rare presence in the law courts and their very limited rights bear testimony. Nonetheless, what is striking is not the women's private domestic orientation, but the restricted male world of *humanitas*, which perhaps resembled Brandes' all-male bar (see §4.1 above) more than any public realm of normative perception. Gender stereotyping has obscured the significance of wealth, poverty, and specialised religious social practices for the perception of women in society.

5   Honour, essentially agonistic

The final element of the model of a normative Mediterranean honour culture is its essentially agonistic character: 'in these honor and shame cultures, social relations are viewed as essentially conflictual in nature'.[145] This feature is predominantly derived from two pieces of anthropology: Bourdieu's essay in the Peristiany volume, which describes honour in Kabyle society in terms of a social game of 'challenge and riposte',[146] and Foster's 'classic peasant society', modelled as a closed system of finite goods.[147] It is alleged that because honour is a public commodity of paramount concern and finite in quantity, all social interactions are necessarily agonistic or competitive. However, like the preceding elements of the model, this element is problematic. The anthropology upon which the model is based does not bear the weight of the interpretation which

---

[145] Elliott, 'Disgraced Yet Graced', p. 168. See also Esler, for whom 'peasant society' is rendered 'viciously agonistic': 'Review', pp. 259f.

[146] 'The Sentiment of Honour in Kabyle Society', in P. Bourdieu, *Honour and Shame: The Values of the Mediterranean* (ed. J. G. Peristiany; London: Weidenfeld & Nicolson, 1965), pp. 191–241.

[147] 'Peasant Society and the Image of Limited Good', *AA* 67 (1965), 293–315.

members of the Context Group have placed on it. Indeed, their particular appropriation obscures the complexity of agrarian societies, which have more usually been discussed in terms of a fundamental duality of both co-operation and conflict, hierarchical social organisations and egalitarian ideologies. Revision of this element underlines the presence of both sides of this duality, not only in the anthropology, but also in the first-century social world.

5.1   The anthropology

The first-century Mediterranean has been characterised by members of the Context Group as a 'viciously agonistic culture of finite goods'.[148] However, whilst it is clear that a section of the anthropological community views conflict as an integral feature of 'agrarian' society, its presentation as a uniformly defining structural feature is unjustified. The anthropology simply does not support the interpretation placed upon it. This element of the model has two sources, and each will now be examined in turn. First, Bourdieu's *homo agonisticus*,[149] whose social interactions are constantly to be viewed as attempts to gain honour at the expense of another, has been crudely appropriated as a normative type.[150] The highly conflictual social relations which Bourdieu observed amongst the Kabyle reflect very particular circumstances. It is the behaviour of the first generation of a pastoral community who were in the pro-cess of being 'settled' into villages in a colonial context.[151] This particularity undermines its applicability to agrarian society in general, and the first-century Mediterranean in particular. There are particular problems with extrapolating from such limited and isola-ted studies to Mediterranean stereotypes.[152] J. Cutileiro contrasts

---

[148] E.g. Esler, 'Review', pp. 259f.

[149] It is labelled as such by G. M. Kressel, 'An Anthropologist's Response', p. 157.

[150] Foundational for this type of presentation are Bourdieu, 'Sentiment', and Neyrey and Malina, 'Honour and Shame', p. 30.

[151] See Bourdieu, 'Sentiment', p. 233.

[152] See §3 above. If we can be sufficiently sensitised to the potential impact of Islam it may nonetheless be possible for Pitt Rivers and Peristiany's studies of Andalusia to be usefully adopted as tools for cross-cultural analysis. However, that is not because of their representative character but because of their very particular qualities, which may resonate with first-century Palestine, e.g. the contrast between Pitt Rivers' 'socio-centric, closed-corporate communities' in the mountains and Gilmore's 'large rural towns, dispossessed rural proletariat, embittered class relations, deep-seated anti-clericism and rural revolutionism' in the plains, as discussed by J. W. Fernandez, 'Consciousness and Class in Southern Spain', *AmEth* 10 (1983), 165.

particular behaviour in Portugal with that noted by Gilmore across the border in nearby Andalusia:[153] 'In the taverns and cafés groups of men are not in constant competition for greater worth; an agonistic element is doubtless present, but it is watered down by the considerations that the system of friendship enforces. The bragger and the man touchy about his honour have no place in this society; *or, when they do, it is as a deviant, pathological case.*'[154] Is this contrast due to the perspective of the anthropologist or to Andalusia's historical exposure to Islam?[155] Or perhaps it was a matter of season! Boissevain, discussing seasonal variation on some Mediterranean themes, notes: 'Winter was thus a time of consolidation, introspection, hardship and peace. Summer, in contrast, brought renewed activity. The tight social control characteristic of small inward looking communities relaxed somewhat in the summer.'[156] The multivalent quality of reflexive honour has been the subject of a historical survey by Stewart,[157] who cites Schopenhauer, arguing that 'Reflexive honour was apparently unknown to the Greeks and Romans.'[158] Indeed, Stewart suggests, whatever the ethos of the system as a whole, some will be quick to see honour impugned, while others will use every evasion possible.[159] It is important to stress that anthropologists, in defining the

---

[153] D. Gilmore, 'Honor, Honesty, Shame: Male Status in Contemporary Andalusia', in *Honor and Shame* (ed. D. D. Gilmore; Washington, DC: AAA Special Publication no. 22, 1987), pp. 90–103. NB: Andalusia is also the focus of Pitt Rivers' discussions.

[154] 'Honra, vergonha e amigos', in *Honra e vergonha: valores das sociedades mediterrâicas* (ed. J. G. Peristiany; Lisbon: Gulbenkian, 1971), p. xxiv, trans. de Pina-Cabral, 'The Mediterranean', p. 402.

[155] See Stewart, *Honor*, p. 77, especially his discussion of J. Schneider, 'Of Vigilance and Virgins: Honour, Shame and the Access to Resources in Mediterranean Societies', *Ethnology* 10/1 (January 1971), 1–24, who makes a comparison between notions of honour amongst the Muslims of Somaliland and those of the Mediterranean basin. This work not only questions the idea of a common cultural region (Somaliland is further from the Mediterranean than Denmark) but also highlights a recurrent link in Mediterraneanist studies. This theme is Arabic culture in general and the Bedouin in particular. Stewart elsewhere notes that increased reflexivity in European notions of honour emerges after the Renaissance, p. 70, although he neglects to make explicit the indebtedness of the European Renaissance to its Islamic cousins.

[156] J. Boissevain, 'Seasonal Variations on Some Mediterranean Themes', *EthEu* 13 (1982/3), 7.

[157] *Honor*, pp. 67ff.

[158] A. Schopenhauer, *Aphorismen zur Lebensweisheit* (ed. A. Hübscher and H. Lankes; Goldman, 1851). The validity of this assertion will be examined in more detail in §5.2 below.

[159] *Honor*, p. 70.

Mediterranean, have tended towards studying, and extrapolating from, the most remote and least integrated villages in the region.[160] The second source for this element of the model is Foster's discussion of the perception of 'limited good'. Foster argued that in 'classic peasant society',[161] 'people share a cognitive orientation in which they perceive their socioeconomic and natural environments to constitute a closed system'.[162] Since their socio-economic and natural environments are perceived as closed, a zero-sum contest ensues where one party's gain is necessarily at the expense of another. This perception apparently leads to the conflict-ridden behaviour which he principally observed in his anthropological studies of the Tzintzuntzan in Mexico. These included a fatalistic outlook, inter- and intra-family conflict, poor co-operation, great ritual expense, and a general lack of motivation.[163] To explain this behaviour Foster postulated the predictive cognitive orientation of 'Limited Good':

> peasants view their social, economic, and natural universes
> – their total environments – as ones in which all of the
> desired things in life such as land, wealth, health, friendship
> and love, manliness and honor, respect and status, power
> and influence, security and safety, *exist in finite quantity*
> and *are always in short supply*, as far as the peasant is
> concerned. Not only do these and all other 'good things'
> exist in finite and limited quantities, but in addition *there
> is no way directly within peasant power to increase the
> available quantities.*[164]

[160] De Pina-Cabral, 'The Mediterranean', p. 405.

[161] 'Classic peasant society' is in inverted commas since it is Foster's particular contruction for analytical purposes, 'Peasant Society', p. 296. The mainstream definition of the term 'peasant society' is that: a substantial majority of the population are occupied in agriculture, their production and consumption are orientated towards the household, and this population finds itself under political and economic obligations to outside power-holders. However, as Spencer notes, 'analytically such a broad category teeters on the verge of incoherence'. 'Peasants', *ESCA*, pp. 418–19.

[162] G. Foster, 'A Second Look at Limited Good', *AQ* 45 (1972), 58. See also p. 62, where he adds the clarification: 'Classic peasants behave the way they do, I believe, because they *perceive* their system to be closed, not because it is closed.'

[163] For observations on characteristic behaviour traits, see 'Interpersonal Relations in Peasant Society', *HO* 19 (1960/1), 174–8; 'The Dyadic Contract: A Model for the Social Structure of a Mexican Peasant Village', *AA* 63 (1961), 1173–92, and 'The Dyadic Contract in Tzintzuntzan, II: Patron Client Relations', *AA* 65 (1963), 1280–94. On how these traits indicate the model of limited good, see 'Peasant Society'.

[164] 'Peasant Society', p. 296, his italics.

It is this predictive cognitive orientation that has been stressed by Malina and members of the Context Group.[165]

However, 'peasant societies' are more complex than in Foster's characterisation. The idea of 'peasant society' has a history that is rarely acknowledged by biblical scholars. The questions that anthropologists ask and the data that they report are shaped by a variety of influences: theoretical, economic, and political. 'Peasants' came to prominence in the late 1960s as a direct consequence of peasant-based revolutionary movements, most notably in Vietnam. 'Peasants' were of particular interest to the academic left because they questioned the certainties of the Marxist-Leninist paradigm.[166] The revolution was coming from the peasants and not the workers of the industrial world. Previously 'peasant studies', following the assumptions of modernisation theory, emphasised attachment to collective norms and values: notably, Redfield's 'sober and earthly ethic',[167] Banfield's 'amoral familism'[168] in Southern Europe, and Geertz's ethos of 'shared poverty' in Indonesia.[169] However, at the height of anti-Vietnam radicalism in reaction to the complacency of modernisation theory, Wolf identified the 'middle peasantry' as potential agents of social transformation.[170] More recent discussion has indicated the diversity of peasant strategies in dealing with exploitation. The work of Adas shows how peasants may simply walk away from oppression, transferring allegiance to another authority.[171] This transference of allegiance, as Ortner's studies in Nepal demonstrate, does not occur solely on a geographical plane. Ortner discusses the founding of the first celibate monasteries as one response to the complex pressures exerted upon this 'agrarian' population.[172] Furthermore, Scott draws attention to the way

---

[165] E.g. *The New Testament World*, p. 90, and Esler, 'Review', pp. 259f.

[166] Spencer, 'Peasants', p. 418. Note that the journals *Peasant Studies Newsletter* and the *Journal of Peasant Studies* were founded in 1972 and 1973 respectively.

[167] R. Redfield, *Peasant Society and Culture* (Chicago: University of Chicago Press, 1956).

[168] E. Banfield, *The Moral Basis of a Backward Society* (Glencoe: The Free Press, 1958).

[169] C. Geertz, *The Interpretation of Cultures: Selected Essays* (New York: Basic Books, 1973).

[170] E. Wolf, *Peasants* (Englewood Cliffs, NJ: Prentice-Hall, 1966).

[171] 'From Avoidance to Confrontation: Peasant Protest in Precolonial and Colonial Southeast Asia', *CSSH* 23 (1981), 217–47. This was also clearly a problem for the colonial powers in antiquity, as the repeated legislation attempting to tie people to the land suggests: see S. Hornblower and A. Spawforth, '*Colonus*', *OCD*, p. 365.

[172] S. B. Ortner, *High Religion: A Cultural and Political History of Sherpa Buddhism* (Princeton: Princeton University Press, 1989), p. 200. See also K. Nadeau,

peasants may employ covert means of resistance like foot dragging and gossip rather than overt confrontation.[173] The broad theoretical trend in peasant studies is towards 'more sophisticated combinations of cultural exegesis, historical research and political economic theorising'.[174] This clearly parallels the theoretical shift within sociology, discussed in the previous chapter, towards a more integrated social paradigm. The very idea of 'peasant society' within anthropology is therefore questioned. It is within this context that Foster's model of 'classic peasant society', developed early in the 1960s, should be read.

Indeed, Foster's model has been subject to sustained critique within the anthropological community, which I have documented elsewhere, and so it will only be briefly noted here.[175] The first objection to the model is its circularity. The perception of limited good is inferred from behaviour said to characterise 'classical' peasant social relations, and this inference is then presented as an explanation of these phenomena without independent verification. Secondly, it is a universal economic truism that 'good' is limited.[176] Thirdly, numerous exceptions to the model have been documented, where particular 'goods' are not perceived to be limited or finite in supply, e.g. land, positive emotions, economic resources, and religious prestige.[177] Foster's model has been described as being 'grossly exaggerated',[178] but perhaps most telling are his own words on the subject where he acknowledges having been guilty of 'dramatizing' and 'hyperbole'. Indeed, he states: 'were I rewriting

---

'Peasant Resistance and Religious Protests in Early Philippine Society: Turning Friars against the Grain', *JSSR* 41/1 (2002), 75–85, on the role of mendicants in social protest and reform.

[173] J. Scott, *Weapons of the Weak: Everyday Forms of Peasant Resistance* (New Haven: Yale University Press, 1985), pp. 28ff., 272f. Also *Domination and the Arts of Resistance: Hidden Transcripts* (New Haven: Yale University Press, 1990), pp. 137–82.

[174] Spencer, 'Peasants', p. 419. See also I. Silber, *Virtuosity, Charisma, and Social Order: A Comparative Sociological Study of Monasticism in Theravada Buddhism and Medieval Catholicism* (Cambridge: Cambridge University Press, 1995), p. 21: 'What is needed is an increasingly interdisciplinary and eclectic approach to the interpretation of collective structures of meaning.'

[175] 'Virtuoso Religion and the Judaean Social Order', in *Anthropology and Biblical Studies* (ed. M. Aguilar and L. Lawrence; London: SCM Press, 2004), pp. 227–58.

[176] Indeed, Foster acknowledges in a footnote that the image of limited good is not exclusively a characteristic of peasants, 'Peasant Society', p. 311: 'I am not even sure it is *more* characteristic of peasants than other groups', his italics.

[177] Ling, 'Virtuoso'.

[178] C. Jayawardena, 'Ideology and Conflict in Lower Class Communities', *Comparative Studies in Society and History* 10 (1968), 440.

this article, I would avoid hyperbole and simply say that "most good" is seen to exist in finite, limited quantities'.[179] Nonetheless, the appropriation of the model by members of the Context Group has focused on Foster's hyperbole and not his later reticence. The 'classic' peasant society adopted presents such a constrained view that its resemblance to any actual community is so limited as to render it an inappropriate framework for comparative analysis. This is perhaps borne out in Malina's adoption, which asserts that both 'beggar and king' share the same 'classic peasant' perceptions.[180] The relations between the city and the village, the elite and the peasant, and their great and little traditions, which are more typically adopted as the defining features of peasant societies, are all presented as a one-way street.[181] There is 'no such thing as a grass-roots movement in peasant societies'.[182] The possibility of any form of 'popular culture'[183] other than as an 'outdated expression of the

---

[179] 'A Second Look at Limited Good', p. 62. This article, although not this quotation, is notably cited by B. Malina, 'Limited Good and the Social World of Early Christianity', *BTB* 8 (1978), 162–76; however, it is absent from all later bibliographies which I have found on the subject.

[180] Malina, *The New Testament World*, p. 90.

[181] *Ibid.*, p. 93. Jesus' ministry is 'essentially a village movement running through the countryside ... even in its pre-industrial city expression, the Christian movement does not make any great impact on the city elites'. Peasants allegedly depend upon the great tradition of the city elite for their cultural forms and values. He also suggests, p. 92, that 'the pre-industrial city had no classes based on wealth, surely no middle class at all'. Freyne, for one, would wish to contradict this impression of a two-dimensional society, suggesting as he does the *tois prōtois tēs Galilaias* of Mark 6:21 as a social class based on wealth, a possible middle class. See his 'The Geography, Politics, and Economics of Galilee and the Quest for the Historical Jesus', in *Studying the Historical Jesus: Evaluations of the State of Current Research* (ed. B. Chilton and C. Evans; Leiden: Brill, 1994), p. 96.

[182] Malina, *The New Testament World*, p. 94. However, Malina's own assertion that Jesus' ministry is 'essentially a village movement' appears to contradict the idea that there were no 'grass roots movements'. It is not at all clear what Malina has in mind by 'grass roots movement'. He does make passing reference to the Zealots, but discounts them since they were not 'after the reshaping of society, but rather the restoration of the subsistence economy', p. 104. This only compounds the confusion. He does not dismiss them as sporadic social bandits – cf. R. A. Horsley and J. S. Hanson, *Bandits, Prophets, and Messiahs: Popular Movements at the Time of Jesus* (San Francisco: Harper & Row, 1985) – but as an ideological movement. However, their ideology, the restoration of the subsistence economy, is insufficient to constitute a 'grass roots movement'. Perhaps the presence of too much spirit in Foster's conservative and acquiescent 'peasants' is unsettling for Malina. His methodological moves, like those of his anthropological source, rather than investigating the relationships evident in 'peasant societies', reinforce a two-dimensional and closed reading.

[183] See Meggitt, *Paul, Poverty and Survival*, pp. 15–18, on 'popular culture' and the problems of defining, illuminating, and obscuring it in our attempts to reconstruct the past.

norms and ideals of the city elites'[184] has been excluded. This is, however, an inadequate conception of such societies, which are made up of 'actors' who, whilst constrained by the structure of their social worlds, nevertheless perceive and act upon what is 'honourable' according to rational interests. There are many publics made up of a multiplicity of actors. Lenski et al. list a whole series of actors who make up 'agrarian' society.[185] The primary distinction is one between the two great antagonistic groups of the 'rich' and the 'poor'.[186] Ortner nuances this elite/non-elite division with a useful third element by talking of 'big', 'little-big', and 'small' people.[187] This third element highlights a neglected dimension to 'agrarian' social order, the possibility of social mobility.[188]

---

[184] Malina, *The New Testament World*, p. 93. This view that the peasantry actually accepts the elite vision of the social order is stated without further comment. However, as Scott has repeatedly observed, the absence of overt resistance in 'agrarian' societies does not necessitate the view that the exploited are in 'substantial symbolic alignment' with elite values. 'Agrarian' peace may well be the peace of repression rather than the peace of consent or complicity: Scott, *Weapons of the Weak*, p. 40.

[185] See Lenski, Lenski, and Nolan, *Human Societies*, pp. 195f., who talk about the 'governing class', 'retainers and priests', 'merchants', 'artisans', 'peasants', and 'expendables'. P. Crone, *Pre-Industrial Societies* (Cambridge, MA: Basil Blackwell, 1989), p. 101, correctly points out that pre-industrial societies were not class societies in the Marxist sense. However, it is to be noted that this is not the manner in which Lenski et al. appropriate the language. Their appropriation is much more inclusive, and like Scott, *Weapons of the Weak*, p. 43, recognises that the explanatory space of social actions includes kinship, neighbourhood, faction, and ritual links. For a tidy definition appropriate to New Testament studies, see P. Cartledge, 'Class Struggle', *OCD*, p. 335, or Hanson and Oakman, *Palestine in the Time of Jesus*, p. 195.

[186] Scott, *Weapons of the Weak*, pp. 172f. The stark division between the 'rich' and 'poor' in 'agrarian' society is neatly illustrated by reference to ritual feasts: the 'well to do validate their status by conspicuous consumption' whilst the 'poor are "led" to the feasts by the smell of meat cooking'. These observations are particularly pertinent to Meggitt, *Paul, Poverty and Survival*, and G. Theissen, *The Social Setting of Pauline Christianity* (trans. J. Schutz; Edinburgh: T&T Clark, 1990), and their discussions of the consumption of 'idol meat' in Corinth.

[187] Ortner, *High Religion*, passim.

[188] This mobility, where it occurs, is predominantly downwards. G. Lenski and J. Lenski, *Human Societies: An Introduction to Macrosociology* (5th edn; New York: McGraw-Hill Book Co., 1987), pp. 289f., note that the rate of downward mobility is not necessarily equal to the rate of upward mobility, and hence, contrary to popular assumption, the rate of upward mobility is not always an adequate measure of total social mobility. They stress that despite the high levels of infant mortality, occasional infanticide, monasticism (less so in Islamic and Protestant societies), prostitution, polyandry, celibacy, and the influence of war, disease, and famine, agrarian societies produce more offspring than there are positions to be filled. This very real problem is presented by Ortner, *High Religion*, who notes that the equal inheritance rule in Sherpa society resulted in land parcelisation, with units being reduced to levels at which the maintenance of families at subsistence level became problematic.

Just as not all 'goods' are perceived as limited, not all 'actors' are programmatically constrained by their structural circumstances. It is notable in Ortner's study that some 'big people' actively function as both patrons of and participants within the specialised, i.e. less normative, religious contexts of their social worlds. In addition, the 'little-big', younger sons of the elite, and 'small', poor, may be seen at times to follow such counter-cultural routes. They adopt and adapt particular historical and cultural resources to the circumstances in which they find themselves. These responses are neither 'essentially' nor 'viciously' conflictual in nature.

Nonetheless, before looking at the first-century text world it is important to stress, whilst notable exceptions have been presented, that agonistic social relations and the perception of 'limited good' are observable social phenomena.[189] However, 'limited good' is not a universally defining feature of 'agrarian' societies. Such societies are marked by both co-operation and competition, by perceptions analogous to limited good and ideologies of equality. The prominence of one element of this duality, i.e. limited good, should not be seen as the defining feature of a particular society but rather as the focus of investigation. How and why does such a conflict-generating perception come to take precedence over co-operation at any particular time and place? Ortner's ethnographic history of Sherpa Buddhism is a rare example of such an investigation. It documents, as a fortuitous by-product, the emergence of a consciousness similar to that of 'limited good', which she clearly describes without labelling it as such, e.g.: 'there seem to be cultural beliefs that specifically embody the notion that the rich are rich illegitimately, as a result of taking resources that belong to others'.[190] This perception even extends to health: 'every time the

Cf. R. L. Rohrbaugh, 'The Pre-Industrial City in Luke–Acts: Urban Social Relations', in *The World of Luke–Acts* (ed. J. Neyrey; Peabody, MA: Hendrickson Publishers, 1991), p. 128, whose emphasis in arguing against Meek's idea of 'status inconsistency' is that 'social mobility was nearly non-existent'.

[189] Du Boulay and Williams suggest that, whilst an ideology approximating that of 'limited good' may be observed, the meaning of individuals' behaviour depends less on images of limited good than on 'images of other goods which accord with, oppose, or complement them ... it is better to view European peasant societies within a more comprehensive framework'. See 'Amoral Familism and the Image of Limited Good', pp. 12f. In the anthropological literature the perceptions of 'limited good' and its European counterpart 'amoral familism' are now conspicuous by their absence, having being replaced by more contingent descriptive approaches.

[190] Anthropology, in its desire to establish itself as an independent and sociologically rigorous inquiry, 'could not tolerate the messy complexities of

ruling family gets married there's a death in the village'.[191] Ortner documents a breakdown of the social and symbolic legitimation of the elite, which previously had sustained the structural dualism between ideologies of egalitarianism and hierarchical social organisation. It appears that repeated colonial rule had heightened the already present contradictory tendencies in this society (the Hindu Gorkha state in the eighteenth century, the Nepal state in the nineteenth century, and the British raj in the late nineteenth and early twentieth centuries).[192] It reinforced the elite, hierarchical structure by providing external military patrons whilst at the same time undermining the indigenous political and religious legitimacy.[193] This position was further exacerbated by the pressure on land caused by a combination of geographical isolation, parcelisation of family land plots, and excessive taxation, which led to increases in debt bondage, tenanted labour, and elite absentee landlords.[194] However, the emergence of this consciousness did not generate a monochrome, 'essentially' agonistic, society. Rather this structural dissonance led social actors to draw upon the historical and cultural resources at hand to respond to this crisis in legitimation; among a number of responses, which included emigration and trading strategies, was the founding of the first celibate monasteries. The 'actors' in this episode all adopted roles which in turn challenged, transformed, and reproduced elements within their social world. What stands out in Ortner's discussion is the complexity of conceiving the social world of an 'agrarian' society and how her combination of cultural exegesis, historical research, and political economic theorising may help us to access this complexity.

5.2   The first century

The essentially agonistic nature of the normative Mediterranean honour culture presented by members of the Context Group implies that since all 'goods' exist in limited amounts, 'which cannot

historical contingency', N. Thomas, 'History and Anthropology', *ESCA*, p. 273. This failure to place culture in historical context was particularly pronounced in the 1960s and 1970s. However, more recently, historical concerns have been addressed: Ortner's cultural and political history of the Sherpa Buddhism is a good example.

[191] Ortner, *High Religion*, p. 121.

[192] *Ibid.*, p. 91.

[193] *Ibid.*, pp. 95f.

[194] *Ibid.*, p. 118.

be increased or expanded',[195] individuals can only improve their social position at the expense of others. Therefore any apparent improvement in an individual's position is viewed as 'a threat to the whole community'.[196] Community stability is maintained only by adopting the highly conservative strategy of perpetuating existing social arrangements, by constantly challenging any social interaction which may be viewed as an inappropriate claim to honour.[197] The Gospels are allegedly full of such exchanges.[198] Jesus' social interactions are all characterised as competitions for honour.[199] Even 'innocent' questions are challenges, and virtually any form of social intercourse – gift giving, dinner invitations, discussions in public places, buying and selling – exposes the participants to the possibility of competition for honour.[200] When a challenge has been posed, 'the challenged *must* make a response'.[201] However, the Context Group's identification of this element in the first-century world, following the pattern set in their reading of the anthropology, is both selective and overstated.

Malina, in his fullest application of this element of the model to date, asserts that 'in the first century Mediterranean world, just as in

[195] Malina, *The New Testament World*, p. 95.

[196] *Ibid.*, p. 95. See also D. E. Oakman, 'The Countryside in Luke–Acts', in *The Social World of Luke–Acts* (ed. J. H. Neyrey; Peabody, MA: Hendrickson Publishers, 1991), p. 159, paraphrasing J. Potter, M. Diaz, and G. Foster, eds., *Peasant Society: A Reader* (Boston: Little, Brown and Company, 1967), pp. 304–5.

[197] *The New Testament World*, p. 96: 'Most people would be interested in maintaining things just the way they are.' See also J. H. Neyrey, 'Questions, *Chreiai*, and Challenges to Honor: The Interface of Rhetoric and Culture in Mark's Gospel', *CBQ* 60 (1998), 669: 'if someone acquires honor by prowess or cleverness, others will perceive themselves as losing'.

[198] J. H. Neyrey, *Honour and Shame and the Gospel of Matthew* (Louisville: Westminster John Knox, 1998), pp. 44–52. He claims to identify this phenomenon throughout the Gospel.

[199] D. de Silva, *Honor, Patronage, Kinship and Purity: Unlocking New Testament Culture* (Downers Grove, IL: IVP, 2000), p. 29.

[200] See Esler, *The First Christians*, p. 27.

[201] De Silva, *Honor*, p. 29 my italics. See also Malina, *The New Testament World*, p. 44, who adds a further intensity to the competition for honour by suggesting that it was highly dishonourable to settle disputes with equals in any legal court. This assertion is undermined by copious material in Roman law on *iniuria* which suggests ready recourse to law on matters of reputation: see R. Zimmermann, '*Iniuria* and defamation', *OCD*, p. 759. See also Stewart, *Honor*, p. 80, on Pitt Rivers and the recourse to law (Malina's source at this point), and how Stewart demonstrates that Pitt Rivers' argument only applies in very particular cases, notably the secret revenges of Spanish drama. However, it must also be noted that the relationship between *iniuria* and honour may indicate a discontinuity between the Greco-Roman linguistic field of honour and the Context Group's conceptual definition.

nearly all peasant societies, all goods are believed to be limited'.[202]
To support this contention he cites Aristotle: 'For the amount of
such property sufficient in itself for a good life is not unlimited'
(*Politics* 3.9, 1256b). However, this citation as evidence of this
perception is at best naive. In the preceding line to that cited by
Malina, Aristotle quotes Solon: 'But of riches no bound has been
fixed or revealed to men.' Aristotle is discussing an idealised natural
limit, not the general perceptions of Athens in the fourth century
BC, or even those of the first-century Mediterranean. Indeed, as
Capper has neatly summarised, there are three clearly distinguish-
able accounts of social and cultural history in early Greek thinking:
the Golden Age – a theory of decline and degeneration; a cyclical
theory of eternal recurrence; and theories of progress.[203] It is clear
that Hellenistic philosophical models did allow that human society
is capable of growth. However, they would often insist that this
improvement is dependent on men embracing the appropriate
philosophical way of life. This is clearly evident in Josephus'
derivative discussion of the three forms of 'Jewish philosophy'
which made up first-century Judaism, *BJ* 2.8.14 (164) (cf. *Ant.*
18.4.9).[204] The picture that Malina presents in his citation of
Aristotle as a proof text is unsustainable.

Neyrey and Rohrbaugh also assert that the first-century social
world was ordered by the perception of limited good, which
consequently led to agonistic social relations.[205] Initially they
appear to present a stronger case than Malina's, offering not one
but a series of illustrative texts. However, upon closer examination
a pattern is apparent in their appropriation. They extrapolate from
very particular passages, presenting their readings as proofs of

---

[202] B. Malina, 'Wealth and Poverty in the New Testament and its World',
Int 41 (1987), 362. Indeed, he presents it as an apparently 'self-evident truth' of the
New Testament world.

[203] 'Reciprocity and the Ethic of Acts', in *Witness to the Gospel* (ed. I. H. Marshall
and D. Peterson; Grand Rapids: Eerdmans, 1998), p. 504, following G. Kerferd, *The
Sophistic Movement* (Cambridge: Cambridge University Press, 1981), p. 125. On
the Golden Age theory of degeneration and the theories of progress, see W. K. C.
Guthrie, *History of Greek Philosophy*, Vol. I (Cambridge: Cambridge University
Press, 1962), p. 400; Vol. II (Cambridge: Cambridge University Press, 1965), pp. 182,
248. See further J. Vallance, 'Anthropology', *OCD*, p. 102.

[204] The presentation of three forms of 'Jewish philosophy' strongly parallels the
first-century Hellenistic schools: see Schürer, *HJPAJC* II, pp. 392f. Also *Vita* 2.12;
Ant. 15.10.4 (371).

[205] See J. H. Neyrey and R. L. Rohrbaugh, ' "He Must Increase, I Must Decrease"
(John 3:30): A Cultural and Social Interpretation', *CBQ* 63 (2001), 464–83.

normative behaviour. Typical of this is their citation of Plutarch, *On Listening* 44B:[206] 'As though commendation were money, he feels that he is robbing himself of every bit that he bestows on another.' However, this passage is not even close to presenting normative perceptions. Plutarch is discussing a particular social type, the 'offensive and tiresome listener',[207] and comment should be contrasted with his comments at 44C: 'For to persons who are truly and consistently good it is the highest credit to bestow credit upon someone deserving of credit, and the most conspicuous honour to honour such a man, since this accrues a superabundant and generous sort of repute.' Honour, in this particular case, is neither perceived to be limited nor the subject of an agonistic reaction. Another feature of Neyrey and Rohrbaugh's proof texts is the preponderance of elite contexts where the concept of honour may more appropriately be described as 'power' rather than 'virtue' or 'repute': see Josephus, *BJ* 1.23.5 (459), *Ant.* 2.11.1 (255); 4.2.4 (32) and Fronto, *Letters* 4.1.[208] Indeed, there is a certain naivety in their reading of Josephus' clearly apologetic account of John, son of Levi's motives in opposing his operations in Galilee, *Vita* 25 (122). In this case the 'perceived' loss is palpable. It is not an abstract repute that is at stake, but survival. Yet on the basis of such 'clearly stated' references to this normative perception Neyrey and Rohrbaugh argue by association that it is 'implied' in a number of New Testament texts.[209] For example, in Mark 6:1–5, Jesus the carpenter's son gains status by speaking with authority in the synagogue, which is interpreted by the Nazareans as their loss.[210] However, this reading accords neither with Plutarch's discussion of praise mentioned above nor with the exceptions to the model outlined in the discussion of the anthropology, which revealed that religious experience may be viewed as unlimited in supply.

The usually more subtle Elliott has also stressed this element of the Context Group's normative honour. He presents the 'essentially conflictual' nature of social relations as a 'crucial feature of Hellenic

---

[206] *Ibid.*, p. 469. Similar problems arise in their handling of Plutarch, *Old Men* 787D.

[207] To be compared with the 'opposite type of person, light-minded and flighty' (44D).

[208] Neyrey and Rohrbaugh, 'He Must Increase', pp. 469f.

[209] See their table 'Ancient Illustrations of Limited Good', *ibid.*, p. 477.

[210] *Ibid.*, p. 473.

(and Hellenistic) culture'.[211] His understanding, drawn from Gouldner's *The Hellenic World*,[212] is notably Hellenic. Yet, whilst it is clear that competition was a significant feature of Hellenistic culture, it was clearly an elite preoccupation.[213] The love of honour, *philotimia*, was a prominent feature of this agonistic drive. However, the sort of honours desired were rather more formal than the conception of public repute promoted by members of the Context Group, and took the form of inscriptions, golden crowns, and statues of bronze (e.g. Josephus, *Ant.* 14 (152–4)). The competition, rather than being regular and reflexive, primarily took the form of orchestrated philosophical, legal, and public debates and so should not be taken as indicative of standard social relations. Indeed, intensely agonistic relations are perhaps more pertinent to the understanding of Homeric society than of the first-century Mediterranean in general.[214] The intensity of Hellenic agonistic society was supplemented in Hellenistic times by 'softer values'.[215] The earlier ideal of the warrior hero was incompatible with the values needed to facilitate effective relations in the more complex Hellenistic states, i.e. the values of justice and moderation.[216] Indeed, Gouldner discusses not only the conflictual

[211] Elliott, 'Disgraced Yet Graced', p. 168. See also K. Hanson, '"How Honorable! How Shameful!" A Cultural Analysis of Matthew's Makarisms and Reproaches', *Semeia* 68 (1994), 81.

[212] A. W. Gouldner, *The Hellenic World: A Sociological Analysis* (Enter Plato: Classical Greece and the Origins of Social Theory; New York: Harper & Row, 1969).

[213] A. Spawforth and S. Instone, 'Agones', *OCD*, p. 41. Notably for the place of Judaea in the Greco-Roman Mediterranean they argue: 'Whatever the qualitative view taken of post-Classical agonistic culture...its power in the shaping of later Hellenism is undeniable, and the limits of its diffusion suggest the limits of Hellenism.' It is notable that 'competition' rather than conflict is the language used by the classicists, whilst Malina wishes to set up a contrast: 'human encounters as competitive (U.S.) versus agonistic or filled with potential conflict (Mediterranean)', 'The Received View', p. 188. This antithesis between competition and conflict, rather than being of any particular heuristic significance, is a false one that is about presenting the Mediterranean as essentially 'other'.

[214] See Finley, *The World of Odysseus*. He argues that Homeric society was characterised by the warrior's quest for honour.

[215] Moxnes, 'BTB Readers' Guide: Honor and Shame', p. 172. Indeed, Moxnes stands out from the Context Group in his sensitive handling of the agonistic dimension of the social world, suggesting, p. 175, that 'honor and shame co-exist with other less competitive values'.

[216] It is perhaps significant that here Hellenic culture was the culture of a maritime society, as opposed to the more hybrid and agrarian societies of Hellenism. However, as Stewart, *Honor*, p. 60, n. 19, observes, there has only been a very limited critical discussion of later ancient Greek notions of honour. Therefore, the significance of this distinction remains conjecture, for the present.

dimension of social relations but also the 'norm of reciprocity'.[217] This is not to suggest that the competition for honours was wholly sidelined. Rather it manifested itself most explicitly in the systems of city honours for public benefactors.[218] This form of competition for honour was not reflexive, however, and was a minority practice, which in itself was not universally welcomed. It is amongst the Cynics that the strongest critiques are found. Dio Chrysostom swings from advocating total withdrawal from public life (*Or.* 66) to urging participation, not for honours but the public good (*Or.* 44.77–8).[219] Indeed, Downing has highlighted the subversion of the agonistic lust for honour, *philodoxia*, as a literary theme.[220] However, the folly of viewing honour as paramount or pivotal was not just evident to the Cynics:[221] 'Now some tickle these men as it were by flattery and puff them up; others maliciously throw out a little tribute as a kind of bait to elicit self praise' (Plutarch, *Moralia: On Inoffensive Self-Praise*, 547C).[222] Honour for honour's sake was viewed as facile, not paramount: 'if you are going to honour anything at all outside the sphere of the moral purpose, you have destroyed your moral purpose' (Epictetus, *Arrian's Discourses*, 4.4.23–4). Furthermore, the wise man was advised not to be touchy about his honour; he should 'never allow himself to pay to the one who offered him an insult the compliment of admitting that it was offered' (Seneca, *De Constantia* 89). For Seneca, the problem is not

---

[217] A. W. Gouldner, 'The Norm of Reciprocity: A Preliminary Statement', in *Friends, Followers and Factions* (ed. S. W. Schmidt, J. C. Scott, C. H. Lande, and L. Guasti; Berkeley, CA: University of California Press, 1977), pp. 28–42. See also T. W. Gallant, *Risk and Survival in Ancient Greece* (Cambridge: Polity Press, 1991), p. 146, who, whilst noting how individuals and individual households are locked into a continual struggle with every other person for access to the resources required for life, observes that: 'Our sources from antiquity focus almost exclusively on the ideational aspects of obligation and reciprocity, stressing in particular the aspect of equality.'

[218] See F. W. Danker, *Benefactor: Epigraphic Study of a Graeco-Roman and New Testament Semantic Field* (St Louis: Clayton, 1982), pp. 26–7; Stewart, *Honor*, pp. 59f. and Moxnes, 'BTB Readers' Guide: Honor and Shame', pp. 172f., who cites Josephus, *Ant.* 15 (152-4) and the honor bestowed on Hyrcanus to suggest that 'even foreigners could receive such honors'. However, Hyrcanus is perhaps more appropriately viewed as the head of a temple state than as a mere 'foreigner'.

[219] Note also that the Epicureans advocated a total withdrawal from public life.

[220] Downing, 'Honour', p. 64, who cites amongst others Socrates laying a counter charge upon the Cynic Antisthenes: 'I spy your love of fame, *philodoxia*, peeping through' (Diogenes Laertius, *Lives* 6.1.8).

[221] Elliott, 'Disgraced Yet Graced', p. 169, notably uses the same sources, Plutarch and Dio Chrysostom, to suggest a purely positive perception of the preoccupation with honour.

[222] Cf. Epictetus, *Arrian's Discourses* 3.26.15–22, and Cicero, *De Officiis* 2.12.

one of potential danger to social standing, but one of dealing with one's feelings.[223] Whilst such advice clearly demonstrates that individuals in the Greco-Roman world were sensitive about their social standing, it is nowhere evident, in the Roman world at least, that a man brought infamy upon himself if he failed to respond to an insult in a reflexive manner.[224] There appears to be a conflict between the conception of a 'viciously agonistic' Mediterranean honour culture and the more nuanced semantic and social fields of Greco-Roman social interactions.[225]

The programmatic application of a 'viciously agonistic' honour culture does fail to give sufficient attention to the particular nature of Greco-Roman honour cultures.[226] This is particularly evident in Malina's discussion of 3 John and hospitality. Hospitality, or the lack of it, is read by Malina within the context of a contest for finite and paramount honour. The issue at stake within the letter is apparently the 'moral brokerage, ability and honor of the Elder'.[227] The letter is the elder's attempt to defend himself from the 'challenge' laid down by Diotrephes in his refusal to offer hospitality. It is his 'culturally required attempt at satisfaction'.[228] However, in the light of the preceding discussion of honour cultures this programmatic reading may be observed as problematic on a number of levels. Whilst Diotrephes fits neatly into the elite honour discourse – he loves to be first, *philoprōteuein*[229] – the elder does not appear to be playing the game. His letter is not obviously public.[230] It is not addressed to his alleged adversary and it appears to

---

[223] Seneca on insults: 'men are not harmed, but angered by it', *De Constantia* 59.

[224] See Stewart, *Honor*, pp. 67f., who discusses *iniuria* and *contumelia* pertaining to *dignitas*, *existimatio*, and *ignominia*.

[225] Cf. §2.2 above.

[226] Even though they note that what counts for honourable can vary within a given culture, their emphasis on honour's primacy obscures consideration of counter values over and against status and patronage: see further Downing, 'Honour', pp. 63f.

[227] Malina, 'The Received View', p. 179.

[228] *Ibid.*, p. 187. In this reading he paradoxically reinscribes the view that he attacks. The letter ends up as a discourse about power.

[229] He behaves very much in the manner of a patron. Indeed, when the elder's characterisation of him as one who loves to be first, *philoprōteuein*, is removed from the distorting discourse on ecclesiastical office, this word has social significance. *Philoprōteuein* is used in Plutarch's *Lives*, Solon 29.3 and Alcibiades 2.1, to mock drive for public office, and similar forms, *philotimos* and *philodoxia*, are used, as we have already noted above, in the contemporary literature to parody preoccupation with public honours.

[230] For Malina's thesis to stand, the letter requires a public audience that can ascribe or withhold honour. The letter must be public. Yet D. Rensberger, *1 John, 2 John, 3 John* (Abingdon New Testament Commentaries; Nashville: Abingdon Press, 1997),

advocate a counter-culture position not too dissimilar to that of the Cynics, doing good, not bad, *to agathon*, not *to kakon*. The letter, rather than demonstrating 'honour spurned and a required attempt at satisfaction', provides a window upon counter values to honour within the first-century social world, which will be addressed further in the following chapter.

5.3   Summary

Once again it is clear that members of the Context Group have tended towards hyperbole in their appropriation and application of anthropological literature. Revision of the anthropology has highlighted how social actors in agrarian contexts may adopt a number of social strategies besides conflict. This practice appears to depend upon the available historical and cultural resources, and not least of these is the manner in which religious discourse is framed within the social world. In this context the prominence of the religious social actor as a centre for alternative values is particularly challenging. This insight is paralleled in the revision of the model's application to the first-century social world. The proof texts offered by members of the Context Group in reality illuminate a breadth of perceptions and practices. Even where the agonistic element of their model appears most discernible as an elite discourse, the focus of the texts is upon actual gains and losses, and it is a universal truism that there are winners and losers. What clearly stands out in this discussion is the presence of competing values, most significantly advocated by specialised religious and philosophical social actors, which problematise the model of a normative Mediterranean honour culture.

6   Conclusion

The preceding critical revision of the model of a normative Mediterranean honour culture summarised by Esler as a 'viciously agonistic, group-orientated and honour-obsessed culture of finite goods'[231] has highlighted a number of problems. The model has

p. 157 (following C.-H. Kim, *The Familiar Letter of Recommendation* (SBL Dissertation Series 4; Montana: Missoula, 1972), and R. Funk, 'The Form and Structure of II and III John', *JBL* 86/4 (1967), 424–30), is in 'no doubt' that this is a private letter.
    [231] Esler, 'Review', pp. 259f.

been shown to be dependent upon a limited reading of particular anthropology. This reading neglects the contingent nature of social practice. Indeed, its dogmatic application obscures the complexity of both contemporary agrarian and first-century social worlds. 'Honour' is not simply a structural ordering principle dictating actors' roles in a fixed social world. It has histories permeated by religious and philosophical, political, and socio-economic narratives, which in turn manifest and form counter values and practices. The preceding discussion has repeatedly observed, within both the anthropology and the first-century social worlds, tensions between values and practices, egalitarian ideologies alongside hierarchical social organisation, co-operation and conflict, and the presence of not only external repute but also moral autonomy. The evident tension between such values and practices, which is no doubt reflected in our New Testament texts, cannot be resolved by crudely imposing this normative model. Rather, it is within this tension that we must attempt to locate our texts. This requires a more integrated approach to the social world, which listens to multiple voices, especially those of the religious social actor whom we have repeatedly observed at the interface of the honour complex of values. It is with the place of such social actors in mind that we now turn our attention to the religious dimension of the social world and the role of the religious social actor therein.

3

JUDAEA AND 'VIRTUOSO RELIGION'

1 Introduction

The previous chapter demonstrated how both agrarian societies and the New Testament text world are more complex than the cultural stereotype of a normative Mediterranean honour culture offered by members of the Context Group. It revealed that social actors are not simply constrained by such allegedly normative values but may also appropriate cultural resources, frequently religious ideologies, to form alternative structures within their social worlds which may provide a means for mediating the cultural contradictions that more customarily define agrarian societies. However, social approaches to New Testament texts have repeatedly neglected the social potential of religious social actors. This chapter reveals a pattern of sidelining such actors which is evident in the normative values promoted by members of the Context Group and is paralleled in current discussions of 'asceticism', which predominantly associate 'asceticism' with the self-mastery of an individual who stands apart from the social world. Indeed, this pattern continues despite an interpretative context within the sociology of religion in which the nature of 'asceticism' is being critically revised. This neglect is addressed, not by offering an alternative overarching model, but rather by focusing on just one form of practice which such religious social actors may manifest: 'virtuoso religion', i.e. forms of piety that may lead to the formation of religious orders. 'Virtuoso religion' is a particularly pertinent focus for study because its loci of operation are frequently prominent at the interface of values and practices. The social-scientific literature (anthropology, sociology of religion, and comparative studies of religion) which provides the basis for this discussion points to a formal resemblance between the contexts in which one may expect the prominence of this social form and first-century Judaea. This resemblance is examined in detail and reveals not only Judaea's distinctive character but also the presence of virtuoso practices, evident amongst the Essenes and other 'pietists', that notably offered cultural resources which challenged normative gender roles, i.e. celibacy, and radically addressed the poor, i.e. a piety of poverty. This confirming presence indicates the heuristic potential of 'virtuoso religion' to assist us in our understanding of elements of the New Testament world.

2   The religious actor

It is a distinctive feature of research into the historical Jesus, recently observed by D. S. du Toit,[1] that he tends to be presented as either the founder of an alternative community, standing outside society,[2] or as a reformer who founded a socio-political movement within society.[3] There appears little room for, or understanding of, the potential role of the religious social actor as an active agent within the social world. Indeed, the potential of such actors has frequently been downgraded in discussions of the New Testament world. This is not surprising since frequently the researchers, concerned that too many descriptions of *Sitz im Leben* have lacked concrete non-theological context, have consciously sought to move away from theologically inspired reconstructions.[4] However, Garrett is surely correct in her observation that there has been a tendency to reduce 'theological statements to reflexive expressions of social forces' and thereby minimise the historical importance and creative initiative of religious actors.[5] This tendency finds its origins in, and is reinforced by, a particular focus in foundational works on the sociology of religion, which either totally absorb the religious social actor or place them at the margins of any given social world. This is a clear trend in the work of Weber, which has until recently underpinned much of the scholarship on the religious social actor.[6]

---

[1] 'Redefining Jesus: Current Trends in Jesus Research', in *Jesus, Mark and Q* (JSNTS 214; ed. M. Labahn and A. Schmidt; Sheffield: Sheffield Academic Press, 2001), pp. 82–124.

[2] E.g. G. Theissen, *The First Followers of Jesus* (London: SCM Press, 1978).

[3] E.g. Horsley, *Sociology*.

[4] See J. Z. Smith, 'Too Much Kingdom, Too Little Community', *Zygon* 13 (1978), 123–30.

[5] 'Sociology', p. 90. NB: Garrett's focus, perhaps reflecting the interpretative context, is on the individual leader as opposed to the group.

[6] For critical discussions on the impact of Weber, see V. L. Wimbush and R. Valantasis, eds., *Asceticism* (Oxford: Oxford University Press, 1995), pp. xxivf., and Silber, *Virtuosity*, pp. 25ff.

In discussing such actors Weber introduced the label 'virtuoso religion' to differentiate particular forms of religiosity from 'mass religion'.[7] He made a critical distinction between two types of virtuoso religion: the first, 'otherworldly-mysticism', exemplified by Buddhism and Jainism; the second, 'innerworldly-asceticism', exemplified by Protestantism, especially Calvinism.[8] In 'otherworldly-mysticism', action in the world is perceived as 'essentially inferior'; a gulf lies between the virtuoso and the layman.[9] Their relationship is viewed as one of 'magical anthro-polatry': the layman either worships the virtuoso directly, as a saint, or 'buys' blessings or magical powers to promote his particular interests.[10] The layman is not encouraged to follow the contempla-tive's way of life. His influence is, apparently, simply in the sphere of ritual. In contrast, Weber's discussion of the 'innerworldly-ascetic' does not focus at all on virtuoso–layman interaction. Rather his focus is on what he perceives to be the innerworldly-ascetic's major impact upon the socio-political order and its affinities with economic rationalisation.[11] Here Weber stretches the idea of the virtuoso to the limits, understanding the Protestant ethic as an extension of the demands of innerworldly asceticism, of mediaeval monastic virtuosity, to all members of the religious community. When discussing monasticism he makes no direct reference to the issue of virtuoso–layman interaction. Rather his focus is on the institutional ambivalence towards, and the political advantages of, monasticism for ecclesiastical and secular rulers. Asceticism made monks outstandingly efficient, which led Weber to label them the first 'professionals', who could function as an

---

[7] *The Protestant Ethic and the Spirit of Capitalism* (trans. T. Parsons; London: Unwin Hyman, 1930), pp. 162–5. The term 'virtuosity' sometimes has the negative connotations of 'mere' technical brilliance and superficial, 'soulless' performance. This is not the meaning attached to the term by Weber, for whom it denoted first some form of religious and moral excellence and only secondly the idea of expertise. It is this understanding, without any negative connotations, which is adopted here. On the divergent semantic development of 'virtuosity', see Silber, *Virtuosity*, p. 25, esp. n. 3.

[8] Wimbush and Valantasis, eds., *Asceticism*, use these terms for Weber's contrasting types, p. xxiv. They have been variously described: e.g. Silber, *Virtuosity*, labels the two types 'contemplative-orgiastic' and 'activist-ascetic', p. 25.

[9] See Silber, *Virtuosity*, p. 26.

[10] C. Wright Mills, *From Max Weber: Essays in Sociology* (New York: Oxford University Press, 1975), p. 289.

[11] The theme of his *Ethic*.

apparatus of officials and a counterweight against the nobility.[12] In the mediaeval West, monasticism functioned, he famously argued, to create a check-and-balance type of civilisation: 'authority was set against authority, legitimacy against legitimacy, one office charisma against another'.[13] Thus, he portrayed Western asceticism as being profoundly related to the West's uniquely dynamic rationalisation, an interpretation greatly served by his characterisation of the role of virtuoso-asceticism in non-Western civilisations as simply contemplative and otherworldly.

In Weber's foundational schema, the ascetic in the West is subsumed within the social world, whilst in the East the ascetic stands apart from their social world. This imbalance in his treatment of the virtuoso is now widely recognised.[14] He consistently downplayed the significance of otherworldly-mysticism, which he credited with little sociological significance, and treated much less extensively.[15] This legacy has notably infected biblical interpretation and has resulted in the tendency for religious social actors to be either absorbed into the social world or located on its margins as otherworldly individuals or sectarians. The role of such actors, as agents of social transformation, has been obscured by this paradigm, and this has resulted in a failure to appreciate the particular significance of such individuals or groups. Despite attempts to move beyond this polarisation it has been carried over, as we will now see, into discussions of asceticism in the New Testament.

2.1 Asceticism in the New Testament

Asceticism is generally discussed, following its Greek root *askēsis*, 'exercise or training', in terms of the self-mastery of the individual. Kaelber's definition is typical: 'a voluntary, sustained and at least partially systematic programme of self-discipline and self-denial in which immediate, sensual, or profane gratifications are renounced in order to attain a higher spiritual state or a more thorough

---

[12] M. Weber, *Economy and Society: An Outline of Interpretative Sociology* (New York: Bedminster, 1968), p. 1171.

[13] *Ibid.*, p. 1192.

[14] Silber, *Virtuosity*, p. 26.

[15] On Weber's relative neglect of mysticism, see W. R. Garret, 'Maligned Mysticism: The Maledicted Career of Troeltsch's Third Type', *SA* 36/3 (1975), 205–23, and S. J. Tambiah, 'Buddhism and This-Worldly Activity', *MAS* 7 (1973), 1–20.

absorption into the sacred'.[16] However, the continued discussion of asceticism in such terms serves to perpetuate an impression that the religious social actor is to be located in sacred space outside the social world. More recent discussions of 'asceticism', from a group of scholars who call themselves the 'Asceticism Group', have sought a clearer understanding of its distinctive character.[17] It has been recognised that discussions based on somewhat arbitrarily identified 'ascetic' themes such as celibacy, poverty, and discipline fail to provide an adequate basis for critical discussion. Indeed, the subject is notable for the limited nature of its theoretical resources, which, until recently, have been dependent upon Weber's theoretical legacy.[18] This legacy is reasonably described by Wimbush and Valantasis as a 'legacy of academic and culture specific biases and prejudices regarding the origins, essence and value of asceticism'.[19] There have been two main theoretical responses. The first has been to adopt an abstract, all-encompassing definition, as done by Valantasis, whose approach is heavily indebted to Foucault and Harpham.[20] Valantasis defines asceticism as 'performances designed

[16]'Asceticism', *The Encyclopedia of Religion* (New York: Macmillan, 1987), Vol. I, p. 441.

[17] On the 'Asceticism Group' see: V. L. Wimbush, ed., *Ascetic Behaviour in Greco-Roman Antiquity: A Source Book* (Studies in Antiquity and Christianity; Minneapolis: Fortress, 1990); V. L. Wimbush, ed., *Discursive Formations, Ascetic Piety and the Interpretation of Early Christian Literature* (*Semeia* 57–8; Atlanta: Scholars, 1992); V. L. Wimbush and W. Love, eds., *The Sexual Politics of the Ascetic Life: A Comparative Reader* (*Union Seminary Quarterly Review* 48:3-4, 1994 [1995]); and Wimbush and Valantasis, eds., *Asceticism*. For a summary of the work of the Group, see L. E. Vaage and V. L. Wimbush, eds., *Asceticism and the New Testament* (London: Routledge, 1999), pp. 2f. For more traditional historical-interpretative works on early Christianity, see Peter Brown's *The Body and Society: Men, Women and Sexual Renunciation in Early Christianity* (New York: Columbia State University Press, 1988); also J. D. M. Derrett, *Ascetic Discourse: An Explanation of the Sermon on the Mount* (Eilsbrunn: Koʾamar, 1989).

[18] Discussed above; see Weber, *Ethic*; *Sociology*, pp. 166–83. See also O. Hardman, *The Ideal of Asceticism: An Essay in the Comparative Study of Religion* (London: SPCK, 1926), who defines asceticism according to three types: the mystical ideal–fellowship, pp. 74–118; the disciplinary ideal–righteousness, pp. 119–61; and the sacrificial ideal–reparation, pp. 162–85. Typical of other, less focused discussions is W. James, *The Varieties of Religious Experience* (New York: Mentor, 1958).

[19] Wimbush and Valantasis, eds., *Asceticism*, p. xxv. For a historical survey of the literature on asceticism, see pp. ixff.

[20] 'A Theory of the Social Function of Asceticism', *ibid.*, pp. 544–52, following M. Foucault, *The Use of Pleasure*, Vol. II, *The History of Sexuality* (trans. R. Hurley; New York: Vintage Books, 1985) and 'On the Genealogy of Ethics: An Overview of Work in Progress', in *The Foucault Reader* (ed. P. Rabinow; New York: Pantheon Books, 1983), and G. Harpham, *The Ascetic Imperative in Culture and Criticism* (Chicago: University of Chicago Press, 1987).

to inaugurate an alternative culture, to enable different social relations, and to create a new identity'.[21] The second response has been to adopt a generalist strategy of discussing 'vague categories' of ascetic themes, e.g. prayer, or meditation, fasting, vigils, celibacy, poverty, etc., with the hope that this will facilitate comparative study.[22] However, neither of these approaches wholly escapes the danger of either drifting into generalisation or the mere listing of intuitively derived practices and sayings.[23] Nonetheless, it is in this theoretical context that the 'novel' application of the category of asceticism to the New Testament has predominantly occurred.[24] Whilst such interpretation has acknowledged the current theoretical discussions, it has tended towards a reinscription of Greco-Roman conceptions of asceticism, focusing upon the self-mastery of the individual.[25] Indeed, despite contributors' often lengthy theoretical introductions, the recent Asceticism Group volume on the

---

[21]'Theory', p. 548.

[22] E.g. A. J. Saldarini, 'Asceticism and the Gospel of Matthew', *ANT*, p. 13, who advocates a form of 'vague abstraction', following R. Neville, *Normative Cultures* (Albany: SUNY Press, 1995), esp. chap. 3.

[23] On the difficulty of defining asceticism, see the excellent discussion in S. Fraade, 'Ascetical Aspects of Ancient Judaism', in *Jewish Spirituality* (ed. A. Green; London: Routledge, 1986), pp. 253–7.

[24] On the 'novel' application, see *ANT*, p. 7. That discussion of asceticism is considered a novelty in current scholarship is perhaps due to a historical antipathy in Protestant scholarship towards perceiving any excessive asceticism in the tradition: see D. Allison, *Jesus of Nazareth, Millenarian Prophet* (Minneapolis: Fortress Press, 1998), p. 216, n. 8. Another factor is perhaps the tendency to discuss ascetic forms such as the charismatic without any reference, in the social sense, to their ascetic antecedents; see, e.g., J. D. G. Dunn, *Jesus and the Spirit* (London: SCM, 1975). On this tendency to understate the presence of ascetic forms within Judaism, see J. Montgomery, 'Ascetic Strains in Early Judaism', *JBL* 51 (1932), 183–213.

[25] Whilst the stated aim of Vaage and Wimbush in *ANT* is to 'explore how the phenomenon of asceticism in Greco-Roman antiquity can serve as a theoretical framework' (p. 5), they leave the particular theoretical apparatus open to their contributors. The principal response is to acknowledge the discussions in Wimbush and Valantasis, eds., *Asceticism*, and proceed by relating particular New Testament texts to somewhat intuitive categories derived from readings of Greco-Roman asceticism. For example, S. R. Garrett, 'Physician of the Soul?' p. 72, talks of the 'flourishing self'; A. Smith, ' "Full of Spirit and Wisdom" ': Luke's Portrait of Stephen (Acts 6:1–8:1a) as a Man of Self-Mastery', p. 106, of 'self-mastery'; T. K. Seim, 'Children of the Resurrection', p. 116, of 'the philosophical ideal of disciplined pursuit (*askesis*) of certain acclaimed virtues to achieve well-being'; and D. Rensberger, 'Asceticism', p. 129, of 'Self-denial'. This emphasis is even stronger in the contributions made to Part Two of the volume, tellingly entitled 'Paul (The Real Thing)', p. 157. It is notable that the only reference to the Essenes in *Ascetic Behaviour* is in a quotation from Philo, p. 136, in which he is stating that he will not be discussing them!

New Testament displays a tendency to isolate the ascetic from their social world.[26] The place of such individuals within their social worlds, their relations with the 'laity', and their communal identity are often neglected.[27] When the composition of the social world is necessarily touched upon, the weakness of the theoretical underpinning becomes apparent in the recourse to models of sectarianism.[28] Indeed, the neglect of the communal dimension of the ascetic is evident in the examples used for comparative analysis, which are dominated by reference to the Cynics.[29] When consideration is given to more communal forms, e.g. the Therapeutae, they are arbitrarily and erroneously presented as anomalous and therefore inappropriate for any understanding of first-century practices.[30]

[26] This is evident amongst both those who accept and those who reject ascetic readings. Focus falls on such issues as fasting, celibacy, wealth, and rigour; e.g., debates over the nature of Jesus' ascetic practice argue over such texts as Mark 2:18–20 and Luke 7:31–5. For Crossan, Jesus comes eating and drinking: *The Historical Jesus: The Life of a Mediterranean Jewish Peasant* (Edinburgh: T. & T. Clark, 1991), p. 260. Cf. Allison, *Jesus*, pp. 173f., who notes that Luke 7:31–5 is adopting the 'polemical language of Jesus' adversaries'; that at Luke 17:26–30 Jesus uses 'eating and drinking' in a pejorative sense; and that Mark 2:18–30 is not a blanket denial of fasting; see also Luke 4:1–13 and Matt. 6:16–18, where Jesus fasts and instructs others on fasting respectively. See further the discussions on fasting in J. D. M. Derrett, 'Primitive Christianity as an Ascetic Movement', in Wimbush and Valantasis, eds., *Asceticism*, pp. 89f. Such foci eclipse the communal dimension, which is predominantly absent.

[27] See Tolbert in *ANT*, p. 30, who views Mark's ascetic and counter-ascetic qualities in the context of a 'marginal group within a hostile dominant society'. However, she gives no indication as to what she means by 'marginal group'. Yet within the social sciences the idea of marginality is a potent theoretical resource that has significant potential for illuminating Christian origins: see D. Duling, 'The Matthean Brotherhood and Marginal Scribal Leadership', in Esler, ed., *Modelling*, pp. 159–82. Likewise, Patterson's discussion in *ANT*, pp. 49f., considers the social impact of the performance of the ascetic. However, the ascetic's relation to the social world is discussed in terms of isolated individual itinerant social radicals, following G. Theissen, *Sociology of Early Palestinian Christianity* (trans. J. Bowden; Philadelphia: Fortress Press, 1978).

[28] See Saldarini, 'Matthew', p. 19, and Rensberger, 'Asceticism', pp. 132f.

[29] See Tolbert, 'Mark', p. 30; Garrett, 'Physician of the Soul?' p. 72; and A. Smith, 'Self-Mastery', p. 98. On the Cynics as a backdrop for Christian origins, see F. G. Downing, 'The Jewish Cynic Jesus', in Labahn and Schmidt, eds., *Jesus, Mark and Q*, pp. 184–215. On the problems surrounding such readings, see C. Evans, 'The New Quest for Jesus and the New Research on the Dead Sea Scrolls', in *Jesus, Mark and Q*, pp. 180ff.

[30] On the Therapeutae, see further Tolbert, 'Mark', p. 47, n. 12. This telling note betrays an apparent ignorance of Essene practices within Judaea: 'The authorship and dating of text are disputed, in part because the otherwise unknown ascetic Egyptian community the text discusses embodies so very much communal practices of the later (third to fourth century CE) asceticism that it seems out of place in relation to other religious practices of the first century CE.'

The historical social context of particular religious social actors appears secondary to inter-textual discussions.[31] The contributors either lack knowledge of Essene practices, erroneously characterising the Essenes as a sect in the desert fleeing the world,[32] or simply fail to acknowledge their presence. The role of the religious social actor within any particular social world is not considered. It is in this context that I wish to advocate a critical return to Weber's discussion of religious virtuosity, which will function as the starting point for a more socially integrated discussion of asceticism.

2.2   Virtuoso religion

The critical revision of the model of a normative Mediterranean honour culture highlighted that the liminal space at the interface of values and practices is one which is frequently marked by the presence of the religious social actor.[33] However, the preceding review of the discussion of asceticism in the New Testament reveals that the social significance of such actors has been neglected. They have either been fully integrated into their social worlds or marginalised. This sub-section draws on more recent discussions of 'virtuoso religion' that help generate a more integrated picture of the roles which such actors may perform within their social worlds. These discussions clarify the nature of the virtuoso and provide the necessary theoretical resources for examining their relational aspects. Virtuoso religion is revealed to be distinct from sectarianism by virtue of its ability to function as an alternative community not outside society but within it. Indeed, its capacity to maintain an alternative community within society means that such religious minorities should not be viewed as marginal vis-à-vis their social worlds, but as having the potential to perform as cultural variables of far-reaching macrosociological significance. Finally, contexts predisposed towards the emergence of virtuoso

---

[31] This is the weakness with Patterson's otherwise excellent contribution to the discussion, '*Askesis* and the Early Jesus Tradition', *ANT*, pp. 49–70. It attempts to relate ascetic practice to traditions in Q and the Gospel of Thomas. Both are sayings sources (if you accept the Q hypothesis), which provide very limited scope for discussing social setting beyond the theoretical constructions imposed upon them.

[32] See Tolbert, 'Mark', pp. 30 and 45, who makes a direct connection between the Essenes and Qumran and understands the 'Qumran community's goal' as to withdraw from society.

[33] See chapter 2 above.

religion are outlined and revealed to be particularly pertinent for the understanding of first-century Judaea.

2.2.1   *Virtuoso religion, an alternative community within society*

Hill and Silber have significantly revised Weber's theoretical category 'virtuoso religion' in recent years.[34] This revision provides a powerful resource to assist our understanding of the potential roles the religious social actor may have adopted in the New Testament world. Hill and Silber argue that the sharp contrast between the 'innerworldly' and 'otherworldly' virtuoso obscures a commonality which had originally led Weber to identify them as expressions of the same phenomenon. In an attempt to address this problem and clarify the core features of 'virtuoso religion' Hill advocates that virtuosity should be distinguished from both 'mass religion' and 'charismatic religion'.[35] Whilst the 'virtuoso' and the 'charismatic' may be related, basic differences exist. The virtuoso rigorously restates an existing tradition, whilst the charismatic represents an entirely new basis of normative obligation: 'Charismatics proclaim a message: virtuosi proclaim a method.'[36] Hill's clarification has been further elaborated by Silber, who, whilst stressing the relatedness of virtuosity and charisma, sets out the ideal-typical differences between the two.[37] The first difference lies in the virtuoso's disciplined and methodical character, which is to be contrasted with the basic feature of charisma, its resistance to rational planning and discipline.[38] This discipline lends virtuosity a sustained character alien to volatile

---

[34] M. Hill, *Religious Order*, and Silber, *Virtuosity*.

[35] Whilst Weber used the term 'charisma' in connection with 'virtuosity', he never articulated the relationship between the two; see *Sociology*, pp. 162–5.

[36] *Religious Order*, p. 2.

[37] *Virtuosity*, pp. 190f. Whilst broadly accepting Hill's distinction, she notes that he only contrasts virtuosity with subversive charisma. He ignores other forms, in particular what Weber called 'official' or institutionalised charisma – whereby charisma comes to reside in the position or office rather than in the person. She further notes that 'Virtuosi may develop into charismatic figures, and the latter may in turn give rise to new forms of virtuosity. Virtuosi, however, do not as a rule turn into charismatic figures; and as long as they do not, they constitute a sociological type with distinctive, if indeed "quieter" (but not necessarily less socially significant), features.' The 'quietist' approach of the virtuoso may be of significance for the understanding of the continued occupation of the Essene quarter in Jerusalem: see B. J. Capper, '"With the Oldest Monks". Light from the Essene History on the Career of the Beloved Disciple?', *JTS* 49/1 (April 1998), 47.

[38] *Virtuosity*, p. 191.

charisma, which typically cannot be sustained for long and either disappears or undergoes routinisation.[39] The next difference concerns their source of differentiation from the 'mass religion'. Whilst the virtuoso's state may be achieved, acquired, and developed, the charismatic's tends to be conceived as spontaneous, extraordinary, and personal.[40] Another distinction is that the virtuoso is less dependent on external recognition than the charismatic, who is by definition dependent on attribution, confirmation, and maintenance by an audience.[41] Finally, clear differences are evident in their orientation to normal patterns of social relations. The charismatic displays outreaching, communicative social tendencies, whilst the virtuoso's tendency to dissociation can take the form of radical withdrawal. However, the virtuoso's dissociation does not negate their 'potential for charismatization vis-à-vis or within the outside world'.[42] Indeed, it is their combination of a single-minded commitment to the realm of ultimate concerns and the consequent attempts to re-establish a pure, rigorous enactment of religious tradition which makes them apt to develop counter tradition and dissent. For Silber, the virtuoso's defining capacity is their ability to maintain alternative structures which present a reversed image of society, whilst remaining within its ideological and institutional boundaries. The significance of this subversive potential for the understanding of religious social actors in the New Testament social world has, however, been subsumed by the repeated focus upon the charismatic ascetic, i.e. a focus on the personal and innovative.[43]

Virtuoso religion because of its antithetical character vis-à-vis the wider social world, its tendency towards dissociation, and its attempts to form pure, rigorous enactments of religious tradition has frequently been marginalised.[44] Whilst studies on the social impact of saints and holy men are multiplying, they have been

---

[39] Potentially adopting a virtuoso form.

[40] *Virtuosity*, p. 192.

[41] *Ibid.*

[42] *Ibid.*, pp. 193f. Silber's significant contribution is to assert that virtuosity may take on the form of an institutionalised charisma with subversive potential. It may perform, in Hill's words, a revolution by tradition: see *Religious Order*, pp. 85f.

[43] See §2.1 above.

[44] Weber consistently neglected the virtuoso–layman interaction: see Wright Mills, *Weber*, pp. 290–1.

limited to individual forms of virtuosity.[45] Social studies of institutional forms of virtuoso religion, i.e. religious orders and monasticism,[46] have repeatedly neglected their interactions with their social worlds and focused instead on their internal organisation.[47] Hill, in his discussion of religious orders, is notable for making the first attempt to relate virtuoso religion to the wider sociological context.[48] He presents a typological comparison with the sect type and suggests that whilst they share similarities, the virtuoso are distinct. The religious order is understood in terms of virtuosity, not as a sect of the church, but as a 'sect within' and not opposed to the church.[49] It both legitimates and is legitimated by the church and often serves the wider society. This combination of subversive and conservative elements has also been emphasised in Seguy's discussion of monasticism. It encompasses both a 'utopia', an alternative perfect mirror society, and an 'implicit protest', dissent within the established order of things.[50] The most comprehensive treatment to date of the virtuoso's relations with the social world has come from Silber, who adopts and adapts Turner's notion of anti-structure to encapsulate the antithetical qualities of virtuoso religion.[51] Anti-structure usually refers to

[45] E.g. J. Wach, *Sociology of Religion* (Chicago: The University Press, 1962); D. Weinstein and R. Bell, *Saints and Society* (Chicago: University of Chicago Press, 1982); and J. Hawley, ed., *Saints and Virtues* (Berkeley: University of California Press, 1987).

[46] The virtuoso and virtuoso religion may be illustrated by reference to the monk and monasticism. However, the language of monasticism is intentionally downplayed since it carries with it Western cultural resonances, which may distract from the ideal-typical quality of 'virtuoso religion'.

[47] Attention has focused on the internal features of virtuoso institutions and comparisons made with 'total institutions' such as prisons. On the total institution, see E. Goffman, *Asylums: Essays on the Social Situation of Mental Patients and Other Inmates* (Harmondsworth, Middlesex: Penguin Books, 1968), and for their application to virtuoso institutions, G. J. Hillery, 'The Convent: Community, Prison or Task Force', *JSSR* 8 (1969), 140–51. This focus continues despite the fundamental and obvious difference that remains in the voluntary nature of virtuoso social forms. On the fundamental differences between total institutions and virtuoso institutions, see M. Hill, *Religious Order*, p. 7.

[48] *Religious Order.*

[49] *Ibid.*, pp. 12–13, notably picking up Wach's language from his discussion of protest movements, and his idea of 'protest within', *Sociology*, pp. 173–93.

[50] J. Seguy, 'Une sociologie des sociétés imaginées: monachisme et utopie', *Annales E.S.C.* 26 (1971), 328–54. Cf. the common critique of 1QS and the community of goods in Acts, which argues that they are utopian idealisations rather than evidence of actual social practices.

[51] For Turner on 'anti-structure', see the chapter 'Metaphors of Anti-structure in Religious Culture', in *Dramas, Fields and Metaphors: Symbolic Action in Human Society* (Ithaca, NY: Cornell University Press, 1974), pp. 272–300.

temporary, transitory, and liminal conditions or situations in social life which are conducive to solidary, non-hierarchical modes of fellowship.[52] Within virtuoso religion, this anti-structure is not a passing phase but rather becomes a structure in itself, which eventually may become part of the wider social structure. Virtuoso religion is marked out by the 'dense interweaving of structure and antistructure' which distinguishes it from other forms of social institution such as sects and makes it a form of 'alternative structure *within* society at large'.[53] Its liminality means that it is faced with a number of dilemmas.[54] It must define and control its degree of insulation versus involvement within the wider social environment. In addition, the virtuoso must confront the potential problems of laxity, corruption, and decline; and of radicalism, which may engender its own criticism, making it vulnerable to successive waves of reformism.[55] Nonetheless, the virtuoso's withdrawal from the world generates not only communal institutions, but also prestige that has the potential to be converted into power in the world.[56] This power may be manifested in either conservative[57]

---

[52] See *Virtuosity*, p. 40.

[53] *Ibid.*, p. 41, my italics.

[54] Essentially virtuoso religion is fragile, which raises the question how, and why, do religious virtuoso groups emerge and persist? Durkheim has suggested that virtuoso asceticism constitutes in symbolic form the basic asceticism inherent in all social life. It functions to keep 'norms too high, so that they should not sink too low'. E. Durkheim, *The Elementary Forms of Religious Life* (Glencoe, IL: Free Press, 1965), p. 356; cf. the more recent discussion by Harpham, *Imperative*. Another, more complex function attributed to virtuoso asceticism is as a 'safety-valve': see Silber, *Virtuosity*, pp. 44f. It provides society with an insulated sector where roles and practices whose legitimacy cannot be totally denied may be segregated; see E. Shils, *Center and Periphery: Essays in Macrosociology* (Chicago: University of Chicago Press, 1975), p. 130. However, as Silber, *Virtuosity*, p. 45, notes, both these positions present a monolithic view that neglects the dynamism and tensions evident amongst the virtuoso.

[55] Cf. the *Tapasa Bhikku* (lit. beggars) discussed by N. Yalman, 'The Ascetic Buddhist Monks of Ceylon', *Ethnology* 1 (1962), 315–28, who claim that the original charisma of the Buddha has been lost in the formal edifice of the church and attempt to return to its original source through taking on more extreme forms of 'poverty'.

[56] See G. Hamel, *Poverty and Charity in Roman Palestine, First Three Centuries C.E.* (Berkeley, CA: University of California Press, 1990), p. 178, n. 76; Nadeau, 'Peasant Resistance'; and Silber, *Virtuosity*, pp. 164f.

[57] On the conservative manifestation of power, see P. Brown, 'The Rise and Function of the Holy Man in Late Antiquity', *JRS* 61 (1971), 91, for whom the virtuoso functions to fill the institutional vacuum. For an example of the virtuoso's potency in institutional form, see Capper, 'With the Oldest Monks', p. 28. Capper underlines the social/political significance that the religious group initially had on the ascendancy of Herod.

or innovative forms.[58] Virtuoso religion forms alternative structures; culturally specific forms of segregation and practices; and
material and symbolic forms of exchange with the laity.[59] These
structures may take the form of distinct communities, which may
take a lead, at the very least theoretically, both in forms of social
provision and in the provision of centres for the perceived
preservation of undefiled tradition.[60] These virtuoso institutions,
religious houses or monasteries, frequently generate both patronage
and membership from a broad range of social actors.[61] Virtuoso
religion is therefore 'not merely the characteristic of a religious
minority – but also a cultural variable of far reaching macrosociological significance'.[62] It is a cultural variable of potential
significance, as we will now see, for our understanding of social
relations in first-century Judaea.

2.2.2   Virtuoso religion and first-century Judaea –
a preliminary view

Comparative studies have illustrated that, whilst the religious
virtuoso's single-minded commitment to the realm of ultimate
concerns (and consequent attempts to establish pure, rigorous
enactments of religious tradition) can lead to dissociation and
radical withdrawal, this social practice is neither sectarian nor
'ascetic' in the sense predominantly adopted by the Asceticism
Group.[63] In contrast, the defining capacity of the virtuoso is their
ability to maintain alternative structures which present a reversed
image of society whilst remaining within its ideological and
institutional boundaries. Notably, this form of religious social
practice occurs most prominently in contexts where cultural
orientations encourage belief in the perfectibility of the individual
and allow voluntary commitment to that goal; and where central

---

[58] On the innovative ascetic, see L. Dumont's 'World Renunciation in Indian
Religions', in *Religion, Politics and History in India* (The Hague: Mouton, 1970),
p. 46, who supports the 'safety-valve' model, but combines with it a stress on the
innovative potential of the ascetic.
[59] *Virtuosity*, p. 196: such relationships are 'rich in ambivalences and dilemmas';
also Ortner, *High Religion*, pp. 148ff.
[60] See *Virtuosity*, pp. 148 and 213. She observes that charitable relief is specially
mentioned in the foundational charters of many monasteries.
[61] *Ibid.*, pp. 66f., 145–50.
[62] *Ibid.*, p. 2.
[63] See §2.1 above.

cultural premises are fundamentally incompatible with the concerns of ordinary life.[64] Indeed, Silber concludes from her comparative study of monasticism in Theravada Buddhism and mediaeval Catholicism that 'the virtuoso complex is apt to become an overarching generalised structure in agrarian societies where macrosocietal, state structures may be present, but rather weak or inefficient, and where the degree of cultural ideological pluralisation and elite differentiation is relatively limited'.[65] She also observes that when in the twelfth century state and church structures became more dominant, there was clearly a corresponding decline in the scope and centrality of virtuoso religion in the mediaeval West. The identification of these features is confirmed by Ortner's more discursive ethnographic study of Sherpa Nepal, which observes a growth in virtuoso practices and structures that corresponds with the emergence of these features.

Ortner's study is particularly suggestive in that it exposes striking structural and cultural parallels with first-century Judaea.[66] Both were land-locked marginal lands with agrarian economies, which historically emerged from a context of pastoral agriculture.[67] In addition, they were both confronted with the problem of land pressures and land parcelisation,[68] which they both addressed through attempts to increase productivity, adopting terraced agriculture, and by emigration.[69] They were also societies embedded in the religious dimension of their social worlds, which encouraged belief in the perfectibility of the individual,[70] and had the Temple

---

[64] *Virtuosity*, p. 199.

[65] *Ibid.*, p. 208.

[66] See further §3 below.

[67] G. A. Smith, *Geography*, p. 297; cf. Ortner, *High Religion*, pp. 26f.

[68] D. A. Fiensy, *The Social History of Palestine in the Herodian Period: The Land is Mine* (Studies in the Bible and Early Christianity, 20; Lampeter: The Edwin Mellen Press, 1991), p. 85; cf. Ortner, *High Religion*, pp. 155f.

[69] Hanson and Oakman, *Palestine*, pp. 21; cf. Ortner, *High Religion*, p. 75.

[70] Judaea was an agrarian society marked by its limited cultural pluralisation, elite differentiation, and compromised macrosocietal structures (on the political and economic geography of Judaea, see chapter 4, §2 below). In addition, its cultural elements encouraged belief in the perfectibility of man and allowed for the possibility of voluntary commitment to the search for such perfection. On the perfectibility of human beings, see Philo, *De Somniis* 2.234 and *Spec. Leg.* 4.140; and on Moses as archetype *Leg. All.* 3.91; *De Ebrietate* 94; *Vit. Mos.* 1.1. Also, Wisdom 3:6; 4:13; 9:6; 15:3; Sirach 45:8. Indeed, for the people of God the cultural impetus towards perfection was a command: 'Be holy, for I, Yahweh your God, am holy', Lev. 19:2. See also Fraade, 'Aspects', p. 269, who describes the Essenes' practices as 'elitist *askēsis*'.

at the centre of their states.[71] This religious dimension stressed an egalitarian ideology seemingly at odds with hierarchical political structures. The legitimation of these structures was repeatedly undermined by the state's dependence for political autonomy upon changing external military 'patronage'.[72] This 'patronage' undermined the legitimacy of the elite by subverting religious institutions,[73] and by distilling elite offices and imposing alien forms of taxation.[74] Furthermore, in these contexts they both experienced increases in debt bondage, tenanted labour, and the emergence of elite absentee landlords.[75]

The combination of these structural conditions, a stark dichotomy in the social hierarchy between the elite and non-elite, and a culture which stressed the intrinsic value of the whole nation before God[76] provides a typical backdrop to the emergence of virtuoso religion. The honourable situation of the elite, undermined by perceptions of impiety and naked greed, and the inability of the non-elite to participate in the 'public' discourse of honour are both addressed by the emergence of this anti-structure.[77] Such anti-structure provides a locus for mediating the cultural contradictions within the social world.[78] Virtuoso religion generates a set of counter values within which both elite and non-elite may honourably participate.[79] It provides a new set of potential roles for the social actor to practise. For the elite, the legitimacy of their honourable status was challenged on two fronts; competition from

---

[71] *HJPAJC* II, p. 215, and Goodman, *Ruling Class*, p. 46; cf. Ortner, *High Religion*, p. 8.

[72] *HJPAJC* I, pp. 330–5; cf. Ortner, *High Religion*, pp. 58, 112f.

[73] *HJPAJC* I, pp. 237, 377; cf. Ortner, *High Religion*, p. 97.

[74] Hamel, *Poverty and Charity*, p. 149; cf. Ortner, *High Religion*, pp. 40ff., 91f.

[75] Fiensy, *The Land is Mine*, p. 160; cf. Ortner, *High Religion*, pp. 118f.

[76] On the egalitarian ideal at the heart of Jewish tradition, see Hollenbach, *Defining Rich and Poor*, pp. 57f.

[77] The emergence of such an anti-structure does not require the emergence of a middle class as A. I. Baumgarten has suggested in his *The Flourishing of Jewish Sects in the Maccabean Era: An Interpretation* (SJSJ 55; Leiden: Brill, 1997). Indeed, his close following of C. Hill, *The World Turned Upside Down: Radical Ideas during the English Revolution* (London: M. T. Smith, 1972), leads him to some uncomfortable manoeuvres. He struggles with and stretches his nomenclature, 'sect', pp. 5ff. and acknowledges that factors proposed as explanations were not 'as widespread in their consequences as one might want', p. 198.

[78] See Ortner, *High Religion*, p. 126.

[79] On participation in the virtuoso complex, see the particularly detailed examination *ibid.*, passim. These observations are repeated in Silber's more theoretically orientated comparative analysis, *Virtuosity*, pp. 66ff., 150, 180. See esp. pp. 6, 34, 213f. on the Maussian perspective of gift giving.

political elite rivals, and intensifying self-doubt about personal moral worth and social value. Involvement in virtuoso religion, in the form of gift giving, could illustrate not only their power and altruism but also their 'smallness' in their desire to serve rather than dominate.[80] For the non-elite their support for the virtuoso represented a form of self-empowerment and social assertion. In contrast to the elite it was a statement of their 'bigness', indicating their ability to harness the gods, defeat demons, and control their own fate.[81] In addition, both elite and non-elite could become active participants. This was a particularly attractive option for the downwardly mobile younger sons of the elite, for whom it provided an alternative to the parcelisation of family lands or emigration.[82] It was also an option for the non-elite who were unable to care for their offspring. These observations lead to the conclusion that 'virtuoso religion' may be a highly appropriate social-scientific resource for any attempt to reimagine the role of the religious social actor in first-century Judaea.

2.3   Summary

The previous chapter's revision of the model of a normative Mediterranean honour culture advanced by members of the Context Group has illustrated the presence of the religious social actor at the liminal interface between values and practices. Nonetheless, such actors have been frequently obscured in programmatic applications of the model. Whilst this neglect is a by-product of social-scientific interpretation's self-conscious strategy of moving away from the theologically conceived *Sitz im Leben*, its consequence is to denude their model of much of its heuristic force. This neglect is intensified by Weber's theoretical legacy to the sociology of religion, which has been shown to result in either the assimilation or the marginalisation of the religious social actor. The review of the Asceticism Group's discussion of the 'ascetic' in the New Testament has illustrated that despite an acknowledgement of the theoretical problems with Weber's legacy it has been reinscribed with the religious social actor identified on the margins as an otherworldly individual or sectarian. In order to

---

[80] Ortner, *High Religion*, pp. 148f.
[81] *Ibid.*, p. 164. Also Silber, *Virtuosity*, pp. 211f.
[82] Ortner, *High Religion*, pp. 168f.

move beyond this position, and to realise the voice of the religious social actor, recent literature from the social sciences on 'virtuoso religion' not previously discussed in New Testament studies has been introduced. Virtuoso religion has been shown to provide a means of discussing and discriminating between the possible roles and potential significance of such social actors. Indeed, it has highlighted how a religious minority may emerge as a cultural variable of far-reaching macrosociological significance. Furthermore, it shows that the particular social form of the religious virtuoso is potentially highly significant for the understanding of first-century Judaea. It is therefore to Judaea that we now turn our attention.

3   The Judaean social world

The preceding discussion has noted that 'virtuoso religion' is not a normative model to be applied to the New Testament world in general, but a social form that is most likely to feature significantly in particular circumstances. These circumstances have been documented by Silber, on the basis of her comparative studies, and confirmed by Ortner, in her ethnographic studies. These studies suggest a flourishing of virtuoso institutions in agrarian societies where: (i) cultural orientations encourage belief in the perfectibility of the individual and allow voluntary commitment to that goal; (ii) central cultural premises are fundamentally incompatible with the concerns of ordinary life; (iii) macrosocietal, state structures may be present but rather weak or inefficient; and (iv) the degree of cultural ideological pluralisation and elite differentiation is relatively limited. This section reveals how these features particularly resonate with first-century Judaea and how the heuristic potential of 'virtuoso religion' is confirmed by clear evidence of such practices in the Judaean social world.

3.1   Judaea, an agrarian society

The following discussion of first-century Judaea, its land, and its people reveals that it clearly conformed to most standard understandings of agrarian societies.[83] Its population were predominantly

---

[83] On agrarian society, see A. Barnard and J. Spencer, eds., *Encyclopedia of Social and Cultural Anthropology* (London and New York: Routledge, 1996), pp. 418f.

agriculturalists for whom production was orientated towards the household and who were under economic and political obligations to outside power holders.

3.1.1 The land

The character of the land of Judaea has been neatly encapsulated by G. Smith:

> It is singular how much of an island is this inland province. With the gulf of the Arabah to the east, with the desert to the south, and lifted high and unattractive above the line of traffic, which sweeps past her on the west, Judaea is separated as much as by water from the two great continents, to both of which she otherwise belongs.[84]

This assessment parallels Josephus' apologetic:

> Well, ours is not a maritime country; neither commerce nor the intercourse which it promotes with the outside world has any attraction for us. Our cities are built inland, remote from the sea; and we devote ourselves to the cultivation of the productive country with which we are blessed.[85]

However, Josephus' rhetoric requires some clarification. Judaea was, as it is still to this day, troubled by a preponderance of stone complemented by a deficiency of water.[86] It is borderland made up of hill country, which stands in close proximity to the desert.[87]

---

[84] See *Geography*, pp. 297. On the traffic 'sweeping by her on the west', see B. Beitzel, D. Graf, B. Isaac, and I. Rolls, 'Roads and Highways', *ABD* V, pp. 776–87. It is clear that neither of the principal ancient highways, the 'Great Truck Road' and the 'King's High Road', passed through Judaea; and that the local road networks in Judaea were not 'upgraded' until the late first century. Cf. D. E. Oakman, 'Economics of Palestine', *DNTB*, pp. 303–8, who is typical in discussing the 'limited' Judaea within the later Roman designation of Palestine and therefore in a Mediterranean context.

[85] Josephus, *Ag. Ap.* 1.12 (60). On the need for caution about the actual condition of agricultural land expressed in Josephus *BJ*. 3.35–8 and *Ep. Arist.* 112–18, see E. Gabba, 'The Social, Economic and Political History of Palestine 63 BCE–CE 70', *CHJ* III, p. 106.

[86] See the sections on 'Geological structure' and 'Climate' (with its charts of mean annual rainfall) in D. Wood, ed., *New Bible Atlas* (Leicester: IVP, 1985). Also the discussion in D. E. Oakman, *Jesus and the Economic Questions of his Day* (Studies in the Bible and Early Christianity; Lewiston, NY: The Edwin Mellen Press, 1986), pp. 20f.

[87] See further §3.2 below.

The pressure on land caused by population growth, poor communications, and regional insecurity meant that it was necessary
for Judaea to have 'every square inch of land under cultivation'.[88]
This is evident in the extensive use of terracing,[89] in contrast to
Galilee, where the more promising land, climate, and communications did not necessitate this form of agriculture.[90] Whilst pockets
of land were capable of producing good yields of grain, these
areas were predominantly outside Judaea in Galilee.[91] On the
whole, yields were low.[92] In times of scarcity, grain was imported
from Egypt.[93] Legumes rather than grain were the substance of the
popular diet;[94] fruit, dates, figs, wine, oil, and balsam were also
produced, for both internal consumption and export.[95] The other
principal use of the land was for the raising of livestock required by
the Temple for sacrifices.[96]

---

[88] S. Applebaum, 'Judaea as a Roman Province: The Countryside as a Political
and Economic Factor', *ANRW* II/8 (1989), 363, n. 86.

[89] See Oakman, *Economic Questions*, p. 21 and M. Broshi, 'The Role of the
Temple in the Herodian Economy', *JJS* 38 (1987), 32. Also Z. Ron, 'Agricultural
Terraces in the Judaean Mountains', *IEJ* 16 (1966), 33–49, 111–22, whose survey of
the 'Jerusalem corridor' identified some 56 per cent of the land as having been
terraced. Cf. Ortner's discussion of Sherpa Nepal, *High Religion*, p. 75.

[90] See Oakman, *Economic Questions*, p. 21, who notes the use of 'strip lynchets',
where the plough was run obliquely at a shallow angle along the hills, and enclosed
fields.

[91] In Judaea, Michmas and Zanuha are commended for their quality, whereas
Hapharaim in Galilee is renowned for the abundance of its crops: see M. M^{c}n. 8,1.

[92] On average a fivefold return was expected: see J. Klausner, 'The Economy of
Judea', in *The World History of the Jewish People*, Series I, Vol. VII, *The Herodian
Period* (ed. M. Avi-Yonah and Z. Baras; London: Allen, 1975), pp. 180f. For a
comprehensive discussion on the problem of calculating yield, see Hamel, *Poverty
and Charity*, pp. 125–37.

[93] Josephus, *Ant.* 15.9.1ff. (305–14).

[94] See Hamel, *Poverty and Charity*, p. 15, 'Legumes were the poor man's meat.'
On their significance in the diet of the poor see also P. Garnsey, *Cities, Peasants
and Food in Classical Antiquity* (with addenda by Walter Scheidel; Cambridge:
Cambridge University Press, 1998), pp. 214–55.

[95] Hamel, *Poverty and Charity*, pp. 9f., and Klausner, 'The Economy of Judea',
pp. 181f., with a helpful map detailing the principal areas of production on p. 182.
The single most important of Judaea's very limited exports was balsam, found only
in Jericho, En-Gedi, and probably across the Jordan: see Broshi, 'The Role of the
Temple in the Herodian Economy', pp. 32f., n. 89.

[96] On animal husbandry see A. Büchler, *The Economic Conditions of Judea after
the Destruction of the Second Temple* (London: Jews' College, 1912), p. 45. Other
natural resources derived from the 'land', including the Dead Sea, were salt, pitch,
asphalt, and bitumen: see Josephus, *BJ* 4.8.4 (476ff.), and Pliny, *Nat. Hist.* 16.25.

3.1.2   The people

The majority of the Judaean population made their livelihood by working the land for the elite.[97] The smallholder who worked his own land served the elite through his payment of taxes, probably bearing most of the burden of taxation.[98] Most of his produce went in feeding the family; any surplus was used for barter in the nearest market for household necessities and the payment of taxes.[99] Owning his land, he was in a paradoxically precarious situation.[100] After prolonged drought or war, having no savings, he often lost his land, his security, and became a hired labourer.[101] Even if a smallholder succeeded in holding on to his plot until he died, his sons were confronted with the problem of parcelisation.[102] Only his eldest son, who inherited a double share,[103] could hope to support himself and a family on the land. His brothers would often sell him their portion and join the swollen ranks of the hired labourers.[104]

---

[97] On landholdings, see M. I. Rostovtsev, *The Social and Economic History of the Roman Empire* (2nd edn; rev. by P. M. Fraser; Oxford: Clarendon Press, 1957), Vol. I, p. 270, Vol. II, p. 663, n. 32. Also Oakman, *Economic Questions*, pp. 37ff., Hamel, *Poverty and Charity*, pp. 151ff., and Klausner, 'The Economy of Judea', pp. 189ff. On other occupations, i.e. slaves and artisans, see Fiensy, *The Land is Mine*, pp. 90f., and Hamel, *Poverty and Charity*, p. 153, respectively.

[98] Fiensy, *The Land is Mine*, p. 92.

[99] On the basic loads on the freeholder's output, see Oakman, *Economic Questions*, pp. 49f.

[100] Fiensy, *The Land is Mine*, p. 93; he rightly observes that the relationship between the smallholder and the elites was 'just as much an asymmetrical power relationship as that between the landlord and tenant'.

[101] On this view of land loss, see Oakman, *Economic Questions*, p. 55, and Goodman, 'The First Jewish Revolt'. For other causes of land loss and a survey of the recent literature, see Fiensy, *The Land is Mine*, pp. 77f., who highlights the practices of encroachment, extortion, and fraud, p. 79. In addition, he emphasises the impact of the breakup of the extended family and the resulting further loss of control over the land by traditional kinship networks, p. 133.

[102] On the problem of parcelisation, see Klausner, 'The Economy of Judea', p. 189. On calculating the size of land plots, see Fiensy, *The Land is Mine*, pp. 93f., and for Judaea, in particular S. Gibson, 'Jerusalem (North-East), Archaeological Survey', *IEJ* 32 (1982), 156f. Cf. Ortner, *High Religion*, discussed in §2.2.2 above.

[103] On rules of inheritance, see Hanson and Oakman, *Palestine*, pp. 46f.

[104] The growing tendency towards large estates in the Herodian period meant that there were a great number of day labourers: see Fiensy, *The Land is Mine*, p. 85. Applebaum, 'Judaea', suggests that this situation was further exacerbated, first by Pompey's expropriation of the coastal plain and transjordan, Josephus, *Ant.* 14.4.4 (75f.), the land returning to their original inhabitants, and secondly, by Herod's confiscations, *Ant.* 16.5.4 (154–6), 17.9.2 (305f.). On the assessing of actual population pressure, see the survey of recent literature in Gabba, 'The Social, Economic and Political History of Palestine 63 BCE–CE 70', p. 113, n. 85.

In contrast, large landowners produced more than enough.[105] From their surplus, they could lend money, seed, or food to the impoverished smallholders with the land as surety. In lean years, the smallholder would eventually become so indebted as to lose control of his land.[106] Landowners could also lease out their fields. They could be put into the hands of a contractor who would provide a predetermined return on the harvest; or into the hands of a lessee, a poor farmer with an insufficient plot, who would till the land himself for an agreed portion of the produce. Alternatively, the leaseholder and the tenant paid in produce and cash respectively and bore the loss if the land produced less than the agreed fee.[107] This, however, is a somewhat top down view of land tenure.[108] Three notions concerning tenure were evident in first-century Judaea: rights in the land were sacred,[109] they were achieved through conquest, or they were the product of an economic 'entrepreneurial' land grab.[110] From the perspective of the non-elite, the asymmetrical relations of power meant that differentiation between tax and rent was probably meaningless. It was a burden that stood in opposition to their perspective of the sacred and inalienable right to the land.[111]

---

[105] On large estates, see Oakman, *Economic Questions*, p. 47; S. Applebaum, 'Economic Life in Palestine', in *The Jewish People in the First Century: Historical Geography, Political History, Social, Cultural and Religious Life and Institutions* (ed. S. Safrai and M. Stern; Assen and Amsterdam: Van Gorcum, 1976), p. 657; J. Jeremias, *Jerusalem in the Time of Jesus* (trans. F. Cave and C. Cave; London: SCM Press, 1969), p. 91; Hamel, *Poverty and Charity*, p. 151; and M. Gil, 'Land Ownership in Palestine under Roman Rule', *RIDA* 17 (1970), 11–53.

[106] Jeremias, *Jerusalem*, pp. 98f., suggests that such mechanisms were actively adopted by the High Priests to enrich themselves: see Josephus, *Ant.* 20 (181). On the use of debt contracts as a means to wrest land generally, see G. E. M. de Ste Croix, *The Class Struggle in the Ancient Greek World: From the Archaic Age to the Arab Conquests* (London: Duckworth, 1981), p. 225. Cf. the inclusion of 'landlords' in 1 Enoch 61–2.

[107] On the rabbinic sources for describing the condition of such labourers and their relations to the land, see Klausner, 'The Economy of Judea', pp. 189–95, and Fiensy, *The Land is Mine*, pp. 75–105.

[108] On the view of land tenure 'from above' and 'from below', see Oakman, *Economic Questions*, p. 37.

[109] Hamel, *Poverty and Charity*, p. 161: 'Because God was believed to be the supreme authority, any proper dominion needed some form of religious sanction.'

[110] Fiensy, *The Land is Mine*, p. 105.

[111] Oakman, *Economic Questions*, p. 38: 'It is not accidental that the elites of antiquity thought territorially and the small proprietors relationally.' Cf. J. Neil, *Palestine Life* (London: Simpkin, Marshall, Hamilton, Kent & Co., 1916), pp. 339–62, whose discussion of nineteenth-century landholdings in Palestine strongly resonates with Oakman's discussion of perceptions of rights in the land.

3.1.3   Jerusalem and the Temple

Jerusalem and the Temple stood at the centre of Judaea, a land striking in its 'natural unfitness for the growth of a great city'.[112] Jerusalem was the only major urban centre in Judaea.[113] It was the centre for the cult and administration. It was where the elite 'owners' of the land lived;[114] where land was appropriated in the courts;[115] where legislation was formed to assist in the monetisation of the economy;[116] and where taxes and tithes were accrued.[117] It was the focus for both consumption[118] and expropriation of revenues.[119] Perhaps the only mitigating factor for the rural population was that it was also the centre for pilgrimage and therefore trade.[120] However, it is not at all clear whether the rural population would have accrued any benefit from these activities. Indeed, they may even have increased the pressure on the local economy.[121] Jerusalem was a veritable parasite feeding off the rural

[112] G. A. Smith, *Geography*, p. 317. Indeed, the physical nature of the hill country made communications highly problematic: see P. Ferris, 'Judah, Hill Country of', *ABD* III, pp. 1036–7: 'Topography seems to have made the area somewhat 'closed' and provincial. The deep E–W canyons make travel from N to S in Judah most difficult if not impossible except along the ridge.'

[113] *HJPAJC* II, p. 197.

[114] On the concentration of the elite in Jerusalem, see Applebaum, 'Judaea', p. 373; Fiensy, *The Land is Mine*, p. 160; and Jeremias, *Jerusalem*, pp. 224–6.

[115] On land appropriation, see Hamel, *Poverty and Charity*, p. 161, who notes how the Temple could be used 'to maintain exploitation by insisting on the sacred character of debts'.

[116] Most notoriously in the form of the *prosbul*: see Goodman, 'The First Jewish Revolt', p. 418.

[117] On Roman taxation and the problems of assessing it, see Applebaum, 'Judaea', p. 373, and Hamel, *Poverty and Charity*, p. 144, and on their relation to tithes and the question of double taxation, p. 149; also, Freyne, 'Geography', and F. C. Grant, *The Economic Background of the Gospel* (Oxford: Oxford University Press, 1926), p. 89. On tithes, see Hamel, *Poverty and Charity*, p. 148; Fiensy, *The Land is Mine*, p. 161, and *HJPAJC* II, pp. 257–74.

[118] Most obviously, on the Temple, see Goodman, 'The First Jewish Revolt', p. 420. Further, on the High Priest's houses and opulent rock-cut tombs, see Fiensy, *The Land is Mine*, p. 161.

[119] On the nature of tribute payments, see Hamel, *Poverty and Charity*, pp. 145f. The question of burden is somewhat unclear under Archelaus, 4 BC to AD 6. What is clear from the polemic against him is that his reign was problematic – indeed, that Judaea may have been somewhat of a poisoned chalice, since he had to maintain Jerusalem without the benefits of Galilee, the richest region of his father's kingdom. See Gabba, 'The Social, Economic and Political History of Palestine 63 BCE–CE 70', pp. 129ff., and *HJPAJC* I, pp. 354f.

[120] See Gabba, 'The Social, Economic and Political History of Palestine 63 BCE–CE 70', p. 111.

[121] Applebaum, 'Judaea', p. 372, argues that it was only in Jerusalem that a 'corner' could be created to raise prices and squeeze out the small man.

populace of Judaea. In comparison with Galilee, Judaea was a strikingly closed social world. Galilee's physical geography placed it in closer proximity to the Mediterranean, to key road networks and to the Decapolis.[122] It had a more diverse economy and less centralised urban settlement, which meant that it lacked such a wide social division between the elite and non-elite.[123] Furthermore, it was literally set apart from Jerusalem and the Temple, separated by the physical and political barrier of Samaria.[124] In contrast, Judaea was closed, physically remote, and rooted in sacred space.[125] It was dominated by Jerusalem and the Temple, which bled the rural economy dry.

This brief survey of Judaea's land, its people, and its city underlines its agrarian character. Indeed, it was perhaps a particularly closed society, which in contrast to other New Testament locations most closely approximates to Foster's model of a 'classic peasant society', discussed in chapter 2, §5 above. It was an unpromising, isolated land marked by asymmetrical relations of power between its elite and non-elite, which were the source of significant cultural contradictions.

3.2   Judaea, social organisation

Judaea in the first century was clearly an agrarian society. This sub-section builds on this observation and examines Judaea's external relations, its internal organisation, and its degree of ideological pluralisation. It argues that Judaea was only nominally independent, possessed weak internal structures, and was marked

---

[122] On the cities of the Decapolis acting as a safety valve for the landless poor by providing a locus for emigration, see *HJPAJC* II, pp. 144, 150, and Goodman, 'The First Jewish Revolt', p. 418.

[123] A. Sherwin-White, *Roman Society and Roman Law in the New Testament* (Oxford: Clarendon Press, 1963), p. 141, and S. Freyne, *Galilee from Alexander the Great to Hadrian 323 B.C.E. to 135 B.C.E.* (Wilmington, DE: Glazier, 1980), pp. 155–207. On the impact of Tiberias and Sepphoris on the relations between the *plēthos* and *dynatoi* in the second half of the first century, see S. Schwartz, 'Josephus in Galilee: Rural Patronage and Social Breakdown', in *Josephus and the History of the Greco-Roman Period* (ed. F. Parente and J. Sievers; Leiden: Brill, 1994), pp. 290–306, and M. Smith, 'The Troublemakers', *CHJ* III, pp. 520ff.

[124] On the political and administrative distinctiveness of Galilee, see M. Goodman, 'Galilean Judaism and Judaean Judaism', *CHJ* III, p. 598.

[125] On its rootedness in sacred space, see M. Weinfeld, *Social Justice in Ancient Israel and in the Ancient Near East* (Publications of the Perry Foundation for Biblical Research in the Hebrew University of Jerusalem; Jerusalem: The Magnes Press, 1995), pp. 97–119.

by its limited ideological pluralisation and elite differentiation: indeed, that the distinctive nature of its social organisation particularly resonates with those features associated with the flourishing of virtuoso religion.

3.2.1 'Independent' Judaea

The rededication of the Temple in Jerusalem in 164 BC perhaps marks the best starting point for understanding the Judaea of the first century.[126] It neatly delineates the beginnings of an 'independent' Judaea, which endured until its suppression as a consequence of the great revolt marked by the destruction of the Temple in AD 70.[127] The word 'independent' is in inverted commas because whilst during this period Judaea gains religious freedoms, greater political autonomy and lands, it remains highly vulnerable and dependent upon external authorities.[128] In the Maccabean period, Judaea's 'independence' is principally under the authority of Syria.[129] However, it also becomes a 'friend' of Rome, a somewhat ineffectual relationship which failed to address its inherent political weaknesses.[130] The periods of greatest stability and 'independence' come when Syria is distracted by its own political intrigues.[131] It is such intrigues that eventually lead to Rome's greater involvement with Judaea.[132] This resulted in loss of lands and authority

[126] *HJPAJC* I, pp. 1f.

[127] *HJPAJC* I, pp. 501f.

[128] On the nature of its 'independence' and Judaea as a 'holy estate', see Weinfeld, *Social Justice*, pp. 114f.

[129] Various episodes neatly demonstrate this dependent relationship: 1 Macc. 10:51–66; Josephus, *Ant.* 13.4, 1–2 (80–5): Jonathan as client to Alexander Balas; Josephus, *Ant.* 13.8.2 (236): John Hyrcanus' tribute to Antiochus; and Josephus, *Ant.* 13.16, 3–4 (418–21): Alexandra's gifts to Tigranes. Judaea was also briefly dependent upon Nabataea: Josephus, *Ant.* 13.15, 2 (392); *BJ* 1.4.8 (103).

[130] 1 Macc. 12:1–4; Josephus, *Ant.* 13.5.8 (163–70); 1 Macc. 15:16–24. For a full discussion of the *senatus consultum* guaranteeing the Jews undisputed possession of their territory see *HJPAJC* I, pp. 194f., also pp. 204f. On the unique nature of this settlement, see Weinfeld, *Social Justice*, p. 116. For a more general discussion, see Sullivan, 'Judaea', 297–9.

[131] *HJPAJC* I, pp. 206–7.

[132] Antipater, the *stratēgos* of Idumaea, successfully meddled in the succession after the death of Alexandra. The ensuing war between Hyrcanus II and Aristobulus II, with corresponding appeals to Rome for support from both sides, led eventually to the direct intervention of Pompey: Josephus, *Ant.* 14.3.2ff. (41ff.). See *HJPAJC* I, pp. 232–42. The dominance of Rome is then only significantly interrupted by the Parthians, 40–37 BC, Josephus, *Ant.* 14.14–16 (370–491); *BJ* 1.14–15 (274–375).

under Pompey in 63 BC,[133] but also their later restoration by
Antonius to Herod in 39 BC.[134] Judaea's dependence upon Rome
is underlined by the active petitioning over Herod's succession
which ultimately led to its becoming a procuratorial province in
AD 6.[135] The resulting political situation represents a return to
the start of the Maccabean period. Judaea initially corresponded
approximately to the former Kingdom of Judah.[136] Whilst in the
intervening years expansion of the borders occurs, initially to
towns in Samaria[137] and eventually to the expanse of Herod's
kingdom, its arrival as a procuratorial province of Rome returns the
boundaries to a broadly comparative situation.[138] This weakness
in Judaea's external relations is also reflected on the level of
internal organisation.

---

[133] The loss of land included all the coastal towns, all the non-Jewish towns east
of Jordan, and Scythopolis and Samaria. These were all placed under the jurisdiction
of the governor of the new Roman province of Syria and Judaea awarded
to Hyrcanus II as High Priest without royal title, Josephus, *Ant.* 14.4.4 (73–6); *BJ*
1.7.6–7 (153–6). See *HJPAJC* I, p. 240.

[134] Although declared king in late 40 BC, in a formal session of the Roman
Senate, it was not until 37 BC that with the help of Sosius he was able to take control
on the ground, Josephus, *Ant.* 14.14–16 (370–491); *BJ* 1.14–15 (274–5). See *HJPAJC*
I, pp. 281ff.

[135] Josephus, *Ant.* 17.9–11 (206–323); *BJ* 2.1–6 (1–100); see *HJPAJC* I, pp. 330–5.

[136] In 1 Maccabees, 'Judaea' is described as the region south of Samaria, the
northernmost limits marked by the *nomoi* of Lydda, Ramathaim, and Ephraim (not
ceded to Judaea until 145 BC, 1 Macc. 11:34). To the east, Jericho is mentioned
among the cities in Judaea (its border position is suggested in 1 Macc. 9:50–2 by
the actions of Bacchides, who garrisons gentile troops there to keep the Jews in
check). To the south, Beth-zur is garrisoned to defend the people against Idumaea
(1 Macc. 4:61; cf. 6:7, 26). To the west, the coastal cities and their interior territories
were wholly gentile, and the furthest limits were Lydda (1 Macc. 11:34), Adida
(1 Macc. 12:38), and Emmaus (1 Macc. 9:50). See further *HJPAJC* I, pp. 140f.
and *HJPAJC* II, pp. 1ff.

[137] These were the three *nomoi* 'districts' in the southern region of Samaria ceded
by Demetrius II to Jonathan, 1 Macc. 11:34, on account of their cultic association
in Jerusalem.

[138] See Josephus, *BJ* 3.3.5 (53). In this description of Judaea the gentile cities
of the coast are not attributed to Judaea; it is simply said that Judaea is not without
the benefits that come from the sea since it extends as far as the coastal lands. Jewish
Joppa is not once assigned to Judaea, but it is very characteristic that after the
description of the four Jewish provinces of Galilee, Peraea, Samaria, and Judaea,
the following are named by way of supplement: the territory of Jamnia and Joppa,
the only coastal cities occupied predominantly by Jews, and the provinces
of Agrippa. For full discussion, see *HJPAJC* II, pp. 6f. Cf. the discussion of the
Maccabean borders in *HJPAJC* I, p. 141.

3.2.2   Internal organisation

In Judaea, the High Priestly families dominated the internal political organisation.[139] The High Priest was the head of a Temple state[140] – a theocracy.[141] The High Priest's was initially a hereditary position.[142] However, from the Maccabean period onwards the legitimacy of the succession was repeatedly undermined, most notably under Herod.[143] Subsequent appointments to the office of High Priest were made by either the monarch or the procurator.[144] Nonetheless, the sensitivity of the role meant that all incumbents still came from restricted aristocratic lines[145] with greater and lesser degrees of legitimacy.[146] The degree of 'elite pluralisation' was strictly limited. The evidence for the precise function and form of the political organisation which the High

---

[139] Fiensy, *The Land is Mine*, pp. 158ff.

[140] Josephus expressly indicates that the High Priest was the political head of the nation, *Ant.* 20.10.5 (251) and speaks of him as the supreme judge, *C.Ap.* 2.23 (194); see *HJPAJC* II, p. 215.

[141] When Pompey abolishes the monarchy in 63 BC, the High Priest becomes *prostasia tou ethnous*, *Ant.* 20.10.4 (244) (see further *HJPAJC* II, p. 204), a result which addresses the concerns of the Judaean people, *Ant.* 14.3.2 (41–5). Following the return to monarchy under Herod and Archelaus, Josephus describes the constitution as 'aristocratic under the leadership of High Priests', *Ant.* 20.10.5 (251); see *HJPAJC* I, pp. 237, 377. See Goodman, *Ruling Class*, p. 46: 'Jerusalem was peculiar as a *polis* ... because it was to a large extent administered from the Temple in its midst.' Significantly, Josephus' reference to a 'theocracy' is one 'proof text' that E. P. Sanders, *Judaism: Practice and Belief 63 B.C.E.–66 C.E.* (London: SCM Press, 1992), p. 405, feels comfortable with. Cf. Stern, *Greek and Latin Authors*, Vol. I, pp. 113–14, no. 32: Polybius speaks of the Jews in Antiochus III's time as 'dwelling around the Temple of Jerusalem'.

[142] The Maccabean uprising replaced the old High-Priestly dynasty with an equally hereditary High Priesthood of the Hasmonaeans, 1 Macc. 14:41. See *HJPAJC* I, p. 193.

[143] Herod removed Hananel and installed in his place the seventeen-year-old Aristobulus, Josephus, *Ant.* 15.2.5–7 (23–38); 3.1 (39–41). On the actions of Archelaus removing High Priests at will, see *HJPAJC* I, pp. 354f.

[144] Josephus suggests that twenty-eight were appointed in this manner, *Ant.* 20.10.5 (250). For a full list of High Priests and who appointed them, see *HJPAJC* II, pp. 229–32.

[145] Notably from the old-established houses of Phiabi, Boethus, Ananus, and Camithus; see E. Smallwood, 'High Priests and Politics in Roman Palestine', *JTS* 13 (1962), 14–34.

[146] On the 'legitimacy' of the role of High Priests from AD 6 to 66, see Goodman, *Ruling Class*, pp. 111f. Whilst the authority of the High Priest was severely undermined, the actions of the Romans in placing Judaea under a High Priest were clearly based on the belief that with the role came paramount authority within Judaea.

Priest led is diverse and complex.[147] The idea that Judaea was simply governed by a Sanhedrin made up of seventy-one men has now come under sustained attack, most notably from Sanders, Goodman, and McLaren.[148] The evidence for such a Great Sanhedrin standing in continuity with the Hasmonean *gerousia* is unsustainable.[149] Nonetheless, it is clear that the High Priest stood at the head of a political elite centred on the Temple made up of *archiereis*, members of the noble families from which the High Priests were selected;[150] the *grammateis*, the professional lawyers; and the influential *presbyterion*, a general designation for both priests and laymen.[151] Furthermore, we find that the Pharisees and Sadducees were significant for their representation in these groups.[152] Whilst Josephus makes mention of a *boulē* in Jerusalem, it is most unlikely that it functioned in a manner comparable to a *polis*.[153] In practice, the political classes under the High Priest

---

[147] The problems revolve around the possible meanings and relationships between the Greek titles *synedrion, gerousia, presbyterion,* and *boulē*. See *HJPAJC* II, pp. 199–226.

[148] For such 'traditional readings' of the Sanhedrin and its composition, see E. Lohse, 'συνέδριον', *TDNT* VII, pp. 860–71, esp. §B.2. Also *HJPAJC* II, pp. 210–18. On the recent critique, see E. P. Sanders, *Jesus and Judaism* (London: SCM Press, 1985); Goodman, *Ruling Class,* and J. McClaren, *Power and Politics in Palestine: The Jews and the Governing of their Land 100 BC–AD 70* (JSNTS 63; Sheffield: Sheffield Academic Press, 1991). For a summary of their positions, see E. P. Sanders, *Judaism,* pp. 472–81.

[149] See Goodman, *Ruling Class,* pp. 113ff.; also McClaren, *Power and Politics,* pp. 10–34, whose review of the literature reveals the absence of agreement on such fundamental questions as the functions or numbers of Sanhedrins or councils during this period. It is incontrovertible that Herod significantly undermined the Sanhedrin's authority and that of the High Priesthood. In coming to power he executed 'all' its members: see Josephus, *Ant.* 14.9.4 (175) and cf. *Ant.* 15.1.2 (5), which states that he executed forty-five of the most prominent supporters of the Hasmonean Antigonus. See M. Stern, 'Social and Political Realignments in Herodian Judaea', in *The Jerusalem Cathedra 2* (ed. L. Levine; Jerusalem and Detroit, 1982), pp. 40–62.

[150] On the *archiereis,* see Fiensy, *The Land is Mine,* pp. 159, and *HJPAJC* II, pp. 235f.

[151] McClaren identifies seven distinct groups dominated by the priests: see his *Power and Politics,* pp. 199f.

[152] The significance of religious groupings in the circle of the elite should not be understated. Their influence is evident in the actions of Salome Alexandra, Josephus, *Ant.* 13.16.2 (408–9), *BJ* 1.5.2, and those of Herod, Josephus, *Ant.* 14.9.4 (175); cf. *Ant.* 15.1.2 (5). These actions are motivated by a need for legitimacy and authority which Salome and Herod, at the very least, thought they helped provide.

[153] For a negative assessment of the *polis* status of Jerusalem and the constitutional status of its *boulē,* see V. Tcherickover, 'Was Jerusalem a *"polis"*?', *IEJ* 14 (1964), 61–78; cf. *HJPAJC* II, p. 197. Also E. P. Sanders, *Judaism,* pp. 473f.

appeared to operate in the manner of a 'provincial assembly'.[154] The responsibilities of such an assembly included the maintenance of the provincial emperor cult and the protection of the interests of the citizens of the province.[155] In Judaea, these functions were clearly appropriated by the Jerusalem elite.[156] Notably, on these matters the Samaritans and Galileans acted independently.[157] Civil authority appears to have been restricted to the eleven toparchies of the limited Judaea.[158] Nonetheless, within this limited area the Judaean *archiereis* seem to have formed the 'supreme indigenous tribunal'.[159] They exercised civil jurisdiction, appearing responsible

[154] See J. Kennard, 'The Jewish Provincial Assembly', *ZNW* 53 (1962), 25–51; cf. *HJPAJC* I, p. 377, on the status of non-autonomous communities in the Roman Empire. This type of comparative analysis is absent from McClaren's discussion, which is perhaps too ready to downplay the possibility of functioning institutional structures in his case-study approach.

[155] See S. Cohen, 'The Political and Social History of the Jews in Greco-Roman Antiquity: The State of the Question', in *Early Judaism and its Modern Interpreters* (ed. R. Kraft and G. Nickelsburg; Philadelphia: Scholars Press, 1986), p. 45. The *archiereis*, the *gnōrimoi*, the *dynatoi*, and the *pharisaiōn gnōrimoi* were according to Josephus responsible for the sacrifices on behalf of the Emperor, *BJ* 2.17.2–3 (410–11), and those who after failing to persuade Eleazer Ananias to resume the offering informed the governor, *BJ* 2.17.4 (418). In addition, the *archontes* and *archiereis* made accusations of the malfeasance of Florus to Rome, *BJ* 2.16.1 (333) and 2.16.3 (342).

[156] What is not so clear is the actual nature of the political organisation. This lack of clarity, especially the obfuscation of the sacred and secular roles, perhaps should not be viewed as a problem but rather as a distinctive feature of Judaean polity vis-à-vis the Greco-Roman world.

[157] Josephus makes mention of the Samaritan *boulē* (cf. *Ant.* 14.90–1 and *BJ* 1.169–70), which complains to the governor of Syria about the actions of Pilate, *Ant.* 18.4.2 (87–9). Galilee was of course governed by Antipas until AD 39. He built his capital, Tiberius, with a constitution modelled on a Hellenistic pattern with *boulē*, *archōn*, and council of the *deka prōtoi*: see *Ant.* 18.2.3 (36ff.); *BJ* 2.9.1 (168). On the distinctiveness or otherwise of Judaea and Galilee, see R. A. Horsley, *Galilee: History, Politics, People* (Valley Forge, PA: Trinity Press, 1995), and R. A. Horsley, 'Jesus and Galilee: The Contingencies of a Renewal Movement', in *Galilee through the Centuries – Confluence of Cultures* (ed. E. Meyers; Winona Lake, IN: Eisenbrauns, 1999), pp. 57–74, who advocates their radical separation; and Freyne, 'Behind the Names: Galileans, Samaritans, *Ioudaioi*', who notes that, whilst they were separated geographically, the importance of their being co-religionists remains.

[158] On the division of Judaea into toparchies and the differences between the descriptions of Josephus and Pliny, see *HJPAJC* II, pp. 190ff., esp. p. 218 on the limits of the Sanhedrin's authority. The limits are neatly illustrated by the variations, slight as they may be, between Judaean and Galilean manners and customs: these relate to marriage laws, relations between betrothed couples, different weights, and observance of the Passover. See further *HJPAJC* II, pp. 13f. and p. 23, and M. Goodman, 'Galilean Judaism and Judaean Judaism', *CHJ* III, pp. 596–617, who makes a detailed examination of these differences.

[159] Josephus, *Ant.* 20.10.5 (251); *HJPAJC* I, p. 377; *HJPAJC* II, p. 218.

for the collection of taxes throughout Judaea;[160] possessed an independent militia;[161] and judged non-capital cases.[162] Ultimately, though, this power was exercised through the Roman, authorities which, whilst displaying particular deference to Judaean religious sensibilities, could still intervene at any time.[163] Judaea's state structures both externally and internally may therefore be appropriately described as 'rather weak or inefficient', with only nominal 'independence' and with limited 'elite differentiation'. This identification plainly resonates with the features set out by Silber as ones in which virtuoso religion may flourish.

3.3   Judaea, virtuoso religion

In the previous sub-sections, we have noted the extent to which we might expect to find forms of virtuoso religion in Judaea. The discussion of its land, people, and city highlighted that as an agrarian society Judaea displayed a striking resemblance to Malina's 'classic peasant society', which he problematically conceived of as a closed system (see chapter 2, §5). If there was a region in the first-century Mediterranean where a population perceived its socio-economic and natural environments to be a closed system, then perhaps Judaea is the best approximation. However, in contrast to Malina's assertion that this perception would lead to an essentially agonistic society competing for 'limited good', we have also noted that non-agonistic responses may be practised in such contexts.[164] Indeed, Ortner in her discussion of Sherpa Nepal highlighted one such response in the founding of the first celibate monasteries, i.e. virtuoso religion.[165] In addition, the discussion of Judaea's social structures clearly demonstrated the presence of all the key features which Silber highlighted as pertinent to the prominence of virtuoso religion. This sub-section now explores Judaea's cultural resources and social practices to illustrate the presence of this particular social form.

---

[160] Josephus, *BJ* 2.17.1 (405). See also Goodman, *Ruling Class*, p. 116.

[161] Matt. 26:47 / Mark 14:43.

[162] Acts 4:5–23; 5:21–40. On the debate as to whether they could try capital cases, see *HJPAJC* II, pp. 221f.

[163] *HJPAJC* I, p. 379. The residence of the procurator was notably in Caesarea and not Jerusalem, Josephus, *BJ* 2.9.2 (171); *Ant.* 18.3.1 (55, 57).

[164] Discussed in chapter 2, §5.

[165] *High Religion*.

3.3.1   Judaea, a religious social world

Contrary to the presentation by members of the Context Group of a New Testament world in which kinship and politics subsume other dimensions of the social world, i.e. religion and economics, in our limited Judaea, kinship, economics, and politics appear to be embedded in religion.[166] In comparison to the mixed populations of the surrounding regions, the absence of any significant gentile population in Judaea was distinctive.[167] Cultural ideological pluralism was clearly limited, as illustrated by the sensitivities of Herod's building programme within Judaea – see, e.g., Josephus *Ant.* 15 (328–9).[168] The Judaeans' identity was a religious one resulting from the common experiences of exile and return, experiences understood by reference to their monotheism.[169] It was a society in which Temple and land were at the centre.[170] The High Priest, chief priests, and scribes who principally made up the recognised political body held religious offices affiliated to religious parties, the Sadducees and Pharisees respectively.[171] Furthermore, the kinship basis of social and political organisation was undermined on two fronts. For the elite, the monarchy was abolished, Judaea was placed under external Roman rule, and the hereditary High Priest became an appointee. For the non-elite, the pressures on the land progressively undermined traditional kinship structures.[172] Finally, the economic engines of Judaean society, the land and the Temple, were also heavily under the influence of religious

[166] E.g. B. Malina, 'Interpreting the Bible', p. 154; cf. Josephus, *C. Ap.* 2.170–3: 'Religion governs all our actions and occupations and speech.'

[167] On gentile populations in Judaea, see *HJPAJC* II, pp. 1–15, 29–52, esp. p. 13.

[168] Josephus notes that whilst Herod built extensively, this practice was 'not in Judaea indeed, for that would not have been borne'. On Herod's building programme, see the discussion in chapter 2, §3.2.

[169] E. P. Sanders, *Judaism*, pp. 168f. 'What was *peculiar* to the situation was not taxation and a hard-pressed peasantry, but the Jewish combination of theology and patriotism. Any disregard of national tradition was offensive to God, and people loyal to God knew that he would save them' (his italics).

[170] See Goodman, *Ruling Class*, p. 106; E. P. Sanders, *Judaism*, pp. 294f.; also K. S. Han, *Jerusalem and the Early Jesus Movement: The Q Community's Attitude toward the Temple* (JSNTS 207; London: Sheffield Academic Press, 2002), pp. 51–4.

[171] See §2.2 above.

[172] See §2.2 above and J. Turner, *Societal Stratification: A Theoretical Analysis* (New York: Columbia University Press, 1984), p. 86. Turner notes from the study of advanced agrarian societies that 'Kinship, while still important, becomes less dominant as the organization axis of the society as alternate structures proliferate and expand.'

social actors; the priests who owned land and administered the Temple and legal system.[173]

The atypical religious framing of political and economic considerations within Judaea undermines any normative presentation of its social organisation. It is typical now in social histories of the Jesus movement to adopt the Lenskis' model of the class structure of agrarian society and simply overlay it with religious parties.[174] However, questions of power, privilege, and prestige, the vertical axis of their model, are not necessarily determined in the same manner in diverse social worlds.[175] Within a social world dominated by religion, as opposed to economics and politics, questions of legitimation are overlaid with theological considerations.[176] Religious narratives present a series of counter values, which potentially undermine the sort of hierarchies that, otherwise, typify agrarian societies.[177] This is clear from Ortner's ethnographic study of Sherpa Nepal, which highlighted the adoption of virtuoso religion and its interactions with the layman as a means of mediating the cultural contradictions that had emerged in the social world. In first-century Judaea it is also clear that a tension had emerged between the cultural ideal of egalitarianism and the concentration of power and wealth in the hands of a religious elite. This situation rendered the central cultural premise that the Judaeans were one people before God incompatible with the realities of everyday life. In such contexts, the dominant order

---

[173] On priestly land ownership, see Fiensy, *The Land is Mine*, pp. 51ff.

[174] Lenski, Lenski, and Nolan, *Human Societies*, p. 196. On the application of the model, see E. Stegemann and W. Stegemann, *The Jesus Movement: A Social History of its First century* (trans. O. Dean; Edinburgh: T. & T. Clark, 1999), p. 72, 185. On the problems of overlaying this model on religious groups in Judaism, see S. Cohen, 'The Political and Social History of the Jews in Greco-Roman Antiquity: The State of the Question', p. 48.

[175] It is not possible simply to overlay religious parties on the Lenski model. Sanders, in a discussion of 'Judaism', is surely correct in fostering a view of Judaism which encapsulates both unity and diversity: see E. P. Sanders, *Judaism*. Here he demonstrates how the thesis of Pharisaic dominance (Schürer and Jeremias) cannot be maintained in any simplistic form. They neither created religious zeal nor decided when others would display it, p. 449. Nonetheless, the Lenski model has a certain resonance when applied to parties within first-century Judaism that operated within the dominant polity: see A. J. Saldarini, *Pharisees, Scribes, and Sadducees in Palestinian Society: A Sociological Approach* (Wilmington, DE: Michael Glazier, 1988), and Duling, 'Brotherhood', p. 176.

[176] Herod's association with the Essenes is indicative of such considerations; see the discussion in Capper, 'With the Oldest Monks', p. 28.

[177] On the widespread hope of a new age in which the one God will reign supreme, see E. P. Sanders, *Judaism*, p. 303.

represented by the Lenskis' model may prove unsatisfactory as a representation not only of social actors' perceptions of prestige, or honour, but also of their potential practices. Whilst social practice may take the form of an agonistic response to the dominant social order, alternative responses informed by divergent perceptions of dominion, and therefore honour, may also be evident.[178] The latter are clearly of particular interest for understanding the distinctive nature of Judaea.

3.3.2 Non-agonistic responses to the dominant polity

The non-agonistic responses to the dominant polity, particularly evident in Judaea, questioned the legitimation of the incumbent hierarchy through moral and passive means.[179] Those who made them appealed to an alternative dominion. They were 'pietists'.[180] Their ascetic practices offered an alternative to the Temple and its hierarchy and thereby challenged their legitimacy and efficacy.[181] This is evident in the texts adopted by 'pietists' in which social and religious dimensions appear indistinguishable at times.[182]

---

[178] On agonistic responses, see M. Smith, 'The Troublemakers', *CHJ* III, p. 505. It is notable here that the types of protest which occur in the context of Herod's succession take two forms. The first may be described as intra-elite/retainer-class conflicts over political power, i.e. top down in nature. These occur in Idumaea and Galilee, *BJ* 2 (55); *Ant.* 17 (270, 297). The second form may be described as bottom up. The rural populace of Judaea and Peraea engaged in opportunistic banditry, *BJ* 2 (56); *Ant.* 17 (271–2, 288–9), and a general revolt in Jerusalem occurred to protect the treasury, *Ant.* 17 (251–68).

[179] E. P. Sanders, *Judaism*, p. 455: passive as opposed to violent resistance.

[180] On 'pietists', see E. P. Sanders, *Judaism*, p. 452. He adopts the label to refer to those groups other than the Pharisees, Sadducees, and Essenes. In this discussion, because of the considerable overlap, the label also encompasses the Essenes. See also Fraade, 'Aspects', pp. 258f., which develops the work of Y. Baer, *Yisraʾel ba-ʿamim* (Jerusalem: Bialik Institute, 1955), and A. Büchler, *Types of Jewish-Palestinian Piety* (London: Oxford University Press, 1922), on piety in early Judaism by moving beyond retrospective readings developed from later rabbinic texts.

[181] One striking example of this is the actions of the ascetic Judaean John the Baptist: see K. Rudolf, 'The Baptist Sects', *CHJ* III, p. 479: 'baptism replaces for all *practical purposes* the normal form of sacrificial worship in the Temple' (his italics).

[182] On texts other than the Dead Sea Scrolls adopted by 'pietists', see E. P. Sanders, *Judaism*, p. 452, who highlights the Psalms of Solomon and the Assumption of Moses. Note also D. P. Seccombe, *Possessions and the Poor in Luke–Acts* (Linz: A. Fuchs, 1982), p. 40, who, following E. Bammel, 'πτωχός', *TDNT* VI, p. 896, notes the common thinking between the Psalms of Solomon and Qumran. Also Fraade, 'Aspects', pp. 261–3.

Whilst they identified themselves in the Psalms of Solomon with 'the poor' (10:6), their opponents were characterised as 'the sons of Jerusalem' (2:1), 'those who please men' (4:8), and 'the wicked' (12:1).[183] This contrast between the oppressed pious and the unrighteous elite is even more explicit in 1 Enoch, where the sinners are clearly the wealthy and powerful (91–2, 96), and the righteous are those who keep themselves from worldly wealth and will be received by God (107).[184] However, the group of 'pietists' most clearly identifiable with Judaea were the Essenes.[185] They claimed to embody the new covenant within their community.[186] Dispersed throughout rural Judaea, they were distinctive in

---

[183] On the date and provenance of the Psalms of Solomon, see E. P. Sanders, *Judaism*, p. 452, and *HJPAJC* III.1, pp. 192ff. Whilst the communal perspective of the Psalms is clear, it is probably not prudent to say more than that they were the product of a Jewish party who had in the course of their history fled to the desert, 17:16–17. Cf. Han, *The Q Community*, pp. 95f., who views them as pious Jews living in Jerusalem in the first-century BC.

[184] On the provenance of 1 Enoch in the second century BC, see *HJPAJC* III.1, pp. 250ff. Also Han, *The Q Community*, pp. 98ff. and J. H. Charlesworth, ed., *The Old Testament Pseudepigrapha*, Vol. 1, *Apocalyptic Literature and Testaments* (London: DLT, 1983), p. 7.

[185] On the association of the Essenes with Jerusalem, see B. Pixner, 'An Essene Quarter on Mount Zion?', *Studia Hierosolymitana in onore di P. Bellarmino Baatti, 1, Studi archelogici* (Studium Biblicanum Franciscanum, Collectio Major, 22; Jerusalem: Franciscan Printing Press, 1976), pp. 254–84, and Capper, '"With the Oldest Monks"', pp. 19–25. On the presence of Essenes throughout rural Judaea, see B. J. Capper, 'The New Covenant in Southern Palestine at the Arrest of Jesus', in *The Dead Sea Scrolls as Background to Postbiblical Judaism and Early Christianity* (ed. J. R. Davila; Leiden: Brill, 2003), pp. 90–116. First, he notes that Josephus is quite clear that there were over four thousand celibate male Essenes, *Ant.* 18.1.5 (20–1); cf. Philo, *Quod Omnis Probus* 75, and that these celibate Essenes lived 'in no one town, but settle in large numbers in every one', *BJ* 2.8.4 (124). Secondly, he notes that Philo explicitly links these male celibate Essenes to Judaea. Philo writes that they lived 'in many towns of Judaea, and in many villages in large and numerous societies', *Hypothetica* 11.1. He correctly gives weight to Philo's earlier account over Josephus' post-revolt account, which was written after the resulting population movements. Thirdly, on the basis of archaeological surveys he calculates the probable distribution of villages in the region and argues that three thousand celibate males would have been sufficient to provide viable community houses in most if not all the villages and towns of the Judaean heartland. (Since the Essenes occupied themselves as day labourers in the rural economy, Philo, *Hypothetica* 11.10, such a distribution was probably a necessity as much as from design.) He concludes that all Judaea must have had a good understanding of Essene ideas and community practices, indeed arguing 'that the Essenes were the dominant religious and social force in rural Judaea'.

[186] CD 6.19, cf. 1QS 1.6–2.18. See O. Betz, 'The Essenes', *CHJ* III, p. 448. Their communal orientation is more pronounced than that of the Therapeutae to whom they are often compared, pp. 468f.

practising community of goods.[187] In addition, they identified with,[188] and displayed a profound concern for, the poor.[189] The 'poverty' of the Essenes is not, however, solely an economic focus, but is perhaps best understood in relation to their total dependence upon God.[190] This is underlined in their striving for perfection.[191] This group of 'pietists' has recently been recognised as a significant cultural influence on Second Temple Judaism.[192] Indeed, it has become increasingly clear, especially since previously unpublished material from Cave 4 at Qumran has become available,[193] that uncritical attachment to a past consensus,[194] which marginalised the

---

[187] Josephus, *Ant.* 18.1.5 (20–1); *BJ* 2.8.4 (124) and Philo, *Quod Omnis Probus* 75. Hamel, *Poverty and Charity*, p. 178, n. 76, makes the important observation in relation to the surrendering of property that such an act 'could bring someone more political power and material services than before'.

[188] On their simple life, see Josephus, *BJ* 2 (130).

[189] Concern for the vulnerable is clear on both the practical level of social organisation, CD 14.12–17, and the ideological level of enacting ideals of justice and righteousness, 1QH 5.21–2. See also 1QpPs 37.1.8–10; cf. 2.9–12. On their self-designation as 'the poor' see the detailed discussion in Hamel, *Poverty and Charity*, pp. 177ff.; Capper, 'Two Types'; and also Seccombe, *Possessions and the Poor*, p. 43: 'at least two groups (perhaps related [the Essenes and those behind the Psalms of Solomon]) in the inter-testamental period seemed to have understood that salvation was the property of the poor and of no others'. *Contra* L. E. Keck, 'The Poor among the Saints in Jewish Christianity and Qumran', *ZNW* 57 (1966), 68–75, who suggests that 'Poor' may not have been a 'technical title' for the community. Yet it was clearly an honourable self-designation: see 1QM 11.9, 13; 13.14. On the Essene network of poor-houses and the significance of Bethany, see Capper, 'Two Types' and 'The New Covenant'; see also Hamel, *Poverty and Charity*, pp. 186, who suggests that the contributions of the 'simple folk' of 1QHab 12.3–6 may have functioned as reciprocation for the moral protection provided by the 'Wise'. Indeed, he makes a comparison with the Mendicant Orders of the Middle Ages.

[190] 1QS 9.23–6.

[191] 1QS 2.2; 3.9f.; 8.9, 17f.; 9.9 and 19. See Fraade, 'Aspects', pp. 266–9, on Essene asceticism.

[192] See especially H. Stegemann, 'The Qumran Essenes – Local Members of the Main Jewish Union in Late Second Temple Times', in *The Madrid Qumran Congress* (ed. J. Trebolle Barrera and L. Vegas Montaner; Leiden: Brill, 1992), pp. 83–166, and his *The Library of Qumran* (English translation; Grand Rapids: Eerdmans, 1998), pp. 140–53. Stegemann argues that Essenism represents the main Jewish Union of Second Temple times.

[193] On the significance of the Cave 4 material for scrolls scholarship, see C. Hempel, 'Qumran Communities: Beyond the Fringes', in *The Scrolls and the Scriptures* (ed. S. Porter and C. A. Evans; Sheffield: Sheffield Academic Press, 1997), pp. 50f.

[194] On the problematic nature of the 'past consensus', see P. R. Davies, *Sects and Scrolls: Essays on Qumran and Related Topics* (South Florida Studies in the History of Judaism, 134; Atlanta: Scholars Press, 1996), p. 2, and L. L. Grabbe, 'The Current State of the Dead Sea Scrolls: Are there More Answers than Questions?', in *The Scrolls and the Scriptures*, pp. 54f.

Essenes and the Qumran scrolls, has become unsustainable.[195] The Essenes and the virtuoso religion that they embodied were a major cultural phenomenon within first-century Judaea.

3.4   Summary

First-century Judaea was a religious social world in which asymmetrical relations of power undermined the fundamental cultural premise that it was an egalitarian nation which stood as one people before God. It was also a context in which belief in the perfectibility of the individual was encouraged and voluntary commitment to that goal allowed. It is clear that it was a context in which, according to our social-scientific resources, we may expect the presence and flourishing of virtuoso religion. Indeed, we have observed that this was a reality, embodied in the virtuoso practices of the Essenes and other 'pietists'. In addition, the presence of prominent virtuoso practices is significantly not dependent on a tentative adoption of material from Qumran, but is clearly attested in Josephus and Philo.

4   Conclusion

The preceding chapter's critical revision of the model of a normative Mediterranean honour culture revealed the repeated neglect of the religious social actor in such social-scientific approaches to conceiving the New Testament world. This chapter started by showing how this neglect, following foundational works in the sociology of religion, is paralleled in current discussions of asceticism in the New Testament, which predominantly associate 'asceticism' with the self-mastery of the individual who stands apart from the social world. In response to this interpretative climate, social-scientific resources describing 'virtuoso religion'

---

[195] Whilst the critical insights that virtuoso religion may bring to the subject are not, I believe, insignificant, it is not within the scope of this book to attempt a reconstruction of Qumran/Essene history. Rather I am proceeding on the basis of a relationship between a broadly conceived Essene movement and the scrolls; see, e.g., T. S. Beall, 'Essenes', *EDSS*, pp. 262–9. It is clear that the witness of the scrolls is not necessary for the identification of Essene virtuoso practice and its significance throughout Judaea: see Capper, 'The New Covenant'. Capper's discussion is notable in that its argument for the prominence of Essene cultural practices is not dependent upon the scrolls but is predominantly advanced on the basis of classical sources, archaeological surveys, and the *Damascus Document*.

which have not previously been discussed in New Testament studies have been introduced, e.g. works by Hill, Ortner, and Silber. This material makes it explicit that social actors are not simply constrained by normative values, and illustrates how the religious actor frequently appropriates cultural resources to form alternative structures within their social worlds which may provide means for mediating the cultural contradictions present in their particular contexts. In addition, this material details the particular circumstances in which such religious social actors may become particularly significant within their social worlds. These strongly resonated with first-century Judaea, and this impression was confirmed by more detailed analysis. It is clear that Judaea was a distinct social world within the first-century Mediterranean. It was an unpromising, isolated land marked by the asymmetrical relations of power between its elite and non-elite, an agrarian society. The weakness of its state structures and its limited ideological and elite differentiation, combined with the religious framing of all these features, made it stand out. Indeed, this Judaea clearly resonates with the key elements, identified by Silber and Ortner, which may indicate the prominence of the religious virtuoso in the social world. This formal resemblance is confirmed by the presence of the Essenes and other 'pietists', which provides concrete evidence of distinct virtuoso practices. Furthermore, these practices reveal an alternative structure within society, which radically addressed the poor through the embodiment of an apparent piety of poverty. The presence of such an alternative structure for the potential practices and perceptions of the religious social actor in Judaea is clearly heuristically significant and will be the focus of the remaining chapters.

4

THE JUDAEAN 'POOR'

1   Introduction

The preceding chapter's discussion of a first-century Judaea permeated by forms of 'virtuoso religion' which potentially offered cultural resources that radically addressed the 'poor', i.e. a piety of poverty, is clearly of heuristic significance for understanding the New Testament's poor. It is also clear from recent 'social approaches' to the 'poor' surveyed in this chapter that a more nuanced social-scientific view of the 'poor' is desirable. Indeed, this survey of recent approaches reveals a paradoxical disregard for the social location of the 'poor' in favour of crude intra-textual analysis of formulaic motifs concerning the 'blind, the lame and the poor...'. In contrast to these approaches, this chapter re-presents the social world of the New Testament's 'poor', and revisits the earlier social approaches' intra-textual analyses. It argues that, rather than being suitable material for such analysis, these texts illustrate the contested nature of their subjects, which include the 'poor'. In this context an *excursus* on the first makarism is presented, which argues against Q^{Lk}'s priority. Furthermore, beyond the formulaic motifs, the 'poor' in the earliest traditions are also examined and two apparently interrelated themes revealed: an association between the 'poor' and piety, and a Judaean focus, or location, for these traditions. This Judaean context is further underlined in the references to the 'poor' as recipients of alms. Throughout this re-presentation of the 'poor' in the New Testament world, the insights gained from a more integrated view of religious social actors within their social worlds, facilitated by the social-scientific material on the 'religious virtuoso', prove highly illuminating.

2   Social approaches to the 'poor'

Before I examine the significance of the presence of virtuoso religion in first-century Judaea as a backdrop to New Testament presentations of the *ptōchoi*, the 'poor', this section reviews recent social approaches.[1] These have sought to answer the question of the identity of the 'poor' in the New Testament by exploring their place within the social world. Three distinct strategies for identifying the 'poor' are presented in this review. The first is an economic approach, which views the 'poor' quantitatively, asking whether they constituted a minority within an otherwise prosperous society or whether a majority of the population were 'poor'. The second is a more exclusively social approach, which views the 'poor' qualitatively, subordinating economic considerations to kinship and politics in an attempt to understand the nature of the status designation. The final strategy discussed combines elements of both these quantitative and qualitative approaches with a more inclusive socio-economic reading. The review of each of these strategies reveals not only the consistent oversight of the religious social actor but also a paradoxical neglect of the social context of the 'poor' in favour of the intra-textual analysis of formulaic motifs.

2.1   The economic 'poor'

The economic view of the 'poor' in the New Testament discusses them in quantitative terms. Schottroff and Stegemann are typical of this form of presentation.[2] The 'poor' are considered *a priori* as an economic category. The question of identity is one of number: do the poor represent a minority or a majority of the social world?

---

[1] The social discussion of the 'poor' is not always sensitive to the Greek: see especially the discussion of Malina and Hollenbach in §§2.2 and 2.3 below. The 'poor' therefore remain in inverted commas to reflect not only the contested nature of their identity but also the practice in particular discussions, which neglects their linguistic root.

[2] They suggest that the older form-critical approaches to questions of *Sitz im Leben* have 'thought too narrowly in terms of religious and literary institutions'. They seek to extend this inquiry to include the economic and social conditions of life, and therefore they attempt a social description of groups who played important roles in the Jesus movement: tax collectors, sinners, prostitutes, beggars, and the poor. See *Hope*, pp. 5ff. Cf. R. A. Horsley, *Jesus and the Spiral of Violence: Popular Jewish Resistance in Roman Palestine* (San Francisco: Harper & Row, 1987), pp. 209–45, who concludes that there is no evidence that Jesus either recruited or especially welcomed such social outcasts.

They note that in the Gospels a 'poor' person is referred to as *ptōchos* and not *penēs*,[3] the former being destitute, the latter a poor person who must earn his living through unremitting labour. This is a commonplace contrast, which is repeatedly stated as normative.[4] It is typically illustrated by reference to classical Greco-Roman texts, especially Aristophanes, *Plutus* 511, 532ff., where the *ptōchoi* appear as a relative minority. However, for Schottroff and Stegemann, these *ptōchoi* were not a relative minority of destitute people. The discussion of these two scholars focuses upon a structural economic situation in which large numbers of people lived in dire economic straits. Widespread poverty, they suggest, was a feature of first-century Palestine.[5] The Gospels' exclusive use of *ptōchoi* for the 'poor' is therefore explained as an accurate reflection of a first-century context in which destitution was the condition of a sizeable part of the population. This reading is further sustained by arguing that not all of these *ptōchoi* are destitute in the 'strict sense'. Rather *ptōchoi* may also refer to 'starving groups a cut "above" beggary: unemployed day labourers, fugitive slaves, or individuals rendered homeless by economic forces'.[6] Jesus' blessing of the 'poor' is therefore read as a promise of economic reversal, which has been tangibly manifested in his feeding and healing miracles. His ultimate aim is utopian, to end all need.[7]

Schottroff and Stegemann's economic presentation of the 'poor' is not, however, without problems. The case that they present to explain the Gospels' exclusive adoption of *ptōchoi* is unconvincing. Because they understand *ptōchos* and *penēs* to refer to absolute and relative poverty respectively, they may unjustifiably expand the proportion of the population who live in absolute poverty. This is evident in their argument that not all of the *ptōchoi* are destitute in the 'strict sense'. It is also evident in their negative reading of the economic situation in first-century Palestine. The evidence

---

[3] This distinction is made concrete by Stegemann and Stegemann, *The Jesus Movement*, pp. 71f., who locate them on the lower sections of a 'Social Pyramid' derived from Lenski and Lenski, *Human Societies* (see §2.3.1 above).

[4] For normative presentations of this contrast, see Neyrey, 'Loss', pp. 139f.; U. Luz, *Matthew*, Vol. I (Edinburgh: T. & T. Clark, 1989), p. 231; A. R. Hands, *Charities and Social Aid in Greece and Rome* (Ithaca, NY: Cornell University Press, 1968), pp. 62f.; and P. F. Esler, *Community and Gospel in Luke–Acts* (Cambridge: Cambridge University Press, 1987), pp. 180f.

[5] *Hope*, p. 16.

[6] *Ibid.*

[7] *Ibid.*, p. 32.

presented for this reading focuses on events preceding the Jewish revolt[8] and the famines of 25 BC and AD 46–8.[9] However, even if the reading of the economic situation is accepted at face value,[10] both famine and war were commonplace features of ancient agrarian societies. Indeed, Meggitt has amply demonstrated that crippling poverty was an almost universal feature of the Greco-Roman world.[11] Yet, within the Greco-Roman world, the distinction between *ptōchos* and *penēs* appears to be maintained.[12] It is notable here that within the distinct world of Judaism these two Greek words appear to be used, in the LXX at least, as 'equivalents', and the language of poverty had acquired 'strong religious values'.[13] The economic reading of the 'poor' obscures such subtlety. Whilst Schottroff and Stegemann rightly highlight the structural economic element of the social world in their discussion, they fail to ask how these 'poor' were understood culturally. It is to such cultural sensitivities that we now turn.

2.2   The social 'poor'

The more exclusively social view of the 'poor' attempts a qualitative description. This approach, which has been seminally presented by Malina, subordinates economic considerations to kinship and politics.[14] He makes a distinction between four basic social institutions, 'kinship', 'economics', 'politics', and 'religion', and suggests as a general rule that in societal relations one or another of these maintains primacy over the others. He illustrates this by reference

---

[8] They consider attempted revolts as an important economic indicator, illustrated by the burning of the records office in Jerusalem in AD 66, in which the debenture bonds of creditors were destroyed: see Josephus, *BJ* 2 (425ff.). Also *BJ* 3 (532–42); 4 (241); and 7 (438), on the economic context of the rebellions.

[9] See Josephus, *Ant.* 18 (36ff.) and *BJ* 2 (84ff.); see also Hamel, *Poverty and Charity*, p. 173, n. 41, who is reluctant to accept such material as evidence of distinct hardships.

[10] For dissenting views, see E. P. Sanders, 'Jesus in Historical Context', *ThT* 50 (1993), 429–48.

[11] *Paul, Poverty and Survival*, p. 73: 'The underdeveloped, pre-industrial economy of the Graeco-Roman world created enormous disparities of wealth, and within this inequitable, rigid system the non-elite of the cities lived brutal and frugal lives, characterised by struggle and impoverishment.'

[12] On 'Classical Greek usage', see Hamel, *Poverty and Charity*, pp. 168–9.

[13] See *ibid.*, pp. 171f. Cf. F. G. Downing, *Cynics, Paul and the Pauline Churches* (London: Routledge, 1998), p. 154, who plays down the religious dimension in favour of a Cynic background.

[14] B. Malina, *The New Testament World*, pp. 103–7; 'Wealth and Poverty'; and 'Interpreting the Bible'.

to the religious primacy of Islamic republics, the political primacy
of Marxist states, and the economic primacy evident in the US, and
finally observes that in 'Latin America and most Mediterranean
countries, religion, politics, and economics are embedded in
kinship'.[15] The New Testament, according to Malina, is a
Mediterranean text, and economic considerations are therefore to
be found embedded in issues of kinship.[16] Wealth and poverty are
not economic considerations since 'the "socioeconomic" destitution
of the "little people" is a modern construct, since by all accounts,
the poor had enough for the necessities of life'.[17] New Testament
references to the 'poor'[18] where the word occurs without further
description are therefore to be disregarded as being of no heuristic
value. Indeed, he somewhat pessimistically abandons Matt. 19:21;
26:9, 11; Mark 10:21; 14:5, 7; Luke 18:22; John 12:5–8; 13:29; Rom.
15:26; 2 Cor. 6:10; 8:9; 9:9; and Gal. 2:10 as texts where 'we simply
cannot get any idea of what the authors are referring to except by
reading our own ideas into their words'.[19] The solution which he
proposes is to examine texts in which the word 'poor' is used in
company with words that describe the condition of the person who
is labelled 'poor', e.g. Matt. 5:3–5; 11:4–5; Mark 12:42–3; Luke
4:18; 6:20–1; 14:13–21; 16:20–2; 21:2–3; Jas. 2:3–6; Rev. 3:17. These
'linguistic collocations' apparently indicate that 'poor' people are
those who have an unfortunate personal history: captives, the blind,
the oppressed, mourners, the humble, the hungry, the thirsty, the
lame, lepers, the deaf, the dead, the maimed, widows, the homeless,
and beggars.[20] The label 'poor' is not an economic category but

---

[15] 'Interpreting the Bible', p. 154.

[16] This view finds a degree of support in a school of thought which has alleged the
absence of economics in antiquity: see M. Finley, *The Ancient Economy* (London:
Chatto and Windus, 1973), p. 22, who is perhaps one of the strongest advocates of
this view: 'ancient society did not have an economic system'. See also T. F. Carney,
The Shape of the Past: Models and Antiquity (Lawrence, KS: Coronado Press, 1975),
p. 149, and R. Heilbroner, *The Making of Economic Society* (8th edn; Englewood
Cliffs and London: Prentice-Hall, 1989).

[17] 'Interpreting the Bible', p. 155, a claim vigorously challenged below.

[18] Malina's discussion of the 'poor' does not consider the original text and
therefore makes no comment on the distinction between *ptōchos* and *penēs*.

[19] 'Wealth and Poverty', p. 355.

[20] He notably omits from these references collocations which may suggest an
economic dimension, e.g. the *plousioi* of Mark 12:44; Luke 6:24; 14:12; 16:19, 21, 22;
Jas. 2:5, 6; and Rev. 3:17. He also omits to acknowledge their evident religious
dimension, e.g. 'he who is not offended', Matt. 11:5, and those 'persecuted' in Matt.
5:11//Luke 6:22. This omission is notably carried over by Hollenbach, *Defining Rich
and Poor*, p. 55; see §2.3 below.

rather a status designation in a world dominated by perceptions of honour and shame. For Malina,

> the 'poor' rank among those who cannot maintain their inherited status due to circumstances that befall them and their family, such as debt, being in a foreign land, sickness, death, or some personal physical accident. Consequently, from the viewpoint of the vast majority of people, the poor would not be a permanent social class but a sort of revolving class of people who unfortunately cannot maintain their inherited status.[21]

In a limited-good society, with its status-maintenance orientation, the label 'poor' is not indicative of economic rank or class.[22] The status into which one was born, regardless of how high or low, was normally honourable. The majority of people were neither 'rich' nor 'poor', just equal in that each had a status to maintain in some honourable way. Thus those born into the position of the day labourer, landless peasant, or beggar are not considered 'poor persons' in Malina's first-century 'Mediterranean', and 'poor' would not be an economic designation.[23] Jesus' blessing of the 'poor' was therefore addressed to a minority of those who could not maintain their honourable status in life. He promised them a restoration of their inherited status, a restoration of lost honour.

This exclusively social reading of the 'poor' in the New Testament, like the previous economic reading, is also problematic. Whilst its challenge for us to read the text within its social context is a helpful one, the context which Malina constructs strips the social actor of both historical and religious narratives. First, the choice of the Mediterranean's primacy of kinship over all other social institutions appears somewhat dogmatic. In Malina's descriptions of societal organisation he discusses the dominance of religion as one possibility but gives it no further consideration. Yet first-century Judaea was practically a Temple-state: see chapter 3, §3.2 above. In addition, the radical subordination of economics to kinship is not sustainable. On the level of the social actor, Theophrastus' 'Boaster' was keen to tell all who would listen of his investments in overseas trade, of his gains and losses, and of

---

[21] 'Wealth and Poverty', p. 356.
[22] For a comprehensive discussion of the 'limited-good' society see chapter 2, §5.
[23] *The New Testament World*, p. 106, and 'Wealth and Poverty', p. 356.

a licence for tax-free export and only secondly of public benefactions; even these were discussed in pecuniary terms.[24] Whilst
Theophrastus was clearly not writing in first-century Palestine, he
wrote from the heart of Malina's mythical ancient Mediterranean
honour culture with its embedded economics. Furthermore, on the
level of social structures, Malina's presentation of an embedded
economy as one in which 'economic goals, roles, production, hiring,
firing, planning and the like, are determined by kinship or political
considerations, either alone, or primarily'[25] appears less certain
when consideration is given to the exploitative taxation policies
of the Ptolemies, which were specifically designed to extract the
greatest possible 'surplus'.[26]

Secondly, Malina's strategy of 'linguistic collocation', which
restricts his discussion to those texts in which the word 'poor' is
used in company with words that describe their condition, appears
to ignore redactional interests. Whilst it is inappropriate to go as far
as Roth, who focuses exclusively on 'the blind, the lame, the poor
and others' as literary types,[27] Malina's equally exclusive focus on
this group in terms of their honour status is unsustainable. A
reading of this group without some consideration being given to
their historical antecedents in the religious narrative which underlies
the text is not credible.[28] Neither can the dismissal of all other
references to the 'poor' be acceptable. These references are marked
by strikingly common features, which may provide a greater scope

---

[24] Theophrastus, *The Characters. Alazoneia* 23. It is as a rebuttal of Malina's
hyperbole that I cite him rather than as a 'normative' source.

[25] 'Interpreting the Bible', p. 154.

[26] See Pastor, *Land and Economy*, pp. 34ff. On the debate about the nature of
ancient economics, see S. Meikle, 'Modernism, Economics and the Ancient
Economy', *Proceedings of the Cambridge Philological Society* 41 (1995), 174–91,
who contrasts the primitivist and modernist perspectives of Finley, *The Ancient
Economy*, and T. Lowry, 'Aristotle's "Natural Limit" and the Economics of Price
Regulation', *Greek, Roman and Byzantine Studies* 15/1 (Spring 1974), 57–63,
respectively. It is clear from his discussion that the primitivists have minimised the
importance of 'economic activity' in the ancient world.

[27] J. Roth, *The Blind, the Lame and the Poor: Character Types in Luke–Acts*
(JSNTS 144; Sheffield: Sheffield Academic Press, 1997), p. 26; see further §3 below.

[28] For an example of the significance of the historical antecedents of such 'types',
see J. A. Sanders, 'From Isaiah 61 to Luke 4', in *Christianity, Judaism, and other
Greco-Roman Cults: Studies for Morton Smith at Sixty* (ed. and compiled by
J. Neusner; Leiden: Brill, 1975), pp. 75–106, who compares Luke's midrash on who
'the poor, the captives and the blind' would be with Qumranic literature. See also
A. Ceresko, 'The Identity of "the Blind and the Lame" (ʿiwwēr Ûpissēah) in Samuel
5:8b', *CBQ* 63/1 (January 2001).

for social reconstruction than Malina's more literary lists. These will be highlighted in §3 below.

Finally, the view that the label 'poor' operates exclusively as a status designation and not as an economic category is unsustainable. The argument initially appears to have some merit on the basis of the classical Greco-Roman antithesis between the *ptōchos* and the *penēs*, where the 'poor' person (*ptōchos*) may be viewed as standing outside the shared social space of the *plousios* and the *penēs*.[29] However, we noted in the preceding discussion that this antithesis does not appear to have operated unambiguously within a Jewish context.[30] In addition, to remove the 'poor' from an economic context, Malina asserts that 'No one goes without necessities.'[31] Except in drought, famine, or war, when everyone lacked the basic necessities, no one was, allegedly, destitute. Two pieces of evidence are presented to support this declaration. First, Matt. 6:25–32, the parable of the lilies of the field, apparently 'certainly indicates' that all things necessary for human subsistence were quite at hand.[32] This is an extraordinarily brash reading. Why tell the disciples not to worry if subsistence was such a self-evident reality? Why teach them to pray for their daily bread (Matt. 6:11/Luke 11:3)? Besides the eschatological dimension of this text,[33] there are significant socio-economic realities that Malina appears blind to. Even Oakes' moderate reading of first-century Philippian society estimates that 20 per cent of the peasant population were living below a healthy subsistence level.[34] Secondly, Malina cites Clement of Alexandria,

---

[29] Hamel, *Poverty and Charity*, p. 195: 'Whereas the *ptōchos*, who was viewed with a mix of awe and fear, could become the object of pity, the *penēs* was a participant in the race for status.' See also Hands, *Charities*, pp. 78–81.

[30] See §2.1 above, and Hamel, *Poverty and Charity*, p. 171.

[31] B. Malina, 'Wealth and Poverty', pp. 362f. See also Neyrey, 'Loss', p. 139, who cites Plutarch, *On Love of Wealth* 523F and Seneca, *Ep. Mor.* 25.4 to support this apparent 'self-evident truth'. However, these texts do not describe normative conditions, but advocate a sufficiency in an elite context. This is particularly clear in the Plutarch passage, which discusses the infectious nature of wealth and at 524A contrasts not borrowing to buy cheese and running into debt to buy a splendid house.

[32] B. Malina, 'Wealth and Poverty', p. 362.

[33] W. Davies and D. Allison, *A Critical and Exegetical Commentary on the Gospel according to Saint Matthew* (ICC; Edinburgh: T. & T. Clark, 1988), pp. 649ff.

[34] P. S. Oakes, *Philippians: From People to Letter* (Society for New Testament Studies, Monograph Series, 110; Cambridge: Cambridge University Press, 2001), pp. 40–50, who discusses in detail the various merits of the arguments advanced by P. Garnsey and G. Woolf, 'Patronage and the Rural Poor', in *Patronage in Ancient Society* (ed. A. Wallace-Hadrill; London: Routledge, 1989), pp. 153–70. See also Meggitt, *Paul, Poverty and Survival*, pp. 53–73, for an assessment of levels of destitution.

The Teacher 2.14.5, and Plutarch, *On Love of Wealth* 523F, who both suggest that no person is destitute or overlooked. Both these references, however, are problematic. The former is a later Christian and apologetic text,[35] and the latter an elite Hellenistic text that eulogises an idealised philosophical good.[36] They also share a common appreciation of Middle Platonism and a corresponding polemical attitude towards both the Epicurean identification of pleasure with the highest good and Stoic materialism and determinism.[37] They represent a particular later tradition, and their use as proof texts without further comment or contextual analysis is an inadequate basis from which to advance such a brave declaration. Furthermore, the view which Malina presents that the 'poor' refers to a minority 'revolving class' is also problematic. The idea that those born to be 'day labourers, landless peasants or beggars' are somehow honourable is advanced by reference to 'limited good', society's apparent status-maintenance orientation, and the assertion that no one was destitute. This primitive 'wantlessness'[38] is a questionable anthropological construct which overwrites any consideration of either ethnic or religious consciousness; all is subordinated to this structural ordering of 'classic peasant society'.[39] The idea that one's honourable status is simply a matter of one's position at birth is a highly constrained view of honour, which neglects both historical and religious dimensions of the social world.[40] It is to this historical dimension that we now turn.

---

[35] This is most evident in the following maxim from Malina's source, which implies both situations of want and the apologetic nature of the text: 'If one says that he has often seen the righteous man in need of food, this is rare, and happens only where there is not another righteous man' (Clement of Alexander, *The Teacher* 3.8).

[36] See helpful introductory notes in Plutarch, *Moralia: On Love of Wealth* (trans. P. DeLacy and B. Einarson; London: Heinemann, 1959), pp. 1–5.

[37] See S. Lilla, *Clement of Alexandria: A Study in Christian Platonism and Gnosticism* (London: Oxford University Press, 1971), pp. 44f., e.g. Clement, *Protr.* 1.51.6–7, cf. Plutarch, *Adv. Col.* 1111b10–12. This appreciation of Middle Platonism is a marked feature of the culture of the second century AD: see J. Dillon, 'Platonism, Middle', *OCD*, p. 1193.

[38] T. F. Carney, *The Shape of the Past: Models and Antiquity* (Lawrence, KS: Coronado Press, 1975), pp. 198f.

[39] On 'classic peasant society', see chapter 2, §5.1 above.

[40] See the extensive critique of the idea of a normative honour culture in chapter 2 above.

2.3 The socio-economic 'poor'

The socio-economic view of the 'poor' combines elements of both quantitative and qualitative approaches. This approach, advocated by Hollenbach,[41] understands the 'poor' not only as the temporarily unfortunate but also as the more permanently structurally oppressed. Whilst Hollenbach accepts Malina's characterisation of a first-century Mediterranean where economics is embedded in kinship and politics,[42] he suggests that if the 'poor' are to be understood properly, the economic dimension should be retained. In his desire to reopen the question of the economic dimension, he argues that 'distinctive features of Jewish tradition' need to be considered; in addition, that the context of this tradition 'might have had particularly distinctive features that distinguished it to some extent from other Mediterranean traditions'.[43] He therefore supplements Malina's strategy by introducing to the discussion the particular Jewish sabbatical-jubilee traditions. Whilst he argues that all facets of these traditions may still be viewed as being embedded in kinship or politics,[44] the distinctive element for Hollenbach is that now the 'poor' may be viewed both as unfortunates and as the oppressed peasant class.[45] The sabbatical-jubilee regulations address a social structure that has 'fallen' from an original utopian egalitarian ideal,[46] which now takes the form of an oppressive aristocratic–peasant structure in which the peasants, the 'poor', are dominated by the aristocrats, the 'rich'. The 'poor' are therefore most appropriately viewed as a permanent group within society.[47] Developing this reading, Hollenbach adopts Luke 4:16–30 as his hermeneutical key since it is here that the 'poor' in the New

---

[41] Hollenbach, *Defining Rich and Poor*.

[42] Indeed, he appears seduced by Malina's intra-textual analysis: see *ibid.*, p. 55.

[43] *Ibid.*, p. 57.

[44] On sabbatical-jubilee traditions of 'care', 'redemption', and 'release', see P. Hollenbach, 'Liberating Jesus for Social Involvement', *BTB* 15 (1985), 154f. Kinship ties provide 'care' and 'redemption' through immediate response to hunger and short-term response to landlessness respectively. Political actions provide 'release' through a long-term response to landlessness.

[45] *Defining Rich and Poor*, p. 57.

[46] Here he follows N. Gottwald, *The Tribes of Yahweh: A Sociology of a Liberated Israel* (London: Orbis, 1979), who describes such a historical development in ancient Israel. Notably, this egalitarian ideal appears more generally throughout anthropological discussions of most if not all agrarian societies: see chapter 2, §5.1 above.

[47] *Defining Rich and Poor*, p. 58.

Testament are allegedly 'unambiguously' defined.[48] The quotations from Isa. 58:6–7 and 61:1–2 clearly express the traditional prophetic concern for 'economic-political justice'.[49] The 'poor' are those 'captive' as debt prisoners, and the 'oppressed' are those pulled down by structural economic deprivation. They encompass the peasantry as a whole who have fallen into 'covenantally unjustified economic conditions'.[50] They are not merely the general class of unfortunates. He concludes on the basis of this reading that when Jesus addresses the 'poor', he proclaims:

> Among temporary unfortunate people, the blind receive their sight, the lame walk, the lepers are cleansed, the deaf hear, and the dead are raised up, and the more permanent structurally oppressed poor have good news (of liberation) preached to them (Matt 11:5//). Blessed are you structurally oppressed poor, for the kingdom of liberation belongs to you. But woe to you structurally oppressing rich, for you've had all the good you'll ever get (Luke 6:20, 24).[51]

In contrast to Malina, Hollenbach's 'poor', like those of Schottroff and Stegemann, once again represent the major part of society.

Hollenbach's reintegration of structural economic considerations in the discussion of the 'poor' is to be welcomed. However, his approach eclipses rather than supplements Malina's focus on honour. It is not clear that Hollenbach has fully grasped the significance of Malina's argument. His insight that the peasantry as a whole have fallen into 'covenantally unjustified economic conditions' powerfully complements Malina's view that the 'poor' are those who cannot maintain their inherited status. It potentially weds Malina's honour discourse with a more culturally sensitive view of dominion, which does not embed the social world in kinship, politics, or even economics, but rather views dominion in terms of a religious covenant. The structural economics which Hollenbach identifies indicates not simply an economic reality but also a breach in covenant. The structurally oppressed were

---

[48] He rejects the beatitudes, Matt. 5:3f. and Luke 6:20f., parables about humility at banquets, Luke 14:13f. and 16:19f., and Jesus' answer to John's question, Matt. 11:5, as all being ambiguous; see *Defining Rich and Poor*, pp. 59f.

[49] *Defining Rich and Poor*, p. 60.

[50] *Ibid.*

[51] *Ibid.*

unable to maintain their inherited status as a people of the covenant. Yet Hollenbach maintains a distinction between qualitatively different 'poor', the temporarily unfortunate, and the permanently oppressed. This is perhaps a result of Malina's rather narrow view of 'inherited status', which is driven by his dogmatic understanding of a Mediterranean honour culture. Hollenbach remains wedded to a picture of the New Testament world in which economic considerations are embedded in kinship and politics. Whilst he wants to see economics, kinship, and politics all given due consideration, he fails to see that his highlighting of the sabbatical-jubilee tradition potentially provides one answer. Economics, kinship, and politics may be embedded in the religious dimension. This would have been the case in Judaea in particular. Yet only the most limited consideration is given to any concrete context for the 'poor'. The nearest he gets is to refer to 'Jesus' Palestine'.[52] This lack of concrete context is further evidenced in his adoption of Luke 4:16–30 as his hermeneutical key. Luke's redactional interests are not considered.[53] Yet Hollenbach extrapolates from this particular theological motif to his social reading. His concern to reintegrate economic considerations in the discussion of the 'poor' by focusing on historical features of Jewish tradition paradoxically neglects to consider how such religious narratives may have been embodied in the first-century social world.[54] It is such questions that we will address in §3 below.

2.4   Summary

The social approaches reviewed tackle the question of the identity of the 'poor' in the New Testament from different perspectives. Schottroff and Stegemann concentrate on social actors and conclude that the 'poor' are a major part of the population living in dire economic straits. Malina focuses on normative social values recontextualising the 'poor' and presenting them as a minority unable to maintain their inherited status. Hollenbach, whilst nominally marrying the approaches of Schottroff, Stegemann, and Malina, focuses on the historical, understanding the 'poor' to

---

[52] *Ibid.*, p. 57.

[53] Yet neither Matt. 13:54–8 nor Mark 6:1–6 includes the Isaiah references in their versions of the Nazareth rejection.

[54] See Seccombe, *Possessions and the Poor*, pp. 24–43, and J. A. Sanders, 'From Isaiah 61 to Luke 4'.

be a combination of the temporarily unfortunate and the permanently structurally oppressed. Whilst it may be legitimate, in a critique of theologically conceived *Sitz im Leben*, to stress 'economic' and 'social' elements of the New Testament world, it is, I believe, an error to overwrite its religious dimension. There are merits in each of the social approaches outlined; however, one of the challenges taken up in this book is to attempt a more integrated approach to conceiving New Testament social worlds. It seeks an understanding of how social actors' practices are informed not only by the structural ordering of their lives but also by historical narratives which may facilitate a transformation or reinscription of their world. Schottroff and Stegemann, by focusing on 'texts that take a position on social problems', immediately place their 'poor' in an economic box and exclude this dynamic possibility.[55] Likewise, the 'social-scientific' strategies of Malina and Hollenbach, which favour inter- and intra-textual readings of the 'poor' and dogmatically adhere to a vision of the social world that ignores its religious dimension, effectively strip the 'poor' of their context. Their paradoxical neglect of the social context of the 'poor', or of their traditions, in favour of the analysis of formulaic motifs locks them into an abstract world upon which are imposed supposedly normative values. However, as I will now demonstrate, these texts, rather than being appropriate subjects of such analysis, appear to illustrate the contested nature of their subjects. Furthermore, the heuristic potential of the references so casually abandoned by Malina for their alleged 'ambiguity' is revealed, and they are shown to provide particular access to the social world of the 'poor'.

3   The social world of the *ptōchoi*

Judaea was a distinct social world in which virtuoso religion appears to have been practised and to have provided an alternative structure within society which radically addressed the 'poor' through its embodiment of an apparent piety of poverty. Recent social approaches to the 'poor' in the New Testament have neglected such particularity, however. Instead they have focused, as we have just seen, on more broadly conceived social and

---

[55] L. Schottroff and W. Stegemann, *God of the Lowly: Socio-Historical interpretation of the Bible* (Maryknoll, NY: Orbis, 1984), p. 6. They take the view that the 'poor' are most appropriately considered 'poor in the economic sense of the word'.

economic considerations which have tended towards homogenising the first-century Mediterranean and obscuring the religious dimension of the social world. In contrast, this section seeks to explore the particular social world of the New Testament's *ptōchoi*. It starts by revealing the contested nature of the motif, which appears so favoured in Malina and Hollenbach's social approaches: see §§2.2 and 2.3 above. Moreover, in an *excursus* on the first makarism (Matt. 5:3/Luke 6:20) it reveals that social approaches to the 'poor' have reinscribed a consensus which promotes Luke's unqualified blessing to the 'poor' as the more 'original'. It is argued that this homogenising approach not only neglects redactional interests but also obscures particular traditions concerning the piety of poverty. The *excursus* concludes by inverting the consensus position on the makarism. It argues Matthew's 'poor in spirit' is most plausibly understood against a context of Judaean virtuoso religion and that Jesus uttered it using a language formulation derived from his experience of such piety. The section continues by highlighting that the *ptōchoi* in the New Testament are closely associated with piety and Judaea. This reading is complemented with insights from the theoretical framework concerning the nature of lay/virtuoso interactions.

3.1   The contested 'poor' motif

Malina and Hollenbach in their strategy of 'linguistic collocation', which understands the 'poor' on the basis of words that occur in close proximity to *ptōchoi* and that appear to describe social conditions, have primarily focused their discussion on formulaic motifs concerning the *ptōchoi*, e.g. Matt. 5:3–5; 11:4–5; Luke 4:18; 6:20–1; and 14:13–21.[56] This is particularly clear in Hollenbach's choice of Luke 4:17–19 as the hermeneutical key to his identification of the 'poor'. The *ptōchoi* in the majority of these references are clearly part of formulaic constructions. Indeed, such constructions are a prominent element in Luke's redaction, e.g. 4:16–30, cf. Matt. 13:54–8 and Mark 6:1–6; also Luke 14:15–24, cf. Matt. 22:1–10. Therefore the social reality, or otherwise, of the *ptōchoi* cannot simply be a matter of highly constrained intra-textual analysis. Rather, to understand these *ptōchoi* it is necessary to attempt to understand how this formula may have been perceived in its

---

[56] See §§2.2 and 2.3 above.

first-century context. This involves not only the sort of inter-textual analysis advocated by Roth but also the rooting of that inter-textual analysis in a social context.[57] The importance of understanding the context of these traditions is evident upon a cursory reading of Luke 4:16f. and 7:22f./Matt. 11:5. In Luke 4:16f. Jesus' proclamation in a synagogue in Nazareth of 'good news to the poor' does not appear to be expected; it is rejected, and a comparison made with the rejection of the prophets. In Luke 7:22f./Matt. 11:5 Jesus adopts this proclamation to identify the nature of his ministry in reply to the disciples of the Baptist, a particular constituency. He concludes by declaring *makarios*, 'blessed', the one who is not 'offended' because of him (7:23). This particular constituency is presented as being challenged by Jesus' 'offensive' identification with this motif.

Further examination of these texts highlights the contested nature of such formulaic motifs within first-century Judaea. Flusser, Miller, and Sanders have clearly demonstrated the importance at Qumran of such motifs, which predominantly derive from Isaiah 61.[58] For our purposes it is sufficient to note that the motif functioned here as an in-group appellative. The *ptōchoi* from this particular perspective would not have been perceived either as the temporarily unfortunate or as the structurally oppressed peasant but rather as a specific constituency within first-century Jewish pietism.[59] The New Testament notably provides one occasion on

---

[57] *The Blind*, p. 26. Roth's approach is too dogmatic, insisting that the motif should be 'interpreted in the context of the LXX rather than on the basis of extra-textual historical or social constructs'. This side-stepping of historical questions in favour of literary study leads him to view the poor functionally as an element in Luke's christological rhetoric. Roth here follows closely the strategy of D. A. Neale, *None but the Sinners: Religious Categories in the Gospel of Luke* (JSNTS 58; Sheffield: JSOT Press, 1991), sharply critiqued for such sidestepping by B. J. Capper, 'Review: "None but the Sinners", Neale, D. A. JSNTS 58, 1991', *JTS* 43/2 (1992), 389–94. See also J. Barton, *Oracles of God: Perceptions of Ancient Prophecy in Israel after the Exile* (London: DLT, 1986), p. 151.

[58] D. Flusser, 'Blessed are the Poor in Spirit', in *Judaism and the Origins of Christianity* (compiled and ed. by D. Flusser with S. Safrai and B. Young; Jerusalem: Magnes Press, The Hebrew University, 1988), pp. 102–14; M. Miller, 'The Function of Isa 61:1–2 in 11QMelchizedek', *JBL* 88 (1969), 467–9, and J. A. Sanders, 'From Isaiah 61 to Luke 4', in *Luke and Scripture* (ed. C. Evans and J. Sanders; Minneapolis: Fortress, 1993), p. 59.

[59] On competing constituents for this appellation, see Seccombe, *Possessions and the Poor*, pp. 35ff. To identify this designation with a constituency within first-century pietism is not to deny a socio-economic dimension, as has been previously noted in discussions of virtuoso religion; such groups provide not only soteriological subtleties but also concrete social services. See Silber, *Virtuosity*, p. 213. Also chapter 3, §2.2 above and chapter 5, §3.2.2 below.

which the motif is addressed to a particular constituency (Luke 7:22f./Matt. 11:5);[60] the remaining references occur within units of tradition which are more problematic to place and will be examined in the following sections. In this context, the motif is addressed to the disciples of the Judaean Baptist. There are many links, geo-graphical and ideological, that connect the Baptist with the Essenes; although the Baptist may not have been an Essene, he may well have been influenced by contact with them.[61] This is most evident in Matthew and Luke's inclusion in their renditions of the motif of the 'raising of the dead', which is not present in the Isaianic passages (35:5–6 and 61:1–2). This element of the motif is, however, present in 4Q521.[62] It appears that, in his reply to the Judaean Baptist, Jesus not only alludes to texts important to the Qumran communities,[63] but also paraphrases them as they did. However, there is also a profound difference between Jesus' and the Essenes' midrash on who the *ptōchoi* were.[64] Jesus' actions undermine any expectation which the disciples of the Baptist may have held that addressed this expression exclusively to their particular in-group.[65] Rather, the expectation is 'offensively' addressed (Luke 7:23) to those to whom God wishes it to apply: to those who turn to Jesus.[66] However, simply because Jesus appears to reject a narrowly con-ceived exclusivist appropriation of the Isaian motif does not mean,

---

[60] On the integrity of the tradition, see Dunn, *Jesus and the Spirit*, p. 60, and Nolland, *Luke*, Vol. I, p. 327.

[61] See A. Geyser, 'The Youth of John the Baptist: A Deduction from the Break in the Parallel Account of the Lucan Infancy Story', *NovTest* 1 (1956), 70–5; R. E. Brown, *The Gospel according to John (I–XII)* (New York: Anchor Bible, 1966), p. 49; and B. Pixner, 'Jesus and his Community: Between Essenes and Pharisees', in *Hillel and Jesus* (ed. J. H. Charlesworth and L. L. Johns; Minneapolis: Fortress Press, 1997), p. 215.

[62] C. Evans, 'The Recently Published Dead Sea Scrolls and the Historical Jesus', in *Studying the Historical Jesus* (ed. B. Chilton and C. Evans; Leiden: Brill, 1998), p. 553. See also M. Goodacre, 'How Blessed are the Poor?', unpublished manuscript of draft chapter for his *The Case against Q*, p. 16, n. 27.

[63] E.g. Isaiah 61; cf. 11QMelch 2.4, 6, 9, 13, 18; 1QH 15.15; 18.15.

[64] J. A. Sanders, 'From Isaiah 61 to Luke 4', p. 62.

[65] See Pixner, 'Essenes and Pharisees', pp. 215f.

[66] See L. Crockett, 'The OT in the Gospel of Luke with Emphasis on the Interpretation of Isa 61:1–2' (unpublished doctoral dissertation, Brown University, 1966). Crockett raises the question whether the controversy might have occurred because Jesus interpreted the *ptōchoi* to mean those whom the Essenes viewed as impure of spirit and flesh: see J. A. Sanders, 'The Ethic of Election in Luke's Great Banquet Parable', in *Luke and Scripture* (ed. C. Evans and J. Sanders; Minneapolis: Fortress, 1993), pp. 116–20, and the discussion of Crockett in Seccombe, *Possessions and the Poor*, pp. 37ff.

as we will see below, that the appellation should be understood as being unconditionally inclusive and therefore addressed to the structurally or temporarily 'poor'. It is clear that any attempt to understand the *ptōchoi* in such formulaic expressions cannot credibly depend on an intra-textual reading. Rather, the location of the tradition within its social world reveals that the very nature of who the *ptōchoi* were was the subject of debate.

3.2   *Excursus* on the first makarism, Matt. 5:3/Luke 6:20

In the previous section we started to argue that when the *ptōchoi* are located within their social world, their very nature is the matter of debate. The ambiguities and possibilities of comprehending the *ptōchoi*, as this *excursus* will now demonstrate, are perhaps most evident when examining the redactional interests surrounding the first makarism. However, a consensus has settled over this makarism which appears to preclude any possible fresh insight.[67] It has become almost universally held that Luke's 'Blessed are the poor' (6:20) originates with Jesus and that Matthew's *'in spirit'* (5:3) is a 'spiritualising gloss'. Indeed, Luke's *hoi ptōchoi* without qualification is deemed 'potentially misleading',[68] and even 'shocking to the Greeks', for whom it would have caused perplexities which Matthew sought to avoid.[69] This reading depends heavily upon social understandings of the makarism and the *ptōchoi* in the New Testament social world.[70] However, it is not at all clear

[67] On arguments for the consensus position, see the classical statement by Davies and Allison, *Saint Matthew*, p. 442.

[68] *Ibid.*, pp. 435f., 442. See also J. Fitzmyer, *The Gospel according to Luke* (New York: Doubleday, 1985), pp. 631f., who suggests that Matthew has adapted the 'original beatitude', and F. W. Danker, *Jesus and the New Age: A Commentary on St. Luke's Gospel* (St Louis: Clayton, 1988), p. 139, who writes of an 'interpretative addition'.

[69] Hamel, *Poverty and Charity*, pp. 174 and 193.

[70] This is perhaps the most prominent means for arguing for Luke's 'originality'. However, two other notable strategies are also advanced. The first is to argue from absence: *hoi ptōchoi* occurs elsewhere in Matthew without qualification, Matt. 11:5; 19:21; 26:9, 11. This argument is augmented by making reference to Luke 6:24, the first 'woe' that has the rich, *tois plousiois*, without qualification, apparently implying an unqualified *hoi ptōchoi* in at least Q^Lk. The second is literary: Matthew's qualification disrupts what would otherwise be perfect parallelism in Q. In Q, *makarioi hoi ptōchoi, makarioi hoi peinōntes*, and *makarioi hoi klaiontes* allegedly exemplify perfect parallelism that is disrupted by Matthew's qualification. However, the absence of qualification to *hoi ptōchoi* elsewhere in Matthew does not demand the conclusion that *tō pneumati* is redactional. Indeed, it may be indicative of

that such an understanding has informed this consensus. Indeed, even recent discussion of the makarism by Hanson and Neyrey,[71] members of the Context Group, has failed to challenge this consensus. Hanson takes as his subject the cultural function of the makarisms, which he argues belong to the word-field and value system of honour and shame. Their function is therefore deemed to be as declarations of community honour. Neyrey builds on this reading by examining the content of the makarisms, particularly the *ptōchoi* in Q. He rejects the idea of viewing *ptōchos* as an economic term in favour of examining the cultural meaning of such labels and develops a cultural scenario which facilitates an exclusively secular reading of the *ptōchoi*. The *ptōchoi* in Q were 'dishonoured' as a result of being ostracised by their families for following Jesus. In return, the *ptōchos* was reciprocally deemed *makarios*, 'honourable', by Jesus. In contrast to these approaches, which have simply ignored or reinscribed the consensus position, this *excursus* will illustrate the heuristic strengths of a social approach that is sensitive to cultural particularity. It briefly reviews Hanson and Neyrey's arguments in the light of the earlier chapter's critical revision of the Context Group's model of normative honour culture. This discussion underlines the need for cultural sensitivity and helps expose the inadequacy of the social assumptions upon which the consensus reading of the first makarism is based. It argues that Matthew's 'gloss', rather than illuminating the *ptōchoi*, may well have been perceived to be culturally incoherent.

3.2.1   Hanson: the makarism as a declaration of community 'honour'

Hanson argues that makarisms do not refer to a 'blessing' and that they are not expressions of 'happiness' or statements of another's 'enviable' position.[72] Indeed, he is particularly concerned over the

a pre-Matthean tradition. See I. Broer, *Die Seligpreisungen der Bergpredigt: Studien zu ihrer Überlieferung und Interpretation* (BBB 61; Bonn: Hanstein, 1986), pp. 70–1; also I. H. Marshall, *The Gospel of Luke: A Commentary on the Greek Text* (Exeter: Paternoster Press, 1978), p. 250, who argues that the Semitic antecedents of the phrase, in 1QM 14.7, count against an editorial expansion. Further, the constructed Q's perfect parallelism is neither self-evident nor proof of precedence in tradition. Indeed, it may be indicative of literary handling, much as Luz postulates a π-alliteration in the tradition's development: see *Matthew*, pp. 226f.

[71] See K. Hanson, ' "How Honorable! How Shameful!" A Cultural Analysis of Matthew's Makarisms and Reproaches', *Semeia* 68 (1994), and Neyrey, 'Loss'.

[72] K. Hanson, ' "How Honorable! How Shameful!" ', p. 81.

failure to differentiate between 'blessings' and 'makarisms'. Such imprecision obscures their particular functions. He stresses, following Janzen and Westermann, that whilst the Hebrew *barûk* and its Greek equivalents in the LXX, *eulogeō* and *euloēmenes*, may be related to *ʿaśrē* and *makarios*, they are not synonymous.[73] Whilst 'blessings' are formal pronouncements set in the context of ritual, 'makarisms' are 'not limited to pronouncements by God or cultic mediators'.[74] They only refer to humans and 'never to God', they do not have their setting in ritual, and one does not pray for or refer to oneself with a makarism.[75] Makarisms are not ritual blessings.[76] Rather the affirmations which they embody are exclamations of honour. They are social imputations of esteem to an individual or group for manifesting desirable behaviour and commitments: '*whatever their context*, all makarisms are formally unified, and they articulate the values of the community...and pronounce the subject/s "honorable"'.[77] The makarisms are therefore only comprehensible in terms of the honour values and challenge–riposte transactions of the agonistic ancient Mediterranean.[78] He concludes that Matthew's makarisms 'must be interpreted as a programmatic statement: the conditions and behaviours which the community regards as honorable'.[79]

---

[73] 'How Honorable! How Shameful!', pp. 85f., following W. Janzen, *ʿaśrē* in the Old Testament', *HTR* 58 (1965), 215–26; *Mourning Cry and Woe Oracle* (*BZAW* 125; Berlin: Töpelmann, 1972) and C. Westermann, *Blessing in the Bible and the Life of the Church* (trans. K. Crim; Philadelphia: Fortress Press, 1978).

[74] ' "How Honorable! How Shameful" ', pp. 89f.

[75] On these fundamental differences he is following Janzen, *ʿaśrē*', pp. 223–4.

[76] Neither are they to be associated with 'happiness': see J. Moulton and G. Milligan, *The Vocabulary of the Greek Testament Illustrated from the Papyri and Other Non-Literary Sources* (3rd edn; Grand Rapids: Eerdmans, 1957), p. 386. They are not expressions of positive human emotions: 'one does not feel good who mourns or who is persecuted (Mt. 5:4, 10)', Hanson, ' "How Honorable! How Shameful!" ', p. 89, again following Janzen, *ʿaśrē*', p. 226. This is a strangely ethnocentric assertion for a member of the Context Group; see *contra* Downing, *Making Sense*, p. 40. Similarly, 'To be envied is the man' is also rejected: see Janzen, *ʿaśrē*', p. 225. This translation is deemed misleading since from his 'Mediterranean' perspective 'envy' is associated with casting the evil eye, misfortune, and greed. Hanson here follows J. H. Elliott, 'The Fear of the Leer', *Forum* 4/4 (1988), 42–71. For an anthropologist's perspective on whether this really is as problematic as Hanson suggests, see Kressel, 'An Anthropologist's Response', pp. 157f. Kressel suggests that Hanson errs in interpreting the casting of the evil eye as a malevolent (purposeful) activity.

[77] ' "How Honorable! How Shameful!" ', p. 92, my italics.

[78] *Ibid.*, p. 82. In his confidence in his ability 'to summarise the value orientation of the ancient Mediterranean' he notably assumes a cultural continuity from the Old to the New Testaments as well as the extra-canonical texts.

[79] ' "How Honorable! How Shameful!" ', p. 100.

However, Hanson's exclusive focus on the makarisms' function within a normative Mediterranean honour culture has distorted his reading.[80] Makarisms are not simply about public validation. The alleged pivotal values of honour and shame that involve competition and public validation are about determining society's internal hierarchy.[81] It is not at all clear that this secular orientation is appropriate for understanding biblical literature where the predominant concern is one's relationship with God and not man, *theos*, not *laos*. The assertion that makarisms are 'never' applied to God and 'only refer to humans' is overstated.[82] Within the wider milieu of the ancient Near East *makarios* designated a state of being that pertained to the gods.[83] Whilst the distinction Hanson makes holds firm for *'ašrē*, it is not entirely clear that this narrow reading of *'ašrē*, derived from Janzen, is the appropriate background for *makarios*. Indeed, Leske, following Schweizer, has pointed out that even the sharp distinction between *'ašrē* and *barûk* is not sustainable.[84]

---

[80] This focus on form and function over content and context is largely the result of his argument developing as a counter thesis to Janzen, thereby inheriting his material and its focus on the Hebrew Bible. When he starts to address Matthew, his central text, it is therefore his stated intention not to address specific contents or sources: ' "How Honorable! How Shameful!" ', p. 99.

[81] Kressel, 'An Anthropologist's Response', p. 158.

[82] Hanson is required to make the immediate clarification that the New Testament has two non-formulaic instances in which *makarios* is applied to God, 1 Tim. 1:11; 6:15. Indeed, his secular bias is underlined by the assertion that makarisms are '*not limited* to pronouncements by God or cultic mediators': see ' "How Honorable! How Shameful!" ', p. 89, my italics.

[83] On the wider context of the makarism, see H. D. Betz, *The Sermon on the Mount* (Hermeneia; Minneapolis: Fortress Press, 1995), pp. 92f. If the Mediterranean values outlined by Hanson are to parallel any phenomena, they are perhaps elements within Hellenistic honour culture. However, makarisms in the Hellenistic context are clearly used of divine nature: Hauck and Bertram, 'μακάριος', *TDNT* IV, p. 362. While makarisms therefore appear to have Hanson's subjective and relative sense of public validation, they also have a transcendental dimension. Man can have a part in divine blessedness. In Philo, *makarios* almost always applies to a transcendental reality which impinges on the earthly sphere for the righteous. Hence it is often used of the divine nature, *Deus Imm.* 161; *Spec. Leg.* 1.329; 2.53; 3.178; 4.48. Here Hanson's 'fundamental difference' between makarisms and blessings appears to have broken down just at the point of closest contact with Mediterranean conceptions of honour!

[84] A. Leske, 'The Beatitudes, Salt and Light in Matthew and Luke', *SBL Seminar Papers* (1991), pp. 816–39, following E. Schweizer, 'Formgeschichtliches zu den Seligpreisungen Jesu', *NTS* 19 (1972–3), 121–6. Intertestamental literature provides evidence of mixed patterns of use where *'ašrē* and *barûk* are adopted indiscriminately with no real difference in meaning. Leske complements Schweizer's material with additional insights from the Psalms: of interest is Ps. 1:1, 3, where the *'ašrē* formula is used, as it is in an allusion to that Psalm in Isa. 32:20. But the same saying in Jer. 17:7, 8 has *barûk*. See also Marshall, *Luke*, p. 248.

In addition, the LXX is not a definitive guide to New Testament meanings. For example, the Hebrew word behind both *ptōchoi* and *praeis*, 'poor' and 'meek', in Matthew's first and third beatitudes is clearly *anawim* (Isa. 61:1 and Ps. 37:11). Notably the 'blessing' that the *anawim* of Psalm 37 received was *barûk* and not ʿ*ašrē* (verse 22).[85] It is neither necessary nor desirable to restrict ourselves to an ethical and secular reading of the makarisms derived from a narrow adoption of ʿ*ašrē* in the Hebrew Bible. Indeed, the idea of the challenge–riposte game of honour is to be rejected. Men can easily go astray in their judgement.[86] The difference between the Context Group's 'honour' and the status of the people of God is neatly illustrated in Ps. 143:15 LXX: 'Men declare blessed (*makarios*) the people to whom these things belong [i.e. the good things of verses 12–14] [but][87] blessed are the people whose God is the Lord.'[88] The makarisms, especially in the New Testament, overwhelmingly refer to a distinctive state that accrues to man from his share in the salvation of the Kingdom of God.[89] Their location, predominantly in Revelation and the Synoptic tradition, underlines a context of eschatological proclamation. Whilst they do represent ideals, their orientation is not the public validation stressed in the model of a normative Mediterranean honour culture, but rather the individual's state before God. Thus there is often contrast with a false estimation of who is truly blessed; all secular goods and values are now completely subsidiary to the one supreme good, the Kingdom of God.[90] Whilst acknowledging an individual as *makarios* may indeed honour them, in the sense of the model of a normative

---

[85] Leske, 'Beatitudes', p. 823.

[86] See Isa. 3:12; 9:15. They go too much by outward success, Mal. 3:15. Rash judgement according to appearance is warned against, Sir. 11:14–28.

[87] The LXX renders the suffixed nouns of the MT verses 12–14 with third-person plural pronouns, making them descriptions of the enemies, whose good fortune is disdained for a higher blessing: see L. C. Allen, *Word Biblical Commentary 21: Psalms 101–150* (ed. D. Hubbard and G. Baker; Waco, TX: Word Books, 1983), p. 288, for full textual analysis.

[88] Notably in verses 8 and 11 the people who have these good things are characterised as 'speaking vanity', *mataiotēs*, and being the right hand of iniquity, *adikias*: cf. Ps. 4:3; 40:4; Eccles. 4:7; 6:11. It is not the 'empty words' of men that are important but their *dikē* or *adikia*, depending upon perspective, which is the subject of the makarism. It is a right attitude before God that is important.

[89] Hauck and Bertram, 'μακάριος', p. 367; Marshall, *Luke*, p. 248, and Davies and Allison, *Saint Matthew*, p. 434.

[90] See Matt. 5:3–6, 10f.; Luke 11:28; John 20:29; 1 Pet. 3:14; 4:14.

Mediterranean honour culture, it is clear that their orientation is towards God and not the public.[91]

3.2.2   Neyrey: The ptōchoi and status maintenance

Neyrey seeks to build upon Hanson's location of the makarisms within the field of honour by revisiting the *ptōchoi*. He presents an intra-textual reading of Q's 'original' makarisms which is informed by his understanding of a normative Mediterranean honour culture.[92] Neyrey's appropriation of this model is notable in that whilst it considerably overlaps with Malina's discussions of the 'poor' in the New Testament,[93] even drawing the same conclusion that *ptōchos* was not an economic term, he nonetheless takes a diametrically opposed view on 'wealth'. Where Malina, on the basis of his model of 'limited good',[94] argues that the rich were perceived to be inherently wicked, Neyrey argues that because honour required public display, it also required wealth to enable that display. Therefore, wealth symbolised honour. However, the passages which he cites to support this view, Plutarch, *On Love of Wealth* 528B and *Table Talk* 679B, and Josephus, *Ant.* 11.254, do not reveal any common perception that honour is symbolised by wealth. Josephus recounts an exceptional elite discourse, a reward within the gift of the King, and Plutarch actually mocks the wealthy because of their need for ostentation.[95] This mocking neatly illustrates that it is the nature of the public display which is important and not necessarily the wealth that backs it up. Indeed,

---

[91] Makarisms are not simply interchangeable with conventional terms of respect: see Downing, *Making Sense*, p. 40.

[92] 'Loss', p. 144. This consensus position is represented amongst others by Nolland, *Luke*, Vol. I, p. 280, and Luz, *Matthew*, pp. 226–9. Nonetheless, there are dissenting voices: see E. Bammel, 'The Poor and the Zealots', in *Jesus and the Politics of His Day* (ed. E. Bammel and C. F. D. Moule; Cambridge: Cambridge University Press, 1984), pp. 120ff., and Leske, 'Beatitudes', p. 826.

[93] See §2.2 above.

[94] Malina, 'Wealth and Poverty', p. 363. He argues that in a 'peasant society' a zero-sum game is played out in which any individual or group advancement is to the detriment of others and that the wealthy person is therefore viewed as being inherently wicked.

[95] E.g., in *On Love of Wealth* 528A, Plutarch argues: 'Such is the felicity of wealth – a felicity of spectators and witnesses or else a thing of naught. How different are self-mastery, the pursuit of wisdom, the knowing what we should about the gods... these have in the soul a luminousness of their own and a surpassing radiance... Such is the nature of virtue, truth and beauty... and with what of these do your trappings of wealth compare?'

within such elite philosophical discourse, honour is closely related to ideas about justice and righteousness.[96] Whilst Malina's thesis is equally problematic, he is nonetheless correct to emphasise that perceptions of wealth have a moral determinant. It is clear that the elite nature of Neyrey's references to wealth leads him into some awkward and unconvincing manoeuvring. This is especially clear in his discussion of land.[97] If wealth is essential to honour, and wealth resides in the land and the elite control most of the land, how can the non-elite have honour? His solution is to argue that *all* land equals wealth: size and quality are not an issue: 'peasants with small plots of land also enjoyed some "wealth" because of their land'.[98] However, to view the non-elite's subsistence plot as 'wealth' is to stretch the imagination. The elite certainly would not have considered it as wealth. They held the free peasant in such contempt that Ambrose had to persuade them of the economic benefits of providing them with famine relief, *De Offic. Ministr.* III (vii) 45–51.[99] Likewise, it is doubtful that the landed peasant would perceive that they enjoyed some 'wealth' because of their land. Whilst they most probably held a high estimation of the land, the emergence, for the Jews, of such levelling mechanisms as the jubilee and sabbatical year as images for the eschatological future are useful indicators of perceived injustices in relation to landholdings.

Neyrey initially appears on firmer ground when he suggests that honour is derived in a large part from membership of a family or clan.[100] Once again, his view is predominantly derived from elite Greco-Roman texts, e.g. Aristotle, *Rhet.* 1360b31–8. It is notable

---

[96] This is evident in another of Neyrey's citations, 1 Kgs. 10:1–10, in which he suggests that the Queen of Sheba's praise of Solomon is based upon his 'sumptuous palace' and that this leads to further wealth and public honour, 'Loss', p. 157. However, the declaration actually focuses on Solomon's wisdom, his justice, and his righteousness before God. It is notable that it is the servants and wives who are declared *makarios* and not Solomon. Where the Queen does address Solomon, in 1 Kgs. 10:6f., it is never solely in response to his wealth. Rather wealth is always seen in the context of his wisdom and piety.

[97] On wealth residing in the land he follows Carney, *The Shape of the Past*, pp. 181–2: 'It was land, not capital, that produced resources in antiquity.'

[98] 'Loss', p. 142

[99] Ambrose points out to the 'men of rank and wealth' that if the free peasants died of starvation, it would be fatal to their own corn supply and, significantly for an estimation of the perceived 'wealth' of the landed peasant, if the actual men of rank and wealth were deprived of their peasants, they would have to buy cultivators, 'slaves', to replace them at additional cost. On the particular vulnerability of the small landowner, see Fiensy, *The Land is Mine*, pp. 92–104, and de Ste Croix, *Class Struggle*, p. 220.

[100] Neyrey, 'Loss', pp. 142, 155.

that Aristotle is here discussing the nature of happiness. This discussion is framed in such a manner, presuming the necessity of an 'abundance of possessions and slaves', that it is clear that 'happiness' is not a quality for general attainment, but rather for the 'gentleman'. In addition, in an unsettling manner for Neyrey's argument, which suggests that honour derives from lineage, this is not Aristotle's concern. Aristotle's concern is to discuss what constitutes 'happiness': 'its component parts must necessarily be: noble birth, numerous friends, good friends, wealth, good children, numerous children, a good old age; further, bodily excellences, such as health, beauty, strength, stature, fitness for athletic contests, a good reputation, honour, good luck, virtue', 1360b 19–20. The relationship that Neyrey claims to derive from this text between honour and good birth is simply not substantiated. Both honour and good birth are constituents of happiness. Nonetheless, the text does affirm a relative importance to lineage. This is also a Jewish theme, one adopted by Philo in his discussion of the special place of the *epēlytos*, 'incomer', where he stresses the importance of family and kin, *Spec. Leg.* 4.176–82. The incomer deserves special attention because 'he has turned his kinsfolk, who in the ordinary course of things would be his sole confederates, into mortal enemies', 4.178. However, this is not the whole case: 'let no one think that good lineage is a perfect blessing and then neglect noble actions', 4.182. Again the family, like wealth, are secondary to 'the honouring of One who alone is worthy of honour', 4.178. Furthermore, Neyrey's stress on the importance of the family and clan pays little attention to the social upheavals caused by Herodian economic policies. Freyne has argued that one consequence of these policies was the diminution of the relative importance of the family.[101] Whilst the extended family was central to the redistributive system, it was wholly unsuited to the market economy. Fiensy, focusing on the control of the land in the Herodian period, puts it in even stronger terms. He talks of a trend towards the break-up of the *beth an* in Jewish society, with the medium social unit becoming the neighbours of a courtyard, many of whom were probably not relatives. Indeed, he asserts that the clans or *mishpahoth* 'completely ceased to function as effective socio-kinship units'.[102] The situation

---

[101] On the development of a market economy in the first century AD, see S. Freyne, 'Herodian Economics in Galilee: Searching for a Suitable Model', in Esler, ed., *Modelling*, p. 43, following Carney, *The Shape of the Past*.

[102] Fiensy, *The Land is Mine*, p. 178.

in the Greco-Roman urban context was perhaps even starker.[103] It is in such a context that the consequences of family ostracism should be read. Neyrey's case for the family unit as utterly dominant in social relations and in total control of the land is overstated.

The final element to Neyrey's argument is that because honour is embedded in the family, who control the land and wealth, any break with the family would have resulted in a loss of access to such land and wealth. This would lead to an inability to maintain inherited status, i.e. honour. This is the cultural context for understanding the *ptōchoi*. Such 'poverty' was not simply an economic designation. Here Neyrey follows Malina's earlier argument.[104] He cites Plutarch and Seneca to argue that whilst we might consider that most of the non-elite in antiquity would qualify as 'poor' in an economic sense, 'In what suffices, no one is poor'.[105] He relates this distinction to the contrast between the *penēs*, who has little wealth yet a sufficiency and is not apparently 'poor', and the *ptōchos*, who lacks social standing and sufficiency and is 'poor'. The *ptōchoi* of the makarisms are not therefore simply an economic category. Rather, the cultural meaning of such a label points to the inability of the *ptōchoi* to maintain their inherited status, their honour. The cultural constraints of such a reading have already been discussed in §2.2 above. It is sufficient to note here that Neyrey's focus upon classical Greek usage and elite texts to support his normative view is inappropriate. Indeed, Downing helpfully points out that these wealthy essayists have turned a 'Cynic conviction into a moral platitude... Neither writer intended to act on the axiom, neither indicates that others believed it'.[106] Neyrey's argument is simply overstated. It is driven by a combination of an elite Greco-Roman view of 'poverty' and a conviction that in the first century, Mediterranean economics was embedded in kinship. Whilst he is surely correct to state

---

[103] Meggitt, *Paul, Poverty and Survival*, pp. 169f.

[104] However, surprisingly for a fellow member of the Context Group, Neyrey does not cite Malina's 'Wealth and Poverty', which arrives at an almost identical conclusion.

[105] Neyrey, 'Loss', p. 139, citing Plutarch, *On Love of Wealth* 523F and Seneca, *Ep. Mor.* 25.4.

[106] *Making Sense*, p. 39. However, his reading of poverty in the Gospels against a Cynic backdrop is perhaps almost as problematic as Neyrey's elite Greco-Roman context: see Evans, 'The New Quest', pp. 180f.

that *ptōchos* was not simply an economic category, he excludes *a priori* the religious dimension of the social world. Neyrey repeatedly neglects the strong religious values that accrued not only to Jewish views of poverty but also to Greco-Roman notions of honour. Before examining the first makarism in detail, I will now attempt briefly to reintegrate these elements of the social world.

3.2.3   The makarisms and the Jews in the New Testament World

Hanson and Neyrey, following the pattern set by other members of the Context Group, place a consistent emphasis on the public dimension of honour. This emphasis, as chapter 2 has amply demonstrated, is unsustainable. It is clear that the stress upon external repute obscures both a more complex Greco-Roman and first-century reality. Within this reality, honour was conceived of not simply in terms of external repute but more prominently as a virtue, which was closely related to ideas of justice and righteousness. The honourable man was characterised by his *megalopsychia*, 'great-spiritedness'. He was as polite to those of moderate fortune as he was to the great. He cared more for truth than for what people thought. His sense of honour related to what was truly honourable, *aretē*, a conception that had moved on from its Homeric heroic connotations to a clear stress upon being and doing good. It is therefore clear that honour cannot be comprehended in an exclusively functional view of the individual within the social world but needs to be related to religious and philosophical dimensions of the cultural context. This understanding underlines the Jews' uneasy relationship with Greco-Roman honour culture, in which the religious exclusivity of many Jews set them apart. Whilst their apologetics sought to present them as being *megalopsychoi*, 'great-spirited', they were clearly vulnerable to being characterised as being *mikropsychoi*, 'poor-spirited'. Indeed, the active participation of a religiously orientated Palestinian within the publicly orientated discourse of Greco-Roman honour culture cannot be taken as a given.

The misanthropic characterisation of the Jews has already been discussed in chapter 2 above. Whilst this characterisation is not normative, it is important because it highlights how their religious exclusivity represented both a social and political obstacle to their acceptance as an honourable people and exposed them to the charge of being *mikropsychoi*.[107] It is against such a backdrop that both Philo and Josephus write their apologetics. The perception of the Jews within educated Greco-Roman classes is a negative one, of social exclusivity. In their defence Philo notes that they offer up prayers for 'all humanity', *Spec. Leg.* 2.167, and that their laws expressly forbid that they should hate other peoples, *Virt.* 51ff. However, as Conzelmann notes, the Jews, in answering the charge of *amixia*, 'inhospitality', by referring to their law, repeatedly contradicted themselves: on the one hand, it provided a defence against the charge; on the other hand, the very law which they appealed to as their defence differentiated them all the more.[108] Typical of this double bind is Josephus' suggestion that the Jewish openness to proselytes illustrated their *philanthrōpia* and *megalopsychia*, *Contr. Ap.* 2.261. However, their openness was not the only thing being illustrated; so also was their insistence that it was on their own terms, their law. The use of language is interesting. Josephus in presenting the Jews as displaying *megalopsychia* wants them to be viewed as great-spirited, honourable people. We may contrast this language with the accusations that he makes of the Egyptians, whom he identifies as the source of the negative presentations of the Jews. They are characterised by their 'folly and poor-spiritedness', *anoias kai mikropsychias*, *Contr. Ap.* 1.226. It is not the Jews who are poor-spirited: rather, the Jews are great-spirited. It is the Egyptians, who have spread this gossip about the Jews, who are guilty of *mikropsychia*. In the context of his apologetics and the allegations made against the Jews it is conceivable that Josephus is simply inverting a charge made against the Jews themselves. It is clear that they were both sensitive and vulnerable to such allegations.

3.2.4   Luke's 'shocking' ptōchoi in context

The first step in attempting to understand the makarism within a Greco-Roman context is to re-examine the assertion that Luke's unqualified *ptōchos* would have been 'shocking'. It has been stated by Hamel that the *ptōchos* was held in contempt.[109] However, this

---

[107] Stern, *Greek and Latin Authors*, pp. 181f., no. 63. Note the contrast in Diodorus Siculus, *Bibliotheca Historica* between the Jews and Antiochus, who is described as *megalopsychos* for not obliterating the Jews completely.

[108] H. Conzelmann, *Gentiles, Jews, Christians: Polemics and Apologetics in the Greco-Roman Era* (trans. E. Boring; Minneapolis: Fortress Press, 1992), p. 144.

[109] *Poverty and Charity*, pp. 174, 193.

view is a problematic one which leads Hamel to contradict himself. It is clear that the predominantly elite textual sources generally held the *penēs* in contempt. The selling of one's work was not seen as different from the selling of oneself.[110] Yet whilst the *penēs* and the *plousios* belonged to the same world and determined each other's identities, the *ptōchos* was a stranger to their world. His identity was wrapped up in traditions concerning hospitality and the belief that he was under the protection of the gods.[111] In this respect, in particular times and contexts, the *ptōchos* could evoke pity, unlike the *penēs*, who, despite his economic deprivation, remained a participant in the race for status.[112] Hamel would have been correct to speak of 'shock' if the makarism had been addressed to the *penēs*, but this was not the case.

Shocking 'poverty' in the Greco-Roman world was perhaps most closely associated with the 'Cynics'.[113] This has been advocated as one possible understanding for the New Testament *ptōchoi*.[114] The 'Cynics' viewed poverty as 'constitutive of the good life'.[115] However, the constitution of this 'poverty' and the prevalence of this perception of the 'poor' are problematic.[116] The focus of 'Cynic' injunctions on possessions and on being poor was freedom through self-sufficiency. In contrast, Luke's first makarism does not extol the life of poverty and hunger but rather promises that in an eschatological future present needs will be fully met.[117] Where the 'Cynics' advocated dependence on the self, Jesus advocated dependence on God. Indeed, within the diversity of 'Cynic' teaching on poverty, the degree of austerity commended varied widely, and the word of choice to describe this poverty was not *ptōcheia* but

[110] *Ibid.*, pp. 167f.
[111] *Ibid.*, p. 170.
[112] *Ibid.*, p. 195.
[113] 'Cynics' is in inverted commas to highlight 'the complexities and discontinuities' involved in the label: see D. E. Aune, 'Jesus and the Cynics in First Century Palestine', in *Hillel and Jesus: Comparative Studies of Two Major Religious Leaders* (ed. J. H. Charlesworth and L. L. Johns; Minneapolis: Fortress Press, 1997), p. 178.
[114] Downing, *Making Sense*, p. 40.
[115] Downing, 'Cynic', p. 201.
[116] On the wider debate with regard to Cynicism and Christian origins, see the critical responses to the work of F. G. Downing, *Cynics and Christian Origins* (Edinburgh: T. & T. Clark, 1992), and B. Mack, *A Myth of Innocence: Mark and Christian Origins* (Philadelphia: Fortress Press, 1988), made by C. Tuckett, 'A Cynic Q', *Biblia* 70 (1989), 349–76; H. D. Betz, 'Jesus and the Cynics: Survey and Analysis of a Hypothesis', *JRel* 74 (1994), 453–75; Aune, 'Cynics'; and Evans, 'The New Quest'.
[117] Tuckett, 'A Cynic Q', p. 373.

penia.[118] It is therefore not at all clear that Luke's first makarism would have been immediately recognisable in terms of the 'Cynics' call to self-sufficiency.

In contrast to the general contempt in which the 'Cynics' were held, it is clear that *ptōchoi* in particular circumstances might evoke pity. It is, however, necessary to note that the pity which the *ptōchoi* might evoke was dependent on context. It was most evident and comprehensible in the familiar Greco-Roman motif which heralded a reversal of conditions. Danker's analysis of such 'benefactor' motifs highlights the traditional antithetical form that such expressions took.[119] The reversal of conditions was, as Dodd has observed, a 'contemporary pattern of thought in the Hellenistic world'.[120] Luke's version of the makarisms with their emphasis on contrasting fortunes would have appealed 'especially' to a Greco-Roman public.[121] Indeed, Luke makes frequent use of this 'topos of transposition', e.g. 1:46–55; 14:7–24; 16:19–31; 18:9–14 and 22–4.[122] Rather than being 'shocking', Luke's makarism is clearly culturally comprehensible from a Greco-Roman perspective.[123] Whilst from such a perspective they were more frequently expressive of the altruistic impulses of the elite than indicative of fundamental changes in the social world, they also took more idealistic forms, most notably in the context of the accession of a king.[124]

---

[118] On the degree of austerity advocated, see H. D. Betz, 'Jesus', p. 472. On the vocabulary of poverty, note the evidence cited by both H. D. Betz, *The Sermon on the Mount*, p. 117, and Downing, *Making Sense*, p. 41. Nonetheless, polemic against early Christians did make use of similarities between Christian and Cynic preachers, polemic that the Christians themselves used to stereotype their adversaries. However, it is notable that in this context Lucian in his *De Morte Peregrini* 11 does not characterise Jesus as a Cynic but rather as a *theios anēr*, and the founder of a mystery cult.

[119] Danker, *Benefactor*, p. 338. He also suggests that this form represents a 'particular concern' of Luke's.

[120] C. Dodd, 'The Beatitudes: A Form-critical Study', *More New Testament Studies* (ed. C. Dodd; Manchester: Manchester University Press, 1968), p. 6.

[121] Danker, *New Age*, p. 138.

[122] J. B. Green, *The Gospel of Luke* (NICNT; Grand Rapids, MI: Eerdmans, 1997), p. 264. Also the discussion of the theme of 'eschatological reversal' in Goodacre, 'Blessed'.

[123] D. L. Balch, 'Rich and Poor, Proud and Humble in Luke–Acts', in *The Social World of the First Christians: Essays in Honor of Wayne A. Meeks* (ed. L. M. White and O. L. Yarbrough; Minneapolis: Fortress Press, 1995), pp. 214–33.

[124] J. Dupont, *Les béatitudes*, Vol. II (Louvain: Nauwelaerts, 1969), pp. 60–1; Weinfeld, *Social Justice*, pp. 57–74; and C. C. McCown, 'The Beatitudes in the Light of Ancient Ideals', *JBL* 46 (1927), 50–61. For a summary of Dupont, see Leske, 'Beatitudes', p. 822.

However, whilst Luke's redactional interest appears quite comprehensible from a Greco-Roman perspective, this reading does not require us to place his *ptōchoi* in a narrowly conceived economic box. It is clear from both Luke 4:16f. and 7:22f. that the identity of these *ptōchoi* was contested and people's expectations challenged. The motif was adopted in a manner which not only resonated with themes of eschatological reversal but also functioned as a prophetic comment on the identity of the elect. This is clearly a feature of Luke 6:20f. The *ptōchoi* are not only associated with those who 'hunger' and 'mourn' but also with the 'hated' (6:22). This antagonism is not directed against a group defined as either unfortunate or structurally excluded but rather expressed in terms of religious practice: 'for great is your reward in heaven, for so men persecuted the prophets who were before you' (6:23, cf. 4:24f.). Indeed, it appears that it is the disciples themselves who are being directly addressed as the *ptōchoi*. Luke's makarism is not addressed to the 'poor' in general but to those who have 'left everything' (5:11 and 23). The prophetic comment on the identity of the elect is also a theme in evidence in Luke's remaining appropriation of the motif, the parable of the great banquet (14:13, 21). This parable is immediately preceded by teaching on humility (verses 7–14), which ends on the same eschatological note that introduces the parable: 'resurrection of the just' (verse 14) and 'shall eat bread in the kingdom of God' (verse 15).[125] In this section of teaching, Jesus completely inverts the guest list and the seating arrangement stipulated for a messianic meal in the Qumran documents, e.g. 1QSa 2.5–22.[126] This apparent critique of Essene eschatological expectation strongly parallels Jesus' expectation that his remarks would offend the disciples of the Baptist (7:22) (see §3.1 above). This section of teaching is once again immediately followed with remarks on the costs of discipleship (verses 25–7) and the giving up of possessions (verse 33; cf. Luke 4:24f.; 6:23; and 7:22). It is clear from this brief discussion that an intra-textual reading of the motif is wholly inadequate. The *ptōchoi* need to be understood in their cultural context where it is clear that their identity was contested. What is also clear is that those to whom the motif is addressed are most appropriately understood as religious social actors who

---

[125] On the links between this pericope and the parable itself, see J. A. Sanders, 'The Ethic of Election', p. 114.

[126] See *ibid.*, p. 118, especially his discussion of 1QSa 2.5–22 and 1QM 7.4–6.

are challenged to respond in the form of potentially costly discipleship.

3.2.5   Matthew's 'qualifying gloss' in context

The argument for Matthew's 'qualification' depends to a large extent upon its being a meaningful clarification. However, the phrase *hoi ptōchoi tō pneumati* is an obscure literary construction,[127] which is perhaps most comprehensible in a Jewish context, against the backdrop of traditions that elevate the place of the *anawim* in Deutero-Isaiah. Nonetheless, the argument that the qualification was added to draw out the true significance of the *ptōchos* as the *conditio humana* is still presented despite these clear Jewish antecedents. In contrast, it will be demonstrated that the very prevalence of this topos underlines the highly problematic case for qualification. *Hoi ptōchoi tō pneumati*, rather than evoking an honourable insight into the *conditio humana*, would have resonated, for the Greco-Roman hearer, with the negative state of *mikropsychia*, 'poor-spiritedness'.

Matthew's *hoi ptōchoi tō pneumati* would have been highly problematic in a Greco-Roman context, especially if the makarisms locate the phrase in a context that may be interpreted as a claim to honour. Matthew's makarisms do not adopt the familiar reversal motif. He has, according to many, 'ethicised' them.[128] He has turned Luke's eschatological blessings into entrance requirements for the Kingdom of God. He has modified his makarisms along wisdom lines; *hoi ptōchoi tō pneumati* become ideal characters to be imitated. In contrast to Luke's makarism, which avoids the potentially 'shocking' nature of *hoi ptōchoi* by placing them in a context of eschatological reversal, Matthew's version appears to be advocating a state at the very least related to socio-economic destitution. This elevation of the *ptōchos* was not a familiar cultural form in the Greco-Roman world, where the *ptōchos* was at best an object of pity and in a condition not to be replicated. In contrast, in the Jewish world 'poverty' had religious overtones, which went well

---

[127] On its obscurity, see H. D. Betz, *The Sermon on the Mount*, p. 112, who notes that the expression is unique in the Greek language and, although grammatically possible, the Greek of the expression 'was difficult to understand'.
[128] J. Dupont, *Les béatitudes*, Vol. I (Louvain: Nauwelaerts, 1958), pp. 254–8; Dodd, 'The Beatitudes: A Form-critical Study'; G. Strecker, 'Die Makarismen der Bergpredigt', *NTS* 17 (1971), 255–75.

beyond the Greco-Roman concern for the stranger under the protection of the gods. The whole people of Israel through deportation and exile had become, and were so characterised in Deutero-Isaiah, the afflicted, the oppressed, despised and rejected by the nations.[129] This language once used of all exiles came exclusively to focus on those faithful to Yahweh. The terms for the faithful in Deutero-Isaiah are all brought together into the one makarism. They are the *anawe-ruah*, the 'afflicted of spirit'. This language is notably a feature of the Qumran literature, where it is addressed to those who are waiting for the fulfilment of the reign of God (1QH 14.3; 1QM 14.7).[130] The phrase *hoi ptōchoi tō pneumati* is simply a literal translation of this Semitic concept. It is most plausible to suggest that Matthew either received this tradition in this form or translated it literally from his source.

Nonetheless, despite clear Jewish antecedents for the phrase, it is still suggested that Matthew is qualifying the *ptōchos*.[131] Betz is typical in presupposing a debate about what Jesus meant by calling the poor blessed. This apparent debate leads to Matthew's qualification, which allegedly provides clarity by bringing to mind the commonplace topos *conditio humana*: 'the expression "poor in (the) spirit" first of all points to an *intellectual insight* into the human condition'.[132] 'Humility' best corresponds to the virtue Matthew seeks to express.[133] He is calling for the virtue of self-examination.[134] Matthew's qualification is thus adopted to clarify Luke's apparently ambiguous *ptōchos*, ambiguity that resulted in the later predominance of the terms for humble, e.g. *tapeinos* and *tapeinophrōn*.[135] This reading of Matthew's makarism plays down its Jewish antecedents by placing the *ptōchos* in the

---

[129] For a survey of the language used and its relation to *ptōchos*, see Leske, 'Beatitudes', pp. 825f.

[130] See further Flusser, 'Blessed', p. 5; G. J. Brooke, 'The Wisdom of Matthew's Beatitudes (4Qbeat and Matt 5:3–12)', *SB* 19 (1989), 35–41.

[131] Betz, *The Sermon on the Mount*, p. 113. He suggests that the addition of 'in (the) spirit' is intended to 'forestall a mis-understanding of the simple adjective "poor"'.

[132] *Ibid.*, p. 115, his italics. He suggests that this topos was familiar 'not only in the Greek philosophers but also the Jewish wisdom and apocalypticism, in Qumran, and in successive literatures, including the church fathers'.

[133] Betz presents the Socratic and Cynic schools as antecedents for this view. However, he acknowledges that this tradition prefers *penēs* to *ptōchos*, *The Sermon on the Mount*, p. 117, n. 183.

[134] *Ibid.*, p. 118.

[135] On the history of interpretation, see J. Dupont, *Les béatitudes*, Vol. III (Louvain: Nauwelaerts, 1973), pp. 399–411.

context of this common topos. However, rather than clarifying the meaning of the expression, the topos highlights the confusion that Matthew's makarism may have generated outside a Jewish context.

Whilst makarisms were not synonymous with 'honour', their proclamation, as we have noted, engendered respect in their subject, placing them by implication in an honour context. In such a context, the 'humility' advocated by Betz as the attitude which best corresponds with *hoi ptōchoi tō pneumati* was directly associated with an appropriate estimation of the self. Betz rightly highlights that such a state was 'opposed to hubris, arrogance, self-indulgence, and over extension of the natural limits'.[136] Yet he neglects to mention that in Greco-Roman discussions on the virtues, the state which best exemplified these qualities was *megalopsychia*, 'great-spiritedness'.[137] In the Greco-Roman field of honour the pious man who knew his own limits found this mean in respect to honour and dishonour; the excess was *chaunotēs*, vanity, and the deficiency was *mikropsychia*, 'poor-spiritedness'. The Jewish susceptibility to accusations of *mikropsychia* has already been noted (see §3.2.2 above). The first makarism's *ptōchoi tō pneumati*, besides its awkwardness in the Greek, bears a striking resemblance to *mikropsychia*. It is my opinion that if Matthew is 'clarifying' the 'potentially misleading' or allegedly 'shocking' *ptōchos*, he fails. Matthew's crude and difficult *hoi ptōchoi tō pneumati* is most comprehensible within the context of Jewish traditions surrounding the piety of the poor in Deutero-Isaiah, most clearly stressed in the virtuoso religion of first-century Judaea. Rather than Matthew 'ethicising' the tradition, it is more credible to suggest that it has been 'ethnicised' by Luke, who displays a consistent interest in presenting the tradition in a manner amenable to Greco-Roman sensibilities. Luke, by turning Matthew's makarisms into the less culturally constrained reversal motif, both maintains the makarisms' roots in the ethos of Deutero-Isaiah and renders the first makarism comprehensible to the Greco-Roman world.

3.2.6   Summary

Unfortunately, Hanson and Neyrey's reading of the makarisms in the light of their normative Mediterranean honour culture fails to

---

[136] *The Sermon on the Mount*, p. 116.
[137] See Lloyd-Jones, 'Honour and Shame', pp. 274f.

engage with the evangelists' redactional interests and simply reinscribes the critical consensus. However, when the first makarism is liberated from this homogenising model, and the distinctive nature of Jewish traditions concerning the *ptōchoi* acknowledged, these interests are illuminated. Indeed, the heuristic fruit of viewing these *ptōchoi* within a more broadly conceived social world has been to invert the consensus that Matthew's first makarism is glossing Luke's 'shocking original'. Matthew's troubling *ptōchoi tō pneumati* is revealed to be most plausibly understood from an indigenous perspective. It is clear from this examination of the Gospel references to the *ptōchoi*, which are located within formulaic motifs, that Jesus' adoption of this language challenged expectations about the identity of the elect. In addition, this challenge was framed in language particularly associated with the Qumran literature.[138] Furthermore, all of these references underline the challenging nature of Jesus' appropriation of this language by making explicit references to the costs of discipleship, which include the leaving of homes, families and possessions, e.g. Luke 4:24; 5:11, 23; 6:23; 7:22; 14:25–7, 33, and Matt. 5:11–12. They reveal a critical-prophetic engagement that is most credibly understood against the backdrop of the prominent social reality of first-century Judaea, which was virtuoso religion.[139] This is not to deny economic, kinship, or political dimensions in the language of the *ptōchoi*. Social justice necessarily touches on each of these elements of the social world. The virtuoso is frequently found at the forefront in the provision of social services and potentially functions as a cultural variable of macrosociological significance. What is clear from the preceding discussion is that the language of the *ptōchoi* is consistently framed in religious terms and addressed to religious constituents of the New Testament social world.

3.3   The *ptōchoi*, piety, and Judaea

The preceding discussion of the 'collocations' of the *ptōchoi* has highlighted their contested nature and in particular that Jesus,

---

[138] See Matt. 5:3, cf. 1QH 14.3 and 1QM 14.7; Luke 7:22/Matt. 11:5, cf. 4Q521; Luke 14:13–27, cf. 1QSa 2.5–22. In addition, the more general appropriation of Isaiah 61 in Luke; cf. 11QMelch. 2.4, 6, 9, 13, 18 and 1QH 15.15; 18:15.

[139] See Ps. Clementine, *Homilies* 15.10.4, where the Gospel of Thomas' 'Blessed are the poor' (1.54) is interpreted as applying not to the poor in general, but to the faithful, who have become voluntarily poor (*pistous penētas*). They will not be condemned for not having given alms because they have no money.

in using such motifs, was challenging expectations about the nature of the elect which were particularly associated with Judaean virtuosity. In addition, this discussion demonstrated the association of these *ptōchoi* motifs with the rejection of the prophets and the costs of discipleship. This sub-section examines the remaining references to the *ptōchoi* in the New Testament. It starts with the extant 'collocations' of the *ptōchoi*, which are predominantly not part of formulaic expressions: Mark 12:42f./Luke 21:3; Jas. 2:3–6 and Luke 16:19f., cf. Rev. 3:17. These references notably underline an association of the *ptōchoi* with virtuosity and secondly with Judaea. The sub-section continues with those references dismissed by Malina and Hollenbach as being of little heuristic value: see §2.2 above.[140] These fall into two categories: the Pauline witness, 2 Cor. 6:2, 10; 8:9; Rom. 15:26 and Gal. 2:10, and references which present the *ptōchoi* as recipients of apparent alms, Matt. 19:21; 26:9; Mark 10:21; 14:5, 7; Luke 18:22; 19:8; John 12:5–8 and 13:29. Throughout this discussion, it becomes increasingly clear that the *ptōchoi* when examined in their social context are particularly associated with piety and Judaea, associations most credibly understood against the backdrop of Judaean virtuoso religion.

3.3.1   The extant 'collocations' of the ptōchoi

The extant 'collocations' of the *ptōchoi* are predominantly not part of formulaic expressions: Mark 12:42f./Luke 21:1f.; Jas. 2:3–6 and Luke 16:19f., cf. Rev. 3:17. Nonetheless, a continuity may be identified in terms of the contexts in which these 'poor' are presented. The first of these references gives accounts of Jesus' observations of the 'poor widow' at the Temple treasury in Jerusalem (Mark 12:42f./ Luke 21:1f.). What is notable in the social approaches outlined above,[141] which focus on the collocation of 'poor' and 'widow',

---

[140] Malina, 'Wealth and Poverty', p. 355: 'we simply cannot get any idea as to what the authors are referring to except by reading our own ideas into their words'. Hollenbach, *Defining Rich and Poor*, pp. 59f., who less dogmatically but nonetheless repeatedly insists upon the 'ambiguity' of such texts.

[141] In Malina's scheme, the reference to a 'poor widow' is tantamount to a tautology. In his normative Mediterranean society it is natural that 'poor' and 'widow' are 'collocated' since to be widowed is to have lost status whatever the individual's economic position. The designation 'poor' is therefore not an economic one but indicative of this loss: see §2.2 above. Hollenbach rightly criticises this somewhat forced reading and points to the clear contrast between the 'poor' and the 'rich', concluding that the 'widow's' 'poverty' has 'some economic-political and some caste meaning': see §2.3 above.

is that the widow's religious social practice is neglected.[142] Whilst the 'widow' is contrasted with the 'rich', who may be characterised by their clothing, positions of honour, and feasting (Luke 20:46/Mark 12:38f.), this apparently economic contrast is not the whole picture. We have already noted that in the formulaic appropriation of the language of 'poverty', expectations concerning the nature of the elect appear to have been challenged in terms of positions of honour and feasting, *deipnois* (Luke 20:46; cf. 14:12f.). In addition, whilst the 'rich' give out of their 'abundance', the 'widow's' gift to the Temple treasury is presented as her 'whole life' (Mark 12:44/Luke 21:4). Indeed, in Luke this piety is perhaps highlighted by the inclusion of *tou theou* in a number of textual variants. She is said to be giving up her life for God: cf. Anna (2:36-8). Her social practice as one of the *ptōchoi* is characterised in terms of total commitment to God, a typical feature of the virtuoso.[143]

This association of pious commitment with the *ptōchoi* is also evident in the second 'collocation' (Jas. 2:3–6). Here the 'poor' are found 'collocated' with 'dirty clothes' (2:2). The 'poor man' is contrasted with a hypothetical 'rich man' who, similarly to Luke 20:46–7; 21:1f., is characterised in terms of his clothing and taking of a position of honour (Jas. 2:2f.). The context is most probably that of worship in a local assembly, *synagōgēn* (2:2).[144] Once again, we find the *ptōchoi* contrasted with the 'rich' in terms of their religious social practice. This is no simple social or economic opposition. The 'rich' are said to oppress members of the assembly

---

[142] This neglect is also a striking feature of J. M. Arlandson's social reconstruction: see *Women, Class, and Society in Early Christianity* (Peabody, MA: Hendrickson, 1997), pp. 172f.

[143] See chapter 3, §2 above. Cf. the *Diatessaron* of Tatian, which suggests that Anna remained a virgin in her marriage. See further the discussion in L. W. Barnard, 'The Origins and Emergence of the Church in Edessa during the First Two Centuries A.D.', *VC* 22 (1968), 161–75.

[144] The nature of this 'assembly' is the subject of debate, especially following R. B. Ward, 'Partiality in the Assembly, Jas. 2.2–4', *HTR* 62 (1969), 87–97, who argues that it was a judicial assembly, before which two members of the community were coming for judgement. However, it is not at all clear that the actors in the passage are known. Judgements are being made on the actors' appearances, and the 'rich' in James are never referred to as 'brothers'. It is perhaps more credible to view it as a gathering for worship at which different responses of a local community to two incoming strangers are being rehearsed, responses which James feels should be sympathetic to radical itinerant prophets: cf. 3 John 1:5 and the elder's discussion of the appropriate reception of the *xenos*. On this more traditional view and for a more detailed critique of Ward's position, see D. H. Edgar, *Has God Not Chosen the Poor? The Social Setting of the Epistle of James* (JSNTS 206, 2001), pp. 116f.

(2:6) and to 'blaspheme that noble name by which you are called' (2:7). The *ptōchoi* by comparison are due honour (2:6) and have been chosen by God 'to be rich in faith and to be the heirs to the kingdom which he promised to those who love him' (2:5; cf. Matt. 5:3/Luke 6:20). The *ptōchoi* are dissociated from the world (cf. 1:27 and 4:4) and associated with those who love God. These *ptōchoi* are clearly associated with piety, a piety that notably involves social practice, in the form of care for the widows and orphans (1:27).[145] Furthermore, the letter is closely associated with, and most probably emerges from, the community around James in Jerusalem,[146] a location which, as we will see in §3.3.2 below, was associated with holding property in common and with the care of widows. These characteristics of insularity from the world, combined with the love of God and the profound concern for the vulnerable, are notably distinguishing features of virtuoso religion.[147]

The association of pious commitment with the *ptōchoi* is less obvious in the 'collocation' at Luke 16:19–31. Here 'poor' is 'collocated' with 'leper'. Indeed, of all the 'collocations' of the *ptōchoi* this one is perhaps least associated with piety: see, e.g., Roth's observation: 'Lazarus has no personality, certainly no piety.'[148] Predominantly, it is the rich man in this story who has been the focus of attention, especially in the light of extra-biblical parallels. Indeed, Hock has most notably argued for a Cynic background to the tradition, reading the parable in parallel with the

---

[145] See E. Bammel 'πτωχός', *TDNT*, p. 911, and M. Dibelius, *A Commentary on the Epistle of James* (revised by H. Greeven; trans. M. Williams; Philadelphia: Fortress Press, 1976), p. 40. See also Edgar, *Has God Not Chosen the Poor?*, p. 111, who views their dependence upon God in terms of Theissen's radical itinerants – see, e.g., *Social Reality and the Early Christians: Theology, Ethics, and the World of the New Testament* (first English-language edn, trans. M. Kohl; Minneapolis: Fortress Press, 1992), pp. 33–59. However, Edgar remains wedded to the view that radical dependency on God equates with itinerancy and leaves no room for institutionalised forms of virtuosity.

[146] On the association of this Epistle with the earliest congregation in Jerusalem, see F. Mussner, *Der Jakobusbrief* (HTKNT 13.1; 5th edn; Freiburg: Herder Verlag, 1987), and P. Maynard-Reid, *Poverty and Wealth in James* (Maryknoll, NY: Orbis Books, 1987). For a recent survey of the literature and a more modest reading, see Edgar, *Has God Not Chosen the Poor?* Whilst he acknowledges an absence of conclusive evidence, he stresses the importance of such attribution for the understanding of the text, pp. 223f. On their association with the 'poor among the saints' and the community around James in Jerusalem, see Hamel, *Poverty and Charity*, p. 190.

[147] See chapter 3, §2 above.

[148] See Roth, *The Blind*, p. 190.

story of the 'poor' Micyllus in Lucian's *Gallus* and *Cataplus.*[149] He correctly highlights that 'wealth' in the ancient world was not morally neutral, and points to numerous critiques of hedonism.[150] The characterisation of the 'rich man' in terms of clothing and dining habits, i.e. his hedonism, was sufficient on the basis of this parallel for Hock to conclude that this would account for his reception at death (16:19). However, Hock's observation that Lazarus is judged innocent 'not so much because of his assumed faith as because of his poverty, which excluded him from a damning life', is, I believe, untenable. In his parallel, it is Micyllus' *sōphrosynē*, 'safe thinking', i.e. observing the limits set by the gods,[151] which marks him for the Isle of the Blessed, not his 'poverty'.[152] Whilst to be *ptōchos* may prevent one from engaging in hedonism, it does not guarantee *sōphrosynē*, 'safe thinking'. The terms are certainly not synonymous. In addition, it is clear from the other commonly cited extra-biblical parallel, Gressmann's Egyptian folktale,[153] that the 'poor man' is characterised as virtuous. Indeed, there are a number of questions surrounding the account of Lazarus, which suggest that he may not be quite as one-dimensional as Roth suggests: why the personal name Lazarus, a unique feature in Jesus' parables, and why does Lazarus find himself carried off by angels to Abraham's bosom, a scenario only previously associated with Enoch (Gen. 5:24) and Elijah (2 Kgs. 2:11)?

Beyond the extra-biblical parallels the New Testament does present a 'Lazarus' in one other context, at Bethany, where Jesus raises him from the dead (John 11:1–44).[154] This tradition may provide an insight into Luke's particular presentation of this topos of transposition. In Luke, Lazarus is presented as a leper and placed outside the rich man's gate (16:20). The rich man is characterised in

---

[149] R. Hock, 'Lazarus and Micyllus: Greco-Roman Backgrounds to Luke 16:19–31', *JBL* 106 (1987), 447–63.

[150] *Ibid.*, pp. 459f. Also Meggitt, *Paul, Poverty and Survival*, pp. 59f.

[151] On *sōphrosynē*, see Luck, *TDNT* VII, pp. 1097–1104. Also, chapter 2, §2.2 above.

[152] Hock, 'Lazarus and Micyllus', p. 461.

[153] See H. Gressmann, *Vom reichen Mann und armen Lazarus* (Berlin: Königliche Akademie der Wissenschaften, 1918); for discussion see Nolland, *Luke*, Vol. III, pp. 825ff.

[154] On the connection between the Lucan and Johannine traditions, see B. Shellard, *New Light on Luke: Its Purpose, Sources and Literary Context* (JSNTS 215; London: Sheffield Academic Press, 2002), pp. 243f.

terms of his opulent clothing and dining habits (16:19), a familiar
pattern (see, e.g., 14:12 and 20:46). In John, Lazarus is 'sick' and
is located in Bethany. It is argued in more detail in chapter 5,
§3.2.3 below that Bethany was the location for a prominent Essene
'poor-house', set aside as a place for those proscribed as unclean
and therefore unable to enter the holy city (11QTemple 46, 16–18).
John's Lazarus was notably 'loved' by Jesus (11:5) and is raised
from the dead (11:44), yet not even this act persuades the 'Pharisees
and the chief priests', i.e. the Jerusalem elite (11:46f.; cf. Luke
16:30f.), to believe. There is a pattern in Luke's 'collocations' of the
ptōchoi which challenges expectations associated with Judaean
virtuosity concerning the nature of the elect (see, e.g., 14:13f. and
21:1f.). John's witness to Lazarus helps us to see the continuation of
this pattern in Luke's presentation. Lazarus' location in Bethany
places him outside, and apparently to be excluded from, the
site of the messianic banquet. Typically for Luke's presentation
of the *ptōchoi*, it is Lazarus, who has literally been placed outside
the context of eschatological blessing, who is elevated. Now, Luke
clearly does not tell us why Lazarus is elevated, but the unique use
of the first name at the very least precludes automatic application
of this reversal pattern to all the social or economically conceived
'poor'. If Luke's adoption of this topos is consistent, it would
suggest that Lazarus' elevated status was due to his piety. Indeed,
this is clearly implicit in the Johannine account, which suggests
a high degree of intimacy between Jesus and Lazarus.

The final so-called 'collocation' of the *ptōchoi* is found in
Rev. 3:17.[155] Here the 'poor' are 'collocated' with the 'wretched,
miserable, blind, and naked'. However, these intra-textual states do
not expose the true nature of the *ptōchoi*. It is clear from reading
the verse in its context that the supposed 'wealth' of Laodicea is
being unmasked and characterised as 'wretched, miserable, poor
(*ptōchos*), blind, and naked'.[156] This occurrence of *ptōchos* is
evidently one element of a formulaic expression which is using
such language of 'poverty' to comment on the quality of a group's
religious social practice. Indeed, this use of the formulaic expression, whilst negative in character, reinforces the preceding readings

---

[155] This collocation is cited by Malina to support his intra-textual reading but
ignored by Hollenbach, who concentrates on Gospel references: see §2.2 and 2.3
above.
[156] In addition, an antithesis is being set up with the church in Smyrna, whose
'works, tribulation, and poverty (*ptōcheian*)' are accounted as 'wealth' (2:9).

of the 'poor' motif, which underline the contested and profoundly religious character of this language.

3.3.2 Paul and the ptōchoi

The Pauline corpus provides the New Testament's earliest witness to the *ptōchoi*: Rom. 15:26; 2 Cor. 6:10; 8:2, 9, and Gal. 2:10. This witness notably reinforces their association with piety and Judaea. In 2 Corinthians we encounter a now familiar pattern in which the language of 'poverty' is used to describe religious social practice. In the context of *kairō dektō*, an 'acceptable time' (2 Cor. 6:2; cf. Luke 4:17–19), Paul commends himself as 'poor and yet making many people rich; having nothing, and yet owning everything' (6:10).[157] He continues by setting in parallel the generosity of the Macedonians, giving out of their *ptōcheia*, 'poverty' (8:2), with Jesus' own 'poverty': 'although he was rich, he became poor for your sake, so that you should become rich through his poverty (*ptōcheia*)' (8:9). This 'poverty' is not easily disentangled from Jesus' or Paul's religious social practice, and this unsettles any simplistic presentation of 'poverty' either as an economic designation[158] or as the 'situation of humanity'.[159] Jesus leaves his home and calls his disciples to leave theirs and to follow him who has 'nowhere to lay his head' (Matt. 8:18–22; cf. 4:18–22 and 9:9). This life-style choice is not an end in itself, but is adopted in order to facilitate Jesus' ministry.[160] What chokes the spread of the word is the anxieties of this world and the seduction of wealth, which point the heart to earthly rather than heavenly treasures. This emphasis is clearly paralleled in Paul's 'poverty'. He not only seeks 'freedom from worldly concerns' (1 Cor. 7:28–35; 8:1–13, cf. James 1:27–2:5), but also declines financial support to help facilitate his service to the Gospel (1 Cor. 9:12, 15–19; 2 Cor. 11:7–15 and 12:13–18).[161]

---

[157] Cf. Rev. 2:9 and 3:17–18, which also contrast economic status and spiritual wealth. The material poverty of the church at Smyrna is compared to its spiritual wealth, 2:9, whilst the economic wealth of Laodicea is unmasked as poverty, 3:17.

[158] See W. Stegemann, *The Gospel and the Poor* (trans. D. Elliott; Philadelphia: Fortress Press, 1984), p. 15.

[159] See L. E. Keck, 'The Poor among the Saints in the New Testament', *ZNW* 56 (1965), 121. This position is somewhat undermined by the clear parallel with the 'poverty' of the Macedonians in 8:2. Are we to understand this as an extreme form of humanity?

[160] See Matt. 6:19–34/Luke 12:22–34 and 16:13; Mark 4:19/Matt. 13:22/Luke 8:14.

[161] See J. M. Everts, 'Financial Support', *DPL*, pp. 295–300.

The language of 'poverty' adopted by Paul in 2 Corinthians does not simply describe a socio-economic state; rather he appears to be tapping into a practice of 'poverty' for the Gospel's sake, which is patterned on the life of Jesus.

The remaining Pauline references to *ptōchoi* refer to his collection for the Jerusalem church: Rom. 15:26 and Gal. 2:10, cf. 1 Cor. 16:1–4; 2 Cor. 8–9 and Acts 11:27–30 and 24:17.[162] In Gal. 2:10 Paul states that the so-called 'Council of Jerusalem' had placed only one obligation upon him, *tōn ptōchōn hina mnēmoneuōmen*, 'remember the poor', and at Rom. 15:26 Paul affirms the gifts of Macedonia and Achaia, *tous ptōchous tōn hagiōn tōn en Ierousalēm*, 'for the poor among the saints at Jerusalem'. The identity of these 'poor' is contested. Is it a conscious self-designation or simply a reference to their economic plight? Holl seminally argued that 'the poor' functioned as a 'self-designation'.[163] He considered that Paul was using a technical term for the church, which it had appropriated from Judaism's traditional regard for the poor, who felt themselves especially chosen by God.[164] Further, since Rom. 15:26 is clearly a reference to the Pauline 'collection', which elsewhere is not described as social relief but for the *agious*, 'saints' (2 Cor. 9:1), the expression is best taken as explicative: 'the poor *who are* the saints in Jerusalem'.[165] The idea that 'the poor' operated as a self-designation has been strongly criticised by Keck.[166] Keck is predominantly troubled by the absence of the designation in Acts and Matthew.[167] This absence results from his setting up

---

[162] See S. McKnight, 'Collection for the Saints', *DPL*, pp. 143–47.

[163] K. Holl, 'Der Kirchenbegriff des Paulus in seinem Verhältnis zu dem der Urgemeinde', *Sitzungsberichte der Berliner Akademie* (1921), 920–47.

[164] On the traditional regard for the poor, see E. Bammel, 'Πτωχός', *TDNT* VI, pp. 885–915. Holl's thesis was notably complemented with material from Qumran which provided evidence for the self-designation 'poor' in the contemporary literature, e.g. 1QpHab 12.3, 6, 10; 1QM 11.9, 13; 4Q171 37.2–10, and more generally as a self-designation for the Jews, Ps. 69:32; 72:4. This point is most reluctantly conceded by Keck, 'The Poor among the Saints in Jewish Christianity', p. 76.

[165] T. E. Schmidt, 'Riches and Poverty', *DPL*, p. 827.

[166] Keck, 'The Poor' and 'The Poor among the Saints in Jewish Christianity'. Keck particularly attacks the suggestion that the Jerusalem church adopted poverty as an ideal of self-denial. This is something of a straw man which he has set up to attack Holl. However, it is not clear that this is how Holl viewed poverty: see the discussion of Keck in M. D. Goulder, 'A Poor Man's Christology', *NTS* 45/3 (1999), 333f.

[167] 'The Poor', pp. 112f. He dismisses Matthew by insisting on reading *ptōchoi* as an economic designation and by summarily rejecting 5:3 as 'a secondary formulation attributable to the Evangelist himself'; cf. the *excursus* in §3.2 above.

of an antithesis between 'technical self-designation' and 'economic plight', which is so starkly drawn that it precludes any possibility that the title might refer to a group within the church.[168] A similar antithesis is also evident in Goulder's defence of Holl, in which he restates the idea that 'the poor' functions as a self-designation.[169] However, Goulder is keen to state that this poverty, whilst having theological roots, does not emerge from an ideal of self-denial but is a consequence of the early church's community of goods and abandonment of work, Acts 1–5 and 1 Thess. 4:11–12; 2 Thess. 3:6–15; 1 Cor. 4:12.[170] How, then, are we to understand these 'poor'?

The answer lies in their social context, Jerusalem. We know from Acts that the early Jerusalem church practised a community of goods and cared for widows (2:42–7; 4:32, 34–5:11; 6:1–6).[171] Likewise in James, the 'humble brother' who is virtually synonymous with the *ptōchoi* also cares for the widow, 1:27 – a tradition closely associated with the Jerusalem church.[172] Indeed, these practices are well recognised and cited as evidence for the church's economic poverty.[173] However, the idea that the practice of property sharing in a religious community will inevitably result in some form of economic disaster flies in the face of the historical realities of such communities, which suggest that they repeatedly

---

[168] Hamel, *Poverty and Charity*, p. 190, has helpfully argued that the 'poor' may have formed part of the congregation and that their 'poverty' was 'first and foremost a complete dependence on God'.

[169] Goulder, 'A Poor Man's Christology', p. 333. He argues convincingly that the Synoptic Gospels all suggest that the first Christian community in Jerusalem saw itself as fulfilling the prophecy of Isa. 61.1.

[170] On the economic poverty of the Jerusalem church, see R. P. Martin, *2 Corinthians* (WBC 40; Waco: Word, 1986), p. 256. Martin lists several possible causes for this poverty: (1) the relief of more and more widows, Acts 6:1–7; (2) the pilgrimages to Jerusalem of both the elderly and Galileans, who burdened the communities; (3) the potential problems arising from Jerusalem's early experimentation with communal life, Acts 4:32–5:11; (4) the economic hardships caused by famine, Acts 11:27–30; and (5) the personal stresses due to economic persecutions: cf. Jas. 1:9; 2:6–7; 5:1–6.

[171] See B. J. Capper, 'Community of Goods in the Early Jerusalem Church', *ANRW* II/26.2 (1995), 1730–74, and 'The Palestinian Context of the Earliest Christian Community of Goods', in *The Book of Acts in its Palestinian Setting* (ed. R. Bauckham; Grand Rapids: Eerdmans, 1995), pp. 323–56. These treatments defend the historical value of these narratives against the older opinion, which views them as Lucan idealising.

[172] See Edgar, *Has God Not Chosen the Poor?*, p. 169.

[173] E.g. Goulder, 'A Poor Man's Christology', p. 333: 'they were in fact poor because of the way of life described in Acts 1–5'.

become wealthy and that this leads to laxity and/or corruption.[174] This property sharing and care for the widows was no utopian innovation of the early church that led to financial disaster. Rather, it had clear antecedents in the social practices of the Essenes: cf. 1QS 1.7ff.; 6.16ff.; 7.6ff.; War 2.122.[175] Indeed, the 'upper room', the site of the first meetings of the early church, was most probably located in the Essene quarter in Jerusalem.[176] Both the social practices and the geographical location of the Essenes seem to overlap with those of the early Jerusalem community. However, it is also likely that only a small group in the early church surrendered property, as the tensions of Acts 5:13–14 may suggest.[177] Property sharing remained voluntary and did not define the Jerusalem church as a whole. Nonetheless, it is evident that within the church there was a group who took on a particular form of religious social practice, which resonates with prominent elements of the virtuoso piety of the Essenes.[178] If we view the *ptōchoi* of the Jerusalem church within their social context against the backdrop of virtuoso religion, then it becomes most credible to think of them in terms of the piety of poverty. Indeed, it brings clarity to the critical

---

[174] On the virtuoso's tendency to accumulate wealth, see Silber, *Virtuosity*, pp. 42, 51, and 215.

[175] See B. J. Capper, '"In der Hand des Ananias…" Erwägungen zu 1QS VI, 20 und der urchristlichen Gütergemeinschaft', *RevQ* 12 (1986), 223–36, and Pixner, 'Essenes and Pharisees', p. 201. On the care for the vulnerable, see especially Capper, 'The New Covenant'. Capper argues in particular that the story of Ananias and Sapphira (Acts 5:1–11) reveals a process of provisional initial surrender of property resonant with that described in 1QS 6. In addition, the following regulation regarding lies is also present, further underlining the resonance with Acts 5:1–11.

[176] On the association of the Essene quarter in Jerusalem with the early church, see Pixner, 'Essene Quarter'; R. Riesner, 'Essener und Urkirche in Jerusalem', *BK* 40 (1985), 64–76, and C. Grappe, *D'un Temple à l'autre* (Paris: Presses Universitaires de France, 1992), pp. 51–69. For further discussion of the location of the 'upper room' and its possible association with the 'Essene quarter', see Capper, 'With the Oldest Monks', pp. 19–29, 47, and 54–5. See further chapter 5, §3.2.3 below.

[177] On the apparent contradiction 'None of the rest dared join them … and more than ever believers were added to the Lord' (Acts 5:13–14), see D. R. Schwartz, 'Non-Joining Sympathisers (Acts 5.13–14)', *Bib* 64 (1983), 550–5.

[178] See Capper, 'Two Types'. For opposing arguments, see R. Bauckham, 'The Early Jerusalem Church, Qumran, and the Essenes', in *The Dead Sea Scrolls as Background to Postbiblical Judaism and Early Christianity* (ed. J. R. Davila; Leiden: Brill, 2003), pp. 63–89.

[179] On 'two types of discipleship', see H.-J. Degenhardt, *Lukas, Evangelist der Armen* (Stuttgart: Katholisches Bibelwerk, 1965); J.-K. Kim, *Stewardship and Almsgiving in Luke's Theology* (JSNTS 155; Sheffield, 1998), and most recently Capper, 'Two Types'.

discussion of 'two types of discipleship' in the early church.[179] There has been a tendency to view Jesus' radical pattern of discipleship in terms of surrendering property as being necessarily about an itinerant social practice.[180] However, the virtuoso background to Judaea points to the probability of not only itinerant radical discipleship but also institutional forms which powerfully illuminate our understanding of the early Jerusalem church.[181] Furthermore, this insight complements the discussion of the purpose of the 'gift'.[182] It assists our understanding of Paul's anxiety at its reception (Rom. 15:31), which makes little sense against the backdrop of economic tribulations. In contrast, if the *ptōchoi* represent the pious centre of the Jerusalem church, then the 'gift' is clearly charged with significance.[183] These Pauline references to the *ptōchoi* once again underline their association with virtuoso practices and Judaea.

3.3.3   The ptōchoi as recipients of alms

In the remaining references to the *ptōchoi* in the New Testament, they appear as the potential recipients of alms.[184] These references include accounts of the giving up of possessions, Matt. 19:21/Mark 10:21/Luke 18:22; 19:8, the costly anointing of Jesus at Bethany, Matt. 26:9/Mark 14:5, 7/John 12:5–8, and at the 'upper room' in Jerusalem 13:29. If we consider the Synoptics' focus on Jesus'

---

[180] E.g. Edgar, *Has God Not Chosen the Poor?*, following Theissen, *Social Reality*.

[181] Capper, 'The New Covenant'.

[182] On various terms Paul adopts to describe the 'gift', see S. McKnight, 'Collection for the Saints', *DPL*, pp. 143–7.

[183] On the significance of the 'gift' in relation to virtuoso religion, see Silber, *Virtuosity*, p. 214. Silber highlights the delicate combination of 'interestedness' and 'disinterestedness' in such giving. This is perhaps evidenced in the ambiguities that surround Paul's collection, which have resulted in a range of interpretations: see Holl, 'Der Kirchenbegriff'; K. F. Nickle, *The Collection: A Study in Paul's Strategy* (SBT 48; Naperville: Alleson, 1966), pp. 74–99 (temple tax); pp. 101ff. (economic poverty); pp. 112–15 (church unity); K. Berger, 'Almosen für Israel', *NTS* (1976–7), 180–204 (entry rites); and S. McKnight, *A Light among the Gentiles* (Minneapolis: Fortress, 1991), pp. 47f. (eschatological). What is perhaps underlined in these works and the insights from Silber is that the 'gift' was most probably interpreted differently by the various parties.

[184] Evidence for any common practice of 'charity' within first-century Palestine is, as a whole, limited and late: see Hamel, *Poverty and Charity*, p. 218, and D. P. Seccombe, 'Was there Organised Charity in Jerusalem before the Christians?', *JTS* 29 (1978), 140–3.

Galilean ministry, a striking pattern is evident in that none of these references occurs outside Judaea.[185]

The Judaean location of references to the giving up of possessions to the *ptōchoi* is not their only distinctive feature. This practice is also clearly religious in nature and associated with the attainment of *zōēn aiōnion*, 'eternal life' (Matt. 19:16, 29/Mark 10:17, 30/Luke 18:18, 30). In the first account of giving up possessions, a 'rich young man/ruler' approaches Jesus and asks him what he must do to inherit 'eternal life'. The young man claims to have followed the commandments from his youth,[186] a claim left unchallenged by Jesus, who notably 'loved him' (Mark 10:21). He is told that he lacks one thing (Mark 10:21/Luke 18:22) if he wants to be *teleios*, 'perfect' (Matt. 19:21).[187] He is told not only to give all his possessions to the poor but also to follow Jesus; a comparison is then made with the disciples who have 'left all and followed' (Matt. 19:27/Mark 10:28/18:28) and who will inherit 'eternal life' (Matt. 19:26/Mark 10:30/Luke 18:30).[188] In the Synoptic tradition the phrase 'eternal life', a prominent Johannine theme, is only found here and at Matt. 25:46 and Luke 10:25, where it is also associated with radical social practice, i.e. the care for the needy stranger. It is notable that in Luke's account of Zacchaeus, who only gives half of his possessions to the 'poor', no mention is made of 'eternal life'. Rather, 'salvation' is said to come to his house (19:9). The combination of the language of 'eternal life' with the injunction to

---

[185] On their location, see Matt. 19:1, 'He departed from Galilee and came to the region of Judaea', and cf. Mark 10:1; Luke 17:11, Jesus has 'passed through the midsts of Samaria and Galilee'; and Luke 19:1, Jesus has entered and 'passed through Jericho'. The remaining references are to Bethany, in Judaea.

[186] This is reminiscent of the consistent piety of Zechariah and Elisabeth, Simon and Anna: see Nolland, *Luke*, Vol. III, p. 886.

[187] On 'perfect', see G. Delling, 'τέλειος', *TDNT* VIII, pp. 67–78. In conjunction with the use of the word in James and the *Didache* it offers a striking link to the concerns with uncompromising and undivided commitment to God. In the *Didache*, at the end of the teaching of the 'Two Ways', the following injunction occurs: 'If you are able to bear the whole yoke of the Lord, you will be *teleios*, perfect/complete, but if you are not able, do what you can', 6:2, cf. Jas. 1:4. See Edgar, *Has God Not Chosen the Poor?*, pp. 141f.

[188] The injunction to give all his possessions is striking when consideration is given to *bKeth*. 50a, which limits the amount one may give and prohibits such extravagant charity: see Hamel, *Poverty and Charity*, p. 219. Indeed, the closest Judaean parallel to such practice is that of the Essenes, of whom Philo notes that 'they stand almost alone in the whole of mankind in that they have become moneyless and landless *by deliberate action*', *Quod. Omn.* 77. On the Greco-Roman parallels to voluntary renunciation, see M. Hengel, *The Charismatic Leader and his Followers* (trans. J. C. Greig; Edinburgh: T. & T. Clark, 1981), pp. 27–33.

surrender one's possessions to the *ptōchoi* exclusively occurring within Judaea is not perhaps insignificant: see further chapter 5, §4 below. Indeed, the repeatedly neglected social context is perhaps the key to their understanding.[189] Judaea was a location where we have identified the practice of virtuoso piety, where the pious 'poor' cared for the social and economic 'poor'.

The final references in this New Testament review of the *ptōchoi* underline this significance: Matt. 26:9/Mark 14:5, 7/John 12:5–8 and 13:29. What is striking in these references is not so much the identity of the *ptōchoi* as their location and social practices surrounding them. The first thing to observe is that the disciples are discussing the practice of giving alms, most prominently in John, and secondly that they carried a common purse, exclusive to John. These disciples, who, we have noted, have given up all, are discussing giving alms. Why do they assume that they could sell the ointment used? How do you proceed to give such a sum as three hundred denarii to the 'poor', and why are they ever present? What social mechanisms were available to give alms to the 'poor'? The relative absence of such formal social mechanisms and the late date of any witness to such practices have been extensively detailed in Hamel's discussion of 'poverty and charity'.[190] Once again, the answer lies in the social contexts, Bethany and the 'upper room'. It has recently been argued that Bethany was the location for a prominent Essene 'poor-house',[191] also set aside as a place for those proscribed as unclean and therefore unable to enter the holy city (11QTemple 46.16–18). It was a place where the 'poor' may be expected to be ever present. In addition, the 'upper room' was most probably located in or close by the Essene quarter of Jerusalem.[192] The significance of these common locations is given further weight by virtue of the references to the *ptōchoi* also revealing parallels in social practice. The carrying of a common purse and the giving of alms were identifying features of the Essenes.[193] Indeed, the

---

[189] A paradoxical feature of recent social approaches to the New Testament 'poor': see §3 above.

[190] See Hamel, *Poverty and Charity*, pp. 212–21, and Seccombe, 'Charity'.

[191] For the suggestion that the etymology of Bethany is 'house of the poor', see Capper, 'The New Covenant'. The arguments for this identification are fully rehearsed in chapter 5, §3.2.3 below.

[192] On the Essene quarter, see Pixner, 'Essene Quarter', an identification that even Bauckham, 'Jerusalem', p. 69 concedes, despite his desire to restrict the *yachad* to the Qumran site alone.

[193] See Beall, 'Essenes', p. 263.

reaction of the disciples, most notably those of the Judaean 'treasurer' Judas, suggests that the group may have been used to the receipt of 'gifts' for distribution to the needy: cf. Mark 6:37. This is certainly the common experience of the religious virtuoso, and Bethany was perhaps the location *par excellence* for the expression of such piety. Reviewing these references to the *ptōchoi* as the recipients of alms underlines their absence from Galilee. Jesus' injunctions and the disciples' discussions occur exclusively in contexts in which the social mechanisms were present for such practice, in Judaea. Furthermore, such practice was clearly associated with radical discipleship and the striving for eternal life through the surrender of all in an act of total commitment, i.e. virtuoso religion.

3   Conclusions

When the New Testament *ptōchoi* are examined in a broadly conceived social world, their religious social character becomes clear. The term 'poor' does not simply denote an economic category of social actor. It is also clearly a mistake to understand them intra-textually, adopting a strategy of 'linguistic collocation' as practised in recent social approaches (see §3.1 above). The collocations of the 'poor' are most credibly understood against the background of debates about the nature of the elect within first-century pietism, particularly within Judaea. This is clear in Jesus' engagement with the disciples of John (Matt. 11:5/Luke 7:22). This reading has been complemented by the *excursus* on the first makarism, which inverts the crude consensus that suggests that Matthew has ethicised Luke's original 'economic' makarism. Both Luke's redactional interest in presenting the *ptōchoi* in the form of a reversal motif and Matthew's clear indigenous antecedents in Judaean piety have been revealed. Whilst a socio-economic dimension is present in the frequent contrasts made with elite figures, it has also been repeatedly demonstrated that the focus of the contrast is on religious social practice, i.e. the piety of the *ptōchoi* or the impiety of the elite figure. In the Pauline corpus, the earliest traditions of the *ptōchoi* in the New Testament, the piety of poverty is further underlined, and Paul's 'poverty' appears to be patterned on the practice of Jesus. In addition, where reference is made to 'the poor', it is most probably to a distinct group within the early Jerusalem church. There are nonetheless references to the *ptōchoi* that do not necessarily imply their piety, the 'poor' as recipients of alms.

However, what these references demonstrate is a religious social practice of radical discipleship: the surrender of property, sharing a common purse, and giving alms. They illustrate the practice of the pious poor caring for the economic poor. This practice notably occurs exclusively within Judaean locations, especially Bethany, places where the social mechanisms for such practice were already present in the form of Essene virtuosity. The utility of a more integrated approach to conceiving the social world which neither privileges social actors nor normative values, but rather views the social world in its complex mix of actors, histories, structures, and practices, is clear. The *ptōchoi* in the New Testament are not simply social actors constrained by socio-economic forces, but a contested category, which is most credibly understood in the context of Judaean traditions concerning the piety of the poor and indigenous forms of virtuoso practice. Whilst they may have been understood as socio-economic actors, they may more frequently have been understood as religious actors adopting a form of piety indigenous to Judaea.

5

JOHN'S SOCIAL WORLD

1   Introduction

In the previous chapters I have cautioned against overstated claims for the heuristic significance of social models. Indeed, a conscious effort has been made to engage not only with social structures and social histories but also with social actors and their practices, and to consider how all these elements of the social world interact with one another. In this context, the critical revision of the model of a normative Mediterranean honour culture has highlighted the neglect within such social approaches of religious social actors and their impact on perceptions of poverty and gender. Furthermore, it has been demonstrated that such homogenising models have repeatedly obscured the particular nature of first-century Judaea and its cultural resources, most notably its virtuoso practices, in the form of a piety of poverty. This chapter seeks to build on these insights, especially those concerning Judaea's cultural particularity. It takes as its focus the most Judaean of the Gospels, John, and asserts that its distinctiveness is most credibly accounted for in terms of Judaea's indigenous virtuosity rather than by reference to the sectarian thesis, which has emerged as something of an orthodoxy in Johannine studies. It starts by arguing that the sectarian thesis predominantly adopts its sociology anachronistically and that its application to the Gospel is programmatic. In addition, the alleged association with Qumran is based on a false premise. Whilst elements of the sectarian thesis remain suggestive, it is ultimately an inadequate social scenario. If a social thesis is to contribute to the understanding of the Johannine distinctiveness, it must take seriously the Gospel's historical social witness. This witness, it will be argued, repeatedly bears the stamp of Judaea's indigenous religious virtuosity. The Gospel's prominent Judaean antecedents are highlighted, and two sets of social actors and their relative absence and presence in relation to the Synoptic tradition are examined. These are the 'poor' and 'women'. The very particular portrayal of these actors underlines the Gospel's social distinctiveness and confirms the heuristic potential of 'virtuoso religion'. This identification in turn helps us to resolve a number of the tensions evident in the sectarian thesis. It provides a more adequate basis for understanding the social forms that ascetic practice may take within any given social world and avoids the frequent marginalisation of such religious social actors as individual self-disciplinarians, or as sectarians fleeing the world. Virtuoso religion's unique potential to form an 'alternative structure within society at large',[1] which distinguishes it from other social forms such as the 'sect', is clearly of relevance. This more integrated view of the Johannine social world, which draws on social-scientific resources on 'virtuoso religion', enables us to envisage the Gospel's striking ethical and eschatological dualism within a credible indigenous social context without forcing it to the sectarian margins of the social world.

2   Johannine sectarianism

The Gospel's distinctiveness has generated a multiplicity of theories concerning its origin. Its sectarian characterisation, following works by Martyn[2] and Meeks[3] already cited in chapter 1, has become for many a comfortable pigeon hole in which to place this most idiosyncratic of the Gospels. However, as will now be shown, closer examination of the 'sociology of sectarianism' reveals that the theoretical basis for this identification is unsteady. In addition, it will be shown that even the more recent and allegedly more sophisticated appropriations of this material, rather than elucidating particular hermeneutical concerns, crudely adopt the sociology as 'evidence' to support preconceptions about the text. Furthermore, simplistic thematic parallels with a caricature of Qumran are shown to feed this identification. Whilst components of the more sophisticated appropriations of the sociology of sectarianism remain suggestive, they ultimately result in an inadequate social scenario.

[1] Silber, *Virtuosity*, pp. 41. Cf. Hill, *Religious Order*, pp. 12f. and his 'sect within'. See further chapter 3, §2.2 above.
[2] *History*.
[3] 'The Man from Heaven'.

2.1   The 'sociology of sectarianism'

The label 'sociology of sectarianism' refers to the wide range of theoretical materials derived from the social sciences which have been applied to the New Testament in attempts to classify the social form of the early Christian movement.[4] The 'sect' is generally recognised to include a number of defining characteristics such as exclusivity, merit, self-identification, voluntary membership, and legitimation strategies. However, the level of abstraction of such lists renders them of limited heuristic value. The 'sect' is a dynamic social phenomenon, which at specific times in its life history may manifest particular attributes more prominently than others.[5] This dynamism is reflected in the diversity of apparently 'defining' characteristics in such lists.[6] Beyond such generality, both the actual sociology adopted and the form of its application vary widely according to author. Nonetheless, within this variety two main strategies for the understanding of sectarianism may be discerned. These are a narrow view of the 'sect', which following Troeltsch and Weber is defined in its relational opposition to the 'church',[7] and a broader conception, which following Wilson rejects any narrow definition in favour of his own soteriologically orientated typology.[8]

The antithetical approach to the understanding of sectarianism has its origins in the sociology of religion's historical analysis of Western Christendom, which initially identified two types of

[4] See R. Scroggs, 'The Earliest Christian Communities as Sectarian Movement', in *Social-Scientific Approaches to New Testament Interpretation* (compiled and ed. D. G. Horrell; Edinburgh: T&T Clark, 1999), pp. 69–91. On the label 'sociology of sectarianism', see Esler's adoption in his *Modelling*, p. 4. It has more recently been used to describe the field by Luomanen in P. Luomanen, 'The "Sociology of Sectarianism" in Matthew: Modelling the Genesis of Early Jewish and Christian Communities', in *Fair Play: Diversity and Conflicts in Early Christianity* (ed. I. Dunderberg, C. Tuckett, and K. Syreeni; Leiden: Brill, 2002), pp. 107–30.

[5] See B. R. Wilson, *Religious Sects: A Sociological Study* (London: Weidenfeld & Nicolson, 1970), p. 28.

[6] Compare the lists of J. H. Elliott, 'The Jewish Messianic Movement: From Faction to Sect', in Esler, ed., *Modelling*, pp. 84f.; R. Stark and W. Bainbridge, *A Theory of Religion* (Toronto Studies in Religion 2; New York: Peter Lang, 1987), pp. 16–17; Wilson, *Religious Sects*, pp. 28f., and *Religion in a Sociological Perspective* (Oxford: Oxford University Press, 1982), p. 91.

[7] E. Troeltsch, *The Social Teaching of the Christian Churches* (London: George Allen & Unwin, 1931), and M. Weber, *From Max Weber: Essays in Sociology* (trans. and ed. H. H. Gerth and C. W. Mills; London: Oxford University Press, 1954), pp. 302–22.

[8] B. R. Wilson, *Magic and the Millennium: A Sociological Study of Religious Movements of Protest among Tribal and Third-world Peoples* (New York: Harper and Row, 1973), pp. 22–6.

Christian organisation: the church and the sect.[9] This legacy has been variously refined, with the 'church' being reclassified as a 'social environment',[10] 'institution',[11] or 'coalition',[12] and the 'sect' differentiated from other oppositional forms such as 'cult'.[13] Nonetheless, the basic conception remains, with the 'sect' being understood in relational opposition to a parent body of some form.[14] However, this antithesis is historically problematic.[15] The identification of the 'parent body', with which the 'sect' is apparently in relational opposition, is not a clear-cut matter. What is the nature of the Judaism in opposition to which the early Christian 'sect' stands? Which formative cultural context represents the dominant 'social environment' or 'institution' against which we are to read the Gospels? When are we to conceive this context, before or after the destruction of the Temple? Where are we to locate it – in Jesus' Galilean ministry or the wider Greco-Roman world? Each of these questions generates its own set of particular problems, the most telling of which is the absence of any clear indication of a single defining Judaism against which the early Christian 'sect' can stand.[16] This antithesis, which

[9] See Troeltsch, *Social Teaching*, and Weber, *Sociology*.

[10] On the 'church' as 'social environment', see B. Johnson, 'On Church and Sect', *ASR* 28 (1963), 542. On the 'church' as a 'religiously defined dominant culture', see L. White, 'Shifting Sectarian Boundaries in Early Christianity', *BJRL* 70 (1988), 14.

[11] E.g. Stark and Bainbridge, *Theory*, p. 126.

[12] On the 'church' as 'parent body' or 'coalition', see Elliott, 'From Faction to Sect', p. 77, n. 6. Elliott adopts the language from the anthropologist Boissevain's work on interpersonal relations in social networks, *Friends of Friends: Networks, Manipulators and Coalitions* (Oxford: Blackwell, 1974), pp. 170–205. Elliott notably identifies the earliest 'Jesus movement' not as a 'sect' but rather as a 'faction'. It is apparently not until the death of Jesus that this faction becomes 'dissociated' from 'the corporate body of Judaism', p. 79.

[13] See Stark and Bainbridge, *Theory*. 'Sects' are understood as coming into existence through a schism with an existing institution, p. 128, and 'cults' through the social acceptance of new religious ideas, p. 156.

[14] See A. Overman, *Matthew's Gospel and Formative Judaism* (Minneapolis: Fortress Press, 1990); see also Luomanen, 'The "Sociology of Sectarianism"', n. 4.

[15] Wilson, on Troeltsch, describes it as an 'anachronism of Western Christian intellectualism', *Magic*, p. 13, n. 8. See also T. Seland, 'Jesus as a Faction Leader: On the Exit of the Category Sect', in *Context* (ed. P. Bøckman and R. Kristiansen; Trondheim: TAPIR, 1987), pp. 197–211.

[16] On 'Judaism', see Sanders' etic perspective *Judaism*. Cf. Martin Hengel and Roland Deines' 'complex Judaism', 'E. P. Sanders' "Judaism", Jesus, and the Pharisees', *JTS* 46 (1995), 60–7; and Neusner and Chilton's 'Judaisms', which results from a more emic perspective focusing on the groups' self-understanding, *Judaism in the New Testament: Practices and Beliefs* (London: Routledge, 1995).

underlies most discussions of sectarianism, is rooted in the sociology of sectarianism's 'christocentric culture-bound character'.[17] Consequently, the 'sect' is automatically understood in its relational opposition. It is the 'other', standing at the margins of the social world as deviant.

The degree to which the historical constraints of the sociology of religion may be transcended depends upon how broadly any comparative framework will allow the 'church' and the 'sect' to be conceived. It finds its most promising resolution in the second of our strategies for conceiving the 'sect', Wilson's soteriologically orientated typology. Wilson has consciously designed and refined his typology to enable the broadest possible application.[18] This is facilitated by understanding the 'sect' not in its relational opposition to a parent body but primarily in its soteriological orientation and only secondly in its response to the 'world', understood as 'items that lie beyond the self conception of the sect'.[19] He identifies seven 'types' of soteriological strategy: conversionist, manipulationist, thaumaturgical, reformist, revolutionist, utopian, and introversionist.[20] However, even in this, its most refined form, the hermeneutical value of the 'sociology of sectarianism' is to be questioned. Wilson, recognising the dangers of any definitive definition, has loaded his discussion with caveats and reservations.[21] The complexity of the 'sect' radically dilutes its explanatory force. Which feature, at what time, generates what response?[22] Furthermore, as will now be illustrated by reference to Esler's application of the typology to the Gospel of John,[23] it is all too easy even when adopting Wilson's typology

---

[17] Wilson, *Magic*, p. 20.

[18] Wilson seeks to generate a heuristic framework which transcends its creator's context: 'it is essential that our categories should be freed from the presuppositions of one particular cultural tradition or of one historical period', *ibid.*, p. 17.

[19] *Ibid.*, p. 19.

[20] *Ibid.*, pp. 22f.

[21] He recognises that any particular 'sect' will combine elements of more than one of his types and that these may in turn change over time, *ibid.*, p. 49.

[22] This problem is evident in the diversity of features that the sectarian identification is used to explain: see the survey of approaches in B. Holmberg, *Sociology and the New Testament: An Appraisal* (Minneapolis: Fortress Press, 1990), pp. 112f. Even if all the purported explanations are deemed valid, their sheer diversity suggests that when the 'sectarian' character of a particular text is being examined, scholars are looking at different aspects of their object rather than investigating the same phenomenon.

[23] P. F. Esler, 'Introverted Sectarianism at Qumran and in the Johannine Community', *The First Christians*, pp. 70–91.

to slip into the stereotypical antithesis of church/sect, which obscures more than it reveals.[24]

2.2   'Introversionist sectarianism' and the Gospel of John

The Gospel of John has widely,[25] although not unanimously,[26] been characterised as 'sectarian': 'It can probably be agreed that on any reading of the Gospel and Epistles there appears a sectarian consciousness, a sense of exclusiveness, a sharp delineation of the community from the world.'[27] The application of the social sciences to help account for the Gospel's distinctive character was first attempted by Meeks, who postulated a 'Johannine sectarianism'.[28] However, in making this identification he acknowledged the absence of adequate theoretical categories for describing the formation of a 'sect' of the sort he perceives the Johannine group to be.[29] In the decades that have passed since the publication of this seminal article, few have followed his social-scientific path.[30] Rather, the label 'sect' has been adopted in a piecemeal and uncritical manner. Therefore, Esler initially appears atypical in offering his application of Wilson's typology to the Gospel as a response to Meeks' earlier call for more 'developed theoretical categories' to apply to Johannine sectarianism.[31] He identifies the

---

[24] For a particularly pessimistic assessment of the utility of the 'sociology of sectarianism', see J. T. Sanders, *Schismatics, Sectarians, Dissidents, Deviants: The First One Hundred Years of Jewish–Christian Relations* (London: SCM Press, 1993), pp. 114–25, following V. Murvar, 'Towards a Sociological Theory of Religious Movements', *JSSR* 14 (1975), 229–56. For a more hopeful outlook, see Holmberg, *Sociology*, pp. 114f. Whilst he is sceptical of its explanatory value, he nonetheless commends its utility for formulating new hypotheses.

[25] On the sectarian identity of Johannine Christianity, see E. Käsemann, 'Ketzer und Zeuge: zum johanneischen Verfasserproblem', *ZTK* 48 (1951), 292–311; Martyn, *History*, and Meeks, 'The Man from Heaven'.

[26] On the mainstream character of Johannine Christianity, see R. E. Brown, *The Community of the Beloved Disciple* (New York: Paulist Press, 1979), pp. 16f., and M. Hengel, *The Johannine Question* (trans. J. Bowden; London: SCM Press, 1989).

[27] D. M. Smith, *Johannine Christianity* (Edinburgh: T&T Clark, 1984), pp. 3f.

[28] 'The Man from Heaven'.

[29] *Ibid.*, p. 70, n. 79.

[30] It is notably Rensberger who is the first to apply Wilson's sectarian typology to the Gospel: see his *Overcoming the World, Politics and Community in the Gospel of John* (London: SPCK, 1989), pp. 27f. However, he explains that he is not attempting sociological analysis: 'I have no wish to enter fully into sociological debates as to what constitutes a "sect"', p. 27. He has no desire to 'explain [his] observations on the basis of a theoretical model', p. 30.

[31] Esler, 'Sectarianism', p. 84.

Johannine community behind the Gospel as reflecting the consciousness of Wilson's 'introverted' sectarian type, which sees the world as

> irredeemably evil and salvation to be attained only by the fullest possible withdrawal from it. The self may be purified by renouncing the world and leaving it. This response might be an individual response, of course, but as the response of a social movement it leads to the establishment of a separated community preoccupied with its own holiness and its means of insulation from the wider society. Even if the ideology posits only its future realisation, in practice, salvation is sociologically a *present* endeavour. The community itself becomes the source and seat of all salvation. Explicitly this prospect of salvation is only for those who belong.[32]

He makes this identification on the basis of the Gospel's presentation of 'profound conflicts' with Judaism, which he argues are indicative of 'symbolic boundary setting' that serves to legitimate the community's identity.[33] He substantiates the Gospel's sectarian status on the basis of its use of *aposynagōgos*, 'banished from the synagogue' (9:22; 12:42; 16:2).[34] It is further underlined by the frequency of Jewish attacks on Jesus in the Gospel, as compared with the Synoptics,[35] and the controversy over Abraham in 8:31–59.[36] This identification is then used as an explanation for the Gospel's realised eschatology,[37] and by implication its prominent dualism.[38] However, Esler's adoption of Wilson's typology is, as will now be demonstrated, problematic.

2.2.1   Esler's Jewish 'church' and the Johannine 'sect'

Esler's adoption of Wilson appears to be strained from the very start. Wilson self-consciously sought to avoid the church/sect dichotomy of previous analysis by delineating sects in terms of their

---

[32] *Ibid.*, p. 73, citing Wilson, *Magic*, pp. 23–4. His italics.
[33] 'Sectarianism', p. 85.
[34] Esler approvingly cites Martyn, *History*. Indeed, it appears that Martyn's two-level reading of the Gospel is programmatic for Esler.
[35] 'Sectarianism', pp. 85f.
[36] *Ibid.*, pp. 86f.
[37] *Ibid.*, pp. 89f.
[38] *Ibid.*, pp. 90f.

soteriological strategies and only secondarily in terms of their particular 'response to the world'.[39] In addition, for Wilson, 'response to the world' suggested 'items that lie beyond the self conception of the sect'.[40] Yet Esler in his identification of the Johannine community as Wilson's 'introversionist' type constantly refers to categories that lie at the heart of its self-conception. He argues that the community's 'response to the "world" largely means... Judaism'.[41] The Johannine community allegedly perceived 'Judaism' as 'irredeemably evil' and held that salvation was only to be 'attained by the fullest withdrawal from it'.[42] However, the Gospel is marked by the paradox that whilst it certainly appears to be anti-Jewish, it is also profoundly Jewish,[43] seeing the world and thinking in Jewish categories.[44] Indeed, when it appears at its most anti-Jewish it is also at its most Jewish.[45] Esler's particular adoption of Wilson's typology overwrites such subtlety and clearly collapses back into the church/sect dichotomy of previous analysis. In spite of his repeated references to 'Judaism' and 'Jews', he attempts neither to define them nor even place them in inverted commas.[46] Their identity is apparently self-evident. It appears from his approving citation of Martyn and the adoption of 'Judaism' and 'Jews' as synonymous terms that he means the official representatives of a normative Jewish religion.[47] However, neither this view of a normative and antagonistic 'Judaism'[48] nor its uniform

---

[39] *Magic*, pp. 18f.

[40] *Ibid.*, p. 19.

[41] 'Sectarianism', 85. This identification of the 'world' with 'Judaism' is further complicated by his location of the Johannine community in 'one of the cities of the Greco-Roman East', a culturally and religiously diverse social environment.

[42] *Magic*, p. 23, cited by Esler, 'Sectarianism', pp. 72f.

[43] J. H. Charlesworth, 'The Dead Sea Scrolls and the Gospel of John', in *Exploring the Gospel of John* (ed. R. Culpepper and C. Black; Louisville, KY: Westminster John Knox Press, 1996), p. 90.

[44] C. K. Barrett, *The Gospel of John and Judaism* (trans. D. Smith; London: SPCK, 1975), p. 71, and G. M. Burge, 'Situating John's Gospel in History', in *Jesus in the Johannine Tradition* (ed. R. T. Fortna and T. Thatcher; London: WJK, 2001), pp. 39f.

[45] W. Meeks, '"Am I a Jew?" Johannine Christianity and Judaism', in *Christianity, Judaism, and other Greco-Roman Cults* (ed. and compiled by J. Neusner; Leiden: Brill, 1975), p. 172.

[46] Cf. Esler's more recent injunctions with relation to *Christianos*, in his 'The Mediterranean Context of Early Christianity', *The Early Christian World*, Vol. I (ed. P. Esler; London: Routledge, 2000), p. 3, n. 1.

[47] 'Sectarianism', p. 84, citing Martyn, *History*.

[48] See T. Donaldson, who argues that Judaism, up to AD 100, was in 'a state of flux, with numerous religious movements, all laying claim to the traditions of Israel', 'Moses Typology and the Sectarian Nature of Early Christian Anti-Judaism',

attribution to the 'Jews' of the Gospel is satisfactory. There is a definite variation in the meaning of the 'Jews' in the Gospel.[49] They appear not only as the Jerusalem elite (18:14, cf. 11:47–53; 19:12–15), but also as the non-elite (6:41–2; 11:31; 12:11) and as a broad ethnic or religious designation (4:22; 11:55; 18:20). It is clear that the 'Jews' of John's Gospel cannot be simply characterised as 'irredeemably evil' (4:22)[50] or as a uniform entity (11:8, cf. 11:19–45; 12:9, 12f.).[51]

In addition, both the efficacy of the twelfth benediction[52] and the confidence with which 'two-level' readings of community history have been conducted are questionable.[53] The uses of *aposynagōgos*,

---

JSNT 12 (1981), 44. Meeks, following J. Neusner, *From Politics to Piety* (Englewood Cliffs, NJ: Prentice-Hall, 1973), advocates that the reinstitutionalisation of Judaism did not begin until the Bar Kochba crisis, and a uniformly, pharisaically defined Judaism did not become instantly normative after AD 70: see 'Breaking Away: Three New Testament Pictures of Christianity's Separation from Jewish Communities', in *To See ourselves as Others See us* (ed. J. Neusner and E. Friechs; Chico, CA: Scholars Press, 1985), p. 102. For surveys and summaries of the variety of 'Judaisms' in the late first century AD, see J. D. G. Dunn, 'Judaism in the Land of Israel in the First Century', in *Judaism in Late Antiquity*, Vol. II: *Historical Synthesis* (Der Nahe und der Mittlere Osten 17.2; ed. J. Neusner; Leiden: Brill, 1995), p. 230; S. Motyer, *Your Father the Devil?* (London: PBTM, 1997), pp. 74–104; and D. G. Horrell, 'Early Jewish Christianity', in *The Early Christian World*, Vol. I (ed. P. Esler; London: Routledge, 2000), pp. 136–97.

[49] On the nuanced portrayal of 'the Jews' in the Gospel, see S. Motyer, 'The Fourth Gospel and the Salvation of Israel: An Appeal for a New Start', in *Anti-Judaism and the Fourth Gospel* (ed. R. Bieringer, D. Pollefeyt, and F. Vandecasteele-Vanneuville; Assen, The Netherlands: Royal Van Gorcum, 2001), p. 95.

[50] Indeed, as Johnson notes, the polemical edge of the Gospel's anti-Judaism is somewhat blunted when placed in a broader historical and literary context: 'this language is everywhere in the fragmented Judaism of the first century', 'The New Testament's Anti-Jewish Slander and the Conventions of Ancient Polemic', *JBL* 108/3 (Fall 1989), 441.

[51] See J. D. G. Dunn, 'The Embarrassment of History: Reflections on the Problem of "Anti-Judaism" in the Fourth Gospel', in Bieringer et al., eds., *Anti-Judaism and the Fourth Gospel*, p. 50, n. 49: 'This is the fact that the key phrase, *the Jews*, is not at all so consistently negative in use as is sometimes suggested.'

[52] Indeed, Esler in his earlier *Community* is reticent about linking the 'definite Jewish policy' of expulsion with the *birkath ha-minim*, p. 55. See R. Kimelman, ' "Birkat Ha-Minim" and the Lack of Evidence for an Anti-Christian Jewish Prayer in Late-Antiquity', in *Jewish and Christian Self-Definition*, Vol. II: *Aspects of Judaism* (ed. E. P. Sanders, A. I. Baumgarten, and A. Mendelson; London: SCM, 1981), pp. 226–44, and W. Horbury, 'The Benediction of the Minim and Early Jewish-Christian Controversy', *JTS* 33 (1982), 19–61. Nonetheless, Esler seems intent on following Martyn in a strategy which Meeks has helpfully labelled 'a red herring in Johannine research', 'Breaking Away', p. 102.

[53] See R. Bauckham, ed., *The Gospels for All Christians: Rethinking the Gospel Audience* (Edinburgh: T&T Clark, 1998), especially Bauckham's opening essay, pp. 23f. Also 'The Audience of the Fourth Gospel', in *Jesus in the Johannine Tradition* (ed. R. T. Fortna and T. Thatcher; London: WJK, 2001), pp. 101–11.

'banished from the synagogue' (9:22; 12:42; 16:2) do not necessarily indicate a defining social schism. The word used to describe the action at 9:34f., *ekballein*, 'to throw out', is common and is used of Jesus himself (Luke 4:29); of Stephen (Acts 7:58); of Paul (Acts 13:50); and of 'Christians' by 'Christians' (3 John 10).[54] Although the term *aposynagōgos* is unparalleled, it can hardly be said to describe anything particularly distinctive: cf. Luke 6:22; Acts 13:45–50; 14:2–6, 19; 17:5–9, 13; 18:6f., 12–17; 1 Thess. 2:14f. Hare notes that exclusion was already a regular discipline at Qumran, 1QS 5.18; 6.24–7.25; 8.16f., 22f.; CD 9.23; and Josephus, *BJ* 2.143.[55] Indeed, the relative absence from the Gospel of the synagogue (John 6:59; 18:20) is perhaps more worthy of comment. The Gospel's references lack the Synoptics' polemical edge where a persecution motif associated with the 'synagogue' is discernible. Here confession of Christ[56] brings followers of Jesus before the synagogue where they are beaten,[57] flogged,[58] or punished[59] for their *apologia*[60] and *martyrion*.[61] It is not clear that John's presentation of the 'synagogue' is qualitatively any more 'sectarian' vis-à-vis 'Judaism' than the Synoptic tradition. Moreover, Esler's presentation of John 8:31–59 as being indicative of the 'soteriological irrelevance' of Abraham for the Johannine community, and therefore indicative of their isolation from Judaism,[62] continues to obscure the Johannine paradox that its soteriological exclusivity is rooted in Jewish exclusivity.[63] Rather than simply nullifying Abraham, Jesus claims him as a witness (8:56; cf. *Apocalypse of Abraham* 29.14–31; 30–1).[64] Rather than 'renouncing' Judaism as

[54] See J. A. T. Robinson, *Redating the New Testament* (London: SCM, 1976), p. 273.

[55] D. R. A. Hare, *The Theme of Jewish Persecution of Christians in the Gospel according to Matthew* (Cambridge: Cambridge University Press, 1967), pp. 48–56.

[56] Mark 13:9; Matt. 10:18; Luke 21:12.

[57] Mark 13:9; Acts 22:19.

[58] Matt. 10:17; 23:34.

[59] Acts 26:11; cf. Luke 12:11.

[60] Luke 12:11; 21:14; cf. Mark 13:11; Matt. 10:19.

[61] Mark 13:9; Matt. 10:18; Luke. 21:13. On the persecution motif in the Synoptic tradition, see W. Schrage, 'συναγωγή', *TDNT* VII, pp. 798–852.

[62] He views the passage as a 'contest of honour' in which the soteriological significance of Abraham is progessively reduced, 'Sectarianism', pp. 86f.

[63] See R. A. Culpepper, 'Anti-Judaism in the Fourth Gospel as a Theological Problem for Christian Interpreters', in Bieringer et al., eds., *Anti-Judaism and the Fourth Gospel*, p. 73.

[64] J. Ashton, *Understanding the Fourth Gospel* (Oxford: Clarendon Press, 1991) pp. 141f.

'irredeemably evil', Jesus engages with, even embodies, its traditions. This is not a debate *with* 'Jews' but rather *between* 'Jews'
on the soteriological significance of Jesus.[65] The result of this
engagement is not an exclusivist retreat. Rather, Jesus' 'contest of
honour' functions to broaden his acceptability to the wider 'world'.

Furthermore, Esler only lists John's most explicitly hostile
references to the 'Jews',[66] curiously including the High Priests'
plan to kill Lazarus, 12:10–11.[67] This is curious because the High
Priests plan this action on account of the 'many Jews' believing
in Jesus, 12:11. Indeed, his attempt to draw a contrast with an
apparent absence of hostility from the 'Jews' in the Synoptics
underlines the crudity of his argument. He cites Luke 4:29 as the
'only' indication of Jewish hostility towards Jesus in the Synoptic
tradition, apart from the action of the 'Jewish authorities which led
to his crucifixion at Roman hands'.[68] This identification exposes his
normative understanding, since the passage refers to 'all those in the
synagogue' (i.e. in Nazareth) and no mention is made of the 'Jews'.
In addition, Esler's casual contrast does little justice to the quantity
of sociological material in the parables. Just as extended discourses
in John may be said to serve a legitimating function, so too may
the parables and their interpretation in the Synoptics.[69] Esler's
eagerness is driven by the contemporary conceit that the sort of
cosmic dualism evident in the Gospel was necessarily the product of
a social schism, inevitably qualitatively distinct from that witnessed
in the Synoptic tradition.[70] Even if his view were sustainable, the
resulting characterisation of 'Judaism' as a 'church' against which
the Johannine 'sect' stands, on the basis of doctrinal confession,

---

[65] S. Pedersen, 'Anti-Judaism in John's Gospel: John 8', in *New Readings in John*
(JSNTS 182; ed. J. Nissen and S. Pedersen; London: Sheffield Academic Press, 1999),
pp. 188f.
[66] They seek to kill Jesus, 5:18; 7:19; 8:37, 40, and 44; Jesus avoids Judaea on their
account, 7:1; they attempt to stone Jesus, 8:59 and 10:31, cf.11:8; they repeatedly
attempt to apprehend him prior to his arrest, 7:30, 32, 44; 8:20; 10:39 and 11:57;
and the High Priests plan to kill Lazarus, 12:10–11.
[67] See Esler, 'Sectarianism', pp. 85f.
[68] *Ibid.*, p. 85. Cf. Mark 12:12.
[69] E.g. the parable of the wicked tenants, Matt. 21:33–45/Mark 12:1–12/Luke
20:9–19, and the interpretation of the parable of the sower, Matt. 13:18–23; Mark
4:13–20/Luke 8:11–15. In the latter example, we again find the theme of 'persecution
for the word's sake'.
[70] On the 'modern prejudice' that cosmic dualism is necessarily a secondary
reflection of a social schism, see T. S. Dokka, 'Irony and Sectarianism in the Gospel
of John', in *New Readings in John* (JSNTS 182; ed. J. Nissen and S. Pedersen;
London: Sheffield, Academic Press, 1999), p. 100.

misconstrues Wilson's theoretical agenda, which sought to escape the 'theological echoes of the earlier classification and their christo-centric culture-bound character'.[71] Esler has slipped into the very culture-bound classifications of Troeltsch and Weber's earlier analysis that Wilson's more sophisticated typology sought to avoid. He appears, as we will now see, to adopt Wilson's typology as 'evidence' to support his preconceptions about the Gospel's status rather than to elucidate the text.

2.2.2   *The Gospel and Wilson's typology*

The characteristic of Wilson's 'introversionist' sect type, which most closely resonates with the concerns of the Gospel, is the feature that Esler seeks to explain: its realised eschatology. However, the remaining characteristics of this type are at best ambiguously evident. First, the Gospel[72] does not advocate that the individual is to be 'purified by renouncing the world and leaving it'.[73] The Gospel engages not only with Esler's 'world' (John 4:22; 5:34b and 12:36)[74] but also with the more literal 'world' (3:16–17; 4:42; 6:33, 51; 17:21; and cf. 12:32; 1 John 2:2; 4:9).[75] Indeed, Martyn notes that in the Gospel 'we see *both* agreement and tension' with Jewish thought, Esler's 'world'.[76] In addition, 'sending' in the more general 'world' is paradigmatic for the Gospel: as the Father sent the Son, so too the Son sends his disciples into the world (3:16–17; 17:18 and 20:21).[77] This hardly represents 'renouncing' and 'leaving'. Secondly, it is a distortion to characterise the Gospel's soteriology

---

[71] *Magic*, p. 20.

[72] It is notable that throughout this apparently social reading no reference is made to the Johannine Epistles.

[73] *Magic*, p. 23.

[74] On the Gospel's engagement with Judaism, see Meeks, who comments: 'The Fourth Gospel is indeed one of the most Jewish of the early Christian writings', '"Am I a Jew?" Johannine Christianity and Judaism', p. 185. De Boer underlines the point: 'neither Jesus in John nor the Evangelist in editorial comments counsels hatred or contempt for the "Jews" or their beliefs': see 'The Depiction of "the Jews" in John's Gospel: Matters of Behaviour and Identity', in Bieringer et al., eds., *Anti-Judaism and the Fourth Gospel*, p. 143.

[75] See R. E. Brown, *John (I–XII)*, pp. 508f.

[76] See Martyn, *History*, p. 104, my italics.

[77] See A. J. Köstenberger, *The Missions of Jesus and the Disciples according to the Fourth Gospel* (Eerdmans: Grand Rapids, 1998), pp. 190–8. Also Dokka, 'Irony and Sectarianism', p. 85, n. 70: 'There remains, nevertheless, a tension between sending and sect which ought to create uneasiness of sorts in all analysts working with the social world of John.'

as orientated towards the establishment of a 'separated community'.[78] Whilst there is to be 'one flock and one shepherd' (10:16),
an individualistic dimension to the calling is also evident, for 'the
sheep hear his voice, and he calls his own sheep by name' (10:4).
Just as each sheep hears the shepherd's voice individually, each
branch is rooted directly in the vine (15:4ff.).[79] In contrast to the
Synoptic tradition's emphasis on the 'Kingdom of God', the Gospel
emphasises personal 'belief' leading to 'eternal life'.[80] The Gospel
repeatedly stresses the importance of the belief and practice of the
individual; salvation is not unambiguously ecclesiological in character; rather its consistent emphasis is christological.[81] Finally, it is
also not clear that the Johannine community is represented as the
'source and seat of all salvation'.[82] Rather, the Gospel acknowledges the role of others and displays distinct universal tendencies,
which are hard to reconcile with the picture of a community set
apart.[83] The community is not the source and seat of salvation. On
the contrary, salvation is, as just noted, consistently christologically
orientated (10:16; 11:52 and 18:37). Furthermore, the commission
of Peter in John 21 is hardly reconcilable with an exclusivist view
of the community.[84] Whilst the Gospel does betray an often ambivalent or antagonistic relationship with the 'world', it is not at
all clear that its soteriological orientation may be singularly
characterised as 'introversionist'.

The Gospel does, however, display strong affinities with another
of Wilson's types, the 'conversionist' sect, which is 'not concerned

---

[78] *Magic*, p. 24.

[79] Dunn, *Jesus and the Spirit*, p. 354. Dunn goes on to note that the eating of
the flesh and the drinking of the blood, or of the water from his side, are 'addressed
more to a series of individuals than to a community which is itself the body of
Christ', John 6:53–8; 7:37f. However, this is not to deny a community orientation.
There is a mutual belonging to Christ, but salvation is not founded upon a mutual
interdependence.

[80] John 3:15f., 36; 4:14, 36; 5:24, 39; 6:27, 40, 54, 68; 10:28; 12:25, 50 and 17:2f.

[81] See C. F. D. Moule, 'The Individualism of the Fourth Gospel', *NovTest* 5
(1962), 184. Also J. F. O'Grady, 'Johannine Ecclesiology: A Critical Evaluation',
BTB 7 (1977), 36–44. O'Grady argues that 'The Fourth Gospel is basically
Christological and is truly individualistic in that it emphasizes the need for the
individual believer to respond in faith to the final revealer, mediator and envoy of the
Father', p. 43. Also R. E. Brown, *John (I–XII)*, pp. CV–CIX.

[82] *Magic*, p. 24.

[83] Bauckham, 'Audience', pp. 110f, n. 53. See also R. B. Edwards, *Discovering
John* (London: SPCK, 2003), pp. 43f., on such presentations as a 'parody of
Johannine Christianity'.

[84] On the literary integrity of John 21, see Bauckham, 'Audience', p. 111, and
'The Beloved Disciple as Ideal Author', *JSNT* 49 (1993), 21–44.

simply with recruitment to a movement, but with the acquisition of a change of heart'.[85] This sect type is unique in Wilson's scheme; all the other types perceive that it is the 'world' which is corrupt, and that it is the 'world' which must be overcome. In contrast, the 'conversionist' type perceives the self as corrupt. Salvation is not to be achieved through the transformation of, or flight from, the world but through the 'supernaturally wrought' transformation of the self:

> what men must do to be saved is to undergo emotional transformation – a conversion experience. This is the proof of having transcended the evil of the world [the world is corrupt because men are corrupt]. Since it is a permanent and timelessly valid transcendence, some future condition of salvation is often posited in which objective circumstances come to correspond to the subjective sense of salvation, but the believer also knows, from subjective change, that he is saved *now*.[86]

The Gospel notably makes clear the need for conversion, a renewal from above (3:1–21; also 7:38 and 20:17, 22). Salvation is not accomplished by an extraction from the world but by an infusion of the divine life (6:58). Jesus does not pray for the removal of his disciples from the world but that they may be kept safe from the evil one (17:15). It is not the world that changes; rather, the believer is kept safe through a supernaturally wrought transformation facilitated by the Paraclete, 14:16f.[87] The impact of the change appears to be so profound that in 1 John 3:9 it seems that members of the community can no longer sin. Here we may compare Wilson's 'permanent and timelessly valid transcendence'. Another feature of the 'conversionist' type is that some form of eschatology is said to be required to sustain their subjective conversion experience. Wilson notes that this may be promised in the future, either in this world or in the prospect of the individual's transfer to another sphere. The presence of a futurist eschatology is relatively rare in the Gospel (found only at 5:28–9; 6:39–44, 51–8; 11:24

---

[85] *Magic*, p. 23.
[86] *Ibid.*, p. 22. His italics.
[87] On the function of the Paraclete in the Gospel, see R. E. Brown, *The Gospel according to John (XIII–XXI)*, (New York: Anchor Bible, 1970), pp. 1135–43, esp. 1139f.

and 12:46–8),[88] and is more often associated with the Synoptic tradition. Indeed, Esler in his *Community and Gospel in Luke–Acts* argues that Wilson's 'conversionist' sectarian type helps account for that Gospel's more pronounced stress on a delayed eschaton.[89] However, the 'conversionist' type's possible eschatological orientations do not necessarily preclude an identification with John's Gospel since one's subjective conversion experience may also be understood in relation to the prospect of the individual's transfer to another sphere (cf. 14:1–3; 20:17). In addition, the 'conversionist' type also stresses the immediacy of salvation: 'he is saved *now*'[90] (cf. 1:12; 5:24). The identification of these features underlines Wilson's own injunctions, when presenting his sectarian typology, that sects may manifest characteristics of more than one of the types,[91] an observation underlined by Rensberger, who, in passing over the theoretical discussion of sectarianism, identified not only 'introversionist' and 'conversionist' elements in the Gospel but also 'revolutionist' elements![92] It is apparent that Wilson's 'introversionist' sect type is adopted by Esler more for its rhetorical force, as buttressing evidence for his preconceived scheme, than for its hermeneutical potential. Esler appears wedded to a problematic and pervasive view of the Gospel which views it as an in-group document, and, as will now be demonstrated, draws inadequately developed thematic parallels with Qumran.

2.2.3   'Sectarianism', the Gospel, and Qumran

Prior to the discovery of the Qumran scrolls the Gospel was predominantly read against the backdrop of Jewish wisdom literature, Philo, the hermetic books, and the Mandaean writings.[93]

---

[88] A definitive discussion of the Gospel's eschatological orientation is not possible in the context of this discussion. Reference to 'delayed' and 'realised' eschatologies is therefore limited to that which is adopted by Esler in his various discussions of sectarianism (unless otherwise stated).

[89] *Community*, p. 59. Indeed, any description of John's Gospel as 'conversionist' sits uncomfortably with his previous work on Luke–Acts and may explain his reticence in making this identification.

[90] *Magic*, p. 22.

[91] *Ibid.*, p. 26: 'the seven types of response might not appear in any high degree of purity in the real world. The beliefs of religious movements are often volatile, inconsistent, many sided, and internally contradictory.'

[92] Rensberger, *Overcoming the World*, pp. 27f. His brief adoption of Wilson's typology is perhaps one of its most faithful appropriations.

[93] On the history of interpretation, see Ashton, *Understanding*, pp. 9–27.

Such readings led many to regard the Gospel as the most Greek of the Gospels.[94] However, the scrolls acted as a catalyst for recognising[95] the thoroughly Jewish character of Johannine theology and led to the current acknowledgement of the Gospel as the one which is most engaged with Judaism.[96] They have also provided the opportunity for comparative studies which have identified numerous thematic parallels with the Johannine literature, particularly its ethical and eschatological dualism.[97] The identification of such parallels has led to numerous theories postulating some kind of influence upon the Johannine literature, either direct[98] or indirect.[99] However, the enthusiasm for such links has given way to more 'sober analyses'.[100] It has not been possible to prove a direct link to a widely held degree of satisfaction. It is in this more sceptical context that the allegedly complementary social parallel of a common 'sectarian' identity has been proposed.[101] The Qumran and Johannine communities' distinctive dualism is said to be a product of their social circumstances, which are characterised by the sharp division between their communities and the world. Whilst the community at Qumran had fled the world, literally to the desert, the Johannine community found itself estranged from its world, excluded from the synagogue (9:22; 12:42; 16:2).[102] The dualism

[94] E.g. E. J. Goodspeed, *An Introduction to the New Testament* (Chicago: Chicago University Press, 1937), pp. 314–15. He defines the Gospel's purpose as 'to strip Christianity of its Jewish swaddling clothes, its intense anti-Jewish feeling, and its great debt to the mystery religions – combined to show that its author was a Greek not a Jew. In the Gospel of John the Greek genius returns to religion.'

[95] Or perhaps rediscovering: see K. Bornhäuser, *Das Johannesevangelium. Eine Missionschrift für Israel* (Gütersloh: Bertelsmann, 1928).

[96] See J. M. Lieu, 'Anti-Judaism in the Fourth Gospel: Explanation and Hermeneutics', in Bieringer et al., eds., *Anti-Judaism and the Fourth Gospel*, pp. 101f.: 'while not denying the validity of appealing to "parallels" with Graeco-Roman thought, John's conceptual framework, his "culture", is unreservedly "Jewish"'.

[97] See R. E. Brown, 'The Dead Sea Scrolls and the New Testament', in *John and the Dead Sea Scrolls* (ed. J. H. Charlesworth; New York: Crossroad, 1990), pp. 7–8.

[98] See J. H. Charlesworth, 'The Dead Sea Scrolls', and Ashton, *Understanding*, pp. 232–7, n. 43.

[99] See R. E. Brown, *New Testament Essays* (New York: Paulist Press, 1965), pp. 102–31.

[100] A. Pilgaard, 'The Qumran Scrolls and John's Gospel', in Nissen and Pedersen, eds., *New Readings in John*, p. 126.

[101] See Esler, 'Sectarianism'; Ashton, *Understanding*, p. 212, and M. Boismard, 'The First Epistle of John and the Writings of Qumran', in Charlesworth, ed., *John and the Dead Sea Scrolls*, pp. 156–65.

[102] See Martyn, *History*; Meeks, "The Man from Heaven"; R. E. Brown, *Community*; and Rensberger, *Overcoming the World*. These works have helped to generate a consensus that the Gospel bears the marks of a major sociological schism. Pilgaard, 'Scrolls', p. 129, n. 100.

which is common to both allegedly reflects this sectarian detach-
ment.[103] It gives meaning to the social situations in which the two
groups find themselves. It is part of a wider socially exclusive system
of language, which reinforces the Johannine community's sectarian
identity.[104]

However, the case for common social origins for the dualistic
themes in the Qumran scrolls and the Johannine literature is not
well served by the sectarian identification. It is clear that just as the
'sectarian' identification of the Gospel of John is problematic (see
§2.2 above), its application to the scrolls is also disputable. The
identification of the Qumran literature as the product of a radically
estranged community is now widely regarded, in scrolls scholarship
at least, as an unhelpful and untenable caricature.[105] Nonetheless,
the 'sectarian' label remains, and is used to distinguish the community behind particular elements in the literature.[106] However,
the identity and nature of this community, or communities, is the

---

[103] Painter stresses the importance of the parallel between the Gospel and
Qumran. It is 'important because it highlights the sectarian character of both the
Qumran community and the Johannine Christians', *The Quest for the Messiah: The
History, Literature, and Theology of the Johannine Community* (Nashville: Abingdon
Press, 1993), p. 38.

[104] See H. Leroy, *Rätsel und Missverständnis: Ein Beitrag zur Formgeschichte*
(BBB 30; Bonn: Peter Hanstein, 1968); B. Malina, 'John's: The Maverick Christian
Group', *BTB* 24 (1987), 167–82; J. H. Neyrey, *The Ideology of Revolt: John's
Christology in Social-Science Perspective* (Philadelphia: Fortress Press, 1988); and
N. Petersen, *The Gospel of John and the Sociology of Light: Language and
Characterization in the Fourth Gospel* (Valley Forge, PA: Trinity Press
International, 1993).

[105] See P. R. Davies, *Sects and Scrolls*, p. 2: 'The Qumran texts were once peddled
as products of a fringe sect bitterly opposed to a "normative" Judaism. Their
homogeneity was correspondingly emphasized, and theologies were erected out of
various contents. Their historical value as witness to the character of "Judaism"
was mainly as a form of deviation. However, just as the idea of a "normative"
Judaism has been eroded, so has our awareness grown that these Qumran
manuscripts are less cohesive than is desirable for the purposes of constructing
a "Qumran theology".'

[106] Typically, the label 'sectarian' is applied to those texts whose ideology and
vocabulary cohere with 1QS: see, e.g., J. C. R. de Roo, 'Is 4Q525 a Qumran Sectarian
Document?' in Porter and Evans, eds., *The Scrolls and the Scriptures*, pp. 338–67.
However, the significant variations in editions of the Community Rule, especially
the material from Cave 4, where a number of manuscripts of the Community Rule
omit the teaching on the two-spirits in 1QS 3.13–4.26 (frequently identified as
sectarian theology at its most developed), render any identification of what is typically
'sectarian' highly problematic. See C. Hempel, 'Qumran Communities: Beyond
the Fringes', in Porter and Evans, eds., *The Scrolls and the Scriptures*, p. 51, and
P. R. Davies, *Sects and Scrolls*, p. 2, who notes that few who make the distinction
between 'sectarian' and 'non-sectarian' have an agreed set of criteria for applying it.

subject of significant debate.[107] What is clear within these discussions is the growing realisation that the Qumran literature can
no longer be placed on the fringes of Second Temple Judaism.[108]
Indeed, it is my contention in the light of its widespread factionalism that it is unhelpful to apply the label 'sectarian' to
characterise any of the social groups in first-century 'Judaism'.[109]
The appropriation of the label predominantly lacks the sophistication of Wilson's typology. When Dunn can say that a substantial
proportion of our sources are 'sectarian' and Baumgarten feels
comfortable in applying the label to 'the full range of Jewish
groups known from the Second Temple period',[110] then the
language of sectarianism has dissolved to a level of generality that
renders its hermeneutical value questionable. It potentially
obscures the true social character of these groups. In addition,
the allegedly 'sectarian' language which underlines this common
identification is neither necessarily the product of a social
schism[111] nor a uniform feature of the Qumran literature. There
is a growing realisation that the Qumran literature presents
a diverse variety of eschatological teachings.[112] In addition, the
teaching on the two-spirits, 1QS 3–4, the apparent Qumran
doctrine *par excellence*, is notably absent from a number of the
versions of the Community Rule from Cave 4, i.e. 4Q258.[113] It has
been clearly demonstrated that both the Community Rule
and the Damascus Document were subject to complex literary
development and that the two-spirits teaching sits within this

---

[107] On the current lack of consensus in scrolls scholarship, see Grabbe,
'Questions?'. This debate frequently lacks a social dimension. A. I. Baumgarten is
a notable exception: see *The Flourishing of the Jewish Sects*.
[108] See Hempel, 'Beyond the Fringes', p. 49. Note especially H. Stegemann,
'Main Jewish Union' and *The Library of Qumran*, pp. 140–53.
[109] See J. D. G. Dunn, 'Jesus and Factionalism in Early Judaism', in J. H.
Charlesworth and L. L. Johns, eds., *Hillel and Jesus: Comparative Studies of Two
Major Religious Leaders* (Minneapolis: Fortress Press, 1997), p. 157. Dunn touches
upon the question of nomenclature – 'sect', 'faction', or 'school' – and notes that a
large proportion of our sources were 'sectarian'.
[110] *An Interpretation*, pp. 7, 11ff.
[111] As Dokka has noted, it is a 'modern prejudice to believe that "cosmic
dualism" is necessarily a secondary reflection of a social schism', 'Irony and
Sectarianism', p. 100.
[112] P. R. Davies, *Sects and Scrolls*, p. 61.
[113] Cf. Esler, 'Sectarianism', p. 80, who argues that the introverted sectarian
character of the Qumran community is confirmed by it: '1QS manifests a powerfully
dualistic outlook, especially in the teaching on the two-spirits (III.17–IV.1), where
we find a clear enunciation of the notion of the basic division between the sons of
light and the sons of darkness not found in CD.'

literary development.[114] It is therefore not tenable that this most pronounced example of the scrolls' eschatological dualism can be accounted for on the basis of any founding social schism,[115] or be intrinsically linked to the communal legislation of the *communities* (1QS 6.1f., 3f., 6–8). Furthermore, Bauckham, who differentiates between the types of image in which the Gospel's dualism is evident, has forcefully questioned the apparent parallels with dualism in the Gospel of John.[116] These are spatial imagery: 'from above' and 'from below' (8:23); 'not from this world' and 'from this world' (8:23; 18:36); 'not from the world' and 'from the world' (15:19; 17:14, 16); and the imagery of light and darkness (1:4-9; 3:19–21; 8:12; 9:4–5; 11:9–10; 12:35–6, 46; cf. 1 John 1.5–7; 2:8–11). He argues that the Qumran literature provides no parallel to the spatial imagery and that the best parallel for this usage is found in James (1:17, 27; 3:15, 17).[117] The imagery of light and darkness may be quite adequately accounted for by reference to the Hebrew Bible and parallels in Second Temple Jewish literature, rendering a Qumran hypothesis redundant.[118] Finally, the argument that the Gospel's language represents an in-group language is not at all clear; on the contrary, the Gospel appears designed to *introduce* its readers to its special language and symbolism.[119]

[114] Hempel, 'Beyond the Fringes', pp. 48ff., esp. p. 51. Cave 4 revealed ten copies of the Community Rule, 4Q255–64, and eight of the Damascus Document, 4Q266–73.

[115] On the founding of the community, see H. Stegemann, 'Main Jewish Union', p. 104, *contra* the Groningen hypothesis, which starkly differentiates the Essenes (of classical sources) from Qumran and the Dead Sea Scrolls, arguing that the Qumran community was founded as a result of a profound break from a wider Essene movement. Campbell notes that most have not followed this hypothesis and that the 'Qumran-Essene hypothesis [is] likely to win the day': see *Deciphering the Dead Sea Scrolls* (Oxford: Blackwell, 2002), pp. 75 and 100.

[116] 'Qumran and the Fourth Gospel: Is there a connection?', in Porter and Evans, eds., *The Scrolls and the Scriptures*, pp. 267–79.

[117] 'Qumran', p. 269. This parallel is somewhat arbitrarily dismissed: 'Since there are no other resemblances between James and the Johannine literature, these parallels are best explained by common dependence on a Jewish terminology which does not seem to have been preserved in extant Jewish texts.'

[118] Bauckham argues that the correct conclusion has been drawn on the basis of the Qumran discoveries, i.e. the Gospel's Jewish character, but on the basis of the wrong evidence, *ibid.*, p. 279. Bauckham has, however, picked at the soft underbelly of the argument and appears premature in his closing down of the discussion; see Pilgaard's discussion, which raises numerous avenues for further examination, 'The Qumran Scrolls and John's Gospel', pp. 126–42.

[119] See Dokka, 'Irony and Sectarianism'. He concludes that the Gospel, far from being exclusive and impregnable, is 'uniquely readable for outsiders', p. 104. Also, J. Nissen, 'Community and Ethics in the Gospel of John', in Nissen and Pedersen, eds., *New Readings in John*, p. 197, following K. Berger, *Exegese des Neuen*

2.3   Summary

The sociology of sectarianism is deeply embedded in its christo-centric cultural origins, with the 'sect' understood in relational opposition to its 'church'. These origins still shape its appropriation in New Testament studies. Even Esler's appropriation of Wilson's more sophisticated sectarian typology fails to escape this founda-tional antithesis (see §2.2.1 above). Furthermore, the Gospel of John confounds any simple identification with any one of Wilson's types. It displays elements of a number of his types, clouding the typology's possible heuristic potential. Indeed, it is not at all clear that the Gospel's 'sectarian' character is particularly pronounced vis-à-vis the Synoptic Gospels. Rather, it is clear from the growing number of 'sectarian' readings of *all the Gospels* that the force of any argument for 'sectarianism' as the answer to the Johannine distinctiveness has been greatly diluted.[120] Ultimately, the sectarian thesis is driven by two mutually reinforcing yet fundamentally fragile readings of the Gospel: the allegorical two-level reading of community history, which identifies a foundational sectarian social schism, and the alleged sectarian parallel with Qumran. If these elements are not sustainable, the question remains of what, if any, social phenomena may account for the Gospel's distinctive character. If these elements are unsustainable, perhaps it is time to move beyond the theoretical agenda set in train by Meeks' call for more adequate sectarian models and to re-examine the nature of the Johannine social witness.

3   Johannine virtuosity

Social approaches to the Gospel of John have predominantly focused upon reconstructions of the Johannine community.[121]

Testaments: Neue Wege vom Text zur Auslegung (Heidelberg: Quelle & Meyer, 1977), pp. 230-1; Bauckham, 'Audience', p. 109; and P. Phillips, 'A Re-Appraisal of Some Sociolinguistic Approaches to an Understanding of the Prologue of John's Gospel' (BNTC 2002 conference paper).

[120] For example, compare G. N. Stanton's paralleling of Qumran themes with Matthew in *A Gospel for a New People: Studies in Matthew* (Edinburgh: T&T Clark, 1992), pp. 85–107, with Esler's discussions in 'Sectarianism'. Further diluting the sectarian identification is the high level of background polemics evident in the first century: see L. T. Johnson, 'Anti-Jewish Slander'.

[121] E.g. Martyn, *History*; Meeks, 'The Man from Heaven'; R. E. Brown, *Community*; A. J. Matthill, 'Johannine Communities behind the Fourth Gospel: Georg Richter's Analysis', *TS* 38 (1977), 294–315; O. Cullmann, *The Johannine*

These two-level readings have recently become the subject of a methodological refocusing with reader- rather than author-centred approaches dominating comment.[122] The idea that the Gospels were written for distinct communities has been undermined by reference to their genre[123] and to the interrelatedness of the early 'Christians'.[124] These and other significant criticisms have somewhat eclipsed critical reflection upon the nature of the Johannine social world.[125] The question of a distinctive Johannine social witness has been sidelined in favour of imagining its reception in a diffuse and complex late-first-century Judaism.[126] However, such refocusing on the receiver does not circumvent the reality that this Gospel necessarily emerged from a particular social context. Whilst the Gospel may not have been written *for* a community, its internal witness strongly suggests that it was written *from* a community (21:23). This idiosyncratic Johannine feature suggests that it will remain a valid and necessary[127] enterprise to seek to understand Johannine

Circle (London: SCM Press, 1976); M. E. Boismard, *L'Evangile de Jean* (Synopse des quatre evangiles en français, III; ed. M. E. Boismard and A. Lamouille; Paris: Cerf, 1977); W. Langbrandtner, *Weltferner Gott oder Gott der Leibe: Die Ketzerstreit in der johanneischen Kirche* (Beiträge zur biblischen Exegese und Theologie, 6; Frankfurt: Lang, 1977); and D. Rensberger, *Johannine Faith and Liberating Community* (Philadelphia: Fortress Press, 1988).

[122] This methodological refocusing has gained particular emphasis since the publication of Bauckham, ed., *The Gospels for All Christians*.

[123] On the genre of the Gospels, see R. A. Burridge, 'About People, by People, for People: Gospel Genre and Audiences', *ibid.*, pp. 113–46.

[124] On the extensive travel and contact amongst the earliest Christians, see M. B. Thompson, 'The Holy Internet: Communication Churches in the First Christian Generation', in Bauckham, ed., *The Gospels for all Christians*, pp. 49–70, and L. Alexander, 'Ancient Book Production and the Circulation of the Gospels', in Bauckham, ed., *The Gospels for all Christians*, pp. 71–112.

[125] On the 'exegetical circularity' of such readings, especially in the relation to John's Gospel, see Dokka, 'Irony and Sectarianism', p. 90.

[126] This approach finds its antecedents in J. D. G. Dunn, 'Let John be John: A Gospel for its Time', in *Das Evangelium und die Evangelien* (WUNT 28; ed. P. Stuhlmacher; Tübingen: Mohr, 1983), pp. 309–39. Dunn pre-empts the reception-based approach by arguing that John should be read in its 'proper historical location', i.e. late-first-century Judaism. This striking essay and its methodological concerns have recently been further developed by Motyer, *Your Father*, and 'A New Start', pp. 84ff.

[127] Failure to address the question of connections between ideas and their immediate social environments represents a neglect of academic responsibility. For a vigorous defence of such approaches, see A. Baumgarten, *An Interpretation*, pp. 39ff. He concludes by citing Seneca, *Nat. Quaest.* 6.5.2: 'the person who hopes the truth can be found, and therefore dares to act accordingly, and does not cease to ask questions, is likely to make the greatest contribution to its discovery'.

social origins.[128] This section will therefore proceed to argue that the sectarian social thesis has neglected the Gospel's particular witness to a distinct social world, evident in its striking geographical focus on Judaea. It outlines the relative importance for the Gospel of this region, of Jerusalem and of Bethany. Indeed, it argues that the Gospel predominantly presents the Judaean social world from the perspective of an insider. In addition, it is demonstrated that although the Gospel is more often sidelined, even dismissed, in discussions of the New Testament's *ptōchoi*, it actually provides important insights into the nature of, and Jesus' concern for, the *ptōchoi*. These insights are complemented by reference to the Gospel's distinctive presentation of 'women', which, especially in contrast to Luke, gives them a voice that is positive and not stereotyped in character. This social witness, it will be argued, repeatedly possesses the stamp of Judaea's indigenous religious virtuosity and provides a credible social context within which we may understand the Gospel's striking ethical and eschatological dualism without recourse to the sectarian social thesis.

3.1   Judaea

The sectarian social thesis accounts for the Gospel's distinctiveness on the basis of a defining schism with late-first-century 'Judaism'. It is a paradox of such readings that when the Gospel is being read with reference to social history, it is the social history of a speculatively reconstructed Johannine community that is discussed. In contrast, the very particular social world, Judaea, which this sub-section will argue is the social focus of the Gospel's witness is simply ignored. This is despite the Gospel's claims to be an eyewitness account (1:14; 19:35; cf. 1 John 1:1–4 and 4:14). Indeed, the Gospel underlines the importance of historical witness (14:26; 16:4 and 20:31). These claims should not be too readily dismissed as the product of rhetorical flair or wilful deception. Rather, their credibility should be examined.

The frequency of the Gospel's references to, and evident familiarity with, Jerusalem and Bethany are indicative of a particular social witness, one which is qualitatively distinct from

---

[128] This enterprise, as Meeks has noted, produced the odd 'red herring', 'Breaking Away', p. 102. Nonetheless, whilst this is necessarily a tentative venture, such false starts should not be allowed to lead to a failure of nerve.

the Synoptic tradition. The credibility and consistency of this witness to the Judaean social world is clear. It is evident not only in local knowledge[129] but also in the numerous traditions particular to the Gospel, which are rooted in Judaea.[130] It displays an intimate knowledge of Jerusalem, the Temple, and its practices.[131] These details should not be dismissed too readily as simply reflecting the 'theological interests' of the evangelist vis-à-vis the Synoptic tradition.[132] Such details as the name of the High Priest's servant (18:10) or the note that Annas was the father-in-law of Caiaphas (18:13) cannot be easily classified as theological.[133] Rather these details suggest a particular witness distinct from that of the Synoptic tradition. Indeed, in John 4:43–5 Jesus' *patris*, 'homeland', appears to have become Judaea and not the Synoptics' Galilee.[134] In addition, the presentation of the *Ioudaioi*, whilst not wholly transparent or consistent, is most probably indicative of a particular

[129] Local knowledge extends well beyond that of the Synoptics: the Pool of Bethesda, the Pool of Siloam, Solomon's Portico, the Wadi Kidron, the High Priest's house, and the pavement 'Gabbatha'. See C. H. H. Scobie, 'Johannine Geography', *SRel* 11 (1982), 77–84, and the discussion of J. A. T. Robinson, *The Priority of John* (London: SCM, 1985), pp. 48–59. Also, on the original 'Jewish-Palestinian home' of the author of the Gospel, see Hengel, *The Johannine Question*, pp. 110f.

[130] Ruckstuhl, 'Mitglied der essenischen Mönchsgemeinde in Jerusalem', *BK* 40/2 (1985), 78, lists 3:1–2; 7:50–2; 19:39 (all Nicodemus, a member of the Jerusalem establishment); 5:2–9 (the miracle at Bethesda); 9:1–7 (the healing at Siloam); 10:22–3 (the feast of the Dedication of the Temple); 11:1–46 (the raising of Lazarus at Bethany); 11:55–7 (the Chief Priests and Pharisees inquire about Jesus' whereabouts); 18:1–3 (Jesus goes to the garden beyond the Kidron valley); 18:13–24 (the hearing before Annas); and 19:20–42 (details concerning the crucifixion and the tomb). See also Cullmann, *The Johannine Circle*, p. 66: 'the special interest in Judaea indicated by the selection of narratives suggests that he came from Judaea'.

[131] For example, the Gospel knows that Solomon's Portico was a sheltered spot in winter, 10:22–3, and that Jesus' self-identification as the 'light to the world', 8:12, took place in the Court of Women, 8:20, which was where the great candelabra lit during the feast of the Tabernacles stood. See further Motyer, "A New Start', pp. 88f. and Capper, 'With the Oldest Monks', pp. 11.

[132] L. Morris, *The Gospel according to John* (Grand Rapids: Eerdmans, 1995), p. 12.

[133] For these details, we have no authority other than John's, but as Barrett notes of Annas' relationship with Caiaphas: 'It is in itself entirely credible', *The Gospel according to St John* (London: SPCK, 1958), pp. 438. On such details in the Gospel, see further Burge, 'History', pp. 39f.

[134] The logic of the passage, in its Johannine context, seems to demand that Jesus' *patris*, the place of his rejection, is Judaea and not Galilee. See W. Meeks, 'Galilee and Judea in the Fourth Gospel', *JBL* 85 (1966), 165; Motyer, 'A New Start', p. 95; and J. M. Bassler, 'The Galileans: A Neglected Factor in Johannine Community Research', *CBQ* 43 (1981), 247f., *contra* R. E. Brown, *Community*, pp. 39–40.

ethnic awareness.[135] In this context it should be noted that the 'beloved disciple', the claimed source of these traditions (21:24), was most probably not one of the 'Twelve' but rather a 'Jerusalem disciple'.[136] He was most likely a former disciple of John the Baptist's Judaean ministry, the unnamed disciple at 1:35ff.[137] In addition, he appears to have had intimate knowledge of the High Priest's household (18:15–17).[138] Furthermore, he seems to have owned or at least had charge of premises in Jerusalem (19:27). It is here that he may have acted as host of the last supper, at which he reclines in the bosom of Jesus, the honoured guest (13:23). This position in the dining arrangements, as Capper, following Whiteley, has argued,[139] indicates that he was most probably the host. Capper also suggests the possibility, on the basis that Jesus places his mother in the care of the 'beloved disciple' (19:27) and she is then found at prayer in the upper room (Acts 1:12–14), that he was the *oikodespotēs*, 'master', of Luke 22:11 and Mark. 14:14. Whilst the Synoptic accounts of Jesus' last supper are from the perspective of the Galilean disciples and note their unfamiliarity with the location of the 'upper room', the Gospel's narrative appears to be told from the perspective of the *oikodespotēs*.[140]

[135] On the identity of the *Ioudaioi*, see J. H. Charlesworth, 'The Gospel of John: Exclusivism Caused by a Social Setting Different from that of Jesus (John 11:54 and 14:6)', in Bieringer et al., eds., *Anti-Judaism and the Fourth Gospel*, pp. 482ff. On the Gospel's distinctive perspective on Galilee and Samaria, see R. Karris, *Marginalized*, pp. 54–72. See further §2.2.1 above.

[136] On the 'beloved disciple' as a 'Jerusalem' disciple, see Capper, 'With the Oldest Monks', p. 3. Capper develops here Ruckstuhl's thesis that the beloved disciple was an Essene monk in Jerusalem: Ruckstuhl, 'Mönchsgemeinde in Jerusalem'. Capper is notably more circumspect in his assessment of the evidence and prefers to label the 'beloved disciple' a 'member of an ascetic religious quarter in Jerusalem'. Bauckham notes that he is 'not depicted as a Galilean disciple' and that this portrayal is restricted by virtue of its being the remembered career of a historical disciple: see 'Ideal Author', p. 43. Likewise Cullmann notes 'the fact that outside John 21, the "beloved disciple" only appears in narratives set in Judaea corresponds with the special interest of the *whole* Gospel in Judaea' (*The Johannine Circle*, p. 66). See also Hengel, *The Johannine Question*, pp. 124–6, and R. E. Brown, *Community*, pp. 31–4.

[137] On this identification, see Cullmann, *The Johannine Circle*, p. 71; R. E. Brown, *Community*, p. 34; Bauckham, 'Ideal Author', pp. 34f.; and Charlesworth, 'The Dead Sea Scrolls', p. 89.

[138] See R. E. Brown, *John (XII–XXI)*, p. 822. The disciple mentioned was, at the very least, a close associate of the 'beloved disciple': see Hengel, *The Johannine Question*, pp. 78–9, and Bauckham, 'Ideal Author', p. 34.

[139] See Capper, 'With the Oldest Monks', pp. 13f., following D. E. H. Whiteley, 'Was John Written by a Sadducee?', *ANRW* II/25, 3 (1985), 2494.

[140] Matt. 26:17–19, Mark 14:12–26, and Luke. 22:7–13; cf. John. 13:23.

The Gospel's distinct perspective is further evident in the evangelist's discussion of Bethany. In the Synoptic tradition Bethany is essentially an anecdotal location where Jesus 'spent the night' (Matt. 21:17; Mark 11:11) and where he was anointed by an anonymous 'woman' (Matt. 26:7; Mark 14:3, cf. John 12:1–8).[141] In contrast, the Gospel provides not only an explanatory parenthesis[142] (11:2) but also details from the perspective of the recipients of Jesus' visit (11:1–45). The account of the raising of Lazarus is full of emotional tension. Jesus' 'love' for Lazarus, Martha, and Mary is evident (11:5, 36), as is his inner turmoil. He was 'greatly disturbed,' and 'wept' (11:33, 35, 38). Further, whilst the narrative focus is on Jesus, it nonetheless repeatedly reflects Martha and Mary's local perspective and not that of the 'disciples' (11:21–32).[143] Bethany is not an anecdotal location but rather, as will be argued further in §3.3 below, takes a central position in the Gospel. It is clear that this Gospel displays a particular interest in Judaea, Jerusalem, the Temple, and its practices. It preserves particular personal details and narratives which are both rooted in Judaea and told from a local perspective, and in these respects its social witness appears to be qualitatively distinct from the Synoptic tradition.

3.2   The absent *ptōchoi*

In the previous chapters, we have noted that the prominence of the religious social actor within any given social world may influence the perceptions of poverty. In addition, research from the social sciences has been presented which highlights key elements of the social world that may prove highly suggestive for the emergence of virtuoso religion.[144] These elements have been shown to resonate clearly with the distinctive nature of first-century Judaea, and consequently virtuoso religion has proved to be a useful theoretical framework for the understanding of the New Testament's presentation of the *ptōchoi*, references to which are predominantly

---

[141] Luke's enigmatic accounts of Jesus' anointing, 7:36–50, and of Martha and Mary, 10:38–42, lack contextual rooting: see Shellard, *New Light*, p. 245. Shellard in discussing these passages notes how 'Luke's temporal and geographical references are often vague, especially when his sources are at odds.'

[142] On the Gospel's explanatory parentheses, see R. Bauckham, 'John for Readers of Mark', in *The Gospels for All Christians*, pp. 147–72.

[143] Indeed, the only one of the 'disciples' named is Thomas, and his input is an ironical prelude to Jesus' entering Bethany.

[144] See chapter 4, §2.

associated with Judaea. These observations suggest that the Gospel's prominent and particular Judaean witness, outlined in §3.1 above, may be of particular interest for the understanding of the ethos of the New Testament's *ptōchoi*. This is unfamiliar territory. The Gospel has predominantly been sidelined, even dismissed, as being of marginal significance for the discussion of poverty in the New Testament. This is despite the Gospel's portrayal of a blind beggar (9:1–41), rather than a Galilean fisherman, as an archetypal disciple. Indeed, the Gospel does make reference to the *ptōchoi* and typically provides a particular witness, which focuses on 'Bethany', the immediate context for the *ptōchoi*, and the 'upper room', an intimately Johannine context for community ethos. It will be argued in this sub-section that the relative absence, in relation to the Synoptic tradition, of overt discussion of the *ptōchoi* or adoption of the formulaic expressions discussed in chapter 4, §3.1f. above is indicative not of spiritual preoccupations but rather of an indigenous perspective which speaks not of the *ptōchoi* but from their immediate cultural milieu. However, before these areas are examined, the current consensus on the Johannine *ptōchoi* will be briefly addressed.

3.2.1   The neglect of the Johannine ptōchoi

The *ptōchoi* in the Gospel of John are apparently of little significance, if any, for the understanding of their place in the New Testament. Specialist treatments of 'Poverty in the New Testament' largely sideline, or even ignore, the Gospel's references.[145] This lack of interest is also evident in broader treatments of the Johannine tradition.[146] However, the neglect of the Gospel's 'poor' is not a universal phenomenon.[147] Liberation theologians

---

[145] See D. L. Mealand, *Poverty and Expectation* (London: SPCK, 1980), p. 13: 'the Fourth Gospel contains little material of direct relevance to this particular topic'; Schottroff and Stegemann, eds., *God of the Lowly*; Schottroff and Stegemann, *Hope*; B. Malina, 'Wealth and Poverty' (see chapter 4, §2 above); Hollenbach, *Defining Rich and Poor*; and Hamel, *Poverty and Charity*. Mealand's remark is typical of these specialist treatments, which either ignore or dismissively sideline the Johannine literature.

[146] In the major commentaries the references to the *ptōchoi* tend to be discussed in briefest of terms either in relation to the Synoptics or focusing on the role of Judas: see R. E. Brown, *John (I–XII)*, pp. 449f.; Lindars, *John*, pp. 412f.; and Morris, *John*, pp. 513f. No indication is given as to the possibility of a particular Johannine perspective on the *ptōchoi* or poverty more generally.

[147] See the summary of liberationist perspectives on the Gospel in T. Hanks, 'Poor, Poverty', *ABD* V, pp. 414–24.

have highlighted such distinctive elements as the homelessness of the incarnate Word (1:11, 46; cf. 14:2–3).[148] Indeed, Miranda argues on the basis of the close connection within the Johannine literature of love and justice that 'John's love is love of the deprived, the poor, the needy.'[149] This connection is demonstrated in 1 John 3:17–18: 'How does God's love abide in anyone who has the world's goods and sees a brother or sister in need and yet refuses help? Little children, let us love, not in word or speech, but in truth and action.'[150] In New Testament studies this thematic approach to the Gospel's 'poor' appears to have been addressed only by Karris, who argues that the apparent lack of material on the 'poor', in comparison to the Synoptics, results from a false comparison.[151] When the hermeneutical key becomes 'Jesus and the marginalised', Jesus' preferential option for the poor is clear.[152] This preferential option is apparent in the Gospel's concern for those marginalised economically,[153] religiously,[154] physically,[155] geographically,[156] and because of their gender.[157] Karris continues by attempting to relate the Gospel's concern for the marginal to its *Sitz im Leben*. He follows the consensus position, which locates the community in

---

[148] F. Herzog, *Liberation Theology* (New York, 1972), p. 53. See also S. Ryan, 'Jesus and the Poor in the Fourth Gospel', *Biblebhashyam* 4 (1978), 213–28, and J. Comblin, *Sent from the Father: Meditations on the Fourth Gospel* (Maryknoll, NY: Orbis Press, 1979).

[149] J. P. Miranda, *Being and the Messiah: The Message of St John* (Maryknoll, NY: Orbis Books, 1977), p. 95.

[150] Miranda's notably inclusive translation.

[151] *Marginalized*, pp. 17–21.

[152] *Ibid.*, p. 12.

[153] In John 12:5–8 Judas complains about Mary's action. He suggests that alms could have been given to the *ptōchoi*. In John 13:26–30 in the 'upper room' the disciples suggest that Judas has left to give alms.

[154] In John 7:40–52 reference is made to the crowd, which does not know the law' (verse 49), i.e. the marginalised in society, who are favourably contrasted with the religious leaders.

[155] In John 5:1–15 Jesus heals the man lame for thirty-eight years and at 9:1–41 the man blind from birth.

[156] The Samaritans of John 4:4–43 were clearly marginalised people, and Karris wishes to suggest that the royal official of John 4:44–53 was also marginalised because of his geographical, i.e. Galilean, antecedents. He argues that the evangelist is peculiarly redundant in mentioning Galilee in this passage five times and notes the plural 'you' in verse 48, which he suggests enables the royal official to typify the Galileans who seek the benefits of Jesus' signs. Finally, he complements this reading by highlighting how at 7:41 'Galilee' is a derogatory word on the lips of leaders from Judaea, implying geographical marginalisation: see *Marginalized*, pp. 62ff.

[157] E.g. John. 2:1–11; 11:1–12:8; 19:25–7; 20:1–18. The Gospel gives major prominence to women: see further the discussion in §3.3 below.

a post-Jamnian sectarian conflict with the synagogue.[158] However, he suggests that the Gospel's concern for the marginalised indicates that this conflict was about orthopraxy and not orthodoxy and that John's community was being excluded not for its christology but for its extension, following Jesus, of the 'elect' to the marginal in society.[159] The Gospel's presentation of Jesus' extension of God's revelation to the marginalised pertinently demonstrates its consequence, conflict with the religious authorities. These marginalised in turn serve as paradigms of behaviour for the persecuted community.[160] This reading of the *Sitz im Leben* is, however, highly problematic, for reasons acknowledged by Karris. The theme is acknowledged as being 'secondary', 'eclipsed', even 'quickly forgotten';[161] and further the Epistles, according to Karris, 'do not seem to shed significant additional light on the hypothetical life situation'.[162] Notwithstanding these reservations, Karris' highlighting of the marginalised in the Gospel and the greater appreciation of the Gospel's valuable historical witness[163] and its rootedness in Judaism,[164] particularly its resonance with themes emanating from Qumran,[165] indicate that the significance of the Gospel's *ptōchoi* is ready for reappraisal.

3.2.2   The ptōchoi and alms

In §3.1 above we noted that the Fourth Gospel displayed an insider's perspective on Bethany and Jerusalem. This Gospel's references to the *ptōchoi* exclusively occur within these particular contexts (12:5–8; 13:29). Two distinctive features are apparent: Jesus and his disciples gave alms (12:5, 13:29) and they held money in common (12:6; 13:29). It is regularly suggested that the

---

[158] *Marginalized*, p. 102. On the question of the Johannine sectarian identification see §2 above.

[159] *Marginalized*, p. 104. However, even if the significance of Jamnia is uncritically accepted, this reading sits more comfortably with the Gospel of Matthew than it does with John: see Davies and Allison, *Saint Matthew*, pp. 136–8.

[160] *Marginalized*, p. 105.

[161] *Ibid.*, p. 31.

[162] *Ibid.*, p. 106; cf. 1 John 3:17–18 cited above.

[163] On the Gospel's historical witness, see D. Moody Smith, 'Historical Issues and the Problem of John and the Synoptics', *From Jesus to John* (ed. M. C. de Boer; JSNTS 84; London: Sheffield Academic Press, 1994), pp. 252–67.

[164] See C. K. Barrett, *The Gospel of John and Judaism* (London: SPCK, 1975).

[165] On the relationship between the Johannine literature and Qumran, see Charlesworth, 'The Dead Sea Scrolls'. See further §2 above.

first of these features, that Jesus and his disciples gave alms, is nothing more than an expression of common Jewish piety at the time of the Passover.[166] However, this view, which originates from Jeremias, is problematic.[167] It is dependent upon a retrospective reading of M. Pes. 10.1, which prescribed that a poor man should not be given less than four cups of wine on Passover eve, even though he was supported from the daily distribution, the *tamchuy*.[168] Yet, as Seccombe has illustrated, comparison of M. Pes. 10.1 with 5.1, which describes what once happened in the Temple, demonstrates a clear difference in aspect. The former is prescriptive, describing what is to happen now and henceforth; the latter is descriptive of what once happened in the Temple.[169] Indeed, Seccombe convincingly argues that no rabbinic evidence confirms the presence of any such organised charity in Jerusalem in the New Testament period.[170] The almsgiving referred to in the Fourth Gospel (6:5–7; 12:5–8 and 13:29), whilst found in the general context of the Passover, does not take the form of the prescriptive acts found in Jeremias' late sources, which focus on the Temple gates and the home.[171] Besides 13:29 the references to alms occur outside the context of the Temple, in Bethany (12:5–8) and Galilee (6:5–7), and clearly have nothing to do with a host of a supper opening his house. Nonetheless, money and the Passover do appear to be significantly related in the Gospel. In the context of his first Passover, Jesus drives the money changers

---

[166] R. E. Brown, *John (XIII–XXI)*, p. 576, and Barrett, *John*, p. 374.

[167] J. Jeremias, *The Eucharistic Words of Jesus* (trans. N. Perrin; London: SCM Press, 1966), pp. 53f., and *Jerusalem*, pp. 131–4.

[168] On the *tamchuy*, see Jeremias, *Jerusalem*, pp. 131f.

[169] See further Seccombe, 'Charity', p. 141.

[170] Seccombe, 'Charity'. His argument is twofold. First, he re-examines Jeremias' key texts, M. Ket. 13.1-2, M. Pes. 10.1, and M. Shek. 5.6, and debates respectively the public nature of the charity; the period in which the prescription was effective; and the selective nature of the charity. Secondly, he notes the lack of any positive evidence for organised charity before AD 70 and cites material indicating the expressions of pity for the poor (not indicative of a situation of organised relief); the destitution of particular individuals; and the absence from the list of officers who served in the Temple of any mention of formal roles for the care of the destitute. The latter are especially notable by their absence in situations of emergency relief.

[171] *Eucharistic Words*, p. 54. He cites M. Pes. 9.11 and an Aramaic Passover saying from the ninth century to argue that it was not uncommon to invite someone from the street into one's home to share the meal with them. He also cites the report in Josephus that the Temple gates were opened at midnight on the Passover night and speculates that the beggars would congregate there, *Ant.* 18.29f.

from the Temple (2:13–25);[172] at his second, Jesus miraculously feeds the disciples and the crowd and challenges them to trust in him who provides food which truly satisfies (6:35), as opposed to money (6:7);[173] and at his last, the disciples ironically believe that Judas is giving something to the *ptōchoi* (13:1–30).[174] The Temple has become a market (2:16), but no money can buy the bread of life (6:35); the true gift to the *ptōchoi* at Passover is not money but rather Jesus himself (13:29).[175] Whilst a pattern is apparent which resonates with the Gospel's christological device whereby Jesus embodies particular dimensions of Jewish cultural practice,[176] the manner in which we are to understand the practice of the disciples' almsgiving is not. It is not unreasonable to assume that the references to almsgiving reflect particular cultural practice. Nevertheless, the question remains of how we are to understand this practice if the Passover context is unclear. This question will now be addressed.

3.2.3   *The ptōchoi and the common purse*

The second feature of the Gospel's reference to the *ptōchoi*, that they held their money in common, may assist in our understanding of the practice of almsgiving. The keeping of common funds is

---

[172] See R. Bauckham, 'Jesus' Demonstration in the Temple', in *Law and Religion* (ed. B. Lindars; London: SPCK, 1988), pp. 72–89, who argues that Jesus' attack was on the 'whole financial arrangements of the sacrificial system'.

[173] See Karris, *Marginalized*, p. 31.

[174] See R. A. Culpepper, *Anatomy of the Fourth Gospel* (Philadelphia: Fortress Press, 1983), p. 174, who makes explicit the Gospel's use of irony here.

[175] See Karris, *Marginalized*, pp. 22ff. He detects at 13:29 the possibility that the Gospel is responding directly to a post-Jamnian polemical context in which almsgiving has grown in prominence. However, the theme is perhaps too embedded to support a reading of the *Sitz im Leben* were such orthopraxy to have become such a prime issue.

[176] Especially evident in chapters 5–10: see R. E. Brown, *John (I–XII)*, pp. 543f., and Motyer, 'A New Start', p. 88. At the Sabbath Jesus performs works that only God can do at the Sabbath, 5:1–47; at the Passover Jesus gives bread replacing the manna of the Exodus, 6:1–71; at the Tabernacles Jesus figuratively replaces the water and light ceremonies of the feast, 7–9; and as the section starts at the sheep gate, 5:2, where the sheep were brought into Jerusalem for sacrifice, Jesus develops the theme of laying down his own life as the sheep gate and shepherd, 10:1–21; finally, at the Dedication Jesus is consecrated in place of the Temple altar, 10:22–39. Furthermore, this material reflects upon particular details of the Temple and Judaean cultural practices which are not present in the Synoptic tradition, e.g. Matt. 26:5; 27:15; Mark 14:1–2; 15:6; Luke 2:4–3; 22:1; cf. John. 2:23; 4:45; 5:1; 6:4; 7:2–14, 37; 10:22; 11:56; 12:12, 20; 13:1 and 29.

attested not only in the Bethany narrative (12:5–8) and in the upper room (13:29) but also at 6:5–7 in Philip's response to Jesus' question: 'Where shall we buy bread so that these people may eat?' Philip does not respond that they are poor disciples of a peripatetic teacher without resources but rather that two hundred denarii would be insufficient for the purpose. Is it credible that a small band of disciples would have such a resource at their disposal?[177] How are we to understand this common fund in cultural terms? Communal property under the charge of a defined individual was not a unique phenomenon. It was a defining feature of Essene community life, attested in all three first-century sources on the Essenes.[178] Indeed, the daily pooling of the celibates' wages appears to have been sufficient to provide both a frugal common table and the provision of alms to the destitute.[179] In the context of marrying communities, with limited monthly contributions from married Essenes, community life centred on a *beth-hacheber*, 'community house', which cared for, amongst others, 'the needy and the poor, and the elder who is bowed down' (CD 14.12–17).[180] Is this Essene practice a better context for understanding Jesus and the disciples' almsgiving? In the Gospel, we certainly have the appearance of common funds, which were in an individual's charge – in the hands of Judas.[181] Indeed, there is a certain coherence in the estimation that Judas held a formal role in the group. It was perhaps precisely because he held the funds that it is he who protested at Bethany (12:4–6) and that he had a place of honour near Jesus at the last

[177] The figure of two hundred denarii is often discussed in relation to an *individual's* earning potential as a day labourer and therefore considered to be a substantial sum of money: see D. A. Carson, *The Gospel according to John* (Cambridge, MA: Eerdmans, 1991), p. 269.

[178] Josephus, *BJ* 2 (122); *Ant.* 18 (20); Philo, *Hypothetica*, 10.4; *Quod. Omn.* 12.77; and Pliny, *Natural History* 5.15.73. See Beall, 'Essenes', p. 263.

[179] Josephus, *BJ* 2.8.6 (134): 'Two things are left to individual discretion, the giving of assistance and mercy. Members may on their own decision help the deserving, when in need, and supply food to the destitute; but gifts to relatives are prohibited, without permission of the managers.' On the economic activity of the celibate Essene, see B. J. Capper, 'The Church as the New Covenant of Effective Economics', *IJSCC* 2 (2002), 90 and 'The New Covenant', pp. 100–1.

[180] On the social function of the Essene community house, see Capper, 'Economics,' pp. 90–3, and 'The New Covenant', pp. 104–8. Note especially his calculations regarding the possible surplus generated by the pooling of community resources. These lend some credibility to the figure of two hundred denarii mentioned at 6:7.

[181] On the nature of the the *glōssokomon*, 'money box', 12:6; 13:29, see Barrett, *John*, p. 344. Barrett goes as far as to identify Judas as 'treasurer'.

supper (13:26);[182] and it lends plausibility to the disciples' conjecture at 13:27–9. However, the link with the Essenes goes beyond formal resemblance. In Bethany, we appear to have the location of an Essene community house.[183] The 'Temple Scroll' from Qumran prescribes that three villages to the east of Jerusalem should be set aside for those ritually unclean who could not enter the city (11QTemple 46.16–17). Bethany clearly corresponds with this prescription.[184] It is where we find Simon the leper (Matt. 14:3) and the infirm Lazarus (John 11; cf. Luke 10:38–42).[185] This identification is also confirmed by its etymology.[186] The village's name confirms its function. Jerome's *Onomasticon* defines its meaning as *domus adflictionis*, 'house of affliction', deriving the name from the Hebrew *beth 'anî* or the Aramaic *beth 'anyâ*, 'house of the poor' or 'house of affliction/poverty'. The modern semantic equivalent of *beth 'anyâ*, 'Bethany', is 'Poorhouse'.[187] This identification appears to locate Jesus' and the disciples' practice of holding funds in common and the giving of alms in a particular Judaean context in which such practice was clearly familiar. It is also interesting that the only place where concern for the *ptōchoi* is found on the lips of the disciples in the Gospels is Bethany (suggesting that the particular context caused their embarrassment).

The reference to a common fund and almsgiving is not limited to Bethany. It is also directly related to the upper room, the context of the last supper at 13:29. The intimate perspective

---

[182] See Whiteley, 'Sadducee', p. 2494. Whiteley argues on the basis of seating arrangements that if the guest of honour, Jesus, reclined in the 'bosom' of his host, the 'beloved disciple', and Peter was on his right, then this accounts for Peter's asking the 'beloved disciple' to ask Jesus who it was that was going to betray him. In this arrangement it makes sense that Judas, being 'the treasurer of the twelve, and therefore counting as third in precedence, after Jesus and Peter, was reclining in the third most honourable place to the left of his master'.

[183] On Bethany as the location of an Essene community house, see B. Pixner, 'Bethanien bei Jerusalem – eine Essener-Siedlung?', in *Wege des Messias und Stätten der Urkirche* (SBAZ 2; ed. R. Riesner; Giessen: Basel, 1994), pp. 208–18.

[184] See Y. Yadin, *The Temple Scroll*, Vol. I (Jerusalem: IEJ, 1983), p. 305, and Pixner, 'Essenes and Pharisees', pp. 220f.

[185] On the relation between John 11 and Luke 10:38–42, see Shellard, *New Light*, p. 243, n. 161.

[186] On the etymology of 'Bethany', see Capper, 'Economics', p. 96, and 'The New Covenant', pp. 108–11.

[187] Indeed, Capper speculates that because of its prime location, as the last station on the pilgrims' route to Jerusalem 'after crossing the river and taking the road through Jericho up into the highlands', it 'received its name because it was the Essene poorhouse *par excellence*', 'Economics', p. 97.

provided by the Gospel of this room and its key actors has already been touched upon in §2.1 above. The beloved disciple appears either to own or to have charge of these premises, and it is perhaps implicitly where he takes the mother of Jesus, with whose care he has been entrusted at the cross (John 19:25–7). Acts 1:12–14 locates the post-Easter disciples 'together with the women and Mary the mother of Jesus' (1:14) in the *hyperōon*, 'upper room' (1:13). It is from this context of 'prayer and petition' that the 'community of goods' of the first Jerusalem church emerges (Acts 2:42–7; 4:32–5:11 and 6:1–6).[188] Capper has demonstrated how the accounts of the structures of property sharing in Acts show some detailed resemblance to those prescribed by the Essenes.[189] However, once again the association does not end at the level of formal similarity. Contributions to the study of Essene history, including archaeological research, have suggested that the early Christian community in Jerusalem developed in the immediate vicinity of an ascetic or 'Essene' quarter.[190] It is striking that the only references to the *ptōchoi* in the Gospel occur in the contexts of Bethany, the 'house of the poor', and in the 'upper room', a location most probably found in the ascetic quarter of Jerusalem. It is likewise striking that in these particular contexts reference is made to a common fund and almsgiving. In addition in this Gospel's account of the last supper it is in the 'upper room' that Jesus takes the role of a *doulos*, 'slave', washing the disciples' feet (13:1–20), illustrating the total commitment of the new commandment of mutual love (13:33–4; 15:12–15). In these locations associated with a group, one of whose self-designations

---

[188] The connection of the Gospel's presentation of common funds and almsgiving with the practice in the Jerusalem church has not gone unnoticed. Bultmann remarks in a comment on 12:5–6: 'It is then presupposed that the disciple group receives and distributes gifts for the poor, hence perhaps the custom reflected in Acts 4:37', *The Gospel of John* (Oxford: Blackwell, 1971), p. 415, n. 8.

[189] Capper, 'Context' and 'Community'. Perhaps the most striking example set out by Capper is in relation to the apparent novitiate-style regulations governing the surrender of property in the community at Acts 5:3–4, cf. 1QS 6.18–20: see his '"In der Hand des Ananias". Erwägungen zu 1QS VI,20 und der urchristlichen Gütergemeinschaft', *RevQ* 12 (1986), 223–36.

[190] See E. Bammel, 'Sadduzäer und Sadokiden', *ETL* 55 (1979), 107–15; Pixner, 'Essenes and Pharisees', pp. 196–200; Riesner, 'Essener'; 'Josephus' "Gate of the Essenes" in Modern Discussion', *ZDMG* 105 (1989), 105–9; O. Betz and R. Riesner, *Jesus, Qumran and the Vatican* (London: SCM, 1993). On the nature of the label 'Essene' in relation to this quarter, see Capper, 'With the Oldest Monks', pp. 19–25. Capper advocates the label 'ascetic' on account of the rather narrow appropriation of 'Essene' in New Testament studies.

was 'the poor',[191] the 'servant' Jesus is anointed as a gift for the *ptōchoi*.[192] The references to the *ptōchoi* in the Gospel, rather than being of marginal significance, open a window on a cultural context in which both the piety of poverty and care for the poor as an expression of that piety were familiar elements within the social world.

3.2.4   The Judaean ptōchoi

In contrast to the Synoptics, the Gospel of John provides what might be termed an indigenous perspective on Judaea. This cultural context, in which the Essenes were a most prominent cultural force,[193] is highly pertinent for any reading of the New Testament's *ptōchoi*. The Essenes were esteemed because of their profound concern for the vulnerable;[194] one of their self-designations was the 'poor';[195] they understood that poverty was not solely economic but understood in terms of a total dependence upon God;[196] and they viewed salvation as the property of the in-group and no others.[197] It is notable that John's Gospel is unique in its discussion of the *ptōchoi* in presenting the disciples as conforming, in their operation of a common fund, to a 'major tenet' of Essene cultural practice.[198] It appears to speak from a community which, from its connections with the Baptist, Bethany, and the ascetic quarter, was clearly familiar, and most probably had close associations with, particular Essenes. It is also clear that the Essenes adopted the language of 'poverty', especially Isaiah 61, as an expression of their 'self-embodiment of the fulfillable word of God'.[199] In addition, they understood their community to function as an embodiment of a

---

[191] See chapter 3, §3.3.

[192] Capper, 'Economics', p. 98.

[193] On the scope of Essene cultural influence, see chapter 3, §3.3 Also, Hempel, 'Beyond the Fringes', p. 49.

[194] Concern for the vulnerable is clear on both the practical level of social organisation, CD 14.12–17, and the ideological level of enacting ideals of justice and righteousness, 1QH 5.21–2. On their care for the vulnerable, see further Capper, 'Two Types' and 'The New Covenant'.

[195] 1QH 18.14; 1QM 11.9; and 4QPs 37. See Hamel, *Poverty and Charity*, pp. 177ff.

[196] 1QS 9.23–6. See Hamel, *Poverty and Charity*, p. 184.

[197] See O. Betz, 'The Essenes', *CHJ III*, pp. 448–9, and J. A. Sanders, 'From Isaiah 61 to Luke 4', pp. 59–61.

[198] Beall, 'Essenes', p. 263.

[199] Flusser, 'Blessed'; Miller, 'Isa 61:1–2 in 11QMelchizedek', and J. A. Sanders, 'From Isaiah 61 to Luke 4', p. 59. See further chapter 4, §4.1, above.

new Temple.[200] Its rituals and daily activities became commensurate with the atoning sacrificial activities of the Sanctuary.[201] It is striking how the Gospel most associated with Judaea repeatedly portrays Jesus as *personally* embodying key elements of Judaean cultural landscape, most strikingly the Temple (2:19, 21).[202] The theological implications of the association of the body of Christ broken in death with that of the 'new Temple' 'are most clearly expressed' in the Johannine literature.[203] Worship is connected with the Spirit, which proceeds from Jesus (4:14): 'Thus Christ is shown to be the replacement for the old cultus and cult centre.'[204] The presentation of Jesus as the ultimate gift to the *ptōchoi* in the Essene quarter in Jerusalem appears to conform to this pattern. This is not simply a matter of Passover piety. It is in this context that Jesus takes on the role of a 'slave' (13:16), and it is the practice of such service that becomes the subject of the Gospel's makarism. Whilst in Matt. 5:3 and Luke 6:20 it is the *ptōchoi* who are the subjects of the first makarism, in John 13:17 it is those who follow Jesus' example of total submission. The Gospel's particular cultural perspective renders the Synoptics' prominent presentation of the *ptōchoi* redundant: see chapter 4, §3 above. The rhetorical force of blessing or proclaiming good news to the *ptōchoi* in a context in which such motifs are embedded in one's cultural identity is greatly diluted. Those who closely identify themselves with the *ptōchoi* live with expectations, such as those of the disciples of John the Baptist (Luke 7:22/Matt. 11:5),[205] which require particular treatment. The Gospel therefore provides a more indigenously conceived presentation of Jesus, which intimately addresses and embodies elements of the Essenes' piety of poverty. This presentation continues in 1 John, where the practice of almsgiving and a certain

---

[200] On the community's 'self-constitution as a new Temple', see B. Gärtner, *The Temple and the Community in Qumran and the New Testament* (Cambridge: Cambridge University Press, 1965), p. 114, and H. Eshel, 'Worship, Qumran Sect', *EDSS*, p. 995. Also P. R. Davies, *Sects and Scrolls*, pp. 56f. Davies makes the important and subtle point that it is not the case that the Temple was no longer effective but that its validity was restricted to the community. The community therefore constituted the true Temple.

[201] 1QS 8.8–9; 9.3–4.

[202] Note also the Sabbath (chapter 5), Passover (chapter 6), Tabernacles (chapters 7–10) and Dedication (chapters 10–12). See Motyer, 'A New Start', pp. 88f.

[203] See Gärtner, *The Temple*, p. 140, and his comparison of John's approach with that of the Synoptics.

[204] *Ibid.*, p. 119.

[205] See chapter 4, §3.1 above.

mutuality with regard to property are highly significant for community identity and clearly associated with the pattern of Jesus laying down his life. In 1 John 3:16f. the elder expressly links Jesus' laying down of his life with the quality of love amongst the 'brothers', which is to include mutuality with regard to property (verse 17).[206] Jesus' literally life-giving practice trumps all forms of indigenous piety and provides the pattern for the community's religious social practice.

3.2.5   Summary

It is clear that a closer examination of the Gospel's social witness, which is rooted in a particular Judaean milieu, does not require the location of its evident concern for the marginalised in a sectarian post-Jamnian context, *pace* Karris, where almsgiving following the destruction of the Temple has become a major concern.[207] Rather, the Gospel's concern for the vulnerable may be credibly accounted for in terms of the earliest witnesses' reflections on Jesus' ministry against the backdrop of indigenous forms of religious virtuosity. The Gospel does not speak as the Synoptic tradition does *of* the *ptōchoi*, but rather *from* their immediate cultural context. It provides, as I will now continue to argue, a unique witness to a stratum of early Christian social practice which stood in line with the historical reality of Judaean religious virtuosity. Indeed, it is such reflection on and engagement with indigenous virtuoso practices and not some defining social schism which account for the Gospel's distinctiveness vis-à-vis the Synoptic tradition.

3.3   The presence of 'women'

In the previous chapters, we have noted that where the religious social actor is prominent in the social world, perceptions of poverty and gender may vary from what apply elsewhere as cultural norms. In addition, in more specific circumstances religious social actors,

---

[206] To be like Jesus his followers must be merciful, especially towards the needy. S. S. Smalley notes the parallel with the practice of a community of goods in the early Jerusalem community, Acts 2:44–5; 3:26, *1, 2, 3 John* (Word Biblical Commentary; Waco, TX: Word Books, 1984), p. 198. The close association of the community of goods in Acts with both an Essene location and practice has already been highlighted: see §3.2.3 above.

[207] See §3.2.1 above.

i.e. the religious virtuoso, may become prominent in their social worlds. These circumstances have been demonstrated to resonate particularly with first-century Judaea, where the presence of such virtuosity was evident in the practices of the Essenes. It is against this background that we have been addressing the question of the Johannine social witness, which, it has been argued, is rooted in the Judaean social world. In contrast to the previous sub-section, which focused on the absence, relative to the Synoptic tradition, of this Gospel's *ptōchoi*, this sub-section highlights the relative prominence of the Gospel's 'women'. It starts by reviewing how the Synoptic tradition presents women as social actors and relates these observations to our previous discussions of women's roles in the first-century social world: see chapter 2, §4.2 above. It continues by arguing that the Gospel's portrayal of women as primary social agents is clearly distinct from the Synoptics' presentation. These qualitative differences, especially evident in comparison with Luke, raise the question of how the prominent roles attributed to women can be reconciled with the reception of women in the late-first-century church. The solution proposed in this sub-section is that the roles of these women are best understood not within the public world of the church's proclamation, but rather within the more private sphere of pious practices, practices that resonate with Judaea's indigenous forms of virtuoso religion. The very prominence of women points to such a particular social world, which in turn helps us to account for the Gospel's distinctiveness.

3.3.1   Synoptic 'women'

It has been claimed that in the Gospels' presentation of the ministry of Jesus, new religious roles for women are evident.[208] This is allegedly 'especially apparent' in Luke and reflects a late-first-century concern to stress the equality of women with men as objects of God's grace.[209] Indeed, Luke's women have become 'virtually emblematic' of Christian feminism, e.g. Mary and

---

[208] See R. Scroggs, 'Women in the New Testament', *IDB*, pp. 966–8; C. F. Parvey, 'The Theology and Leadership of Women in the New Testament', in *Religion and Sexism* (ed. R. R. Ruether; New York: Simon & Schuster, 1974), pp. 139–46; R. B. Edwards, 'Women', *ISBE*, IV, pp. 1089–97, and M. Alexandre, 'Early Christian Women', *HWW*, I, pp. 407–44.

[209] B. Witherington, 'Women', *ABD*, VI, pp. 957–61.

Elizabeth (1:33–56) and Martha and Mary (10:38–42).[210] However, the suggestion that the Synoptic tradition presents a radical revision of the roles of women depends upon the sort of stereotypical reading of the social world that secludes women within a private world of passivity and views women's discipleship, however limited, as ground-breaking.[211] Whilst it is clear that first-century women's social roles were predominantly limited, it is also clear, especially from inscriptional evidence,[212] that the potential nonetheless existed for them to participate in the social and religious lives of their communities.[213] This potential was most fully realised by the social elite, of whom we have evidence that they functioned as benefactresses,[214] and the religious social actor, evident amongst the Cynics, Therapeutae, and Essenes.[215] The presentation of women in the Synoptic tradition repeats this pattern. Their roles are predominantly orientated towards the private world of the household. They are wives,[216] mothers,[217] widows,[218] and mourners.[219] They are engaged in household activities,[220] or they are

[210] M. R. D'Angelo, 'Women in Luke–Acts: A Redactional View', *JBL* 109/3 (1990), 441.

[211] On the public/private division of the social world along gender lines, see Corley, *Private Women*, and the discussion in chapter 2, §4.2 above.

[212] E.g. the benefactress in Priene in the first century BC (*Pleket 5.G*), who dedicated at her own expense a cistern and the water pipes in the city: see Lefkowitz and Fant, *Women's Life*, p. 158.

[213] See the critical revisions of normative gender roles in R. S. Kraemer, 'Jewish Women and Christian Origins: Some Caveats', in *Women in Christian Origins* (ed. R. S. Kraemer and M. A. D'Angelo; Oxford: Oxford University Press, 1999), pp. 35–49; R. S. Kraemer, 'Beginning', pp. 50–79 in the same volume, and A.-J. Levine, 'Second Temple Judaism, Jesus and Women: Yeast of Eden', *BI* 2/1 (1994), 8–33. Also the discussion in chapter 3, §2.3 above.

[214] E.g. Flavia Publicia Nicomachias from Phocaea, Asia Minor, who is declared in a second century AD inscription (*Pleket 19.G*) as the people's 'benefactor, and benefactor through her ancestors, founder of our city, president for life … ': see *Women's Life*, p. 160.

[215] See Brooten, *Women Leaders*; Batten, 'More Queries for Q'; Lefkowitz and Fant, *Women's Life*; and for a particularly Judaean perspective see Crawford, 'Mothers, Sisters, Elders'.

[216] Matt. 5:27–30 and 19:3–9.

[217] Luke 1–2; Matt. 1:3, 5–6 and Matt. 12:49–50/Mark 3:31–5/Luke 8:19–21. On 'mothers', see further the discussion in §3.3.2 below.

[218] Luke 18:1–8 and Mark 12:41–4/Luke 21:1–4.

[219] Matt. 27:55–6/Mark 15:40–1/Luke 23:49.

[220] Matt. 13:33/Luke 13:20–1; Matt. 24:41/Luke 17:35; Matt. 25:1–13; Luke 8:1–3; 15:8–10. The form of *diēkonoun*, 'support', offered by women followers of Jesus in Luke 8:1–3 is perhaps best understood in terms of women's household activities rather than in terms of church office. Jesus includes under the term *diakonein* many different activities such as giving food and drink, extending shelter, providing

the silent,[221] and frequently passive, recipients of healing.[222] However, when women are neither silent nor passive their witness is doubted,[223] their words corrected,[224] and their actions censured by the disciples, leading to Jesus' intervention, intervention affirming not so much a change in gender status as the individual's expression of faith.[225] The notable exceptions are the occasional appearances of elite women[226] and the specialised religious social actor.[227] Indeed, this initial survey of women's roles appears not to stress their equality with men but rather underlines the prevalent social reality that they were 'seen but not heard'.[228] In addition, as will now be illustrated by a more detailed discussion of Luke's most developed female characterisation, Martha and Mary (10:38–42), far from presenting a liberating perspective Luke's redactional interests appear to advocate the maintenance of such social order. Furthermore, this order appears to conform to the censure of

clothes, and visiting the sick and prisoners, as in Matt. 25:42–4, all of which are not gender-specific but may more generally be understood as tasks undertaken by women, especially women of means, e.g. Joanna. Indeed, it was not unparalleled for women to support Rabbis out of their means: see B. Witherington III, 'On the Road with Mary Magdalene, Joanna, Susanna and Other Disciples – Luke 8, 1–3', *ZNW* 70 (1979), 243–8. Also R. Bauckham, *Gospel Women: Studies of the Named Women in the Gospels* (London: T&T Clark, 2002), pp. 109–202, esp. 110–21. Bauckham notably exposes the problem with domesticating women's service in this passage; however, his arguments do not preclude their household orientation. Notably, the forms of 'patronage' or 'benefaction' (see his discussion, pp. 161–5) evident in the early churches necessarily take place in household contexts in which women have prominent roles.

[221] Matt. 9:22/Mark 5:31–4/Luke 8:48.

[222] Matt 8:14–15/Mark 1:29–31/Luke 4:38–9; Matt. 9:18–26/Mark 5:21–43/Luke 8:40–56; Luke 4:36; 13:11–17.

[223] Matt. 27:61–28:17/Mark 15:47–16:11/Luke 23:55–24:12, 22–4.

[224] Luke 11:27–8.

[225] E.g. Matt. 15:21–8; cf. Mark 7:24–30. It is notable that this woman, probably the most forthright of the Synoptic tradition, is not a Jew: cf. the forthright Samaritan woman in John 4:4–42. In addition, she is clearly censured in Matthew, where her setting is public, but in Mark, where the dialogue occurs in private, in a house, no such censure is present. Furthermore, her witness is totally absent from the more 'orderly' Luke. See Kraemer, 'Caveats', p. 40. Also Matt. 26:1–6/Mark 14:3–9/ Luke 7:36–50; cf. John 12:1–8, where the woman is named and her actions praised, as opposed to her sins being forgiven. On the relationship between these narratives, see B. Shellard, 'The Relationship of Luke and John: A Fresh Look at an Old Problem', *JTS* 46/1 (April 1995), 71–97, and *New Light*, pp. 243f.

[226] Matt. 14:3–12/Mark 6:17–29/Luke 3:19–20 and Matt. 27:19.

[227] Luke 1; cf. Mark 12:41–4/Luke 21:1–4. On Anna, see R. Bauckham, *Gospel Women*, pp. 77–107. On the 'pious widow', see the discussion in chapter 4, §3.3.1 above.

[228] J. Dewey, 'Women in the Synoptic Gospels: Seen but Not Heard?', *BTB* 27 (1997), 53.

women's roles evident in relation to the emergence of the first public congregations (1 Cor. 14:34–5 and 1 Tim. 2:11–12).[229]

It has been argued that Luke's account of Martha and Mary, 10:38–42, highlights the liberation of women from their previous domestic roles and affirms their position as disciples. Indeed, Parvey has described the passage as the 'keystone of the changed status of women'.[230] This reading rests on two primary assumptions. These are that female discipleship was a new cultural phenomenon and that Mary's discipleship sets her free from a domestic setting. However, whilst it was not common for women to operate as religious social actors in the first-century social world, it was certainly not a unique phenomenon: see further chapter 2, §4.2 above. In addition, the latter assumption, which seeks to present Mary's discipleship as liberation from the domestic setting, fails to address the large number of textual variants associated with this pericope.[231] Within these, it is possible to generate both domestic and more neutral readings of the context. The end of verse 38 is textually uncertain and may either include or exclude the phrase 'into her house'. There are no apparent reasons for a deletion, suggesting that it is an addition,[232] which notably serves to domesticate the text. Martha no longer welcomes Jesus into the public world of the village. Rather she welcomes him into the private world of her home. This is in stark contrast to John 11:1–44, where Martha 'went out to meet him, but Mary stayed at home' (11:20). The following verse, Luke 10:39, also has a significant variant, which excludes a relative pronoun that strips Martha of her student role; an inclusive translation would read: 'And Martha had a sister Mary *who also* having sat at the feet of Jesus…'[233] The last two verses have as many as six different variants, which have nearly all found scholarly support.[234] It is possible within these to present either a domestic setting, referring to the

---

[229] See Capper's section on 'The transition of worship to public space and the exclusion of women from public leadership in second generation Christianity' in his 'Public Body', pp. 136–43. Also F. Cardman, 'Women, Ministry, and Church Order in Early Christianity', in Kraemer and D'Angelo, eds., *Women in Christian Origins*, pp. 300–29.

[230] Parvey, 'Women', p. 141.

[231] On the textual variants, see Nolland, *Luke*, Vol. II, p. 600.

[232] See Marshall, *Luke*, p. 451.

[233] See D'Angelo, 'A Redactional View', p. 454.

[234] See Marshall, *Luke*, pp. 452f.; Fitzmyer, *Luke*, pp. 894f.; and A. Baker, 'One Thing Necessary', *CBQ* 27 (1965), 127–35.

number of 'dishes' required for a meal, or a more neutral context where simply one 'thing' is necessary. Furthermore, it is possible from these variants to construct a number of readings. Martha may be read as a high-status woman,[235] who, having sat at Jesus' feet, welcomes him into the village where she is involved in some form of community responsibility,[236] activities into which she seeks to draw Mary. This action prompts Jesus' affirmation of Mary's silent listening. Alternatively, Martha may be read as welcoming Jesus to her home and, being preoccupied with domestic activities, seeking to engage Mary's assistance, actions which lead to Jesus' correction – only one 'dish' is necessary – and to the affirmation of Mary's silent listening.[237] Significantly, the common features of these readings conform to the previous presentation of women's roles in the Synoptics, which predominantly have women's speech corrected and their silent listening affirmed.[238] Indeed, neither reading appears particularly ground-breaking for female roles.[239] Mary's liberation is clearly not as radical as Parvey would have us believe. Indeed, the passage is a literary construction in which Martha and Mary appear to be reduced to the role of ciphers.[240] Nonetheless,

---

[235] 'Martha' is a female form of the Aramaic noun *mare*, 'lord': see Fitzmyer, *Luke*, p. 893.

[236] Such a reading would argue that the Greek noun *diakonian* had a technical sense in the early church, which not only extended to ritual-meal table service but also to ecclesiastical leadership – cf. Acts 6:1–6 – and that Luke would not have been ignorant of such resonant meaning. See J. E. Via, 'Women, the Discipleship of Service and the Early Christian Ritual Meal in the Gospel of Luke', *SLJT* 26 (1985), 44; cf. Nolland, *Luke*, Vol. II, p. 604.

[237] E.g. J. Collins, 'Did Luke Intend a Disservice to Women in the Martha and Mary Story?', *BTB* 28/3 (1998), 104–11.

[238] NB: it is Martha's 'concern' that is the subject of correction: her practice is not criticised, but her self-perception is: cf. Luke 22:24–7, However, such a comparison is undermined by the domestication of the text.

[239] E. Schüssler-Fiorenza observes: 'Mary ... is the *silent* woman, whereas Martha, who argues in her own interest, is *silenced*', *But She Said: Feminist Practices of Biblical Interpretation* (Boston, MA: Beacon Press, 1992), p. 62. Also the more nuanced T. K. Seim, *The Double Message: Patterns of Gender in Luke–Acts* (Edinburgh: T&T Clark, 1994), pp. 116f.

[240] The antitheses which readings of this pericope frequently set up reduce them to theological principles or types rather than treating them as historical social actors. E.g., Martha represents justification by works to Mary's justification by faith; almsgiving to prayer; Judaism to Christianity; synagogue to church; world to spirit. In addition, structural analysis of the pericope appears to support this understanding. The contrasts set up are constant and clear: speaking to listening, movement to rest, argument to receptivity, openness to purposefulness, agency to passivity, and rejection to better choice. However, it is an error to talk on this basis of Luke having a particular agenda, either pro- or anti-female roles: see Seim, *The Double Message*, p. 249.

it does appear that Luke's 'pairing' of male and female narratives is indicative of a particular redactional interest in the place of women, which most probably serves as a catechetical device.[241] The women in Luke serve as examples for the Gospel's readers, who not only illustrate to women their proper place but also to the outside world that within the Christian world good order is maintained (cf. 1Cor. 14:34–5 and 1Tim. 2:11–12).[242]

3.3.2   Johannine 'women'

The Johannine women, upon initial examination, appear to conform to the pattern of female roles identified in the Synoptic tradition. They are all presented in typical female locations, at a wedding (2:1–12), at a well (4:4–42), at a meal (12:1–8), and in the context of mourning (11:1–44; 19:25–7 and 20:1–2, 11–18). However, unlike the Synoptic tradition, there is only one silent woman, Mary, wife of Clopas (19:25),[243] and only one anonymous woman, the Samaritan at the well (4:4–42). Indeed, besides Mary, wife of Clopas, all the Gospel's women are fully rounded characters, each with an individual voice.[244] Whilst they are subject to male correction and comment (2:4; 4:27; 12:7), their consistently positive portrayal is dramatically underlined by comparison with their male counterparts, who are presented as being deficient in perception (3:10; 16:18), hypocritical (12:4–6), conceited (13:37), inconsistent (13:38; 16:31–2), even thoroughly evil (13:2, 27–30). Indeed, such is the Johannine women's qualitative distinction from the Synoptics that a number of studies have sought specifically to understand this distinct feature of the Gospel.[245] It has been

---

[241] See D'Angelo, 'A Redactional View', p. 447.

[242] If Luke's Jesus liberates women from anything, he liberates them from demonic possession, 4:39, 8:2–3, 13:10–13: see S. Davies, 'Women in the Third Gospel and the New Testament Apocrypha', in *'Women Like This'* (ed. A.-J. Levine; Atlanta, GA: Scholars Press, 1991), p. 187, and Kraemer, 'Caveats', p. 46: 'Luke–Acts ... may prefer to represent women around Jesus as marginalized women to minimize women's stature within early Christian Churches.'

[243] On the identity of Mary, wife of Clopas, see Bauckham, *Gospel Women*, pp. 203–33.

[244] See S. M. Schneiders, 'Women in the Fourth Gospel and the Role of Women in the Contemporary Church', in *The Gospel of John as Literature* (ed. W. G. Stibbe; Leiden: Brill, 1993), p. 129, and Karris, *Marginalized*, p. 74: 'John's Gospel is unique in the amount of space he gives to and in the stories he tells about women.'

[245] See Karris, *Marginalized*, pp. 73f. On the literature's relation to contemporary standards of testimony, see R. G. Maccini, *Her Testimony is True* (JSNTS 125; Sheffield: Sheffield Academic Press, 1996).

suggested by Brown that their presence is a part of the evangelist's antipathy towards church orders. They are simply examples of the importance of obedience to God's word, obedience that they exemplify.[246] Alternatively, Schneiders argues that their portrayal is directed against male traditionalist antipathy towards women's active participation within the community.[247] Conversely, Karris contends that the address is focused outside the community, that the Johannine heroines are designed to illustrate to potential converts the roles which women may enjoy.[248] It is clear that these discussions, besides attempting to understand the Johannine women, have also been struggling with contemporary questions of the role of women in the church.[249] This has perhaps drawn the focus of study away from these women's potential to provide insight into the Gospel's particular social witness, and onto attempts either to affirm or to deny particular forms of ecclesiastical offices, e.g. the apostleship of the Samaritan woman and Mary Magdalene.[250] In contrast, the following discussion attempts first to understand their social witness.

The Gospel's distinct social witness is clearly evident in its presentation of women. This is first observed with Jesus' 'Mother' (2:1–12 and 19:25–7). Her particular significance has, however, been somewhat eclipsed by concerns for her symbolic and theological content.[251] Nonetheless, the Gospel's accounts of Jesus' 'Mother' do provide a distinct social perspective. We learn that at the cross she is committed to the 'disciple whom Jesus loved' (19:26–7). It has already been noted that this disciple most probably owned, or at least had charge of, premises located in the ascetic quarter of

---

[246] *Community*, p. 186.

[247] 'Women', p. 142.

[248] *Marginalized*, pp. 75f. Similarly, B. Witherington III, 'Women', *ABD*, who argues that 'at the end of the 1st century AD the role of women in the Christian community was probably still being debated, and in order to further the teaching of Jesus ... the Fourth Evangelist has presented various women as models'.

[249] Whilst Brown's discussion emerged from his preparations for the Pontifical Biblical Commission in April 1975, Schneiders' chapter directly addresses the 'Role of Women in the Contemporary Church'. On the Gospel as the focus of the first attempts to 're-read the gospels in search of authority and more treatment of women', see M. R. D'Angelo, '(Re)Presentations of Women in the Gospels: John and Mark', in Kraemer and D'Angelo, eds., *Women in Christian Origins*, p. 131.

[250] On the distorted focus of many such discussions, see Kraemer, 'Caveats', pp. 36f.

[251] E.g. Schneiders, 'Women', pp. 128f., who denies that any social significance can be discerned from her presentation since her role is allegedly necessarily 'unique to her or universal'.

Jerusalem where the disciples gathered for the last supper.[252] It is in this location that in Acts 1:14 we find her with the 'women' devoting themselves to prayer. In addition, the title 'Mother' used repeatedly of her (2:1, 3, 5, 12; 19:25, 27) – a form of reference particular to John – was also adopted as a title of authority in communities which made use of the Qumran literature (4QD^e).[253] Indeed, the role of the 'Mother' in such communities most probably involved the organisation of the forms of social relief that are also in evidence in the earliest communities of Acts, especially the care of widows (cf. Acts 6:1–6 and 9:36–43).[254] The combination of this location,[255] practice, and language appears to suggest strongly an actual rather than symbolic group to which Jesus' 'Mother' is entrusted, one in which she perhaps has the position of 'Mother'. The adoption of a designation rooted in the forms of fictive-kinship social organisation evident in the practice of Judaean virtuosity is perhaps also evident in the presentation of Mary Magdalene (20:1–2, 11–18). The distinctive element of her social witness is not so much the fact that she was 'sent' and believed (verse 17) as those to whom she was sent.[256] In Matt. 28:1–8 and Mark 16:1–8 she is sent to the 'disciples', and in Luke 24:9–10 she is sent to the 'eleven' and the 'apostles'. In contrast in John's Gospel she is sent by Jesus to the *adelphous*,'brothers' (20:17), a designation which clearly implies the 'disciples' of the following verse. The choice of this language is of interest since it is not only one of the first self-designations of the Jerusalem community (Acts 1:15, 16; 6:3) but also an integral designation for the Johannine self-understanding (21:23; 1 John 2f. and 3 John 5–6).

However, perhaps the most striking social witness is that of the *adelphai*, 'sisters', Martha and Mary (11:1–44 and 12:1–8).

---

[252] See §3.1 above.

[253] See the discussion in Crawford, 'Mothers, Sisters, Elders'.

[254] See Capper and his description of women's roles in Essene communities: 'Though these elderly women did not have the same authority in the community houses as the elderly men, some (if not all) probably had particular roles in the tutelage of young girls taken in by the centre', 'The New Covenant', p. 103. Also B. B. Thurston, *The Widows: The Women's Ministry in the Early Church* (Minneapolis: Fortress Press, 1989).

[255] It is also not insignificant that the other location associated with Jesus' 'Mother' is Cana, a location which is introduced in the Gospel by reference to Nathaniel's piety, 1:47–51, and facilities for the observance of ritual purity, 2:6. It is typically for the Gospel a location unparalleled in the Synoptics.

[256] On the 'apostolic' witness of Mary, see M. R. D'Angelo, 'Reconstructing "Real" Women from Gospel Literature: The Case of Mary Magdalene', in Kraemer and D'Angelo, eds., *Women in Christian Origins*, pp. 105–28.

The picture painted of these women is far removed from the Synoptics' anonymous anointing (Matt. 26:7/Mark 14:3, cf. Luke 7:38) and Luke's catechetical illustrations (10:38–42). The Gospel's narratives are marked by their intimacy: anonymity is uncovered (11:2) and 'secret' meetings revealed (11:28). We are told that Martha and Mary are 'loved' by Jesus (11:5), a distinctive designation for the Johannine literature, which defines those who have and keep Jesus' commandments (14:21), a practice that serves to designate the 'brothers' (1 John 2f.).[257] Besides this designation the Gospel provides an insight on the nature of their *diakonia*, 'service' (12:2; cf. Luke 10:40). Martha, along with her 'sister', appears to be caring for their sick 'brother' in Bethany, a location which we have already noted was particularly associated with the Essenes' care for the needy (see §3.2.3 above). In this capacity, they 'send' for the healer Jesus (11:3), a request to which he responds at some personal risk (11:8). When Jesus is reported to be arriving, Martha goes out to meet him (11:20), evidently outside the village (11:30). She appears to be a formidable woman with social leverage such that she is mentioned first in the list of those whom Jesus 'loved' (11:5).[258] Whilst Mary appears less forthright, she too appears to be of sufficient social stature to have access to the costly 'pistic nard' used to anoint Jesus (12:3). Indeed, Capper characterises Mary as a 'wealthy woman, a member of the Jerusalem elite and patron of Bethany, the poorhouse nearest to Jerusalem'.[259] The high status of these women is perhaps confirmed by their close association with the *Ioudaioi*, 'Jews', 11:31, who are sometimes associated in the Gospel with the Jerusalem elite (18:14;

---

[257] Indeed, D'Angelo has identified numerous female pairings in the New Testament and argued on this basis that their 'sisterhood' may represent a 'shared commitment to mission' rather than a blood relationship, *ibid.*, p. 108; 'Women Partners in the New Testament', *JFSR* 61 (1990), 77–81. Although I do not share her emphasis on 'mission', her discussion is nonetheless an important corrective to readings which automatically assume a blood relationship for 'sisters' whilst remaining open to readings of 'brothers'. Perhaps a reading of 'co-workers' would placate Bauckham's reticence: see *Gospel Women*, pp. 213f.

[258] The observation that Martha is a female form of the Aramaic noun *mare*, 'lord', seems in these circumstances to be of some relevance. See Seim, *The Double Message*, p. 98.

[259] 'The New Covenant', p. 113. Here he also elaborates on the context by arguing, following Daube, that the 'beautiful work' of the Marcan parallel, 14:6–8, functioned as a technical term for an act of charitable work: see *The New Testament and Rabbinic Judaism* (London: Arno Press, 1973), pp. 315–16. It is likely that such an elite status figure would have stood outside the inner circle of the pious poor, as sponsor or patron, and therefore would not have called herself *ptōchos*.

cf. 11:47–53; 19:12–15).[260] It is also apparent in their ability to challenge Jesus with a degree of impunity only apparent in the Synoptics with the elite and the religious social actor (11:21, 32, 39; cf. §3.3.1 above).[261] What makes this episode stand out, though, is not the idiosyncratic Johannine designations, or the forthright nature of their social practice, but rather Martha's presentation in relation to the Johannine literature's theological preoccupations. This perhaps suggests that her practice of care, along with her 'sister', for her 'brother', was not simply an expression of sibling concern but is indicative of a more established pattern of behaviour in Bethany, the house of the poor. Her confession of faith, 'I believe that you are the Christ, the Son of God, the one coming into the world' (11:27), is the most complete christological confession in the Gospel (cf. 20:31).[262] Indeed, this confession not only occurs in a literary context which stresses key Johannine themes – Jesus' delay,[263] his humanity[264] and the importance of belief[265] but also functions as a proleptic climax to the Gospel itself.[266] Its extra-ordinary nature is underlined when it is compared with Peter's confession of Jesus as the 'holy one of God' (6:69). This confession lacks the central place it has in Matt. 16:16 and Mark 8:29,

[260] See the discussion of the 'Jews' in §2.2.1 above.

[261] Jesus' observations at 11:40 do not address Martha's practice or preoccupations but rather reflect upon her understanding of her confession. His words are tame in comparison with those used to correct Peter following his confession, Matt. 16:23/Mark 8:33.

[262] Maccini, *Testimony*, p. 149.

[263] The climax of the narrative, the resurrection of Lazarus, is repeatedly delayed: by Jesus, 11:6, by Martha, 11:39, and again by Jesus, 11:41. Delay defines the plot. Likewise, delay appears to be a primary concern for the community. This is evident in teaching on the Paraclete and the emphases on witness, and that which was from the beginning, 1 John 1:1; 2:7, 13, 14, 24; 3:8, 11; 2 John 5, 6.

[264] The narrator gives both internal psychological and external physical perspectives on Jesus. These range from the physical reality of his presence, 'feet', 11:32, to his emotional reality: 'greatly disturbed', 'wept', and 'again greatly disturbed', 11:33, 35, 38. The physical reality is further underlined by reference to Jesus' journey to Lazarus, which is defined in terms of separation: Jesus is outside Judaea, 11:8, 16, outside Bethany, 11:17–37, and outside the tomb, 11:38. Lazarus' death is at least partly attributed to this separation, 11:21, 32. It is striking that it is in the context of the highest christological confession and Jesus' most dramatic miracle that his humanity is also stressed. This clearly resonates with the christological debates within the Epistles that are key to community identity: see Smalley, *1, 2, 3 John*, pp. xxiiif.

[265] E.g. John 20:31; cf. 1 John 5:13, also 1 John 3:23. On Johannine stress on 'belief', see R. E. Brown, *John (I–XII)*, pp. 512f.

[266] On the narrative functioning as both a coping stone on the series of signs and the beginning of Jesus' journey to his death and resurrection, see Lindars, *John*, p. 383.

a position that has now been accorded to Martha. It is sandwiched between an account of 'many disciples' leaving Jesus on account of his christological claims (6:60–6) and the prediction of betrayal from within the 'Twelve' (6:67–71). The only other use of the title 'holy one of God' in the New Testament is by the demon possessed (Mark 1:24 and Luke 4:34). This hardly represents a clear affirmation of Peter, or the Twelve.[267] In the location where Jesus is anointed as the true gift to the *ptōchoi*, Martha confesses the faith of the 'brothers' (21:23).

There does appear, however, to be a particular anomaly in the Gospel's presentation of women, the anonymous Samaritan at the well, 4:4–42.[268] Initially the narrative displays some formal resemblances with the Synoptic accounts of a forthright foreign woman (Matt. 15:21–8 and Mark 7:24–30), although typically for the Gospel, the portrayal is qualitatively distinct.[269] In Matthew and Mark the woman initiates the contact, seeks healing, and is rebuked by the disciples (Matt. 15:23), whilst in John the contact is initiated by Jesus, the woman does not request healing, and the disciples' rebuke is unspoken (4:27). The pattern we have identified in relation to female roles in the social world suggests that unchecked public roles are most appropriately understood to have been adopted by either the elite or the religious social actor. The Samaritan woman's activity, a simple practical errand, shows that she is not an elite figure. She is found at a 'well' (4:6), a household setting on the margins of the public world from which she clearly enters the 'city' to speak to 'men' (4:28–30). This portrayal requires some explanation. In this context the passage's repeated adoption of the language and symbolism of marriage is of particular interest for the understanding of the Johannine social witness (4:6, 15–18; cf. 3:39). The symbolic resonance of a single man at Jacob's well initiating a conversation with a woman clearly sets up the expectation of Jesus' impending betrothal. It clearly reflects the betrothal scenes found in the Pentateuch in which a betrothal is initiated when a foreign man meets with a woman at a well outside a town

[267] Martyn, *History*, pp. 124f., and R. E. Brown, *Community*, pp. 28f. Both suggest that the episode represents the separateness of the apostolic group from the evangelist's.

[268] Indeed, such is the anomalous character of this passage, especially its location in Samaria and the confession 'Saviour of the world', 4:42, that it is considered to reflect not the ministry of the historical Jesus but the 'history of the Johannine community'. See, e.g., Schneiders, 'Women', p. 132.

[269] On the similarity, see Kraemer, 'Caveats', p. 40.

(Gen. 24:10–52; 29:1–10 and Exod. 2:15–20). Instead, following Jesus' self-revelation (4:26) the woman leaves her water jar (4:28) and brings the Samaritan men to 'belief' through her 'word' (cf. 17:20). Her actions are characterised as sowing the seed for apostolic harvest (4:35; cf. Matt. 9:35–8).[270] Just at the moment one would expect betrothal, the woman is portrayed as displaying insight into Jesus' identity (4:19; cf. 3:10). Indeed, at the moment of expected closure her marital status is rendered meaningless in comparison to her task of proclamation. Her practice of bringing others to belief, to birth from the Spirit,[271] provides an alternative to the female practices of birth from the flesh and child-rearing. Rensberger is surely correct in his observation that 'The woman's relationship with Jesus thus becomes a metaphor for his "betrothal" to the believer'.[272] This raises the question of how such a betrothal may have been understood within the Judaean social world. Whilst the idea of a 'bride of Christ' initially appears anachronistic in terms of Jesus' historical ministry, there are indications of the possibility of such female roles in the practices of the Essenes.[273] In 4Q502 we have a liturgical text 'intended to accompany the entrance of youths into the Yachad when they came of age'.[274] The question of the exact nature of this text has not yet been settled.[275] Nonetheless, it is clear that it is a liturgical work designed for a joyous occasion of thanksgiving in which different members of the group participate, including the 'daughter of truth'.[276] This liturgy has notably been characterised as a 'Rituel de Mariage',[277] an identification which has not received universal acceptance since it apparently runs counter to celibate characterisation of the Qumran community.[278]

---

[270] R. E. Brown, *Community*, pp. 188f.

[271] Cf. 3:3–8; also 1:12–13 and 6:63.

[272] 'Asceticism', p. 142.

[273] See L. B. Elder, 'The Woman Question and Female Ascetics among the Essenes', *BA* 57 (1994), 230–2.

[274] E. Cook, 'A Liturgy of Thanksgiving', in *The Dead Sea Scrolls: A New Translation* (ed. M. Wise, M. Abegg, and E. Cook; New York: HarperCollins, 1996), pp. 407–8.

[275] See the discussion in Crawford, 'Mothers, Sisters, Elders', pp. 180f.

[276] A female equivalent of the 'Sons of Truth', 1QS 4.6; see J. Baumgarten, '4Q502, Marriage or Golden Age Ritual?', *JJS* 34 (1983), 128.

[277] M. Baillet, *Qumrân Grotte 4 III (4Q482–4Q520)* (DJD 7; Oxford: Clarendon, 1982), pp. 81–104, tentatively supported by J. R. Davila, *Liturgical Works* (Eerdmans Commentaries on the Dead Sea Scrolls, 6; Grand Rapids, MI, 2000), p. 184.

[278] On the question of celibacy at Qumran, see E. Qimron, 'Celibacy in the Dead Sea Scrolls and the Two Kinds of Sectarians', in *The Madrid Qumran Congress* (ed. J. Trebolle Barrera and L. Vegas Montaner; Leiden: Brill, 1992), pp. 287–94.

However, this characterisation of the liturgy does not necessarily exclude the possibility of celibacy, which we know to have been a feature of the Essenes, and may provide a context for understanding the Johannine presentation of the Samaritan woman.[279] Whilst it is necessarily somewhat speculative, it is nonetheless credible to imagine that the entrance of the 'daughter of truth' into the community was characterised as a spiritual marriage and that this language was part of the indigenous cultural landscape of the fourth evangelist. The Gospel, as we have already noted, frequently embodies indigenous forms of cultic symbolism and practice, and this may well account for the distinctive presentation of the woman as a 'bride of Christ'. It is not merely a Gospel in which women are unusually prominent, but also one in which Jesus' first miracle was at a wedding (2:1–11). Between the possibility of a believer becoming intoxicated with the miraculous wine of 2:10 (cf. Acts 2:13) and the awkward bride at the well (4:5–42) Jesus is identified as the bridegroom (3:29). It is striking that at Bethany two sisters and a brother, Martha, Mary, and Lazarus, live together, apparently without spouses. If they are all single, this may indicate the practice of celibacy, an aspect of virtuoso religion and certainly 'Essene' in character.[280]

3.3.3   'Women' and the witness of the community

The Johannine presentation of female roles is qualitatively distinct from that of the Synoptic tradition, especially Luke. Women are portrayed as foundational actors in Jesus' historical ministry. The 'Mother' of Jesus leads the disciples to belief (2:1–12) and is committed to the archetypal Johannine disciple at the cross (19:25–7). The Samaritan woman is 'betrothed to Christ' and proclaims his 'word' (4:4–42). The 'sisters' at Bethany between them confess the Johannine faith (11:1–44) and anoint Jesus for his burial (12:1–8). Finally, Mary Magdalene testifies to the 'brothers' (20:17). Indeed, if we follow the logic of the two-level readings of 'community' history, accepting the high representational value of

---

[279] D'Angelo's arguments that Mary's anointing and Mary Magdalene seeking Jesus' body at the tomb echo the woman in Song of Songs 1:12 and 3:1–3 have a particular resonance in this context. Women appear to be presented as 'lovers': see '(Re)Presentations', p. 136.

[280] Indeed, one may ask whether they were really siblings or rather key individuals in a community of fictive kin.

the Gospel's characterisations,[281] then women need to be placed at the end of the trajectory of such reconstructions and not relegated to an appendix.[282] However, the focus of such reconstructions distracts our attention from these women's particular social witness. Their qualitatively distinct prominence in the narrative raises a problematic cultural conundrum, which is reinforced by the frequent attempts to identify them as 'apostles' and 'evangelists'.[283] How do we reconcile their presentation with the reception of women in the first-century churches such as that evidenced in the Pastoral Epistles?[284] The answer to this question has started to emerge in the survey of the Gospel women's particular social witness. They have been predominantly identified in particular locations associated with Judaean virtuosity, Bethany and the Jerusalem upper room and its environs. In addition, their portrayal has included distinctive language, 'Mother', 'brothers', and 'sisters' – language which is associated with Jesus' earliest ministry (Matt. 12:46–50/Mark 3:31–8 and Luke 8:21) and the type of fictive-kinship groups that were probably most evident around the Essene community house (4QD[e] and 4Q 502).[285] Indeed, of all the religious groups within first-century Judaea it is only with the Essenes that we find reference to women as members of a religious grouping (CD 7:6–7; 1QSa 1:4 and 1QM 7:4–5).[286] Furthermore, this language of fictive kinship is clearly evident in the Epistles, where we also observe a certain gender exclusivity, which may be expected in forms of

[281] Culpepper, *Anatomy*, p. 106.

[282] Cf. R. E. Brown, *Community*.

[283] Perhaps best exemplified by Schneiders, 'Women'.

[284] A rhetorical question notably left unanswered by Brown in his *The Churches the Apostles Left Behind* (London: Cassell, 1984).

[285] E.g. the 'Mothers' of 4QD[e]: 'Whoever murmu]rs against the Fathers [shall be expelled] from the congregation and shall not return; [but if] against the Mothers, then he shall be punished te[n] days, because the Mo[th]ers do not have "authority" in the midst of [the congregation].' Also, the 'daughter of truth' in 4Q502. See Crawford, 'Mothers, Sisters, Elders'. Also Capper, 'The New Covenant', p. 103: 'The elderly women constituted an order very much like the widow orders of early Christianity, and were probably cared for by the young girls who were taken in and other unattached women who formed the staff of the community centres.'

[286] Women were also evident in the Therapeutae; however, this group was not associated with Judaea and bears comparison with the Essenes: see C. T. Hayward, 'Therapeutae', *EDSS*, pp. 943–6. On the presence of women in first-century religious movements, see Kraemer, 'Beginning'. It is notable that the inscriptional evidence of women's involvement with the synagogue is external to the land of Israel and that none of it is earlier than the second century AD.

religious virtuosity.[287] In 1 John the label 'brother'[288] designates a member of the community, within which the elder's 'children'[289] appear to be organised into two groups, 'fathers' and 'young men' (2:12–14).[290] The latter is notably a designation paralleled in Acts 5:6, 10 in the context of the Jerusalem congregation's community of goods.[291] However, this reading of 1 John is not without its detractors, notably because 'the naming of "fathers" and "young men" seems to indicate a male-dominated (even monastic?) community'.[292] Despite the presence of such virtuoso practices in the immediate context of the Gospel's witness, such an identification is ruled out *a priori*. This interpretative practice continues with readings of 2 John which view the letter's reference to the 'elect lady' as a personification of the Johannine church.[293] Her anonymity curiously counts against any identification of her as a prominent woman offering hospitality to the early church, as does the presence of the 'elect sister' (2 John 13).[294] This is despite the 'elder' and the 'beloved disciple' providing precedents for anonymity and the evident presence of females who served as householders elsewhere in the New Testament.[295] It is notable that the earliest interpretations of the 'elect lady' do not attempt a symbolic reading but rather attempt to identify the 'lady'

---

[287] See P. Perkins, *The Johannine Epistles* (New Testament Message 21; Wilmington: Glazier, 1979), p. xi, who argues that the author 'clearly conceives his audience as men'.

[288] 1 John 2:9, 10; 3:12, 15, 17; 4:20 and 5:16.

[289] 1 John 2:1, 12, 14, 18, 28; 3:7, 18; 4:4; 5:19, 21.

[290] On this two-class division, see J. Houlden, *A Commentary on the Johannine Epistles* (Black's New Testament Commentaries; London: A. & C. Black, 1973), p. 70, following A. E. Brooke, *A Critical and Exegetical Commentary on the Johannine Epistles* (ICC; Edinburgh: T&T Clark, 1912), p. 43.

[291] On the service of 'young men' in such communities, see B. J. Capper, 'Order and Ministry in the Social Pattern of the New Testament Church', in *Order and Ministry* (ed. R. Hannaford and C. Hall; Leominster, Herefordshire: Gracewing, 1996), p. 88.

[292] Smalley, *1, 2, 3 John*, p. 69. For a reading that does not rule out such a possibility, see J. C. O'Neill, 'New Testament Monasteries', in *Common Life in the Early Church* (ed. J. V. Hills; Harrisburg: Trinity Press International, 1998), pp. 126f.

[293] See Smalley, *1, 2, 3, John*, p. 318.

[294] Houlden asks: 'Is the Johannine community, under the Elder, a multi-headed matriarchal society …?', *Johannine Epistles*, p. 142. Such a thought is clearly anathema to him.

[295] E.g. Phoebe at Cenchreae (Rom. 16:1–2), Nympha of Laodicea (Col. 4:15), and Lydia of Philippi (Acts 16:12–15, 40). On the cellular pattern and multiplicity of household congregations in each city and the presence of wealthy female 'patrons', see Capper, 'Public Body', p. 130. On the 'elect lady' as an actual person, see O'Neill, 'New Testament Monasteries', pp. 128ff., and D'Angelo, '(Re)Presentations', p. 132.

in question.[296] Indeed, this understanding of the 'elect lady' may help account for the contrast with 3 John in relation to the elder's discussions of hospitality (2 John 10–11; cf. 3 John 5–8). The evident reluctance in discussions of the Johannine literature to identify forms of social organisation analogous to monasticism, i.e. religious virtuosity, has perhaps more to do with culturally bound presuppositions concerning the role of women in the church than it does with any fear of anachronism.

3.3.4   Summary

It is clear that the Johannine presentation of women is qualitatively distinct from their portrayal in the Synoptic tradition. It is also clear that the prominence of women in the first-century social world was most closely associated with either the elite or the religious social actor. Indeed, there was most probably some overlap between the two, with the elite woman's patronage and participation in the life of the religious virtuoso functioning as a means of extending social leverage outside the narrowly conceived elite household. The prominence of the Johannine women therefore immediately suggests an elite or virtuoso context. The association with virtuosity is notably reinforced by the Gospel's evident antecedents in a Judaean milieu, a location within which we find the Essenes, the only religious grouping within first-century Judaea to include women in its membership. When the Johannine social witness evident in its distinct language, locations, and practices is considered, this virtuoso identification is unavoidable. The qualitatively distinct portrayal of women is not best understood either as an indication of antipathy towards church orders or as apologetic and propaganda to affirm the presence of women leaders in the first-century churches; rather it is most credibly comprehended in terms of social witness to indigenous forms of female practices evident in Judaea's virtuoso religion. The very prominence of the Johannine women, who are both seen and heard, points to such a particular social world.

3.4   Virtuoso religion and the Johannine social witness

This chapter has sought to re-examine the social witness of the most Judaean of the Gospels, John, and secondarily its Epistles. It has

---

[296] See A. E. Brooke, *The Johannine Epistles*, pp. 167f., on Clement of Alexandria's reading of *eklektē* as the proper name 'Electa'.

exposed the unsuitable nature of the sectarian social thesis, which inadequately accounts for the Gospel's distinctiveness. It has also underlined the Gospel's indigenous perspective on Judaea, especially in contrast to the Synoptic tradition, and observed its idiosyncratic portrayal of the *ptōchoi* and women. This social witness exposes the very features that may be indicative of the presence of virtuoso religion in the social world, i.e. distinctive social roles in relation to poverty and gender. However, social readings of the Johannine literature remain until now dominated by the sectarian thesis, and this has eclipsed discussion of its witness to the religious social actor. Nonetheless, there has been one notable contribution in this area, an essay by Rensberger on 'Asceticism and the Gospel of John'. This sub-section starts by exposing the problematic nature of Rensberger's discussion, which is marked by its limited conception of 'asceticism' and a misconceived reluctance to associate the 'ascetic' themes which he identifies with the Gospel's historical social witness. Following from this review 'virtuoso religion' is presented as a counter thesis to sectarian readings of the Johannine literature and as a means of more adequately understanding these 'ascetic' themes. The application of this framework makes it clear that the Johannine distinctiveness is most credibly understood as a consequence of its emergence from indigenous forms of virtuosity particular to the Judaean social world and not as a product of a late-first-century sectarian schism.

3.4.1   Johannine 'asceticism'

The origin of the Johannine literature from a particular religious social world has only been hinted at in previous scholarship, which has most recently dwelt on resonances between the Gospel's ethical and eschatological dualism and the literature emerging from Qumran.[297] Social-scientific discussions of the Gospel, as previously observed, have predominantly framed this association in terms of a common sectarianism, an association that is dependent upon a caricature of the Qumran literature as the product of a radically estranged community.[298] Literary associations between the

---

[297] On the history of 'religio-historical research', see H. K. Nielsen, 'Johannine Research', in Nissen and Pedersen, eds., *New Readings in John*, pp. 17–21. Such research has not tended to consider the specialised nature of social environments, an exception perhaps being Cullmann, *The Johannine Circle*.

[298] See §2.2 above, especially the discussion of Esler, 'Sectarianism'.

Johannine literature, the Essenes, and Qumran are equally contested.[299] However, perhaps the most striking assessment of the Johannine literature's origins comes from Ashton, who argues that the evangelist was a 'converted' Essene who had dualism in his 'guts'.[300] The scandalous specificity of this identification has been greatly alleviated by Capper's convincing argument that the 'beloved disciple' was a resident of an 'ascetic religious quarter' in Jerusalem.[301] This identification leads him to ask the 'mischievous' rhetorical question: 'Could part of the answer to the question of the distinctive character of the Johannine tradition lie in its conception in a distinctive, intensely contemplative, virtually *monastic* spirituality?'[302] Indeed, he suggests that a particular type of 'ascetic Jewish life' may account for the Gospel's profound difference in character from the Synoptic tradition. However, whilst Capper's argument is highly suggestive, he does not develop his category 'ascetic Jewish life' through a social-scientific methodology, focusing rather on historical questions. The Gospel of John has never been the focus of research on early Christian asceticism.[303] Indeed, Rensberger's discussion in the edited volume emanating from the 'Asceticism Group' stands out as the only detailed treatment of 'asceticism' within the Gospel and will now be appraised.[304]

Rensberger's initial assessment of the Gospel's 'ascetic' credentials is negative.[305] However, as we have already noted in relation to the discussion of the Gospel's *ptōchoi*, initial assessments can be deceiving, as can be inadequately conceived theoretical

---

[299] E.g. Bauckham, 'Qumran'.

[300] *Understanding*, p. 273.

[301] 'With the Oldest Monks', p. 2.

[302] *Ibid.*, p. 1, his italics. For a monastic identification of the Johannine Epistles, see O'Neill, 'New Testament Monasteries'. However, O'Neill's discussion is undermined by its anachronistic and unsophisticated adoption of 'monastic' categories.

[303] Rensberger, 'Asceticism', p. 127. This is clear from the discussions of Derrett, 'Primitive', and Allison, *Jesus*, pp. 172–216. Both of these authors attempt to underline the ascetic nature of Jesus' ministry, and both develop their arguments overwhelmingly from the Synoptic tradition. It is also clear from the theme's total absence from B. Malina and R. Rohrbaugh, eds., *Social Science Commentary on the Gospel of John* (Minneapolis, MN: Fortress Press, 1998).

[304] L. W. Countryman's contribution to the volume which addresses the Johannine Epistles simply recanvasses Grayston's analysis of the Johannine community and adopts such a sceptical line in relation to 'ascetic' practices that it is of little assistance in this discussion: see 'Asceticism in the Johannine Letters?', *ANT*, pp. 383–91.

[305] 'Asceticism', p. 131.

categories.[306] Rensberger, whilst acknowledging the theoretical debates about the nature of 'asceticism', settles upon an understanding that is centred on the practice of self-denial, which encapsulates the lowering of social standing.[307] This definition is an ethnocentric construction that derives from Greco-Roman understandings of asceticism and takes no account of forms of asceticism indigenous to Judaea.[308] Its distorting compass is further exacerbated by the relating of asceticism to the lowering of social standing: 'The lowering of social standing also involves renunciation, a restriction of self, especially in an honor/shame society like that of the ancient Mediterranean.'[309] It has previously been demonstrated that the practice of 'asceticism' does not necessarily involve the lowering of social standing and may even be adopted to maintain social standing, as in the case of the younger sons of the elite.[310] This is nevertheless the course set by Rensberger. It is on this basis that he claims that the Gospel makes no overt references to 'ascetic' practices.[311] The only ascetic discipline that is possibly urged in the Gospel is confession, which leads to expulsion from normative social structures (9:22; 12:42–3; 19:38) and thereby a lowering of social standing, i.e. self-denial.[312] The Gospel encourages the maintenance of confession and therefore the renunciation of the self (20:31). This neatly fits in with his preconceptions about the nature of the Gospel's social witness, i.e. that the 'Johannine community must be considered a sect'.[313]

Nonetheless, Rensberger's analysis does leave room for the 'ascetic interpretation' of the Gospel. Despite his discussion being

---

[306] See §3.2 above.

[307] 'Asceticism', pp. 129f.

[308] See chapter 3, §3.3 above.

[309] Here Rensberger follows B. Malina, 'Pain, Power and Personhood: Ascetic Behavior in the Ancient Mediterranean', in Wimbush and Valantasis, eds., *Asceticism*, pp. 162–77. Malina's discussion is problematic for a number of reasons, not least of which is his dogmatically framed contrast between an ancient group-self and a contemporary Western individual-self. This artificial dichotomy distorts his reading of the ancient world: see further chapter 2, §2.1.f.

[310] See chapter 3, §2.2.2 above. Indeed, Malina acknowledges the potential elevation in status of such social actors: see 'Ascetic Behavior', p. 167, n. 309.

[311] Rensberger, 'Asceticism', p. 131.

[312] *Ibid.*, p. 136. He argues that confession stands out from such themes as baptism, John 3, the eucharist, John 6, and the new command of John 13 because while they function to initiate membership into a counter-cultural community, they lack the dimension of self-denial.

[313] 'Asceticism', p. 132, following his early identification in *Johannine Faith*, pp. 71–7.

marked by a reticence which maintains a distance from historical questions, it remains a highly suggestive reading that exposes important 'ascetic' themes. He highlights the importance of the Gospel's incarnational christology for an 'ascetic interpretation'.[314] The logic of this christology is that the human realm of the 'flesh'[315] has become the realm of divine activity and the body may therefore become the vehicle for eternal life (1:14). It is to be trained and disciplined rather than destroyed. Jesus' fleshly vulnerability, which is rooted in his utter submission to God,[316] sets a pattern for his disciples.[317] Jesus' glorification, which is his ultimate glorification of God, is the exposure of his fleshly humanity at the cross.[318] Thus the Gospel's presentation of Jesus as deliberately offering his body to death, in order to perform God's will and make him known, 'bears resemblance to ascetic self-denial'.[319] Rensberger also observes that the Gospel's treatment of sexual and marital imagery offers possibilities for ascetic interpretation.[320] He identifies a lowering of the estimation of physical birth in favour of the birth that comes from above (3:3–8). Those who seek to bring about this 'spiritual' birth appear to be elevated over those who physically engender birth. Likewise, in the adoption of marital imagery Jesus' bride is the one who believes in him (3:29). Indeed, the following portrayal of the Samaritan woman (4:4–42) appears to validate the pursuit of a spiritual marriage with Jesus. Finally, in relation to food he notes an 'unmistakable similarity' between Jesus, whose food is to do the will of God (4:31–4), and the fasting ascetic, who is nourished by the service of God.[321] In the Gospel Jesus is predominantly the provider of food.[322] It is only at 4:31–4 that we hear of him being in receipt of food. However, this is not physical

---

[314] 'Asceticism', pp. 137f. This discussion of christology introduces his sectarian reading of the Gospel, suggesting that the schismatic nature of their confession rendered it an action in 'resistance to the world'.

[315] John 6:63; 8:15 and 17:2.

[316] His obedience in everything that he has been commanded to do: see John 5:19, 30; 6:38; 7:16–18; 8:28–9; 12:49–50; 14:10, 24 and 17:7–8.

[317] John 14:12; 15:12–13, 18-20 and 16:2.

[318] John 7:39; 12:16, 23–8 and 17:1, 4–5.

[319] 'Asceticism', p. 144. It is also a theme that has been picked up in discussions of the 'poverty' of the divine *logos*: see C. Boff and G. V. Pixely, *The Bible, the Church and the Poor* (Maryknoll, NY: Orbis Books, 1989).

[320] 'Asceticism', p. 141.

[321] *Ibid.*, p. 143. It is striking that when Rensberger does cite John. 2:1–11, it is reference to ascetic food consumption and not spiritual marriage.

[322] John 2:1–11; 4:4–9; 6:1–13, 51–8; 13:23–6 and 21:9–13.

nourishment, but doing the will of the one who sent him. The Johannine disciple is to be nourished by the food that does not perish which is provided by Jesus (6:27; also 2:1–11), the food that endures for eternal life. Rensberger succeeds in identifying clear 'ascetic' themes, but his discussion consistently fails to relate them to any historical social practice.

Despite observing these distinctive 'ascetic' themes, Rensberger's social preoccupation with the Gospel's sectarian origins and his negative preliminary reading of its 'ascetic' credentials preclude him from building on these important insights. Indeed, an examination of his negative preliminary reading reveals how his limited conception of 'asceticism', as the practice of self-denial, obscures and distorts his following assessment of the significance of the themes he has identified. In his preliminary reading, he highlights three areas, which apparently indicate that the Gospel 'gives no indication of any interest in asceticism'.[323] These are prayer, poverty, and relations with John the Baptist. First, in the Gospel, in contrast with the Synoptic tradition, Jesus is never portrayed as retreating from public view for the purposes of prayer (contrast Mark 1:35; 6:45–6 and 14:32–5). When Jesus does pray, it is always in the presence of others (e.g. chapter 17). However, this evidence from absence is also evidence of the presence of extended discourses, i.e. chapters 14–17, a teaching method quite alien to the Synoptic tradition.[324] Indeed, Riesenfeld has argued that such 'discourses and "meditations"' are most probably evidence of the private training and instruction of disciples.[325] Thus Rensberger's evidence from absence may actually point to practice that clearly resonates with the life of the 'ascetic', most notably the virtuoso's preoccupations with discipline and training.[326]

Secondly, Rensberger observes that Jesus associated with the economically prosperous, 2:1–11; 4:46–54; 12:1–8, and does not call on them to renounce their property. Indeed, he believes that Jesus' apparently normative positive attitude towards food

---

[323] 'Asceticism', p. 132.

[324] On the private/public division of Jesus' teaching, see O'Neill, 'New Testament Monasteries', pp. 121f. Although the Synoptic tradition gives us no record of Jesus teaching in extended discourses, it nonetheless clearly indicates that the disciples were taught privately: Matt. 13:11/Mark 4:11/Luke 8:10. Note especially Luke 12:41, where Peter asks whether certain teaching is 'for us or for all'.

[325] H. Riesenfeld, *Studia Evangelica*, Vol. I (ed. K. Aland; Berlin, 1959), p. 59; cf. the Synoptic tradition's record of Jesus' strategy of public teaching in parables.

[326] See chapter 3, §2.2 above.

(2:1–11; 13:23–6; 21:9–13) and the possession of a common purse (12:6; 13:29) indicate that neither he nor his disciples lived in poverty, i.e. that they did not practise self-denial. However, this reading underlines the often-repeated fallacies that surround the discussion of ascetic lives. The caricature of the ascetic living in glorious isolation is just that – a caricature. It is clear from the earlier discussions of religious virtuosos that their association with the laity made them significant social agents, ones who frequently attracted elite association and patronage.[327] The idea that Jesus' limited association with the economically prosperous precludes an 'ascetic' identification is simply erroneous. In addition, the idea that a normative attitude towards food also precludes asceticism is likewise problematic. The references cited (13:23–6; 21:9–13) do not indicate anything other than simple meals, and, of course, ascetics do eat.[328] He appears to be advancing his argument on little more than the absence of instructions directed towards self-denial. Furthermore, Jesus' and the disciples' apparent possession of money does not undermine any 'ascetic' identification, 12:6; 13:29. The idea that the possession of a common purse and the practice of giving alms refutes the possibility of such identification simply exposes the inadequacy of his conception of 'asceticism'.[329] It is clear from the preceding discussions of the Gospel's *ptōchoi* that these social practices were identifying features of Judaea's indigenous forms of virtuosity.[330]

The final element of Rensberger's preliminary assessment of the Gospel's 'ascetic' credentials is its presentation of John the Baptist. He notes that whilst the Gospel displays a particular interest in

[327] See P. Brown, *Society and the Holy in Late Antiquity* (London: Faber & Faber, 1982), p. 113: 'The crowd is an essential element in the life of the Syrian holy man.' Indeed, for a contemporary example one need simply think of the Dalai Lama and his elite patrons.

[328] The only reference that might indicate any form of profligacy is to the miraculous production of wine, 2:1–11, and even this does not preclude the presence of asceticism. Ascetics not only eat but also celebrate. Indeed, I have it on good authority that the only group to drink dry the Old Palace, the Archbishop of Canterbury's residence, at the last Lambeth Conference was that of the Religious Orders. On the fallacy of the contrast between Jesus' free excess and John the Baptist's fasting, see Allison, *Jesus*, p. 173. On the significance of the context of the wedding and the imagery adopted, see Capper, 'With the Oldest Monks', p. 2, n. 4.

[329] It is a paradoxical feature of religious virtuosos, which is obscured by the limited definition of the ascetic in terms of self-denial, that whilst they may individually be 'poor', together they may also be, and often have become, 'wealthy'. On monasticism's tendency to accumulate wealth, see Silber, *Virtuosity*, p. 42.

[330] See §3.2 above.

differentiating between Jesus and John the Baptist,[331] the Synoptics'
contrast between John the ascetic and Jesus' eating and drinking
does not appear.[332] He speculates that because of 'ongoing
competition between the Johannine Christian community and
disciples of the Baptist' its narrative avoids anything that might
'put the spotlight on John'.[333] Therefore, the Gospel intentionally
plays down the Baptist's asceticism. However, in the light of the
attention that the Gospel gives to the disciples of the Baptist, the
fact that their 'ascetic' antecedents are not used to differentiate
them may alternatively indicate a deep-seated commonality in
practice in the social world within which the Gospel's social witness
is embedded, the world of the *ptōchoi*.[334] Rensberger repeatedly
advances his argument on the basis of absences, which upon closer
examination frequently reflect the presence of forms of virtuoso
practice, i.e. teaching in extended discourses, a common purse and
giving alms, and continuity and discontinuity with the practices of
the disciples of the Baptist. His preconceptions of the nature of
'asceticism', which neglect Judaea's indigenous forms of virtuosity,
preclude him from making an 'ascetic' identification. It also results
in his reticence in presenting his 'ascetic' themes as anything more
than possible means of interpretation. However, as we come more
fully to appreciate Judaea's indigenous virtuosity, the significance
of such themes may be more fully realised.

3.4.2   *Transcending Johannine sectarianism*

Theoretical categories for discussing the religious social actor in the
social sciences have been subject to a legacy of 'culture-specific
biases and prejudices' regarding the origins and value of asceticism.[335] These have resulted in a pattern of either totally absorbing
such actors within, or marginalising them in, their social worlds.
In an attempt to address this situation, recent scholarship from
the social sciences has been presented and the theoretical framework 'virtuoso religion' introduced.[336] Comparative studies have

---

[331] John 1:6–8, 15, 19–24; 3:23–30; 5:33–6 and 10:40–1.
[332] Cf. Mark 12:18–19// and Matt. 11:16–19/Luke 7:31–4. On the credibility of
such a contrast, see Allison, *Jesus*, pp. 173f.
[333] 'Asceticism', p. 132.
[334] See §3.2.4 above.
[335] See chapter 3, §2.1 above.
[336] See chapter 3, §2.2 above.

illustrated that whilst the religious virtuoso's single-minded commitment to the realm of the ultimate concerns and consequent attempts to establish pure, rigorous enactments of religious tradition can lead to dissociation and radical withdrawal, this social practice is neither sectarian nor 'ascetic', in the sense generally adopted by the 'Asceticism Group'.[337] The defining capacity of virtuoso religion is its ability to maintain alternative structures that present a reversed image of society whilst remaining within its ideological and institutional boundaries. Its prominence as a social form is a feature of distinct social circumstances which have been demonstrated to resonate particularly with first-century Judaea, with its particular piety of the *ptōchoi*.[338] The alternative structures that it maintains may take the form of distinct communities, which typically take a lead not only in forms of social provision, such as care for the sick, the widow, and the orphan, but also in the provision of centres for the perceived preservation of pristine tradition. These virtuoso institutions, religious houses or monasteries, frequently generate both patronage and membership from a broad range of social actors. However, their defining capacity to provide an alternative structure within society is also profoundly unsettling since the virtuoso must constantly grapple with the competing concerns of insulation versus involvement, laxity and decline versus radicalism and constant reformism. This theoretical framework, as we have seen from the preceding discussion of the Gospel's *ptōchoi* and women, is highly relevant for conceiving the particular religious social milieu from which the Johannine literature emerged. Indeed, as will now be illustrated, it helps reconcile the anomalies which undermine the sectarian social thesis and assists in the comprehension of the apparent intensity of the Johannine religious experience.

In the preceding critique of the sectarian social thesis, it was argued that the Johannine literature does not reflect an 'introverted sect' vis-à-vis 'Judaism'.[339] This 'introversionist' identification not only homogenises 'Judaism' but also neglects the essential 'Jewishness' of the Gospel. The Gospel, as we have noted, is perhaps the most 'Jewish' of all the Gospels.[340] It does not view

---

[337] See chapter 3, §2.1 above.
[338] See chapter 3, §3.3 above.
[339] See the extended critique of Esler, 'Sectarianism', in §2.2 above.
[340] See §2.2.1 above.

'Judaism' as 'irredeemably evil',[341] but rather radically restates its traditions. Indeed, Jesus is presented as embodying key elements of its cultic symbolism and practice. The contested nature of this cultic symbolism and practice has clearly been demonstrated in preceding discussions of the *ptōchoi*.[342] In this context of competing discourses Jesus is presented as the 'truth' (16:6); the true light (1:9); the true bread (6:32); and the true vine (15:1).[343] This radical restatement of tradition does not reflect a sectarian flight from an 'irredeemably evil' parent body but rather the typical practice of the virtuoso whose perception is that they are 'representing or rigorously restoring the pristine purity of an impaired or corrupted tradition'.[344] The nature of the Gospel's antagonism to 'Judaism', rather than providing unambiguous support for a sectarian reading, reveals a defining practice of the religious virtuoso. Similarly, the virtuoso's tension between insularity from and involvement in the world is evident when consideration is given to how the Johannine literature does not reflect an 'introverted sect' vis-à-vis the 'world'.[345] The Gospel does not present the 'world' as 'irredeemably evil' and does not advocate withdrawal from it. The 'world' is the realm of the 'flesh' that becomes the realm of divine activity (8:12; 9:5; 18:37).[346] 'Sending' into the world is a paradigmatic activity in the Gospel: as the Father sent the Son, so too the Son sends his disciples into the world (3:16–17; 17:18 and 20:21).[347] In addition, the language of the Gospel appears designed to initiate its readers and not to alienate them.[348] It is clear that within the Gospel there is a real tension between 'sending'

---

[341] See Esler, 'Sectarianism', pp. 72f.

[342] On the contested nature of the *ptōchoi* in first-century Judaisms, see chapter 4 above. In addition, T. Griffith, *Keep Yourselves from Idols: A New Look at 1 John* (JSNTS 233; Sheffield: Sheffield Academic Press, 2002), pp. 208f., which is of particular interest for understanding this context of contested identities in a Johannine context, especially the observation that the tradition of 'idol polemic', 1 John 5:21, was applied by Jews against Jews in a Jewish Palestinian context.

[343] On the significance of the Johannine identification of Jesus as 'truth', see R. E. Brown, *John*, Vol. I, pp. 499f.

[344] Silber, *Virtuosity*, p. 193; cf. M. Hill, *Religious Order*, and his 'rigorous restatement of tradition', p. 2, and 'revolution by tradition', pp. 85f. The virtuoso's actual relation to tradition may well be at variance from the perceptions of society at large and the religious establishment.

[345] See §2.2 above.

[346] See Rensberger, 'Asceticism', pp. 137f., discussed in §3.4.1 above.

[347] Nissen, 'Community', p. 205. Note especially his reflections on 15:18–16:4 and 'bearing much fruit', i.e. the disciples' witness to Jesus before the world.

[348] Dokka, 'Irony and Sectarianism', p. 104, and Bauckham, 'Audience', p. 109.

and 'sect', which simplistic sectarian identifications obscure (17:11, 14–16). Dokka neatly encapsulates the dilemma:

> In this sense I regard the Gospel of John as an almost self-destructive kind of writing...A truly Johannine community gives, as it were, its words for the world. It must because its very essence and life is determined by the ascending and descending Word, by him who is lifted up and come(s) down. In terms of social relations this would imply two things, a distancing from the world, verging on the absolute, *and* a deep unity with the world, also verging on the absolute.[349]

This unity with the world is not articulated in terms of proclamation but of witness. Indeed, as Bauckham has argued, the 'beloved disciple's' special witness to Jesus (18:15) is ultimately a role of witness to the whole church (21:24) which stands in contrast to Peter's role of mission to the whole church (21:5–11).[350] Likewise, Meeks argues, 'the final discourses of the Gospel give the impression that the primary testimony of the disciples is their very existence as a community'.[351] The Johannine brothers are to bear witness to Jesus, as the Paraclete he sends bears witness (15:26–7). Jesus' fleshly vulnerability, which is rooted in his utter submission to God, sets the pattern for the brothers' life in the world.[352] By their mutual love the world may believe (cf. 17:20–6; 1 John 5:4–5).[353] The Gospel in its relation to the world offers a form of corporate soteriology that is embodied in the brothers' counter-cultural witness, which, whilst it is located in the world, is not of the world. These particular Johannine features are also defining features of virtuoso religion. Whilst the sect may be narcissistic in character, virtuoso religion remains committed to the world.[354] The virtuoso, however, is not preoccupied with proclamation, a feature of the 'charismatic', but is concerned with practice, a rigorous

---

[349] 'Irony and Sectarianism', p. 106.

[350] 'Audience', p. 111, and 'Ideal Author', pp. 41f.

[351] 'The Ethics of the Fourth Evangelist', in W. Meeks, *Exploring the Gospel of John* (ed. R. A. Culpepper and C. Black; Louisville, KY:Westminster John Knox Press, 1996), pp. 323f.

[352] See Rensberger, 'Asceticism', pp. 137f. On Jesus' utter submission to the will of God, see John 5:19, 30; 6:38; 7:16–18; 8:28–9; 12:49–50; 14:10, 24 and 17:7–8. On the disciples' practice, see John 14:12; 15:12–13, 18–20, and 16:2.

[353] Nissen, 'Community', p. 203.

[354] See Hill, *Religious Order*, pp. 28f.

enactment of religious tradition (13:35).[355] This focus renders virtuoso religion a 'precarious sociological phenomenon' caught between the horns of laxity and elitist innovations.[356] It is clear from the Gospel's radical restatement of tradition, its ambivalent yet engaged relations with the world, its focus on witness, and its precarious community, especially evident in the Epistles, that the Johannine distinctiveness is most credibly understood in terms of virtuosity and not sectarianism.

Furthermore, this identification greatly assists in the comprehension of the apparent intensity of the Johannine religious experience. The preceding discussion of the 'conversionist sect' type (see §2.2 above) illustrated that the transformation of the self is a feature of the Gospel and that this transformation literally leads to a new 'life' (e.g. 3:1–21; 6:58 and 7:38). Indeed, the Gospel is marked by its intense vitality (20:31).[357] This vitality is something that transcends human life but nonetheless is a 'life', which is to be presently participated in.[358] It is made possible through the life-giving Spirit (3:5), which provides a continuity between Jesus and the believer and enables the truth to be 're-announced' and 're-proclaimed' (14:15–26; 16:12f.; 1 John 2:27).[359] The Johannine 'life' is one imbued with the virtuoso's preoccupation with the re-presentation of the pristine purity of its tradition (1 John 1:1; 2:7, 13–14, 24; 3:8, 11; 2 John. 1:5–6). Indeed, the 'belief' that leads to Johannine 'life' (20:31) is not a passive receipt of knowledge, but a work to be engaged in.[360] The implications of this Johannine vitality are most fully worked out in the apparent perfectionism of 1 John 3:9, where it appears that members of the community can no longer sin. This religious experience is clearly analogous to the perfectionism of virtuoso religion, which associates an intense personal commitment to ultimate goals with a dissociation from worldly concerns.[361]

---

[355] See *ibid.*, p. 2, and Silber, *Virtuosity*, p. 193.

[356] Silber, *Virtuosity*, p. 197. The utility of 'virtuoso religion' for assisting our understanding of the nature of the elder's conflict with the 'opponents' in the Epistles is not something that can be developed here, but its potential to throw light on these concerns is clear and will become the subject of future research.

[357] See R. E. Brown, *John (I–XII)*, p. 506, for whom the Fourth Gospel 'may be called the Gospel of Life'.

[358] Ashton, *Understanding*, p. 217. 'The new life enjoyed by the faithful is more than ordinary physical existence: it is the life of faith.'

[359] Dunn, *Jesus and the Spirit*, pp. 350f.

[360] Meeks, 'The Man from Heaven', p. 58, and Miranda, *Being and the Messiah*, p. 148, who argues that Johannine belief entails an ethical imperative.

[361] Silber, *Virtuosity*, pp. 190f., and Hill, *Religious Order*, p. 20.

These themes are clearly interrelated in 1 John 3:10ff., where a mutuality with regard to property, i.e. dissociation from worldly concerns, is associated with the self-giving sacrifice of Christ, i.e. personal commitment to ultimate goals.[362] This conjunction constitutes the community's identity. Indeed, the Gospel's first makarism (13:17) is not part of an extended body of teaching as in Matthew's Sermon on the Mount, but rather follows a single enacted parable: Jesus' washing his disciples' feet.[363] The challenge of the makarism is to follow Jesus' exemplary *practice* of total submission. This challenge helps elucidate the Gospel's constitutional 'new commandment' (13:34–5) and sets the pattern for life of the community (15:13). It is a pattern of life by which the believer must 'abide' (6:56; 14:10–11, 23; 15:4–5; 17:11, 21, 23; 1 John 2:24; 4:15–16).[364] Whilst it is a pattern that may appear insular, its mutual love is consistently presented as a continuation of Jesus' practice, his witness before a hostile world:

> The dualism of the Fourth Gospel works not only to distance the community from the world but also affirms both the community's identity and the possibility of conversion and salvation for the people of the world.[365]

Yet sectarian readings predominantly stress features of Johannine insularity and override this tension, which is a defining feature of virtuoso religion:

> It is precisely this dense interweaving of structure and anti structure... that distinguishes [virtuoso religion] from other social institutions and makes it a kind of 'alternative' structure within society at large.[366]

The marginalisation of the religious social actor, as either a sectarian or an ascetic fleeing the world, precludes such subtlety and

---

[362] It is striking that in the Synoptic tradition's limited use of this otherwise distinctly Johannine language of 'eternal life' it occurs only in contexts of renunciation of property, Matt. 19:21/Mark 10:21/Luke 18:22, and the radical love of the other, Matt. 25:46 and Luke 10:25. See chapter 4, §3.3.3 above. It is also striking that in relation to the surrender of property to the *ptōchoi* the social actor is described as a 'young man': cf. the discussion in §3.3.3 above.

[363] Nissen, 'Community', p. 201.

[364] On the distinctive Johannine adoption of 'abide', see R. E. Brown, *John (I–XII)*, pp. 510f.

[365] Nissen, 'Community', p. 210. Also Meeks, 'Ethics', p. 324.

[366] Silber, *Virtuosity*, p. 41.

abandons Rensberger's 'ascetic' themes (see §3.4.1 above) to the category of curiosity. In contrast, the application of the theoretical framework, virtuoso religion, transcends these limited categories and is not only cognisant of the Gospel's indigenous character but also provides a powerful heuristic perspective on Capper's 'ascetic Jewish life' and helps ground Rensberger's 'ascetic' themes. Indeed, it reveals the potential workings of the 'beloved disciple's' 'guts'.[367]

3.4.3   Summary

The sectarian social thesis has eclipsed the Fourth Gospel's social witness to the specialised religious social actor. Nonetheless, the Gospel's 'ascetic' antecedents have been hinted at in Johannine scholarship. However, these discussions have either focused on questions of historical origins (Capper) or when developing a social reading have done so without considering indigenous 'ascetic' practices (Rensberger). It is in this context that a more integrated view of the social world, one marked out by the presence of 'virtuoso religion', has been advanced as a means of transcending the sectarian social thesis. The utility of this approach has been demonstrated by its capacity to place Rensberger's 'ascetic' themes within a credible social context and help invert his argument from absence, by highlighting the significance of the Gospel's extended discourses, mutuality with regard to poverty and potential continuity in practice with disciples of John the Baptist. In addition, the approach greatly assists our comprehension of those features that have been shown to undermine the sectarian thesis critically, not least the consistent tension between being 'sent' into the world and not being of the world. In comparison to the sectarian thesis, which precludes such subtleties and stresses the literature's apparent insularity, the approach adopted helps to reveal an indigenous social form which is defined by such tension: virtuoso religion.

4   Conclusions

In the preceding chapters, the neglect of the religious social actor in discussions of the New Testament social world was highlighted. Indeed, the revision of the Context Group's normative model of

---

[367] See Ashton, *Understanding*, p. 287.

a Mediterranean honour culture revealed that where the religious social actor was prominent within the social world, perceptions of poverty and gender might vary from cultural norms. In addition, the introduction of theoretical resources from the social sciences, especially 'virtuoso religion', helped clarify the roles which religious social actors may practise in their social worlds. It became clear from these discussions that the particular nature of first-century Judaea distinguished it as a context in which forms of religious virtuosity may be expected. The utility of this framework was confirmed in the discussion of the New Testament's *ptōchoi*, which highlighted their close association with indigenous forms of piety. It was revealed that within the earliest 'Christian' communities social practices analogous to those of the religious virtuoso were in evidence and that these practices, along with traditions concerning them, were centred on Jerusalem and Judaea. It is in this context that this chapter has sought to revise critically the understanding of the Johannine social world, which has predominantly been characterised as a product of a late-first-century sectarian schism. This revision started by highlighting anomalies in the sectarian thesis. These included the anachronistic appropriation of the sociology of sectarianism, its programmatic application to the text, and an association with Qumran based on a caricature of scrolls scholarship. It was clear from these discussions that the Gospel's distinctive nature could not be safely accounted for on the basis of a sectarian identification. Following on from this critique the Gospel's social witness was reassessed and its Judaean antecedents highlighted. It was clear that the Gospel betrayed a particular insider's perspective on Judaea, a location that has previously been shown to be closely associated with virtuoso religion. The significance of this association was soon evident. The discussion of the Gospel's *ptōchoi* revealed not only that its limited references were located in areas particularly associated with indigenous virtuosity, the 'ascetic quarter' in Jerusalem and Bethany, the 'house of the poor', but also that they portrayed the disciples as conforming to major tenets of indigenous virtuoso practice, a common purse and giving alms. The Gospel appeared not to be speaking about the *ptōchoi* but rather from their immediate social context. Its evident concern for the marginalised was shown not to require a sectarian post-Jamnian context but rather to be accounted for in terms of the evangelist's reflections on Jesus' ministry against the backdrop of indigenous forms of virtuosity. The discussion of the Gospel's women also revealed a distinct social witness. The very prominence of their portrayal, especially in relation to the Synoptic tradition, suggested the requirement of some form of social explanation that the sectarian thesis could not provide. The distinctive language, locations, and practices used in the description of these women indicated that their portrayal was most credibly understood in terms of indigenous forms evident in Judaea's virtuoso religion. Indeed, the Johannine literature's idiosyncratic portrayal of poverty and gender consistently pointed to such a particular social world. The anomalies of the sectarian social thesis, especially its tendency to obscure the literature's tension between insularity from and involvement in the world, were shown to be reconciled in this particular social world.

6

CONCLUSIONS

This book has argued that forms of piety indigenous to first-century Judaea are particularly pertinent for our understanding of both the New Testament's 'poor' and the Johannine tradition, accounting for the latter's distinctiveness more plausibly than the currently fashionable 'sectarian' interpretations.

In developing this argument a more integrated social-scientific strategy has been advocated, which views the social world as a complex of interacting social dimensions (following Friedrichs, Ritzer, and others). This integrated approach has encouraged a more dynamic understanding of the New Testament world. The utility of viewing the social world in this way has been demonstrated in the critical revision of the model of a normative Mediterranean honour culture as advocated by members of the Context Group of scholars (e.g. Malina, Esler, et al.). This revision has observed how their model obscures both historical and cultural diversity, especially the particular character of first-century Judaea. In addition, the revision has illustrated how attempts to move away from the theologically conceived *Sitz im Leben* have resulted in the neglect of the role of the religious social actor in the transformation and maintenance of social worlds. This has been shown to be reinforced by the particular tendency within foundational works on the sociology of religion either to absorb such actors totally or to place them at the margins of any given social world (e.g. Weber). This tendency has also been shown to be evident in recent discussions of the ascetic in the New Testament.

In response to the neglect of the religious social actor, recent literature from the social sciences on *virtuoso religion*, i.e. forms of piety which typically lead to the formation of religious orders (e.g. Hill, Silber, and Ortner), has been introduced. This more critical literature, which has not previously been adopted in New Testament studies, has taken due consideration of the sociology of religion's tendency either to assimilate or to marginalise the religious social actor. In its analysis of virtuoso religion, it has provided a means of discussing and discriminating between the roles and potential significance of religious social actors, without relegating them to the margins of the social world as sectarians or otherworldly ascetics. Indeed, the defining feature of virtuoso religion, which distinguishes it from other social forms such as that of the sect, has been shown to be its ability to form an 'alternative structure within society at large',[1] what Hill calls a 'sect within the church'.[2] This discussion has also drawn attention to key social variables which may suggest the prominence of virtuoso religion in any given social world. These have been demonstrated to resonate particularly with first-century Judaea, and the presence of virtuoso religion in the practices of the Essenes and other pietists has helped to confirm the potential fruitfulness of this social-scientific resource.

Indeed, the heuristic significance of virtuoso religion has been demonstrated in a survey of the New Testament's *ptōchoi* which has moved beyond the socio-economic categories of previous social analysis (e.g. Schottroff and Stegemann, Malina, and Hollenbach) and underlined the pious practices of the *ptōchoi* and the predominantly Judaean location for these traditions. It has been argued that these features are more credibly understood against the backdrop of the particular Judaean social world, where we have seen forms of virtuoso religion which offered cultural resources that radically addressed the situation of the poor, than any normative New Testament world. In this context it has also been argued, in an *excursus* on the first makarism (Matt. 5:3/Luke 6:20), that a less dogmatic approach to first-century honour culture which recognises cultural difference may help in the understanding of Luke's redactional interests and invert the consensus reading that promotes Luke's alleged 'originality' over Matthew's ethicising 'gloss'.

Finally, the argument that the Johannine literature's distinctiveness may be accounted for by a defining sectarian schism (e.g. Meeks and Martyn) has been rejected, on the basis of both the sociology adopted and a close reading of the text. In contrast, the Gospel's particular social witness, which is conspicuously Judaean and marked by the relative absence of the *ptōchoi* and the relative prominence of 'women' vis-à-vis the Synoptic tradition,

---

[1] Silber, *Virtuosity*, p. 41.
[2] *Religious Order*, pp. 12f.

has been exposed. In place of the often-postulated 'Johannine sectarianism' it has been argued that when the social witness of the Gospel, as opposed to a 'reconstructed' Johannine community (e.g. Brown), is examined, its distinctive character is most plausibly understood in terms of Judaea's cultural particularity. Indeed, it has been advocated that the anomalies of the sectarian reading, especially the evident tension between insularity from and involvement with the world, are most plausibly accounted for on the basis of Judaea's indigenous forms of virtuoso religion.

In summary, this book offers a fresh methodological perspective on the social-scientific interpretation of the New Testament, arguing for a more integrated view of the social world. The recognition of the social world as a complex of interacting social dimensions is clearly of benefit and helps to avoid the often crude stereotyping seen in the model of a normative Mediterranean honour culture. I hope that the critical revision of this model will be viewed as a continuation of the Context Group's attempt to imagine the New Testament world. However, no normative Mediterranean model is offered in replacement. Rather, the critical engagement illustrates the perils of such a strategy. In contrast, the process of engagement has helped draw attention to particular social-scientific resources on 'virtuoso religion' with which to explore tentatively elements of the New Testament world. Indeed, it has helped to expose the particular nature of first-century Judaea and drawn attention to an idiosyncratic, almost religious social world, which in turn helps us to reflect on a neglected location of Jesus' ministry, Judaea. Whilst studies on Jesus and the Gospels have predominantly focused on Jesus' Galilean ministry, so that the quest for the historical Jesus is in danger of becoming the quest for the historical Galilee,[3] this perspective widens the map. The application of the material on 'virtuoso religion' to the question of the identity of the *ptōchoi* in the New Testament, a key element in Jesus' proclamation, draws attention to the predominantly Judaean antecedents of these traditions and moves beyond economic explanations to argue for both their soteriological and socio-economic significance as expressions of the piety of poverty. It also helps explain elements of the Johannine distinctiveness and overcomes the anomalies evident in the sectarian reading. It helps us to envisage the religious social actor as an active social agent rather

---

[3] Freyne, 'Geography', p. 76.

than as an outsider. Indeed, its heuristic significance goes beyond the question of the Johannine distinctiveness and the identity of the *ptōchoi*. It suggests clear avenues, in both Johannine and Synoptic studies, for future exploration which lie beyond the scope of this study, for example the question of the relevance of 'virtuoso religion' to the understanding of Johannine 'mysticism', and the perhaps related question, the literature's potential origins in the milieu of early Syriac monasticism, especially in relation to early Thomasine traditions. In addition, the nature of Jesus' social role, and the possible social character of the Kingdom that he proclaimed, is potentially enhanced by taking a view on virtuoso religion. Du Toit's analysis of current trends in Jesus research is worthy of note at this point. He identifies two general patterns in the various pictures of Jesus as an agent of social change:

> Jesus is either viewed as the founder of a renewal movement which functions as an *alternative community*, that is, as an alternative to a society fraught with oppressive structures [e.g. Theissen, Schüssler-Fiorenza, Crossan, and Borg]; or he is seen as a (radical) reformer who founded a *renewal movement within society* concerned with reforming society itself and its institutions in the face of structural oppression [e.g. Horsley, Kaylor, and Freyne].[4]

The location of the New Testament's witness to the *ptōchoi* and the Johannine literature's distinctiveness within the milieu of Judaean virtuosity prepare the ground for considering a third possibility: that Jesus was, or at least was understood by some of his contemporaries to be, the founder of an 'alternative structure within society at large'.[5] Thus we are left with the tantalising question of the relevance of 'virtuoso religion' for the understanding of Jesus himself.

---

[4] Du Toit, 'Current Trends', p. 122. It is worth observing that the italics in this quotation are his own.
[5] Silber, *Virtuosity*, p. 41.

SELECT BIBLIOGRAPHY

Adas, M. 'From Avoidance to Confrontation: Peasant Protest in Precolonial and Colonial Southeast Asia', *CSSH* 23 (1981), 217–47.

Adkins, A. *Merit and Responsibility: A Study in Greek Values* (London: Clarendon, 1960).

Allen, L. C. *Word Biblical Commentary 21: Psalms 101–150* (ed. D. Hubbard and G. Baker; Waco, TX: Word Books, 1983).

Allison, D. *Jesus of Nazareth, Millenarian Prophet* (Minneapolis: Fortress Press, 1998).

Applebaum, S. 'Judaea as a Roman Province: The Countryside as a Political and Economic Factor', *ANRW* II/8 (1989), 355–96.

Archer, M. *Culture and Agency: The Place of Culture in Social Theory* (Cambridge: Cambridge University Press, 1988).

Arlandson, J. M. *Women, Class, and Society in Early Christianity* (Peabody, MA: Hendrickson, 1997).

Ashton, J. *Understanding the Fourth Gospel* (Oxford: Clarendon Press, 1991).

Baillet, M. *Qumran Grotte 4 III (4Q482–4Q520)* (DJD 7; Oxford: Clarendon, 1982).

Baker, A. 'One Thing Necessary', *CBQ* 27 (1965), 127–35.

Balch, D. L., 'Rich and Poor, Proud and Humble in Luke–Acts', in *The Social World of the First Christian: Essays in Honor of Wayne A. Meeks* (ed. L. M. White and O. L. Yarbrough; Minneapolis: Fortress Press, 1995), pp. 214–33.

Baldry, H. *The Unity of Mankind in Greek Thought* (Cambridge: Cambridge University Press, 1965).

Bammel, E. 'Sadduzäer und Sadokiden', *ETL* 55 (1979), 107–15.

'The Poor and the Zealots', in *Jesus and the Politics of His Day* (ed. E. Bammel and C. D. F. Moule; Cambridge: Cambridge University Press, 1984), pp. 109–28.

Barnard, L. W. 'The Origins and Emergence of the Church in Edessa during the First Two Centuries A.D.', *VC* 22 (1968), 161–75.

Barrett, C. K. *The Gospel according to St John* (London: SPCK, 1958).

The Gospel of John and Judaism (London: SPCK, 1975).

Barton, J. *Oracles of God: Perceptions of Ancient Prophecy in Israel after the Exile* (London: DLT, 1986).

Bassler, J. M. 'The Galileans: A Neglected Factor in Johannine Community Research', *CBQ* 43 (1981), 243–57.

Batten, A. 'More Queries for Q: Women and Christian Origins', *BTB* 24 (1994), 45–51.

Bauckham, R., 'Jesus' Demonstration in the Temple', in *Law and Religion* (ed. B. Lindars; London: SPCK, 1988), pp. 72–89.

'The Beloved Disciple as Ideal Author', *JSNT* 49 (1993), 21–44.

Gospel Women: Studies of the Named Women in the Gospels (London: T. & T. Clark, 2002).

Bauckham, R. ed. *The Gospels for All Christians: Rethinking the Gospel Audience* (Edinburgh: T. & T. Clark, 1998).

Baumgarten, A. I. *The Flourishing of the Jewish Sects in the Maccabean Era: An Interpretation* (SJSJ 55; Leiden: Brill, 1997).

Baumgarten, J. '4Q502, Marriage or Golden Age Ritual?', *JJS* 34 (1983), 125–35.

Benedict, R. *The Chrysanthemum and the Sword: Patterns of Japanese Culture* (London, 1947).

Berger, K. 'Almosen für Israel', *NTS* (1976–7), 180–204.

Exegese des Neuen Testaments: Neue Wege vom Text zur Auslegung (Heidelberg: Quelle & Meyer, 1977).

Berger, P., and Luckmann, T. *The Social Construction of Reality* (Middlesex: Penguin, 1966).

Betz, H. D. 'Jesus and the Cynics: Survey and Analysis of a Hypothesis', *JRel* 74 (1994), 453–75.

The Sermon on the Mount (Hermeneia; Minneapolis: Fortress Press, 1995).

Betz, O., and Riesner, R. *Jesus, Qumran and the Vatican* (London: SCM, 1993).

Bieringer, R., Pollefeyt, D., and Vandecasteele-Vanneuville, F., eds. *Anti-Judaism and the Fourth Gospel* (Assen, The Netherlands: Royal Van Gorcum, 2001).

Boff, C., and Pixely, G. V. *The Bible, the Church and the Poor* (Maryknoll, NY: Orbis Books, 1989).

Boismard, M. E. *L'Evangile de Jean* (Synopse des Quatre Evangiles en français, III; ed. M. E. Boismard and A. Lamouille; Paris: Cerf, 1977).

Boissevain, J. *Friends of Friends: Networks, Manipulators and Coalitions* (Oxford: Blackwell, 1974).

Bornhäuser, K. *Das Johannesevangelium: Eine Missionschrift für Israel* (Gütersloh: Bertelsmann, 1928).

Boulay, J., and Williams, R. 'Amoral Familism and the Image of Limited Good: A Critique from a European Perspective', *AQ* 60/1 (January 1987), 12–24.

Bourdieu, P. *Outline of a Theory of Practice* (trans. R. Nice; Cambridge: Cambridge University Press, 1977).

Brandes, S. *Metaphors of Masculinity: Sex and Status in Andalusian Folklore* (Pennsylvania: University of Pennsylvania Press, 1985).

Broer, I. *Die Seligpreisungen der Bergpredigt: Studien zu ihrer Überlieferung und Interpretation* (BBB 61; Bonn: Hanstein, 1986).

Brooke, A. E. *A Critical and Exegetical Commentary on the Johannine Epistles* (ICC; Edinburgh: T. & T. Clark, 1912).

Brooke, G. J. 'The Wisdom of Matthew's Beatitudes (4Qbeat and Matt 5:3–12)', *SB* 19 (1989), 35–41.

Brooten, B. *Women Leaders in the Ancient Synagogue: Inscriptional Evidence and Background Issues* (Brown Judaic Studies, 36; Chico, CA: Scholars Press, 1982).

Broshi, M. 'The Role of the Temple in the Herodian Economy', *JJS* 38 (1987), 31–7.

Brown, P. *Society and the Holy in Late Antiquity* (London: Faber & Faber, 1982).

    The Body and Society: Men, Women and Sexual Renunciation in Early Christianity (New York: Columbia State University Press, 1988).

Brown, R. E. *New Testament Essays* (New York: Paulist Press), 1965.

    The Gospel according to John (I–XII) (New York: Anchor Bible, 1966).

    The Gospel according to John (XIII–XXI) (New York: Anchor Bible, 1970).

    The Community of the Beloved Disciple (New York: Paulist Press, 1979).

    The Churches the Apostles Left Behind (London: Cassell, 1984).

Büchler, A. *The Economic Conditions of Judea after the Destruction of the Second Temple* (London, 1912).

    Types of Jewish-Palestinian Piety (London: Oxford University Press, 1922).

Bultmann, R. *The Gospel of John* (Oxford: Blackwell, 1971).

Cairns, D. *Aidōs: The Psychology and Ethics of Honour and Shame in Ancient Greek Literature* (Oxford: Clarendon Press, 1993).

Campbell, J. G. *Deciphering the Dead Sea Scrolls* (Oxford: Blackwell, 2002).

Campbell, J. K. *Honour, Family, and Patronage: A Study of Institutions and Moral Values in a Greek Mountain Village* (Oxford: Clarendon Press, 1964).

Capper, B. J. '"In der hand des Ananias." Erwägungen zu 1QS VI,20 und der urchristlichen Gütergemeinschaft', *RevQ* 12 (1986), 223–36.

    'Community of Goods in the Early Jerusalem Church', *ANRW* II/26.2 (1995), 1730–74.

    'Reciprocity and the Ethics of Acts', in *Witness to the Gospel* (ed. I. H. Marshall and D. Peterson; Cambridge, MA: Eerdmans, 1998), pp. 499–518.

    '"With the Oldest Monks." Light from the Essene History on the Career of the Beloved Disciple?', *JTS* 49/1 (April 1998), 1–55.

    'Two Types of Discipleship in Early Christianity', *JTS* 52 (2001), 105–23.

    'The Church as the New Covenant of Effective Economics', *IJSCC* 2 (2002), 83–102.

Carney, T. F. *The Shape of the Past: Models and Antiquity* (Lawrence, KS: Coronado Press, 1975).

Carson, D. A. *The Gospel according to John* (Cambridge, MA: Eerdmans, 1991).

Ceresko, A. 'The Identity of "the Blind and the Lame" (ʿiwwēr ûpissēah) in Samuel 5:8b', *CBQ* 63/1 (January 2001).

Charlesworth, J. H. *The Old Testament Pseudepigrapha*, Vol. I, *Apocalyptic Literature and Testaments* (London: DLT, 1993).

Charlesworth, J. H., ed. *John and the Dead Sea Scrolls* (New York: Crossroad, 1990).

Charlesworth, J. H., and Johns, L. L., eds. *Hillel and Jesus: Comparative Studies of Two Major Religious Leaders* (Minneapolis: Fortress Press, 1997).

Chilton, B., and Evans, C., eds. *Studying the Historical Jesus: Evaluations of the State of Current Research* (Leiden: Brill, 1994).

Chilton, B., and Neusner, J. *Judaism in the New Testament: Practices and Beliefs* (London: Routledge, 1995).

Cohen, S., 'The Political and Social History of the Jews in Greco-Roman Antiquity: The State of the Question', in *Early Judaism and its Modern Interpreters* (ed. R. Kraft and G. Nickelsburg; Philadelphia, 1986), pp. 33–56.

Collins, J. 'Did Luke Intend a Disservice to Women in the Martha and Mary Story?' *BTB* 28/3 (1998), 104–11.

'Cult and Culture, the Limits of Hellenization in Judea', in *Hellenism in the Land of Israel* (Christianity and Judaism in Antiquity Series, Vol. 13; ed. J. Collins and G. Sterling; Notre Dame, IN: University of Notre Dame Press, 2001), pp. 38–61.

Conzelmann, H. *Gentiles, Jews, Christians: Polemics and Apologetics in the Greco-Roman Era* (trans. E. Boring; Minneapolis: Fortress Press, 1992).

Cook, E. 'A Liturgy of Thanksgiving', in *The Dead Sea Scrolls: A New Translation* (ed. M. Wise, M. Abegg and E. Cook; New York: HarperCollins, 1996), pp. 407–8.

Corley, K. *Private Women, Public Meals: Social Conflict in the Synoptic Tradition* (Peabody, MA: Hendickson Publishers, 1993).

Cornwall, A., and Lindisfarne, N., eds. *Dislocating Masculinity: Comparative Ethnographies* (London: Routledge, 1994).

Crockett, L. 'The OT in the Gospel of Luke with Emphasis on the Interpretation of Isa 61: 1–2' (unpublished doctoral dissertation, Brown University, 1966).

Crossan, J. D. *The Historical Jesus: The Life of a Mediterranean Jewish Peasant* (Edinburgh: T. & T. Clark, 1991).

Cullmann, O. *The Johannine Circle* (London: SCM Press, 1976).

Culpepper, R. A. *Anatomy of the Fourth Gospel* (Philadelphia: Fortress Press, 1983).

Culpepper, R. A., and Black, C., eds. *Exploring the Gospel of John* (Louisville, KY: Westminster John Knox Press, 1996).

D'Angelo, M. R. 'Women in Luke–Acts: A Redactional View', *JBL* 109/3 (1990), 441–61.

'Women Partners in the New Testament', *JFSR* 61 (1990), 65–86.

Danker, F. W. *Benefactor: Epigraphic Study of a Graeco-Roman and New Testament Semantic Field* (St Louis: Clayton, 1982).

Jesus and the New Age: A Commentary on St. Luke's Gospel (St. Louis: Clayton, 1988).

Daube, D. *The New Testament and Rabbinic Judaism* (London: Arno Press, 1973).

Davies, P. R. *Sects and Scrolls: Essays on Qumran and Related Topics* (South Florida Studies in the History of Judaism, 134; Atlanta: Scholars Press, 1996).

Davies, S., 'Women in the Third Gospel and the New Testament Apocrypha', in *'Women Like This': New Perspectives on Jewish Women in the Greco-Roman World* (ed. A.-J. Levine; Atlanta, GA: Scholars Press, 1991), pp. 185–97.

Davies, W., and Allison, D. *A Critical and Exegetical Commentary on the Gospel according to Saint Matthew* (ICC; Edinburgh: T. & T. Clark, 1988).

Davila, J. R. *Liturgical Works* (Eerdmans Commentaries on the Dead Sea Scrolls, 6; Grand Rapids, MI, 2000).
The Dead Sea Scrolls as Background to Postbiblical Judaism and Early Christianity (Leiden: Brill, 2003).

Davis, J. *People of the Mediterranean: An Essay in Comparative Social Anthropology* (London: Routledge and Kegan Paul, 1977).

de Silva, D. *Despising Shame: Honor Discourse and Community Maintenance in the Epistles to the Hebrews* (SBLDS 152; Atlanta: Scholars Press, 1995).
Honor, Patronage, Kinship and Purity: Unlocking New Testament Culture (Downers Grove, IL: IVP, 2000).

de Ste Croix, G. E. M. *The Class Struggle in the Ancient Greek World: From the Archaic Age to the Arab Conquests* (London: Duckworth, 1981).

Degenhardt, H. -J. *Lukas, Evangelist der Armen* (Stuttgart: Katholisches Bibelwerk, 1965).

Derrett, J. D. M. *Ascetic Discourse: An Explanation of the Sermon on the Mount* (Eilsbrunn: Ko'amar, 1989).

Dewey, J. 'Women in the Synoptic Gospels: Seen but Not Heard?', *BTB* 27 (1997), 53–60.

Dibelius, M. *A Commentary on the Epistle of James* (revised by H. Greeven, trans. M. Williams; Philadelphia: Fortress Press, 1976).

Dodd, C. 'The Beatitudes: A Form-critical Study', in *More New Testament Studies* (ed. C. Dodd; Manchester: Manchester University Press, 1968), pp. 1–10.

Dodds, E. *The Greeks and the Irrational* (Berkeley and Los Angeles: University of California Press, 1951).

Donaldson, T. 'Moses Typology and the Sectarian Nature of Early Christian Anti-Judaism', *JSNT* 12 (1981), 27–52.

Downing, F. G. 'A bas les aristos: The Relevance of Higher Literature for the Understanding of the Earliest Christian Writings', *NovTest* 30 (1988), 212–30.
Cynics and Christian Origins (Edinburgh: T. & T. Clark, 1992).
Cynics, Paul and the Pauline Churches (London: Routledge, 1998).
' "Honor" among Exegetes', *CBQ* 61 (1999), 53–73.

Making Sense in (and of) the First Christian Century (JSNTS 197; Sheffield: Sheffield Academic Press, 2000).

Dubisch, J. '"Foreign Chickens" and Other Outsiders: Gender and Community in Greece', *AmEth* 20 (1993), 272–87.

Dunn, J. D. G. *Jesus and the Spirit* (London: SCM, 1975).

'Let John be John: A Gospel for its Time', in *Das Evangelium und die Evangelien. Vorträge vom Tübinger Symposium 1982* (WUNT 28; ed. P. Stuhlmacher; Tübingen: Mohr, 1983), pp. 309–39.

'Judaism in the Land of Israel in the First Century', in *Judaism in Late Antiquity*, Vol. II: *Historical Synthesis* (Der Nahe und der Mittlere Osten, 17.2; ed. J. Neusner; Leiden: Brill, 1995), pp. 229–61.

Dupont, J. *Les béatitudes, Vol.I* (Louvain: Nauwelaerts, 1958).

Les béatitudes, Vol. II (Louvain: Nauwelaerts, 1969).

Les béatitudes, Vol. III (Louvain: Nauwelaerts, 1973).

Durkheim, E. *The Elementary Forms of Religious Life* (Glencoe, IL: Free Press, 1965).

Edgar, D. H. *Has God Not Chosen the Poor? The Social Setting of the Epistle of James* (JSNTS 206, 2001).

Edwards, R. B. *Discovering John* (London: SPCK, 2003).

Eisen, U. *Amtsträgerinnen im frühen Christentum. Epigraphische und literarische Studien* (Göttingen: Vandenhoeck & Ruprecht, 1996).

Elder, L. B. 'The Woman Question and Female Ascetics among the Essenes', *BA* 57 (1994), 230–2.

Elliott, J. H. 'Social-scientific Criticism of the New Testament: More on Methods and Models', *Semeia* 35 (1986), 1–33.

'The Fear of the Leer: The Evil Eye from the Bible to Li'l Abner', *Forum* 4/4 (1988), 42–71.

'Disgraced Yet Graced. The Gospel according to 1 Peter in the Key of Honor and Shame', *BTB* 25 (1995), 166–78.

Social Scientific Criticism of the New Testament: An Introduction (London: SPCK, 1995).

Esler, P. F. *Community and Gospel in Luke–Acts* (Cambridge: Cambridge University Press, 1987).

The First Christians in their Social Worlds: Social Scientific Approaches to New Testament Interpretation (London: Routledge, 1994).

'Review: The Social Ethos of the Corinthian Correspondence (Horrell)', *JTS* 49/1 (April 1998), 253–60.

'Models in New Testament Interpretation: A Reply to David Horrell', *JSNT* 78 (2000), 107–13.

Esler, P. F. ed. *Modelling Early Christianity: Social Scientific Studies of the New Testament in its Context* (London: Routledge, 1995).

Evans, C., and Sanders, J., eds. *Luke and Scripture* (Minneapolis: Fortress, 1993).

Fernandez, J. W. 'Consciousness and Class in Southern Spain', *AmEth* 10 (1983), 165–73.

Fiensy, D. A. *The Social History of Palestine in the Herodian Period: The Land is Mine* (Studies in the Bible and Early Christianity, 20; Lampeter: The Edwin Mellen Press, 1991).

Finley, M. *The World of Odysseus* (London: Penguin Books, 1962).
The Ancient Economy (London: Chatto and Windus, 1973).
Fisher, N. *HYBRIS: A Study in the Values of Honour and Shame in Ancient Greece* (Warminster, England: Aris & Phillips, 1992).
Fitzmyer, J. *The Gospel according to Luke* (New York: Doubleday, 1985).
Flusser, D., '*Blessed are the Poor in Spirit*', in *Judaism and the Origins of Christianity* (compiled and ed. by D. Flusser, with S. Safrai and B. Young; Jerusalem: Magnes Press, The Hebrew University, 1988), pp. 102–14.
Fortna, R. T., and Thatcher, T., eds. *Jesus in the Johannine Tradition* (London: WJK, 2001).
Foster, G. 'Interpersonal Relations in Peasant Society', *HO* 19 (1960/1), 174–8.
'The Dyadic Contract: A Model for the Social Structure of a Mexican Peasant Village', *AA* 63 (1961), 1173–92.
'The Dyadic Contract in Tzintzuntzan, II: Patron Client Relations', *AA* 65 (1963), 1280–94.
'Peasant Society and the Image of Limited Good', *AA* 67 (1965), 293–315.
'A Second Look at Limited Good', *AQ* 45 (1972), 57–64.
Fraade, S. 'Ascetical Aspects of Ancient Judaism', in *Jewish Spirituality* (ed. A. Green; London: Routledge, 1986), pp. 253–87.
Freyne, S. *Galilee from Alexander the Great to Hadrian: 323 B.C.E. to 135 B.C.E.* (Wilmington, DE: Glazier, 1980).
Friedrichs, R. *A Sociology of Sociology* (New York: Free Press, 1970).
Funk, R. 'The Form and Structure of II and III John', *JBL* 86/4 (1967), 424–30.
Gallant, T. W. *Risk and Survival in Ancient Greece* (Cambridge: Polity Press, 1991).
Garnsey, P. *Cities, Peasants and Food in Classical Antiquity* (with addenda by Walter Scheidel; Cambridge: Cambridge University Press, 1998).
Garnsey, P., and Woolf, G. 'Patronage and the Rural Poor', in *Patronage in Ancient Society* (ed. A. Wallace-Hadrill; London: Routledge, 1989), pp. 153–70.
Gärtner, B. *The Temple and the Community in Qumran and the New Testament: A Comparative Study in the Temple Symbolism of the Qumran Texts and the New Testament* (Cambridge: Cambridge University Press, 1965).
Geertz, C. 'Ethos, World View and the Analysis of Sacred Texts', *AntRev* 17 (1957), 421–37.
The Interpretation of Cultures: Selected Essays (New York: Basic Books, 1973).
Local Knowledge: Further Essays in Interpretive Anthropology (New York: Basic, 1983).
Geyser, A. 'The Youth of John the Baptist: A Deduction from the Break in the Parallel Account of the Lucan Infancy Story', *NovTest* 1 (1956), 70–5.
Gibson, S. 'Jerusalem (North-east), Archaeological Survey', *IEJ* 32 (1982), 156f.

Giddens, A. *Central Problems in Social Theory: Action, Structure and Contradiction in Social Analysis* (Cambridge: Polity Press, 1979).

Gil, M. 'Land Ownership in Palestine under Roman Rule', *RIDA* 17 (1970), 11–53.

Gilmore, D. D. *Honor and Shame and the Unity of the Mediterranean* (Special Publication no. 22; Washington, DC: AAA, 1987).

Goffman, E. *Asylums: Essays on the Social Situation of Mental Patients and Other Inmates* (Harmondsworth, Middlesex: Penguin Books, 1968).

Goodacre, M. '*How Blessed are the Poor?*' Unpublished manuscript of draft chapter for his *The Case against Q*.

Goodman, M. 'The First Jewish Revolt: Social Conflict and the Problem of Debt', *JJS* 33 (1982), 222–4.

   The Ruling Class of Judaea: The Origins of the Jewish Revolt against Rome AD 66–70 (Cambridge: Cambridge University Press, 1987).

Goodspeed, E. J. *An Introduction to the New Testament* (Chicago: Chicago University Press, 1937).

Gottwald, N. *The Tribes of Yahweh: A Sociology of a Liberated Israel* (London: Orbis, 1979).

Goulder, M. D. 'A Poor Man's Christology', *NTS* 45/3 (1999), 332–48.

Gouldner, A. W. *The Hellenic World: A Sociological Analysis* (Enter Plato: Classical Greece and the Origins of Social Theory; New York: Harper & Row, 1969).

Grant, F. C. *The Economic Background of the Gospel* (Oxford: Oxford University Press, 1926).

Grappe, C. *D'un Temple à l'autre* (Paris: Presses Universitaires de France, 1992).

Green, J. B. *The Gospel of Luke* (NICNT; Grand Rapids, MI: Eerdmans, 1997).

Gregory, J. R. 'The Myth of the Male Ethnographer and the Woman's World', *AA* 86 (1984), 316–27.

Gressmann, H. *Vom reichen Mann und armen Lazarus* (Berlin: Königliche Akademie der Wissenschaften, 1918).

Griffith, T. *Keep Yourselves from Idols: A New Look at 1 John* (JSNTS 233; (Sheffield: Sheffield Academic Press, 2002).

Guthrie, W. K. C. *History of Greek Philosophy*, Vol. I (Cambridge: Cambridge University Press, 1962).

Hamel, G. *Poverty and Charity in Roman Palestine, First Three Centuries C.E.* (Berkeley, CA: University of California Press, 1990).

Han, K. S. *Jerusalem and the Early Jesus Movement: The Q Community's Attitude toward the Temple* (JSNTS 207; London: Sheffield Academic Press, 2002).

Hands, A. R. *Charities and Social Aid in Greece and Rome* (Ithaca, NY: Cornell University Press, 1968).

Hanson, K. '"How Honorable! How Shameful!" A Cultural Analysis of Matthew's Makarisms and Reproaches', *Semeia* 68 (1994), 81–112.

Hanson, K., and Oakman, D. E. *Palestine in the Time of Jesus: Social Structures and Social Conflicts* (Minneapolis, MN: Fortress Press, 1998).

Hardman, O. *The Ideal of Asceticism: An Essay in the Comparative Study of Religion* (London: SPCK, 1926).

Hare, D. R. A. *The Theme of Jewish Persecution of Christians in the Gospel according to Matthew* (Cambridge: Cambridge University Press, 1967).

Harpham, G. *The Ascetic Imperative in Culture and Criticism* (Chicago: University of Chicago Press, 1987).

Hawley, J., ed. *Saints and Virtues* (Berkeley: University of California Press, 1987).

Heilbroner, R. *The Making of Economic Society* (8th edn; Englewood Cliffs, NJ: Prentice-Hall, 1989).

Hengel, M. *The Charismatic Leader and his Followers* (trans. J. C. Greig; Edinburgh: T. & T. Clark, 1981).

Judaism and Hellenism: Studies in their Encounter in Palestine during the Early Hellenistic Period (first English edn; trans. J. Bowden; London: SCM Press, 1981).

The Johannine Question (trans. J. Bowden; London: SCM Press, 1989).

Hengel, M., and Deines, R., 'E. P. Sanders' "Common Judaism", Jesus, and the Pharisees', *JTS* 46 (1995), 60–7.

Herzfeld, M. 'Honor and Shame: Problems in the Comparative Analysis of Moral Systems', *Man* 15 (1980), 339–51.

Anthropology: Theoretical Practice in Culture and Society (Oxford: Blackwell, 2001).

Herzog, F. *Liberation Theology: Liberation in the Light of the Fourth Gospel* (New York, 1972).

Hill, C. *The World Turned Upside Down: Radical Ideas during the English Revolution* (London: M. T. Smith, 1972).

Hill, M. *The Religious Order: A Study of Virtuoso Religion and its Legitimation in the Nineteenth-Century Church of England* (London: Heinemann, 1973).

Hillery, G. J. 'The Convent: Community, Prison or Task Force', *JSSR* 8 (1969), 140–51.

Hock, R. 'Lazarus and Micyllus: Greco-Roman Backgrounds to Luke 16:19–31', *JBL* 106 (1987), 447–63.

Holl, K. 'Der Kirchenbegriff des Paulus in seinem Verhältnis zu dem der Urgemeinde', *Sitzungsberichte der Berliner Akademie* (1921), 920–47.

Hollenbach, P. 'Liberating Jesus for Social Involvement', *BTB* 15 (1985), 151–7.

Defining Rich and Poor Using the Social Sciences (SBL Seminar Papers; ed. Kent Richards; Atlanta, GA: Scholars Press, 1987), pp. 50–63.

Holmberg, B. *Sociology and the New Testament: An Appraisal* (Minneapolis: Fortress Press, 1990).

Horbury, W. 'The Benediction of the Minim and early Jewish–Christian Controversy', *JTS* 33 (1982), 19–61.

Horden, P., and Purcell, N. *The Corrupting Sea: A Study of Mediterranean History* (Oxford: Blackwell, 2000).

Horrell, D. G. *The Social Ethos of the Corinthian Correspondence* (Edinburgh: T. & T. Clark, 1996).
Social-Scientific Approaches to New Testament Interpretation (Edinburgh: T. & T. Clark, 1999).
'Models and Methods in Social-scientific Interpretation: A Response to Philip Esler', *JSNT* 78 (2000), 83–105.
Horsley, R. A., and Hanson, J. S. *Bandits, Prophets, and Messiahs: Popular Movements at the Time of Jesus* (San Francisco: Harper & Row, 1985).
Jesus and the Spiral of Violence: Popular Jewish Resistance in Roman Palestine (San Francisco: Harper & Row, 1987).
Sociology and the Jesus Movement (New York: Continuum, 1994).
Galilee: History, Politics, People (Valley Forge, PA: Trinity Press, 1995).
Houlden, J. *A Commentary on the Johannine Epistles* (Black's New Testament Commentaries; London: A. & C. Black, 1973).
Janzen, W. *Mourning Cry and Woe Oracle* (BZAW 125; Berlin: Töpelmann, 1972).
Jayawardena, C. 'Ideology and Conflict in Lower Class Communities', *CSSH* 10 (1968), 413–46.
Jeremias, J. *The Eucharistic Words of Jesus* (trans. N. Perrin; London: SCM Press, 1966).
Jerusalem in the Time of Jesus (trans. F. Cave and C. Cave; London: SCM Press, 1969).
Johnson, B. 'On Church and Sect', *ASR* 28 (1963), 539–49.
Johnson, L. T. 'The New Testament's Anti-Jewish Slander and the Conventions of Ancient Polemic', *JBL* 108/3 (Fall 1989), 419–41.
Jowkar, F. 'Honor and Shame: A Feminist View from Within', *FI* 6 (1986), 45–65.
Kaelber, W. O. 'Asceticism', in *The Encyclopedia of Religion* (New York: Macmillan, 1987), Vol. I, p. 441.
Karris, R. *Jesus and the Marginalized in John's Gospel* (Collegeville, MN: The Liturgical Press, 1990).
Käsemann, E. 'Ketzer und Zeuge: zum johanneischen Verfasserproblem', *ZTK* 48 (1951), 292–311.
Keck, L. E. 'The Poor among the Saints in the New Testament', *ZNW* 56 (1965), 100–29.
'The Poor among the Saints in Jewish Christianity and Qumran', *ZNW* 57 (1966), 68–75.
'On the Ethos of Early Christians', *JAAR* 42/3 (September 1974), 435–52.
Kennard, J. 'The Jewish Provincial Assembly', *ZNW* 53 (1962), 25–51.
Kim, C.-H. *The Familiar Letter of Recommendation* (SBL Dissertation Series 4; Missoula, Montana: Scholars Press, 1972).
Kim, J.-K. *Stewardship and Almsgiving in Luke's Theology* (JSNTS 155; Sheffield: Sheffield Academic Press, p. 1998).
Kimelman, R. '"Birkat Ha-Minim" and the Lack of Evidence for an Anti-Christian Jewish Prayer in Late-Antiquity', in *Jewish and Christian Self-Definition*, Vol. II: *Aspects of Judaism* (ed. E. P. Sanders, A. I. Baumgarten and A. Mendelson; London: SCM, 1981), pp. 226–44.

Klausner, J. 'The Economy of Judea', in *The World History of the Jewish People*, Series I, Vol. VII, *The Herodian Period* (ed. M. Avi-Yonah and Z. Baras; London, 1975), pp. 179–205.

Köstenberger, A. J. *The Missions of Jesus and the Disciples according to the Fourth Gospel* (Eerdmans: Grand Rapids, 1998).

Kraemer, R. S., and D'Angelo, M. A. eds. *Women in Christian Origins* (Oxford: Oxford University Press, 1999).

Kressel, G. M. 'Shame and Gender', *AQ* 65 (1992), 34–46.

'An Anthropologist's Response to the Use of Social Science Models in Biblical Studies', *Semeia* 68 (1994), 153–60.

Labahn, M., and Schmidt, A. eds. *Jesus, Mark and Q* (JSNTS 214; (Sheffield: Sheffield Academic Press, 2001), pp. 184–215.

Langbrandtner, W. *Weltferner Gott oder Gott der Leibe. Die Ketzerstreit in der johanneischen Kirche* (Beiträge zur biblischen Exegese und Theologie 6; Frankfurt: Lang, 1977).

Layder, D. *Understanding Social Theory* (London: Sage Publications, 1994).

Modern Social Theory, Key Debates and New Directions (London: UCL Press, 1997).

Lefkowitz, M., and Fant, M. *Women's Life in Greece and Rome: A Source Book in Translation* (2nd edn; London: Duckworth, 1992).

Lenski, G., Lenski, J., and Nolan, P. *Human Societies: An Introduction to Macrosociology* (6th edn; New York: McGraw-Hill Book Co., 1991).

Leroy, H. *Rätsel und Missverständnis: Ein Beitrag zur Formgeschichte* (BBB 30; Bonn: Peter Hanstein, 1968).

Leske, A. 'The Beatitudes, Salt and Light in Matthew and Luke', *SBL Seminar Papers* (1991), 816–39.

Levine, A.-J. 'Second Temple Judaism, Jesus and Women: Yeast of Eden', *BI* 2/1 (1994), 8–33.

Lilla, S. *Clement of Alexandria: A Study in Christian Platonism and Gnosticism* (London: Oxford University Press, 1971).

Lindars, B. *The Gospel of John* (London: Oliphants, 1972).

Ling, T. J. 'Virtuoso Religion and the Judaean Social Order', in *Anthropology and Biblical Studies* (ed. M. Aguilar and L. Lawrence; London: SCM Press, 2004), pp. 227–58.

Llobera, J. 'Fieldwork in Southwestern Europe: Anthropological Panacea or Epistemological Straitjacket?', *CritA* 6/2 (1986), 25–33.

Lloyd-Jones, H. *The Justice of Zeus* (Berkeley and Los Angeles: University of California Press, 1971).

Greek Comedy, Hellenistic Literature, Greek Religion, and Miscellanea: The Academic Papers of Sir Hugh Lloyd-Jones (Oxford: Clarendon Press, 1990).

Loizos, P., and Papataxiarchis, A., eds. *Contested Identities: Gender and Sexuality in Modern Greece* (Princeton: Princeton University Press, 1991).

Love, S. 'Women's Roles in Certain Second Testament Passages: A Macrosociological View', *BTB* 17/2 (1987), 50–7.

Lowry, T. 'Aristotle's "Natural Limit" and the Economics of Price Regulation', *Greek, Roman and Byzantine Studies* 15/1 (Spring 1974), 57–63.

Luomanen, P. 'The "Sociology of Sectarianism" in Matthew: Modelling the Genesis of Early Jewish and Christian Communities', in *Fair Play: Diversity and Conflicts in Early Christianity* (ed. I. Dunderberg, C. Tuckett and K. Syreeni; Leiden: Brill, 2002), pp. 107–30.

Luz, U. *Matthew*, Vol. I (Edinburgh: T. & T. Clark, 1989).

Maccini, R. G. *Her Testimony is True: Women as Witnesses according to John* (JSNTS 125; Sheffield: Sheffield Academic Press, 1996).

McClaren, J. *Power and Politics in Palestine: The Jews and the Governing of their Land 100 BC–AD 70* (JSNTS 63; Sheffield: Sheffield Academic Press, 1991).

McCown, C. C. 'The Beatitudes in the Light of Ancient Ideals', *JBL* 46 (1927), 50–61.

McGinn, T. A. J. 'Widows, Orphans and Social History', JRA 12 (1999), 617–32.

Mack, B. *A Myth of Innocence: Mark and Christian Origins* (Philadelphia: Fortress Press, 1988).

McKnight, S. *A Light among the Gentiles* (Minneapolis: Fortress, 1991).

Malina, B. 'Limited Good and the Social World of Early Christianity', *BTB* 8 (1978), 162–76.

    'The Social Sciences and Biblical Interpretation', *Int* 36 (actual issue misprinted and published as 37/3) (1982), 229–42.

    'Interpreting the Bible with Anthropology: The Case of the Poor and the Rich', *Listening* 21 (1986), 148–59.

    'The Received View and What it Cannot Do: III John and Hospitality', *Semeia* 35 (1986), 171–94.

    'John's: the Maverick Christian Group', *BTB* 24 (1987), 167–82.

    'Wealth and Poverty in the New Testament and its World', *Int* 41 (1987), 354–67.

    The New Testament World: Insights from Cultural Anthropology (revised edition; Louisville, KY: Westminster John Knox Press, 1993).

Malina, B., and Rohrbaugh, R. *Social-Science Commentary on the Synoptic Gospels* (Minneapolis: Fortress Press, 1992).

    Social Science Commentary on the Gospel of John (Minneapolis, MN: Fortress Press, 1998).

Marshall, I. H. *The Gospel of Luke: A Commentary on the Greek Text* (Exeter: Paternoster Press, 1978).

Martin, D. *Slavery as Salvation: The Metaphor of Slavery in Pauline Christianity* (London and New Haven: Yale University Press, 1990).

Martin, R. P. *2 Corinthians* (WBC 40; Waco: Word, 1986).

Martyn, J. L. *History and Theology in the Fourth Gospel* (New York: Harper and Row, 1968).

Matthill, A. J. 'Johannine Communities behind the Fourth Gospel: Georg Richter's Analysis', *TS* 38 (1977), 294–315.

Maynard-Reid, P. *Poverty and Wealth in James* (Maryknoll, NY: Orbis Books, 1987).

Mead, M., ed. *Cooperation and Competition among Primitive Peoples* (New York, 1937).

Mealand, D. L. *Poverty and Expectation in the Gospels* (London: SPCK, 1980).

Meeks, W. 'Galilee and Judea in the Fourth Gospel', *JBL* 85 (1966), 159–69.
'The Man from Heaven in Johannine Sectarianism', *JBL* 91 (1972), 44–72.
'Breaking away: Three New Testament Pictures of Christianity's Separation from Jewish Communities', in *To See Ourselves as Others See Us: Christians, Jews, Others in Late Antiquity* (ed. J. Neusner, and E. Friechs; Chico, CA: Scholars Press, 1985), pp. 93–115.
Meggitt, J. *Paul, Poverty and Survival* (Edinburgh, T. & T. Clark, 1998).
Meikle, S. 'Modernism, Economics and the Ancient Economy', *Proceedings of the Cambridge Philological Society* 41 (1995), 174–91.
Meyers, E., ed. *Galilee through the Centuries – Confluence of Cultures* (Winona Lake, IN: Eisenbrauns, 1999).
Millar, F. *The Roman Near East, 31 BC–AD 337* (Cambridge, MA: Harvard University Press, 1993).
Miller, M. 'The Function of Isa 61:1–2 in 11Qmelchizedek', *JBL* 88 (1969), 467–9.
Miranda, J. P. *Being and the Messiah: The Message of St John* (Maryknoll, NY: Orbis Books, 1977).
Moody Smith, D. 'Historical Issues and the Problem of John and the Synoptics', in *From Jesus to John* (ed. M. C. de Boer; JSNTS 84; London: Sheffield Academic Press, 1994), pp. 252–67.
Morris, L. *The Gospel according to John* (Grand Rapids, MI: Eerdmans, 1995).
Motyer, S. *Your Father the Devil? A New Approach to John and 'the Jews'* (London: PBTM, 1997).
Moule, C. F. D. 'The Individualism of the Fourth Gospel', *NovTest* 5 (1962), 171–90.
Moulton, J., and Milligan, G. *The Vocabulary of the Greek Testament Illustrated from the Papyri and Other Non-Literary Sources* (3rd edn; (Grand Rapids, MI: Eerdmans, 1957).
Moxnes, H. 'BTB Readers Guide: Honor and Shame', *BTB* 23 (1993), 167–76.
Murvar, V. 'Towards a Sociological Theory of Religious Movements', *JSSR* 14 (1975), 229–56.
Mussner, F. *Der Jakobusbrief* (5th edn; HTKNT 13.1; Freiburg: Herder Verlag, 1987).
Neale, D. A. *None but the Sinners: Religious Categories in the Gospel of Luke* (JSNTS 58; Sheffield: JSOT Press, 1991).
Neusner, J. *From Politics to Piety: The Emergence of Pharisaic Judaism* (Englewood Cliffs, NJ: Prentice-Hall, 1973).
Neusner, J. ed. *Christianity, Judaism, and other Greco-Roman Cults: Studies for Morton Smith at Sixty* (Leiden: Brill, 1975).
Neville, R. *Normative Cultures* (Albany: SUNY Press, 1995).
Neyrey, J. H. *The Ideology of Revolt: John's Christology in Social-Science Perspective* (Philadelphia: Fortress Press, 1988).
'What's Wrong with This Picture? John 4, Cultural Stereotypes of Women, and Public and Private Space', *BTB* 24 (1994), 77–91.
Honour and Shame and the Gospel of Matthew (Louisville: Westminster John Knox, 1998).

'Questions, *Chreiai*, and Challenges to Honor: The Interface of Rhetoric and Culture in Mark's Gospel', *CBQ* 60 (1998), 657–81.

Neyrey, J. H., ed. *The Social World of Luke–Acts* (Peabody, MA: Hendrickson Publishers, 1991).

Neyrey, J. H., and Rohrbaugh R. L. ' "He Must Increase, I Must Decrease" (John 3:30): A Cultural and Social Interpretation', *CBQ* 63 (2001), 464–83.

Nickle, K. F. *The Collection: A Study in Paul's Strategy* (SBT 48; Naperville: Alleson, 1966).

Nissen, J., and Pedersen, S., eds. *New Readings in John* (JSNTS 182; London: Sheffield Academic Press, 1999).

Nolland, J. *Luke*, Vol. I (Dallas: Word Books, 1989).

Luke, Vol. II (Dallas: Word Books, 1993).

Luke, Vol. III (Dallas: Word Books, 1993).

Oakes, P. S. *Philippians: From People to Letter* (SNTS Monograph Series 110; Cambridge: Cambridge University Press, 2001).

Oakman, D. E. *Jesus and the Economic Questions of his Day* (Studies in the Bible and Early Christianity; Lewiston, NY: The Edwin Mellen Press, 1986).

O'Neill, J. C. 'New Testament Monasteries', in *Common Life in the Early Church: Essays Honoring Graydon F. Snyder* (ed. J. V. Hills; Harrisburg: Trinity Press International, 1998), pp. 118–34.

Ortner, S. B. *High Religion: A Cultural and Political History of Sherpa Buddhism* (Princeton: Princeton University Press, 1989).

Overman, A. *Matthew's Gospel and Formative Judaism* (Minneapolis: Fortress Press, 1990).

Painter, J. *The Quest for the Messiah: The History, Literature, and Theology of the Johannine Community* (Nashville: Abingdon Press, 1993).

Parvey, C. F. 'The Theology and Leadership of Women in the New Testament', in *Religion and Sexism: Images of Women in Jewish and Christian Traditions* (ed. R. R. Ruether; New York: Simon & Schuster, 1974), pp. 117–47.

Pastor, J. *Land and Economy in Ancient Palestine* (London: Routledge, 1997).

Peristiany, J., and Pitt Rivers, J., eds. *Honour and Grace in Anthropology* (Cambridge: Cambridge University Press, 1992).

Perkins, P. *The Johannine Epistles* (New Testament Message 21; Wilmington: Glazier, 1979).

Petersen, N. *The Gospel of John and the Sociology of Light: Language and Characterization in the Fourth Gospel* (Valley Forge, PA: Trinity Press International, 1993).

Pitt Rivers, J. *The Fate of Shechem or the Politics of Sex: Essays in the Anthropology of the Mediterranean* (Cambridge: Cambridge University Press, 1977).

Pitt Rivers, J., and Peristiany, J., eds. *Honour and Shame: The Values of Mediterranean Society* (London: Weidenfeld & Nicolson, 1965).

Pixner, B. 'An Essene Quarter on Mount Zion?', *Studia Hierosolymitana in onore di P. Bellarmino Baatti*, I, *Studi archeologici* (Studium

Biblicanum Franciscanum, Collectio Major, 22; Jerusalem: Franciscan Printing Press, 1976), pp. 254–84.

'Bethanien bei Jerusalem – eine Essener-Siedlung?', in *Wege des Messias und Stätten der Urkirche* (SBAZ 2; ed. R. Riesner; Giessen: Basel 1994), pp. 193–224.

Porter, S., and Evans, C. A., eds. *The Scrolls and the Scriptures* (Sheffield: Sheffield Academic Press, 1997).

Qimron, E. 'Celibacy in the Dead Sea Scrolls and the Two Kinds of Sectarians', in *The Madrid Qumran Congress* (ed. J. Trebolle Barrera and L. Vegas Montaner; Leiden: Brill, 1992), pp. 287–94.

Redfield, R. *Peasant Society and Culture* (Chicago: University of Chicago Press, 1956).

Rensberger, D. *Johannine Faith and Liberating Community* (Philadelphia: Fortress Press, 1988).

Overcoming the World, Politics and Community in the Gospel of John (London: SPCK, 1989).

1 John, 2 John, 3 John (Abingdon New Testament Commentaries; Nashville: Abingdon Press, 1997).

Riesenfeld, H. *Studia Evangelica*, Vol. I (ed. K. Aland; Berlin, 1959).

Riesner, R. 'Essener und Urkirche in Jerusalem', *BK* 40 (1985), 64–76.

'Josephus' "Gate of the Essenes" in Modern Discussion', *ZDMG* 105 (1989), 105–9.

Ritzer, G. *Sociological Theory* (4th edn; New York: McGraw-Hill, 1996).

Robinson, J. A. T. *Redating the New Testament* (London: SCM, 1976).

The Priority of John (London: SCM, 1985).

Rogers, S. 'Female Forms of Power and the Myth of Male Dominance: A Model of Female/Male Interaction in Peasant Society', *AmEth* 2 (1975), 727–56.

Rohrbaugh, R. L. ' "Social Location of Thought" as a Heuristic Construct in New Testament Study', *JSNT* 30 (1987), 103–19.

'The Social Location of the Markan Audience', *Int* 47 (1993), 380–95.

Roller, D. *The Building Program of Herod the Great* (Berkeley: University of California Press, 1998).

Ron, Z. 'Agricultural Terraces in the Judaean Mountains', *IEJ* 16 (1966), 33–49, 111–22.

Rostovtsev, M. I. *The Social and Economic History of the Roman Empire* (2nd edn; rev. by P. M. Fraser; Oxford: Clarendon Press, 1957).

Roth, J. *The Blind, the Lame and the Poor: Character Types in Luke–Acts* (JSNTS 144; Sheffield: Sheffield Academic Press, 1997).

Ruckstuhl, E. 'Mitglied der essenischen mönchsgemeinde in Jerusalem', *BK* 40/2 (1985), 77–83.

Ryan, S. 'Jesus and the Poor in the Fourth Gospel', *Biblebhashyam* 4 (1978), 213–28.

Saldarini, A. J. *Pharisees, Scribes, and Sadducees in Palestinian Society: A Sociological Approach* (Wilmington, DE: Michael Glazier, 1988).

Sanders, E. P. *Jesus and Judaism* (London: SCM PRESS, 1985).

Judaism: Practice and Belief 63 B.C.E.–66 C.E. (London: SCM Press, 1992).

'Jesus in Historical Context', *ThT* 50 (1993), 429–48.

Sanders, J. T. *Schismatics, Sectarians, Dissidents, Deviants: The First One Hundred Years of Jewish–Christian Relations* (London: SCM Press, 1993).

Schmidt, S.W., Scott, J. C., Lande, C. H., and Guasti, L., eds. *Friends, Followers and Factions: A Reader in Political Clientism* (Berkeley, CA: University of California Press, 1977).

Schneider, J. 'Of Vigilance and Virgins: Honour, Shame and the Access to Resources in Mediterranean Societies', *Ethnology* 10/1 (January 1971), 1–24.

Schneiders, S. M., 'Women in the Fourth Gospel and the Role of Women in the Contemporary Church', in *The Gospel of John as Literature* (ed. W. G. Stibbe; Leiden: Brill, 1993), pp. 123–43.

Schopenhauer, A. *Aphorismen zur Lebensweisheit* (ed. A. Hübscher and H. Lankes; Goldman, 1851).

Schottroff, L., and Stegemann, W. *God of the Lowly: Socio-Historical Interpretation of the Bible* (Maryknoll, NY: Orbis, 1984).
Jesus and the Hope of the Poor (trans. J. O'Connell; Maryknoll, NY: Orbis, 1986).

Schüssler-Fiorenza, E. *But She Said: Feminist Practices of Biblical Interpretation* (Boston, MA: Beacon Press, 1992).

Schwartz, D. R. 'Non-joining Sympathisers (Acts 5.13–14)', *Bib* 64 (1983), 550–5.

Schwartz, S. 'Josephus in Galilee: Rural Patronage and Social Breakdown', in *Josephus and the History of the Greco-Roman Period* (ed. F. Parente and J. Sievers; Leiden: Brill, 1994), pp. 290–306.

Schweizer, E. 'Formgeschichtliches zu den Speligpreisungen Jesu', *NTS* 19 (1972–3), 121–6.

Scobie, C. H. H. 'Johannine Geography', *SRel* 11 (1982), 77–84.

Scott, J. *Weapons of the Weak: Everyday Forms of Peasant Resistance* (New Haven: Yale University Press, 1985).
Domination and the Arts of Resistance: Hidden Transcripts (New Haven: Yale University Press, 1990).

Seccombe, D. P. 'Was there Organised Charity in Jerusalem before the Christians?', *JTS* 29 (1978), 140–3.
Possessions and the Poor in Luke–Acts (Linz: A. Fuchs, 1982).

Seguy, J. 'Une sociologie des sociétés imaginées: monachisme et utopie', *Annales E.S.C.* 26 (1971), 328–54.

Seim, T. K. *The Double Message: Patterns of Gender in Luke–Acts* (Edinburgh: T. & T. Clark, 1994).

Seland, T. 'Jesus as a Faction Leader: On the Exit of the Category Sect', in *Context* (ed. P. Bøckman and R. Kristiansen; Trondheim: TAPIR, 1987), pp. 197–211.

Shellard, B. 'The Relationship of Luke and John: A Fresh Look at an Old Problem', *JTS* 46/1 (April 1995), 71–97.
New Light on Luke: Its Purpose, Sources and Literary Context (JSNTS 215; London: Sheffield Academic Press, 2002).

Sherwin-White, A. *Roman Society and Roman Law in the New Testament* (Oxford, 1963).

Silber, I. *Virtuosity, Charisma, and Social Order: A Comparative Sociological Study of Monasticism in Theravada Buddhism and Medieval Catholicism* (Cambridge: Cambridge University Press, 1995).

Sjoberg, G. *The Preindustrial City, Past and Present* (New York: Free Press, 1965).

Smalley, S. S. *1, 2, 3 John* (Word Biblical Commentary; Waco, TX: Word Books, 1984).

Smallwood, E. 'High Priests and Politics in Roman Palestine', *JTS* 13 (1962), 14–34.

Smith, D. M. *Johannine Christianity* (Edinburgh: T. & T. Clark, 1984).

Smith, G. A. *The Historical Geography of the Holy Land, Especially in Relation to the History of Israel and the Early Church* (London: Hodder and Stoughton, 1896).

Smith, J. Z. 'The Social Description of Early Christianity', *RSR* 1 (1975), 19–25.

'Too Much Kingdom, Too Little Community', *Zygon* 13 (1978), 123–30.

Stanton, G. N. *A Gospel for a New People: Studies in Matthew* (Edinburgh: T. & T. Clark, 1992).

Stark, R., and Bainbridge, W. *A Theory of Religion* (Toronto Studies in Religion 2; New York: Peter Lang, 1987).

Stegemann, E., and Stegemann, W. *The Jesus Movement: A Social History of its First Century* (trans. O. Dean; Edinburgh: T. & T. Clark, 1999).

Stegemann, H. 'The Qumran Essenes – Local Members of the Main Jewish Union in Late Second Temple Times', in *The Madrid Qumran Congress* (ed. J. Trebolle Barrera and L. Vegas Montaner; Leiden: Brill, 1992), pp. 83–166.

The Library of Qumran (English translation; Grand Rapids: Eerdmans, 1998).

Stegemann, W. *The Gospel and the Poor* (trans. D. Elliott; Philadelphia: Fortress Press, 1984).

Stern, M. *Greek and Latin Authors on Jews and Judaism: Edited with Introductions, Translations and Commentary* (Jerusalem: Israel Academy of Sciences and Humanities, 1974–84).

'Social and Political Realignments in Herodian Judaea', in *The Jerusalem Cathedra 2* (ed. L. Levine; Jerusalem and Detroit, 1982), pp. 40–62.

Stewart, F. *Honor* (Chicago: University of Chicago Press, 1994).

Strecker, G. 'Die Makarismen der Bergpredigt', *NTS* 17 (1971), 255–75.

Sullivan, R. 'The Dynasty of Judaea in the First Century', *ANRW* II/8 (1989), 296–354.

Tambiah, S. J. 'Buddhism and This-worldly Activity', *MAS* 7 (1973), 1–20.

Tcherickover, V. 'Was Jerusalem a "*polis*"?', *IEJ* 14 (1964), 61–78.

Theissen, G. *The First Followers of Jesus* (London: SCM Press, 1978).

Sociology of Early Palestinian Christianity (trans. J. Bowden; Philadelphia: Fortress Press, 1978).

The Social Setting of Pauline Christianity (trans. J. Schutz; Edinburgh: T. & T. Clark, 1990).

Social Reality and the Early Christians: Theology, Ethics, and the World of the New Testament (first English-language edn, trans. M. Kohl; Minneapolis: Fortress Press, 1992).

Thurston, B. B. *The Widows: The Women's Ministry in the Early Church* (Minneapolis: Fortress Press, 1989).

Torjesen, K. 'In Praise of Noble Women: Gender and Honour in Ascetic Texts', *Semeia* 57/1 (1992), 41–64.

Treggiari, S. M. *Roman Marriage* (Oxford: Oxford University Press, 1991).

Troeltsch, E. *The Social Teaching of the Christian Churches* (London: George Allen & Unwin, 1931).

Tuckett, C. 'A Cynic Q', *Biblia* 70 (1989), 349–76.

Turner, J. *Societal Stratification: A Theoretical Analysis* (New York: Columbia University Press, 1984).

Turner, V. *Dramas, Fields and Metaphors: Symbolic Action in Human Society* (Ithaca, NY: Cornell University Press, 1974).

Vaage, L. E., and Wimbush, V. L., eds. *Asceticism and the New Testament* (London: Routledge, 1999).

Via, V. E. 'Women, the Discipleship of Service and the Early Christian Ritual Meal in the Gospel of Luke', *SLJT* 26 (1985), 37–60.

Wach, J. *Sociology of Religion* (Chicago: The University Press, 1962).

Walcot, P. *Envy and the Greeks:A Study of Human Behaviour* (Warminster: Aris & Phillips, 1978).

Ward, R. B. 'Partiality in the Assembly, Jas. 2.2–4', *HTR* 62 (1969), 87–97.

Weber, M. *The Protestant Ethic and the Spirit of Capitalism* (trans. T. Parsons; London: Allen & Unwin, 1930).

From Max Weber: Essays in Sociology (trans. and ed. H. H. Gerth and C. W. Mills; London: Oxford University Press, 1954).

The Sociology of Religion (trans. T. Parsons; London: Methuen & Co., 1963).

Economy and Society: An Outline of Interpretative Sociology (New York: Bedminster, 1968).

Weinfeld, M. *Social Justice in Ancient Israel and in the Ancient Near East* (Publications of the Perry Foundation for Biblical Research in the Hebrew University of Jerusalem; Jerusalem: The Magnes Press, 1995).

Westermann, C. *Blessing in the Bible and the Life of the Church* (trans. K. Crim; Philadelphia: Fortress Press, 1978).

White, L. 'Shifting Sectarian Boundaries in Early Christianity', *BJRL* 70 (1988), 7–24.

Whiteley, D. E. H. 'Was John Written by a Sadducee?', *ANRW* II/25 3 (1985), 2481–505.

Wikan, U. 'Shame and Honour: A Contestable Pair', *Man* 19 (1984), 635–52.

Williams, B. *Shame and Necessity* (Berkeley: University of California Press, 1993).

Wilson, B. R. *Religious Sects: A Sociological Study* (London: Weidenfeld & Nicolson, 1970).

Magic and the Millennium: A Sociological Study of Religious Movements of Protest among Tribal and Third-World Peoples (New York: Harper and Row, 1973).

Religion in a Sociological Perspective (Oxford: Oxford University Press, 1982).

Wimbush, V. L., ed. *Ascetic Behaviour in Greco-Roman Antiquity: A Source Book* (Studies in Antiquity and Christianity; Minneapolis: Fortress, 1990).

Discursive Formations, Ascetic Piety and the Interpretation of Early Christian Literature (*Semeia* 57–8; Atlanta: Scholars Press, 1992).

Wimbush, V. L., and Love, W., eds. *The Sexual Politics of the Ascetic Life: A Comparative Reader* (*Union Seminary Quarterly Review* 48:3–4, 1994–5).

Wimbush, V. L., and Valantasis, R., eds. *Asceticism: Essays Originally Presented at an International Conference on the Ascetic Dimension in Religious Life and Culture, Held at Union Theological Seminary in New York, 25–29 April 1993* (Oxford: Oxford University Press, 1995).

Witherington, B., III. 'On the Road with Mary Magdalene, Joanna, Susanna and Other Disciples – Luke 8, 1–3', *ZNW* 70 (1979), 243–8.

Wright Mills, C. *From Max Weber: Essays in Sociology* (New York: Oxford University Press, 1975).

Yadin, Y. *The Temple Scroll*, Vol. I (Jerusalem: IEJ, 1983).

Yalman, N. 'The Ascetic Buddhist Monks of Ceylon', *Ethnology* 1 (1962), 315–28.

INDEX OF MODERN AUTHORS

INDEX OF SUBJECTS